W9-AMU-482

# San Antonio & Austin

## 4th Edition

### by Edie Jarolim

**HUNGRY MINDS, INC.**

New York, NY • Cleveland, OH • Indianapolis, IN

## ABOUT THE AUTHOR

**Edie Jarolim** was a senior editor at Frommer's in New York before she indulged her Southwest fantasies and moved to Tucson, Arizona. She has since written about the Southwest and Mexico for a variety of national publications, ranging from *America West Airlines Magazine*, *Art & Antiques*, and *Brides* to the *New York Times Book Review* and the *Wall Street Journal*. She is also the author of *Arizona For Dummies*.

Published by:

## HUNGRY MINDS, INC.

909 Third Ave.
New York, NY 10022
www.frommers.com

ISBN: 0-7645-6201-0
ISSN: 1080-9104

Editor: Justin Lapatine
Production Editor: Heather Gregory
Photo Editor: Richard Fox
Design by Michele Laseau
Cartographer: Roberta Stockwell
Production by Hungry Minds Indianapolis Production Services

Front cover photo: River Walk, San Antonio
Back cover photo: Market Square, San Antonio

## SPECIAL SALES

For general information on Hungry Minds' products and services, please contact our Customer Care department; within the U.S. at 800-762-2974, outside the U.S. at 317-572-3993 or fax 317-572-4002. For sales inquiries and reseller information, including discounts, bulk sales, customized editions, and premium sales, please contact our Customer Care department at 800-434-3422.

Manufactured in the United States of America

5  4  3  2  1

*When should I travel to get the best airfare?*
*Where do I go for answers to my travel questions?*
*What's the best and easiest way to plan and book my trip?*

# frommers.travelocity.com

**Frommer's**, the travel guide leader, has teamed up with **Travelocity.com**, the leader in online travel, to bring you an in-depth, easy-to-use resource designed to help you plan and book your trip online.

At **frommers.travelocity.com**, you'll find free online updates about your destination from the experts at Frommer's plus the outstanding travel planning and purchasing features of Travelocity.com. Travelocity.com provides reservations capabilities for 95 percent of all airline seats sold, more than 47,000 hotels, and over 50 car rental companies. In addition, Travelocity.com offers more than 2,000 exciting vacation and cruise packages. Travelocity.com puts you in complete control of your travel planning with these and other great features:

**Expert travel guidance from Frommer's** - over 150 writers reporting from around the world!

**Best Fare Finder** - an interactive calendar tells you when to travel to get the best airfare

**Fare Watcher** - we'll track airfare changes to your favorite destinations

**Dream Maps** - a mapping feature that suggests travel opportunities based on your budget

**Shop Safe Guarantee** - 24 hours a day / 7 days a week live customer service, and more!

Whether traveling on a tight budget, looking for a quick weekend getaway, or planning the trip of a lifetime, Frommer's guides and Travelocity.com will make your travel dreams a reality. You've bought the book, now book the trip!

## Here's what the critics say about Frommer's:

"Amazingly easy to use. Very portable, very complete."
*—Booklist*

♦

"The only mainstream guide to list specific prices. The Walter Cronkite of guidebooks—with all that implies."
*—Travel & Leisure*

♦

"Complete, concise, and filled with useful information."
*—New York Daily News*

♦

"Hotel information is close to encyclopedic."
*—Des Moines Sunday Register*

♦

"Detailed, accurate and easy-to-read information for all price ranges."
*—Glamour Magazine*

# Contents

# List of Maps

## An Invitation to the Reader

In researching this book, we discovered many wonderful places—hotels, restaurants, shops, and more. We're sure you'll find others. Please tell us about them, so we can share the information with your fellow travelers in upcoming editions. If you were disappointed with a recommendation, we'd love to know that, too. Please write to:

*Frommer's San Antonio & Austin,* 4th Edition
Hungry Minds, Inc.
909 Third Avenue
New York, NY 10022

## An Additional Note

Please be advised that travel information is subject to change at any time—and this is especially true of prices. We therefore suggest that you write or call ahead for confirmation when making your travel plans. The authors, editors, and publisher cannot be held responsible for the experiences of readers while traveling. Your safety is important to us, however, so we encourage you to stay alert and be aware of your surroundings. Keep a close eye on cameras, purses, and wallets, all favorite targets of thieves and pickpockets.

## What the Symbols Mean

### ✪ Frommer's Favorites

Our favorite places and experiences—outstanding for quality, value, or both.

The following abbreviations are used for credit cards:

| | | | |
|---|---|---|---|
| AE | American Express | EC | Eurocard |
| CB | Carte Blanche | JCB | Japan Credit Bank |
| DC | Diners Club | MC | MasterCard |
| DISC | Discover | V | Visa |
| ER | EnRoute | | |

## Find Frommer's Online

**www.frommers.com** offers up-to-the-minute listings on almost 200 cities around the globe—including the latest bargains and candid, personal articles updated daily by Arthur Frommer himself. No other Web site offers such comprehensive and timely coverage of the world of travel.

# Introducing San Antonio & Austin

Call it the Fiesta City or the Alamo City; each of **San Antonio**'s nicknames reveals a different truth. Visitors come here to kick back and party, but they also come seeking Texas's history—and some would say its soul. They come to sit on the banks of a glittering river and sip cactus margaritas, but also to view the Franciscan missions that rose along the same river more than 2½ centuries ago.

Amid San Antonio's typical Southwest sprawl, it is the winding downtown streets most visitors recall. And that river! Few who come to San Antonio leave without a memory of a moment, quiet or heart quickening, sunlit or sparkling with tiny tree-draped lights, when the river somehow worked its magic on them.

**Austin,** that laid-back city in the lake-laced hills, home to cyberpunks and environmentalists, high culture and haute cuisine. A leafy intellectual enclave lying well outside the realm of Lone Star stereotypes, Austin has been compared to Berkeley and Seattle, but it is at once its own place and entirely of Texas.

Many Texans who live in faster-paced cities like Dallas or Houston dream of someday escaping to Austin, which, although it's passed the half-million population mark within its city limits alone, still has a small-town feel. Meanwhile, they smile upon the city as they would on a beloved but eccentric younger sister; whenever an especially contrary story about her is told, they shrug and shake their heads and fondly say, "Well, that's Austin."

## 1 Frommer's Favorite San Antonio Experiences

- **Recapturing Texas's Fight for Independence at the Alamo.** It's hard to imagine the state's prime attraction as a battle site, surrounded as it is today by downtown hotels and shops, until you step inside the Long Barrack, where Texas's most famous martyrs prepared to fight General Santa Anna's troops. See chapter 6.
- **Attending a Mariachi Mass at Mission San José.** You're welcome to watch members of the congregation of this largest of the mission churches raise their voices in spirited musical prayer every Sunday at noon. Come early, as seats are limited and this is a popular thing to do. See chapter 6.
- **Strolling Along the San Antonio River.** Whether you opt to join the throngs at the restaurants and cafes of the South Bank

portion of the River Walk or get away by yourself to one of its quieter stretches, the green, lush banks of San Antonio's river can match your mood, day or night. See chapter 6.

- **People-Watching at Market Square.** The shopping may be tonier in other parts of the city, but the atmosphere at the square's two lively Mexican markets can't be beat. After perusing the colorful wares, take a load off your feet and sip a margarita or a soda at an outdoor table. You'll spot vendors from Mexico and locals who have been coming here since the days when animals and produce were still being sold in the stalls. See chapter 7.
- **Seeing a Show at the Majestic Theatre.** As it happens, the restored Majestic offers top-notch shows of all kinds, but the venue itself, one of the world's last atmospheric theaters, is worth the price of admission alone. Book a seat in the front rows or the upstairs mezzanine, so you can watch the star-studded ceiling. See chapters 6 and 8.
- **Climbing into a Treehouse at the Witte Museum.** You can recapture your youth (or enjoy your kids relishing theirs) at the Witte, where the new HEB Treehouse has interactive science exhibits galore. See chapter 6.
- **Pretending You Live in the King William District.** The gorgeous homes built here by German merchants in the 19th century are eye-popping. You can't enter most of these opulent mansions (unless you're staying at one of the area's many B&Bs), but walk around with assurance and fantasize away. See chapter 6.
- **Riding the Coasters at Six Flags Fiesta Texas.** If you're a fan of stomach-churning adventure, has this theme park got coasters for you! The ever-expanding roster of thrill rides include the Superman Krypton, a gravity-defying coaster of steel; Joker's Revenge, which creates the illusion you're going backward; and the oldie but goodie Rattler, the world's highest and fastest wooden roller coaster. See chapter 6.
- **Climbing the Tower of the Americas in HemisFair Park.** It's a great way to get the lay of the land—no vantage point in the city is higher. And after dark, the lofty bar is an ideal place to sip a drink while overlooking the sparkling array of city lights. See chapters 6 and 8.
- **Buying a Piñata in Southtown.** This Hispanic neighborhood, adjacent to King William, is getting hip, but low-key stores still carry traditional celebration items. If you're lucky enough to be in town for the Day of the Dead, this is definitely the place to go. See chapter 7.
- **Checking out the Headgear at Paris Hatters.** Even if you're not in the market for a Stetson, you should at least wander over to this San Antonio institution that has sold hats to everyone from Pope John Paul II and Queen Elizabeth to Jimmy Smits. See chapter 7.
- **Grooving to Jazz at The Landing.** Jim Cullum and his band play cool jazz at a cool location—the River Walk. It's doesn't get much mellower than this. See chapter 8.

## 2 Frommer's Favorite Austin Experiences

- **Having Coffee at Mozart's.** Caffeine and conversation on a deck overlooking Lake Austin—a great way to end the day. See chapter 12.
- **Joining the Locals Along Austin's Hike & Bike Trails.** Head over to the shores of Town Lake to see why *Walking* magazine chose Austin as America's "Most Fit" city. Speed walkers, joggers, and in-line skaters share the turf with bicyclists and hikers on the many trails set up by the city for its urban athletes. See chapter 13.

- **Swimming at Barton Springs Pool.** The bracing waters of this natural pool have been drawing Austinites to its banks for more than 100 years. If there's one thing that everyone in town can agree on, it's that there's no better plunge pond on a hot day than this one. See chapter 13.
- **Watching the Bats.** From late March through November, thousands of bats emerge in smoky clouds from under the Congress Avenue Bridge, heading west for dinner. It's a mind-boggling sight, and you can thank each of the little mammals for keeping the air pest-free—a single bat can eat as many as 600 mosquitoes in an hour. See chapter 13.
- **Playing in the Water at Lake Travis.** The longest of the seven Highland Lakes, Travis offers the most opportunities for watery cavorting. Whether your thing is Jet-Skiing, snorkeling, or angling, you'll have plenty of choices here. See chapter 13.
- **Touring the Refurbished Capitol.** The country's largest state capitol was pretty impressive even in its run-down state, but after a massive face-lift, visitors can really see that it's a legislative center fit for Texas. See chapter 13.
- **Smelling the Roses at the Lady Bird Johnson Wildflower Center.** Spring is prime viewing time for the flowers, but Austin's mild winters ensure that there will always be bursts of color at Lady Bird Johnson's pet project. See chapter 13.
- **Chuckling over Tall Tales at the LBJ Library.** At the largest and most visited of the country's presidential libraries, a surprisingly lifelike animatronic figure of LBJ, dressed in the actual clothes of the late president and speaking (via recording) in his famed slow drawl, regales visitors with terrific Texas stories. See chapter 13.
- **Ascending Mount Bonnell.** Sure, the 100-odd steps are steep, but the climb is far more rewarding than a Stairmaster: When you reach the top, the view of the city will take away whatever breath you have left. See chapter 13.
- **Taking a Visitors Center Walking Tour.** I wouldn't ordinarily suggest herding activities, but these historic excursions provided free by the city are superb. See chapter 13.
- **Visiting O. Henry's Former Office.** The short-story writer used to work as a draftsman at the General Land Office, Texas's oldest surviving office building. Displays and a life-size cutout photo in what is now the visitors center for the Capitol Complex show how O. Henry spent his days. See chapter 13.
- **Visiting Stevie Ray Vaughan at Town Lake.** The late country rock star looks uncharacteristically stiff in his bronze incarnation, but he has a great view of Austin across the lake, and it's fun to see what kind of stuff his fans have left him. See chapter 13.
- **Listening to the Blues at Antone's.** Antone's may have moved to the trendy Warehouse District, but the music is as timeless as ever. Major blues stars coming through town always end up doing a few sets at Clifford Antone's institution. See chapter 15.
- **Drinking in Some History at Scholz Garten.** The oldest biergarten in Texas has loads of atmosphere—not to mention an up-to-date sound system. Just don't come here after the Longhorns have won (or lost) a game; the place will be packed with singing (or sulking) UT fans. See chapter 15.

## 3 Best San Antonio Hotel Bets

- **Best Historic Hotel:** Who can resist a place that's right across the street from the Alamo and still has the bar where Teddy Roosevelt recruited his Rough Riders?

A 19th-century gem, the **Menger,** 204 Alamo Plaza (☎ **800/345-9285** or 210/223-4361), sparkles now as it did 100 years ago.

- **Best for Business Travelers:** The **San Antonio Airport Hilton and Conference Center,** 611 NW Loop 410 (☎ **800-HILTONS** or 210/340-6060), offers a convenient jet-set location, data ports, a lubricate-those-business-deals sports bar, and an extremely helpful business center staff.

- **Best for Families:** If you can afford it, the **Hyatt Regency Hill Country Resort,** 9800 Hyatt Resort Dr. (☎ **800/233-1234** or 210/647-1234), just down the road from SeaWorld, is ideal for a family getaway. Kids get to splash in their own shallow pool and go tubing on a little river; there's plenty for grownups, too.

- **Best Moderately Priced Hotel:** It's a tossup between the **Ramada Emily Morgan,** 705 E. Houston St. (☎ **800/824-6674** or 210/225-8486), and the **Drury Inn & Suites,** 201 N. St. Mary's St. (☎ **800/DRURY-INN** or 210/212-5200), both economical downtown bets—in historic buildings, yet. You get a bit more for your money if you're traveling on business at the riverfront Drury Inn, but you're closer to all the tourist action (and just a few steps away from the water) at the Ramada. You can't go very wrong with either one.

- **Best Budget Lodging:** If you don't mind sharing a bathroom, you can't beat the rates at **Bullis House Inn,** 621 Pierce St. (☎ **210/223-9426**), a bed-and-breakfast in a historic home near Fort Sam Houston. Three rooms and a suite with private bathrooms are also available. You might even see Geronimo's ghost.

- **Best B&B:** The King William area abounds with B&Bs, but the **Ogé House,** 209 Washington St. (☎ **800/242-2770** or 210/223-2353), stands out as much for its professionalism as for its gorgeous mansion and lovely rooms. You don't have to sacrifice service for warmth here.

- **Best Health Club:** Not only does the health club at the **Marriott Rivercenter,** 101 Bowie St. (☎ **800/228-9290** or 210/223-1000), have the best weight machines and cardiovascular equipment of all the downtown hotels, but it's on the same floor as the free washers and dryers. You can hop on the treadmill while your clothes are in the spin cycle.

- **Hippest Hotel:** With its supercool cigar bar, faux porter trunk–era furnishings, and laid-back atmosphere, the **Havana Riverwalk Inn,** 1015 Navarro (☎ **888/224-2008** or 210/222-2008), is as much a scene as a place to bed down.

- **Best Place to Spot Celebrities:** Everyone from Paula Abdul to ZZ Top has stayed at **La Mansión del Rio,** 112 College St. (☎ **800/292-7300** or 210/225-2581); discretion, a willingness to cater to special requests, and a location that's just slightly away from the action might explain why.

- **Best for River Views:** As their names attest, the Holiday Inn Riverwalk, Hyatt Regency on the River Walk, La Mansión del Rio, the Marriott Rivercenter, and the Westin Riverwalk all have rooms that look out on the water. But the **Hilton Palacio del Rio,** 200 S. Alamo (☎ **800/HILTONS** or 210/222-1400), wins the prize for highest number of accommodations with river views. Stay here, and you can people-watch one of the most bustling sections of the promenade without even leaving your room.

- **Best New Additions to San Antonio's Lodging Scene:** The top new properties in town are both Westins. The **Westin Riverwalk Inn,** 420 W. Market St. (☎ **800/WESTIN-1** or 210/224-6500), upped the ante for elegance and grace on the water, while the **Westin La Cantera,** 16641 La Cantera Parkway (☎ **210/558-6500**), added cachet (and more great golf) to the northwest side of town.

## 4 Best Austin Hotel Bets

- **Best for Conducting Business:** Located near a lot of high-tech companies in northwest Austin, the **Renaissance Austin,** 9721 Arboretum Blvd. (☎ 800/ HOTELS-1 or 512/343-2626), has top-notch meeting and schmoozing spaces, not to mention fine close-the-deal-and-party spots.

- **Best Hotel Lobby for Pretending You're Rich:** Settle in at the lobby lounge at the posh **Four Seasons,** 98 San Jacinto Blvd. (☎ 800/332-3442 or 512/ 478-4500), overlooking Town Lake, and for the price of a Dubonnet, you can act like you stay here every time you fly in on your Learjet.

- **Best Comeback:** Gazing at its glorious, gleaming opulence, you'd never guess that the **Driskill Hotel,** 604 Brazos St. (☎ 800/252-9367 or 512/474-5911), had ever fallen into disrepair. Goes to show what $35 million can do.

- **Hippest Budget Hotel:** Look for the classic neon sign for the **Austin Motel,** 1220 S. Congress St. (☎ 512/441-1157), in Austin's newest cool area. The rooms have been individually furnished, many in fun and funky styles, but the place retains its 1950s character and its lower-than-1990s prices.

- **Best New Arrival:** A great design, chic location, and unexpected touches like Dr. Bronner's soap in the baths have made the **Hotel San José,** 1316 S. Congress Ave. (☎ 800/574-8897 or 512/444-7322), the hottest bed in town.

- **Best Bargain for Extended Stay Business Travelers:** For comfort (including a homey-feeling design, replete with trees), convenience to Northwest high-tech firms, and in-room perks at reasonable rates, you can't beat **Staybridge Suites,** 10201 Stonelake Blvd. (☎ 800/238-8000 or 512/349-0888).

- **Best View of Town Lake:** Lots of downtown properties have nice water views, but the **Hyatt Regency**'s location, 208 Barton Springs Rd. (☎ 800/233-1234 or 512/477-1234), on the lake's south shore, gives it the edge. You get a panoramic spread of the city with the capitol as a backdrop.

- **Best Health Club:** All those high-tech ways to sweat, and all those massage rooms to soothe sore muscles afterward—the **Barton Creek Resort,** 8212 Barton Club Dr. (☎ 800/336-6158 or 512/329-4000), raises exercise to an art form.

- **Greenest Hotel:** Several hotels in Austin take eco-consciousness beyond the old "we-won't-wash-your-towels-if-you-want-us-to-save-water" option, but no one goes nearly as far as **Habitat Suites,** 500 E. Highland Mall Blvd. (☎ 800/ 535-4663 or 512/467-6000).

- **Best for Forgetting Your Troubles:** Stress? That's a dirty word at the **Lake Austin Spa Resort,** 1705 S. Quinlan Park Rd. (☎ 800/847-5637, 800/ 338-6651, or 512/266-4362). After a few days at this lovely, ultrarelaxing spot, you'll be ready to face the world again, even if you don't especially want to.

## 5 Best San Antonio Dining Bets

- **Best for a Romantic Dinner:** On a quiet stretch of the River Walk, **Las Canarias,** at the Mansión del Rio, 112 College St. (☎ 210/518-1063), avoids the noise that plagues most water-view restaurants. You'll enjoy candlelight and superb, discreet service.

- **Best Moveable Feast:** It used to be that you could dine on the river only if you were with a group, but **Boudro's,** 421 E. Commerce St./River Walk (☎ 210/ 224-8484), now offers reservations on its dinner barges to individuals and couples. How sweet it is to drift downstream while enjoying one of the restaurant's excellent meals.

- **Best American Cuisine:** When we give the nod to **Silo,** 1133 Austin Hwy. (☎ 210/824-8686), as tops in American cuisine, we're not talking meatloaf and mashed potatoes (although versions of both dishes may turn up on the menu). Silo's New American recipes, which rely on fresh seasonal and regional ingredients, will dazzle those willing to expand their culinary horizons.
- **Best Continental Cuisine:** Get out those elastic-waist clothes for **Bistro Time,** 5137 Fredericksburg Rd. (☎ 210/344-6626), where wonderfully rich sauces hearken back to the days before the word *cholesterol* entered the national vocabulary.
- **Best Italian Cuisine:** This one goes to hometown favorite **Paesano's,** with two locations: on the River Walk, 111 Crockett, Suite 101 (☎ 210/22-PASTA); and in Lincoln Heights, 550 Basse Rd., Suite 100 (☎ 210/226-9541). The restaurant's cloned itself and relocated, but the fresh, home-style cooking that earned undying devotion hasn't changed since the earliest funky incarnation.
- **Best Mexican Cuisine:** This is a tough one to call in a city with so many worthy contenders, but **Rosario's,** 910 S. Alamo (☎ 210/223-1806), offers great atmosphere along with great food—not to mention some of the most potent margaritas in town.
- **Best New Restaurant:** A chef with an ancestor who cooked for French royalty creates fine French cuisine that even the hoi polloi can afford . . . yes, **Bistro Vatel,** 218 E. Olmos Ave (☎ 210/828-3141), is a very welcome addition to town.
- **Best Ribs on the River Walk:** Okay, so **County Line,** 111 W. Crockett St., Suite 104 (☎ 210/229-1941), is the only barbecue restaurant on the River Walk. But it draws locals downtown in droves for meat platters so good, people used to drive from as far away as Austin to get them.
- **Best Place to Encounter Artists:** Terrific food, a nice selection of libations, good prices, and a fun, funky atmosphere draw creative types of all kinds to the **Liberty Bar,** 328 E. Josephine St. (☎ 210/227-1187).

## 6 Best Austin Dining Bets

- **Best for a Romantic Dinner:** It's a bit of a drive and more than a bit of a wallet bite, but for a no-holds-barred romantic night out, you can't beat **Hudson's on the Bend,** 3509 Hwy. 620 North (☎ 512/266-1369).
- **Best View:** An easy choice—**The Oasis,** 6550 Comanche Trail, near Lake Travis (☎ 512/266-2441), whose multiple decks afford stunning views of Lake Travis and the Texas Hill Country.
- **Best New American Cuisine:** With its just-off-the-farm ingredients, gorgeous presentations, and smashing recipes—not to mention the sounds of indigenous jazz—**Zoot,** 509 Hearn (☎ 512/477-6535), gives American cooking a fresh new name.
- **Best French Cuisine:** Not only do they serve up excellent Gallic food at **Chez Nous,** 510 Neches St. (☎ 512/473-2413), but you don't have to pay an arm and a leg to enjoy it.
- **Best Italian Cuisine:** It's modern, it's cosmopolitan, it's **Mezzaluna,** 310 Colorado St. (☎ 512/472-6770), where the best of new Italian cooking trends and fine Italian wines finds an enthusiastic Austin audience.
- **Best Vegetarian Cuisine:** The **West Lynn Cafe,** 1110 W. Lynn (☎ 512/482-0950), has the largest noncarnivorous selection prepared in the most innovative ways. Vegetarians of all stripes leave here completely sated.

- **Best Place to Spot Celebrities:** You can expect to see the likes of Quentin Tarantino, Emilio Estevez, and Richard Linklater lounging in one of the back booths or hugging a bar stool up front at ultrahip **Güero's,** 1412 S. Congress (☎ **512/447-7688**).
- **Most Quintessentially Austin:** Its laid-back Texas menu, huge outdoor patio, "unplugged" music series, and goofy activities like a Betty Boop festival all make **Shady Grove,** 1624 Barton Springs Rd. (☎ **512/474-9991**), the Platonic ideal of The Austin Restaurant.
- **Most Drop-Dead Gorgeous Dining:** Stylin' from its stunning art nouveau chandeliers down to the arrangement of those little vegetables on the plate, **Sardine Rouge,** 311 W. Sixth St. (☎ **512/473-8642**), will have you fantasizing about redecorating your own place.
- **Best Brunch:** It's a tie between the Sunday buffet at **Green Pastures,** 811 W. Live Oak Rd. (☎ **512/444-4747**), where Austinites have been imbibing milk punch, liberally dosed with bourbon, rum, brandy, ice cream, and nutmeg, for years, and the one at **Fonda San Miguel,** 2330 W. North Loop (☎ **512/459-4121**), where the spread runs deliciously toward Mexico.
- **Sweetest Contribution to the Dining Scene:** Austin's home-grown brand of ice cream, **Amy's,** is wonderfully rich and creamy. Watching the colorfully clad servers juggling the scoops is always a kick. Amy's has six Austin locations, including one on the west side of downtown, 1012 W. Sixth St. at Lamar Boulevard (☎ **512/480-0673**), and one at the Arboretum, 10000 Research Blvd., (☎ **512/345-1006**). And if you don't have a chance to try it in town, you can sample this tasty treat at the airport.

# 2

# Planning a Trip to San Antonio

**S**pontaneity is all well and good once you get to where you're going, but advance planning can make or break a trip. San Antonio is becoming more and more popular; it's best to book your vacation here well in advance. If you're thinking of coming for April's huge Fiesta bash, try to reserve at least 6 months ahead of time to avoid disappointment.

## 1 Visitor Information

Contact the **San Antonio Convention and Visitors Bureau** (**SACVB**), P.O. Box 2277, San Antonio, TX 78298 (☎ **800/ 447-3372;** e-mail: sacvb@ci.sat.tx.us), for a useful pretrip information packet, including a visitors' guide and map, lodging guide, detailed calendar of events, arts brochure, and "SAVE San Antonio" booklet with discount coupons for a number of hotels and attractions. You can also get pretrip information, sans discount coupons, online at the SACVB's Web site, **www.sanantoniocvb.com**.

Phone or fill in an online form on the Web site of the **Texas Department of Tourism** (☎ **800/8888-TEX;** www.traveltex.com) to receive the *Texas State Travel Guide,* a glossy book chock-full of information about the state, along with a statewide accommodations booklet; you can also request it in CD-ROM form. The **Texas Travel Information Center** has a toll-free number (☎ **800/452-9292**) to call for the latest on road conditions, special events, and general attractions in the areas you're interested in visiting; traveler counselors will even advise you on the quickest or most scenic route to your intended destination. *Texas Monthly* magazine, another good source of information, can be accessed at **www.texasmonthly.com**.

## 2 Money

Like most tourist-oriented cities, San Antonio has two price structures: one for locals and one for visitors. You can expect everything from food to hotels to souvenirs to be fairly pricey on the River Walk and at theme parks such as SeaWorld. In general, however, the average San Antonio salary is not terribly high, and the cost of living is about 10% lower than the country's average, so prices tend to be moderate.

Minimal cash is required, since credit cards are accepted universally, and automatic teller machines linked to national networks are strewn around tourist destinations and, increasingly, within hotels. To find

| What Things Cost in San Antonio | U.S. $ | U.K. £ |
| --- | --- | --- |
| Taxi from the airport to the city center | 15.00 | 10.30 |
| Streetcar ride between any two downtown points | 0.50 | 0.35 |
| Local telephone call | 0.35 | 0.25 |
| Long-neck beer | 2.00 | 1.40 |
| Double at La Mansion del Rio (very expensive) | 258.00 | 178.60 |
| Double at Drury Inn & Suites San Antonio Riverwalk (moderate) | 129.00 | 89.30 |
| Double at La Quinta, Market Square (inexpensive) | 69.00 | 47.75 |
| Lunch for one at Rosario's (moderate) | 10.00 | 6.90 |
| Lunch for one at Schilo's (inexpensive) | 6.00 | 4.15 |
| Dinner for one, without wine, at Las Canarias (very expensive) | 45.00 | 31.15 |
| Dinner for one, without beer, at La Calesa (moderate) | 14.00 | 9.70 |
| Dinner for one, without wine, at Earl Abel's (inexpensive) | 9.00 | 6.20 |
| Coca-Cola | 1.00–1.50 | 0.70–1.05 |
| Cup of espresso | 1.30–2.00 | 0.90–1.40 |
| Roll of ASA 100 Kodacolor film, 36 exposures | 6.00 | 4.15 |
| Admission to the Witte Museum | 5.95 | 4.10 |
| Movie ticket | 1.50–7.00 | 1.05–4.85 |
| Ticket to the San Antonio Symphony | 15.00–52.00 | 10.30–35.80 |
| Ticket to a Spurs game | 5.00–55.50 | 3.50–38.40 |

ATMs on the **Cirrus** network, call ☎ **800/424-7787;** for the **PLUS** system, call ☎ **800/843-7587.**

The three major traveler's checks agencies are **American Express** (☎ **800/221-7282**), **BankAmerica** (☎ **800/227-3460**), and **VISA** (☎ **800/227-6811**). See also Appendix B, "For Foreign Visitors."

## 3 When to Go

Most tourists visit San Antonio in summer, though it's not really the ideal season: The weather can be steamy, and restaurants and attractions tend to be crowded. That said, there are plenty of places to cool off around town, hotel rates are generally lower (conventioneers come in the fall, winter, and spring), and some of the most popular outdoor attractions, such as SeaWorld and Six Flags Fiesta Texas are open only—or have far more extended schedules—this time of year. Consider booking a B&B or a hotel that's not business oriented during the week: San Antonio is the single most popular destination in the state for Texans, many of whom drive in just for the weekend.

### CLIMATE

Complain to San Antonians about their city's heat on a sultry summer day and you're likely to be assured that it's far more humid in say, Houston, or anywhere in East Texas.

This may be true—but it won't make you feel any less sweaty. From late May to early September, expect regular high temperatures and high humidity.

Fall and spring are generally prime times to visit; the days are pleasantly warm and, if you come in late March/early April, the wildflowers in the nearby Hill Country will be in glorious bloom. Temperate weather combined with the lively celebrations surrounding Christmas also make November and December good months to visit. January and February can be a bit raw—but if you're from up north, you probably won't even notice.

### San Antonio's Average Monthly Temperature & Rainfall

|  | Jan | Feb | Mar | Apr | May | June | July | Aug | Sept | Oct | Nov | Dec |
|---|---|---|---|---|---|---|---|---|---|---|---|---|
| Avg. Temp. (°F) | 52.0 | 54.5 | 60.8 | 68.2 | 75.3 | 81.9 | 84.0 | 83.8 | 79.3 | 70.5 | 59.7 | 53.2 |
| Rainfall (in.) | 1.66 | 2.06 | 1.54 | 2.54 | 3.07 | 2.79 | 1.69 | 2.41 | 3.71 | 2.84 | 1.77 | 1.46 |

## THE FIESTA CITY

San Antonio's nickname refers to its huge April bash, but it also touches on the city's tendency to party at the drop of a sombrero. It's only natural that a place with strong Southern, Western, and Hispanic roots would know how to have a good time: Elaborately costumed festival queens, wild-and-woolly rodeos, and Mexican food and mariachis are rolled out year-round. And where else but San Antonio would something as potentially dull as draining a river turn into a cause for celebration?

## San Antonio Calendar of Events

Please note that the information contained below is always subject to change. For the most up-to-date information on these events, call the number provided, or check with the Convention and Visitors Bureau (☎ **800/447-3372;** www.SanAntonioCVB.com).

**January**

- **River Walk Mud Festival,** River Walk. Every year, when the horseshoe bend of the San Antonio River Walk is drained for maintenance purposes, San Antonians cheer themselves up by electing a king and queen to reign over such events as Mud Stunts Day and the Mud Pie Ball at Kangaroo Court Restaurant. ☎ **210/227-4262;** www.thesanantonioriverwalk.com. Mid-January.

**February**

- **Stock Show and Rodeo,** Joe and Harry Freeman Coliseum. Starting in early February, San Antonio hosts more than 2 weeks of rodeo events, livestock judging, country-and-western bands, and carnivals. It's been going (and growing) since 1949. ☎ **210/225-5851;** www.sarodeo.com.
- **San Antonio CineFestival,** Guadalupe Cultural Arts Center. The nation's oldest and largest Chicano/Latino film festival screens more than 70 films and videos. ☎ **210/271-3151;** www.guadalupeculturalarts.org. Late February to early March.

**March**

- **Dyeing O' The River Green and Pub Crawl.** Are leprechauns responsible for turning the San Antonio River into the green River Shannon? Irish dance and music fill the Arneson River Theatre from the afternoon on. ☎ **210/227-4262;** www.thesanantonioriverwalk.com. March 17.

**April**

- **Starving Artist Show,** River Walk and La Villita. Part of the proceeds of the works sold by nearly 900 local artists go to benefit the Little Church of La Villita's program to feed the hungry. ☎ **210/226-3593;** www.lavillita.com. First weekend of the month.

❂ **Fiesta San Antonio.** What started as a modest marking of Texas's independence more than 100 years ago is now a huge event, with an elaborately costumed royal court presiding over 10 days of revelry: parades, balls, food fests, sporting events, concerts, and art shows all over town. Call ☎ **210/227-5191,** or 877/ SA-FIESTA within Texas, for details on tickets and events, or log on to **www. fiesta-sa.org**. Starts the third week of the month.

## May

❂ **Tejano Conjunto Festival,** Rosedale Park and Guadalupe Theater. This annual festival, sponsored by the Guadalupe Cultural Arts Center, celebrates the lively and unique blend of Mexican and German music born in south Texas. The best conjunto musicians perform at the largest event of its kind in the world. Call ☎ **210/271-3151** for schedules and ticket information, or check the Web site, **www.guadalupeculturalarts.org**. Mid-May.

• **Fiesta Noche del Rio,** Arneson River Theatre. A colorful revue celebrating Latin culture. The performance takes place on one side of the river while the audience claps from the opposite bank. ☎ **210/226-4651;** www.alamo-kiwanis.org. Every Friday and Saturday from mid-May through July.

• **Return of the Chili Queens,** Market Square. An annual tribute to chili, said to have originated in San Antonio, with music, dancing, crafts demonstrations, and, of course, chili aplenty. Bring the Tums. ☎ **210/207-8600.** Memorial Day weekend.

## June

• **Sí TV Latino Laugh Festival,** Rivercenter Comedy Club and various venues. National and local comedians participate in this 4-day Latino humor fest. Past celebrities appearing for this fun event include Cheech Marin, Edward James Olmos, Jimmy Smits, Daisy Fuentes, and Erik Estrada. ☎ **323/651-2242;** www.sitv.com. Four days in June.

• **Texas Folklife Festival,** Institute of Texas Cultures. Ethnic foods, dances, crafts demonstrations, and games celebrate the diversity of Texas's heritage. ☎ **210/ 558-2300;** www.texancultures.utsa.edu/main/. Four days in June.

• **Juneteenth,** various venues. The anniversary of the announcement of the Emancipation Proclamation in Texas in 1865 is the occasion for a series of African-American celebrations, including an outdoor jazz concert, gospelfest, parade, picnic, and more. Call the San Antonio Convention and Visitors Bureau for details at ☎ **800/447-3372.** June 19.

## July

• **Contemporary Art Month,** various venues. You can pick up a calendar of the more than 70 events that get the city's creative (and acquisitive) juices flowing throughout July at the Blue Star Arts Complex. ☎ **210/227-6960;** www. bluestarartspace.org.

## September

• **Diez y Seis.** Mexican independence from Spain is feted at several different downtown venues, including La Villita, the Arneson River Theatre, and Guadalupe Plaza. Music and dance, a parade, and a *charreado* (rodeo) are part of the fun. ☎ **210/223-3151;** www.agatx.org. Weekend nearest September 16.

• **Jazz'SAlive,** Travis Park. Bands from New Orleans and San Antonio come together for a weekend of hot jazz. ☎ **210/207-3000;** www.ci.sat.tx.us/sapar. Third weekend in September.

## October

- **Oktoberfest,** Beethoven Home. San Antonio's German roots show at this festival with food, dance, oompah bands, and beer. ☎ **210/222-1521.** Early October.
- **Inter-American Bookfair and Literary Festival,** Guadalupe Cultural Arts Center. As many as 50 nationally and regionally acclaimed writers gather for poetry and fiction readings, workshops, panel discussions, and book exhibits. ☎ **210/271-3151;** www.guadalupeculturalarts.org. Changing dates in October.

## November

○ **Lighting Ceremony and River Walk Holiday Parade.** Trees and bridges along the river are illuminated by some 80,000 lights, and Santa Claus arrives on a boat during this floating river parade. ☎ **210/227-4262;** www.thesanantonioriverwalk.com. Friday following Thanksgiving.

## December

- **Fiestas Navideñas,** Market Square. The Mexican market hosts piñata parties, a blessing of the animals, and surprise visits from Pancho Claus. ☎ **210/207-8600.** Weekends in December.
- **Rivercenter Christmas Pageant.** River barges in the Rivercenter complex are the untraditional setting for the traditional Christmas story. ☎ **210/225-0000;** www.shoprivercenter.com. December weekends leading up to the holiday.
- **Las Posadas,** River Walk. Children carrying candles lead the procession along the river, reenacting the search for lodging in a moving multifaith rendition of the Christmas story. ☎ **210/224-6163;** www.saconservation.org. Second Sunday in December.

# 4  Insurance

There are three kinds of travel insurance: trip cancellation, medical, and lost luggage. Trip cancellation insurance is a good idea if you have paid a large portion of your vacation expenses up front.

But the other two types of insurance don't make sense for most travelers. Your existing health insurance should cover you if you get sick while on vacation (although if you belong to an HMO, you should check to see whether you are fully covered when away from home). And your homeowner's insurance should cover stolen luggage if you have off-premises theft. Check your existing policies before you buy any additional coverage. The airlines are responsible for $2,500 on domestic flights if they lose your luggage; if you plan to carry anything more valuable than that, keep it in your carry-on bag.

Some credit cards (American Express and certain gold and platinum Visa and MasterCards, for example) offer automatic flight insurance against death or dismemberment in case of an airplane crash. If you still feel you need more insurance, try one of the companies listed below. But don't pay for more insurance than you need. For example, if you need only trip cancellation insurance, don't purchase coverage for lost or stolen property. Trip cancellation insurance costs approximately 6% to 8% of the total value of your vacation. Among the reputable issuers of travel insurance are:

**Access America,** 6600 W. Broad St., Richmond, VA 23230 (☎ **800/284-8300;** www.accessamerica.com);

**Travelex Insurance Services,** 11717 Burt St., Suite 202, Omaha, NE 68154 (☎ **800/228-9792;** www.travelex-insurance.com);

**Travel Guard International,** 1145 Clark St., Stevens Point, WI 54481
(☎ **800/826-1300;** www.travel-guard.com);
**Travel Insured International, Inc.,** P.O. Box 280568, 52-S Oakland Ave.,
East Hartford, CT 06128 (☎ **800/243-3174;** www.travelinsured.com).

## 5  Tips for Travelers with Special Needs

### FOR TRAVELERS WITH DISABILITIES

**Access-Able Travel Source** (www.access-able.com) is a comprehensive database of
travel agents who specialize in disabled travel; it's also a clearinghouse for information
about accessible destinations around the world, including Texas. Another excellent
resource for travelers with any type of disability is **Mobility International USA,**
P.O. Box 10767, Eugene, OR 97440 (☎ **541/343-1284,** voice and TDD; www.
miusa.org), a nonprofit organization involved in promoting travel awareness for people who have difficulty in getting around. The organization publishes *A World of
Options,* a 658-page book of resources for travelers with disabilities, covering everything from biking trips to scuba outfitters ($35; www.miusa.org).

The new $2 million Riverwalk Trolley Station is a boon for those who use wheel-
chairs, as it has a large elevator to transport people down to the water. Contact the San
Antonio Planning Department (☎ **210/207-7873** voice or 210/207-7911 TDD) for
additional information about accessibility, or click on to the disability access section
of the department's Web site (www.ci.sat.tx.us/planning/disability/) to download a
River Walk map with locations of ramps, elevators and other disabled-friendly access
areas. For VIA Trans Disabled Accessibility Information, phone ☎ **210/362-5050**
(voice) or 210/362-5060 (TDD).

### FOR GAY & LESBIAN TRAVELERS

The Web site of the **Gay and Lesbian Community Center of San Antonio,** 3126 N.
St. Mary's, Suite 400 (☎ **210/732-4300;** www.glccsa.org), is an excellent resource for
information on the city's fairly large, but not exceedingly visible, gay and lesbian population. Features include a calendar of events, listings of gay-friendly businesses, and publications, including the local lesbian newspaper, *Woman Space.* If you stay at the **Painted
Lady Inn,** a gay-owned bed-and-breakfast at 620 Broadway (☎ **210/220-1092;** e-mail:
trvl2sa@earthlink.net), you can also find out all you want to know about the local scene.
**The Esperanza Peace & Justice Center,** 922 San Pedro (☎ **210/641-8123;**
www.esperanzacenter.org), runs a gay and lesbian film series each September. See also
chapter 8 for information about gay bars.

### FOR SENIORS

By joining the **American Association of Retired Persons (AARP),** 601 E St. NW,
Washington, DC 20049 (☎ **202/434-2277),** those over age 50 can get good discounts on many hotels, rental cars, and sights; at extra cost, the Amoco Motoring Plan
offers trip-routing information and emergency road service. (Always remember to ask
about these discounts in advance—for example, when you're booking a room or renting a car, not when you're checking out or returning the vehicle.)

The nonprofit **Elderhostel,** 75 Federal St., 3rd Floor, Boston, MA 02110 (☎ **617/
426-7788;** www.elderhostel.org), has a great variety of inexpensive and interesting
study programs, including room and board, for travelers ages 55 and older; find the
complete catalog online or mail away for one. San Antonio–based courses may range
from a general introduction to Texas history to more specialized subjects, such as the
architecture of the Spanish missions.

# Fighting the Airfare Wars

Airfares are capitalism at its purest. Passengers within the same cabin on an airplane rarely pay the same fare. Rather, they pay what the market will bear.

Business travelers who need the flexibility to buy their tickets at the last minute and change their itinerary at a moment's notice, and whose priority it is to get home before the weekend, pay the premium rate, known as the full fare (at least their companies do). Passengers who can book their ticket long in advance, who don't mind staying over Saturday night, or who are willing to travel on a Tuesday, Wednesday, or Thursday pay the least, usually a fraction of the full fare. On most flights, even the shortest hops, the full fare is close to $1,000 or more, but a 7-day or 14-day advance purchase ticket is closer to $200 to $300. Obviously, it pays to plan ahead.

The airlines also periodically hold sales, in which they lower the prices on their most popular routes. These fares have advance purchase requirements and date-of-travel restrictions, but you can't beat the prices. Keep your eyes open for these sales, which tend to take place in seasons of low travel volume, as you're planning your vacation. You'll almost never see a sale around the peak summer vacation months of July and August, or around Thanksgiving or Christmas, when people have to fly regardless of the fare they have to pay.

**Consolidators,** also known as bucket shops, are a good place to check for the lowest fares. Their prices are much better than the fares you could get yourself, and are often even lower than what your travel agent can get you. You see their ads in the small boxes at the bottom of the page in your Sunday travel section. Some of the most reliable consolidators include **Cheap Tickets** (☎ **800/ 377-1000;** www. cheaptickets.com), which also offers discounts on car rentals and hotel rooms; **Travac Tours & Charters** (☎ **877/872-8221;**

## FOR FAMILIES

The **Family Travel Times** newsletter, *Travel with Your Children,* 40 Fifth Ave., New York, NY 10011 (☎ **888/822-4388** or 212/477-5524; www.familytraveltimes.com), published six times a year, offers good general information, as well as destination-specific articles. Subscriptions cost $39; get one online, by phone, or by snail mail. The free monthly *Our Kids* magazine, published in San Antonio, includes a calendar that lists daily activities oriented toward children; you can find it in San Antonio at Jim's restaurants, HEB supermarkets, Wal-Mart, Toys "Я" Us, Barnes & Noble, and Borders, or order it in advance from the publisher: 8400 Blanco, Suite 201, San Antonio, TX 78216 (☎ **210/349-6667;** www.parenthoodweb.com; e-mail: sanantonioparenting@unitedad.com).

## FOR STUDENTS

You don't have to be a student—or even a youth—to join Hostelling International–American Youth Hostels, 733 15th St. NW, Suite 840, Washington, DC 20005 (☎ **202/783-6161;** www.iyhf.org; e-mail: hiayhserv@hiayh.org), which gives its members discounts at its dorm-style hostels around the world, and also offers rail and bus travel discounts in many places. See chapter 10 for details on the **Council on International Educational Exchange** (**CIEE**), which has an office in Austin but not San Antonio.

Although San Antonio has 12 2- and 4-year institutions of higher education, it's not really a college town, and there's no general gathering place for college-agers, although

www.thetravelsite.com), with useful links to lots of different travel Web sites; and FlyCheap (☎ **800/FLY-CHEAP;** www.flycheap.com), which requires you to provide a lot of information about yourself before you can find out very much about them.

Another way to find the cheapest fare is to scour the Internet. That's what computers do best—search through millions of pieces of data and return information in ranking order. The number of virtual travel agents on the Internet has increased exponentially in recent years.

It would be impossible to go into all the travel booking sites, but a few of the better-respected (and more comprehensive) ones are **Travelocity** (www.travelocity. com), **Microsoft Expedia** (www.expedia.com), and **Yahoo! Travel** (http:// travel.yahoo.com). Each has its own little quirks, but all provide variations of the same service. Just enter the dates you want to fly and the cities you want to visit, and the computer looks for the lowest fares. Several other features have become standard to these sites: the ability to check flights at different times or dates in hopes of finding a cheaper fare; e-mail alerts when fares drop on a route you have specified; and a database of last-minute deals that advertises super-cheap vacation packages or airfares for those who can get away at a moment's notice.

Great last-minute deals are also available directly from the airlines themselves through a free e-mail service called **E-savers.** Each week, the airline sends you a list of discounted flights, usually leaving the upcoming Friday or Saturday, and returning the following Monday or Tuesday. You can sign up for all the major airlines at once by logging on to **Smarter Living** (www.smarterliving.com), or go to each individual airline's Web site. These sites offer schedules, flight booking, and information on late-breaking bargains.

they tend to gravitate toward the entertainment strip on North St. Mary's Street on the weekends. The local branch of the state system, the **University of Texas at San Antonio,** has two campuses, one north of town at 6900 N. Loop 1604 (☎ **210/ 458-4011**), and a newer one on the western side of downtown, at 501 W. Durango (☎ **210/458-2700**). The city's other major universities, **Trinity,** 715 Stadium Dr. (☎ **210/999-7011**); **St. Mary's,** 1 Camino Santa Maria (☎ **210/436-3011**); and **University of the Incarnate Word,** 4301 Broadway (☎ **210/829-6000**), are all private. The best source of local information for student visitors is probably **Hostelling International–San Antonio** (see chapter 4).

## 6 Getting There

### BY PLANE

**THE MAJOR AIRLINES**    The major domestic carriers serving San Antonio are **America West** (☎ 800/235-9292; www.americawest.com), **American** (☎ 800/ 433-7300; www.aa.com), **Continental** (☎ 800/525-0280; www.flycontinental.com), **Delta** (☎ 800/221-1212; www.delta.com), **Midwest Express** (☎ 800/452-2022; www.midwestexpress.com), **Northwest** (☎ 800/225-2525; www.nwa.com), **Southwest** (☎ 800/435-9792; www.iflyswa.com), **Sun Country** (☎ 800/359-6786; www. suncountry.com), **TWA** (☎ 800/221-2000; www.twa.com), and **United** (☎ 800/ 241-6522; www.ual.com). **Aerolitoral** (☎ 800/237-6639; www.aerolitoral.com),

**Aeromar** (☎ 888/627-0207; www.aeromar-air.com), **Continental** (☎ 800/231-0856; www.flycontinental.com), and **Mexicana** (☎ 800/531-7921; www.mexicana.com) offer service to and from Mexico. For the most current information on who jets into town, check the airport Web site: www.ci.sat.tx.us/aviation/index.htm.

Because San Antonio isn't a hub, service to the city has been circuitous in the past, but Southwest currently offers nonstops from Los Angeles, Las Vegas, Phoenix, Nashville, and Orlando; America West flies directly from Las Vegas and Phoenix; American goes straight from Chicago; Sun Country has nonstop service from Minneapolis/St. Paul; TWA flies direct from St. Louis; and Continental has uninterrupted service from Newark, Washington, DC, and Tampa. Both Continental and Mexicana offer direct flights from Mexico City.

**FINDING THE BEST AIRFARES**    The lowest standard fares to San Antonio require a 14-day or 21-day advance purchase, a stay-over Saturday night, and travel during the week. Even with these restrictions, round-trip prices from New York to San Antonio hover around $500; from Chicago, around $350; and from Los Angeles, $200. If you're departing from one of the cities that Southwest services, you're likely to get the lowest rates on that airline. Remember that all the airlines run seasonal specials; look for them as soon as you start thinking about taking a trip. See also the "Fighting the Airfare Wars" sidebar; lots of carriers are now directing their passengers to their own and affiliated Web sites for the best fares.

## BY CAR

As has been said of Rome, all roads lead to San Antonio. The city is fed by four interstates (I-35, I-10, I-37, and I-410), five U.S. highways (U.S. 281, U.S. 90, U.S. 87, U.S. 181, and U.S. 81), and five state highways (Hwy. 16, Hwy. 13, Hwy. 211, Hwy. 151, and Hwy. 1604). In San Antonio, I-410 and Hwy. 1604, which circle the city, are referred to as Loop 410 and Loop 1604. All freeways lead into the central business district; U.S. 281 and Loop 410 are closest to the airport.

San Antonio is 975 miles from Atlanta, 1,979 miles from Boston, 1,187 miles from Chicago, 1,342 miles from Los Angeles, 1,360 miles from Miami, 527 miles from New Orleans, 1,781 miles from New York, 1,724 miles from San Francisco, and 2,149 miles from Seattle. The distance to Dallas is 282 miles, to Houston 199 miles, and to Austin 80 miles.

## BY TRAIN

**Amtrak** provides service three times a week—east to Miami via Houston, Lafayette, and New Orleans, and west to Los Angeles via El Paso and Tucson—from its depot at 350 Hoefden (☎ 210/223-3226). There is also thrice-weekly service between San Antonio and Chicago via Austin, Fort Worth, Dallas, Little Rock, St. Louis, and Springfield. Call ☎ **800/USA-RAIL** or log on to **www.amtrak.com** for current fares, schedules, and reservations.

## BY BUS

San Antonio's **Greyhound** station, 500 N. St. Mary's St. (☎ **210/270-5829**), is located downtown about 2 blocks from the River Walk. The bustling station, which is open 24 hours, is within walking distance of a number of hotels, and many public streetcar and bus lines run nearby. Look for Greyhound's 14-day advance specials, 3-day advance companion special (if you book a round-trip at least 3 days in advance, a companion rides free), and other promotional discounts. For all current price and schedule information, call ☎ **800/229-9424** (☎ 800/345-3109 TDD; 800/752-4841 for assistance for people with disabilities), or log on to **www.greyhound.com**.

# Getting to Know
# San Antonio

**3**

For visitors, San Antonio is really two cities. Downtown, site of the original Spanish settlements, is the compact, eminently strollable tourist hub. The River Walk and its waterside development have revitalized a once-decaying urban center that now buzzes with hotels, restaurants, and shops. And thanks in large part to the San Antonio Conservation Society, many of downtown's beautiful old buildings are still intact; some house popular tourist attractions and hotels, while others are occupied by the large businesses that are increasingly trickling back to where it all began.

The other city is spread out, mostly low-rise, and connected by freeways—more than its fair share, in fact. San Antonio's most recent growth has been toward the northwest, where you'll find the sprawling South Texas Medical Center complex and, farther out, the ritzy Dominion Country Club and housing development, Six Flags Fiesta Texas theme park, and the gorgeous new Westin La Cantera Resort. The old southeast section, home to four of the five historic missions, remains largely Hispanic, while much of the southwest is taken up by Kelly and Lackland Air Force Bases. Whether you fly or drive in, you're likely to find yourself in the northeast at some point: Along with the airport, this section hosts the Brackenridge Park attractions and some of the best restaurants and shops in town.

You'll probably want your own wheels if you're staying in this second San Antonio; downtown, where public transportation is cheap and plentiful, a car tends to be more of a hindrance than a help.

## 1 Orientation

### ARRIVING

**BY PLANE**  The two-terminal San Antonio International Airport (☎ 210/207-3411; www.ci.sat.tx.us/aviation), about 13 miles north of downtown, is compact, clean, well marked—even cheerful. Among its various amenities are a postal center, ATM, foreign-currency exchange, game room, and well-stocked gift shops. Each terminal hosts an unstaffed branch office of the City of San Antonio Visitor Information Center (see "Visitor Information," below) with an electronic panel on which you can pull up descriptions of selected area hotels and a phone that will connect you directly to them. Advantage, Alamo, Avis, Budget, Dollar, Enterprise, Hertz, and National all have desks at both of the airport terminals.

Loop 410 and U.S. 281 south intersect just outside the airport. If you're renting a car here (see "By Car" in "Getting Around," below), it should take about 15 to 20 minutes to drive downtown via U.S. 281 south.

Most of the hotels within a radius of a mile or two offer **free shuttle service** to and from the airport (be sure to check when you make your reservation). If you're staying downtown, you'll most likely have to pay your own way.

**VIA Metropolitan Transit**'s **bus no. 2** is the cheapest (75¢) way to get downtown but also the slowest; it'll take from 40 to 45 minutes. You need exact change. (If you have a long layover at the airport, VIA's Loop 550/551 Limited express bus can take you to the nearby North Star and Central Park malls and let you shop the time away.)

**SA Trans** (☎ **800/868-7707** or 210/281-9900), with a booth outside each of the terminals, offers shared van service from the airport to the downtown hotels for $8 per person one-way, $14 round-trip. Vans run from about 6am until 1am; phone 24 hours in advance for van pickup from your hotel.

There's also a **taxi** queue in front of each terminal. The base charge on a taxi is $1.60; add $1.50 for each mile. It should cost you about $14 to $16 to get downtown, including the 50¢ airport departure fee; from 9pm to 5am the base charge is $2.60, plus the usual $1.50 per additional mile.

**BY TRAIN**    The station is located in St. Paul's Square, on the east side of downtown near the Alamodome and adjacent to the Sunset Station entertainment complex. Drink and snack machines are available in the station, and there's an ATM machine at the Alamodome, within easy walking distance of the station. Lockers are not available (for security reasons), but Amtrak will hold passengers' bags in a secure location for $1.50 per bag. Information about the city is available at the main counter. Both east and westbound trains come into San Antonio at ungodly hours (after 3am and 4am, respectively), so you're not likely to be able to jump straight into any partying, but you can easily pick up a cab from here.

## VISITOR INFORMATION

The main office of the **City of San Antonio Visitor Information Center** is across the street from the Alamo, at 317 Alamo Plaza (☎ **210/207-6748**). Hours are daily 8:30am to 6pm, except Thanksgiving, Christmas, and New Year's, when the center is closed. Two unstaffed satellite offices with brochures are located in Terminals One and Two of the San Antonio International Airport; they both have phones that will connect you to the main office.

Publications such as the free *Fiesta,* a glossy magazine with interesting articles about the city, and *Rio,* a tabloid focusing on the River Walk, are available at the Visitor Information Center, as well as at most downtown hotels and many shops and tourist sights. Both of these advertising-based tourist publications list sights, restaurants, shops, cultural events, and some night life. Also free but less obviously ad-driven is San Antonio's alternative paper, the *Current.* It's pretty skimpy, but it's a good source for night-life listings (although not for movie schedules). Check out the Current's *Visitors Guide to the Alamo City,* published four times a year and available at most River Walk hotels, restaurants, and bars, for its offbeat takes on the standard tourist attractions and its suggestions for unusual things to do around town.

The **San Antonio Express-News** is the local newspaper and it's got a good arts/entertainment section called "The Weekender," which comes out on Friday and is available for free around town.

Arguably the best state-oriented magazine in the country, **Texas Monthly** contains excellent short reviews of restaurants in San Antonio, among other cities; its incisive articles about local politics, people, and events are a great way to get acquainted with Lone Star territory in general. You can buy a copy at almost any local bookstore, grocery, or newsstand.

## CITY LAYOUT

Although it lies at the southern edge of the Texas Hill Country, San Antonio itself is basically flat. As I noted earlier, the city divides into two distinct districts: a compact **central downtown** surrounded by a Western-style, freeway-laced **sprawl.** Neither section is laid out in a neat grid system; many of downtown's streets trace the meandering course of the San Antonio River, while a number of the thoroughfares in the rest of town follow old conquistador routes or 19th-century wagon trails.

**MAIN ARTERIES & STREETS**   Welcome to loop land. Most of the major roads in Texas meet in San Antonio, where they form a rough wheel-and-spoke pattern: I-410 traces a 53-mile circumference around the city, and Hwy. 1604 forms an even larger circle around them both. I-35, I-10, I-37, U.S. 281, U.S. 90, and U.S. 87, along with many smaller thoroughfares, run diagonally, but not always separately, across these two loops to form its main spokes. For example, U.S. 90, U.S. 87, and I-10 converge for a while in an east–west direction just south of downtown, while U.S. 281, I-35, and I-37 run together on a north–south route to the east; I-10, I-35, and U.S. 87 bond for a bit going north–south to the west of downtown. As a result, you may hear locals referring to something as being "in the loop." That doesn't mean it's privy to key information; rather, it lies within the circumference of I-410. True, this covers a pretty large area, but with the spreading of the city north and west, it's come to mean central.

Among the most major of the minor spokes are Broadway, McCullough, San Pedro, and Blanco, all of which lead north from the city center into the most popular shopping and restaurant areas of town. Fredericksburg goes out to the Medical Center from just northwest of downtown. When San Antonians talk about "the Strip," they mean the stretch of North St. Mary's between Josephine and Magnolia, once known for its night life but a bit less lively these days.

Downtown is bounded by I-37 on the east, I-35 on the north and west, and U.S. 90 (which merges with I-10) on the south. Within these parameters, Commerce, Market, and Houston are important east–west thoroughfares. Alamo and Santa Rosa are major north–south streets; the former on the east side and the latter on the west side.

**FINDING AN ADDRESS**   Few locals are aware that there's any method to the madness of finding downtown addresses, but in fact, directions are based on the layout of the first Spanish settlements, when the San Fernando cathedral was at the center of town: Market is the north–south street divider, and Flores separates the east from the west. Thus, South St. Mary's becomes North St. Mary's when it crosses Market, where the addresses start from zero in both directions. North of downtown, San Pedro is the east–west dividing line, although not every street sign reflects this fact.

There are few clear-cut rules like this in loop land, but on its northernmost stretch, Loop 410 divides into east and west at Broadway; at Bandera Road, it splits into Loop

410 north and south. Keep going far enough south, and I-35 marks yet another boundary between east and west. Knowing this will help you a little in locating an address, and will explain why, when you go in a circle around town—you probably won't do this voluntarily—you'll notice that the directions marked on overhead signs have suddenly shifted.

**STREET MAPS**　The Visitor Information Center (see "Visitor Information," above) and most hotels distribute the free street maps published by the **San Antonio Convention and Visitors Bureau** (**SACVB**). They mark the main attractions in town and are useful enough as a general reference, especially if you're on foot; they even indicate which downtown streets are one-way—a bonus for drivers. But if you're going to do much navigating around town, you'll need something better. Both **Rand McNally** and **Gousha's** maps of San Antonio are reliable; you'll find one or the other at most gas stations, convenience stores, drugstores, bookstores, and newsstands.

## Neighborhoods in Brief

A sure sign of urban sprawl is when areas stop acquiring names and begin getting geographical designations. The older areas described here, from downtown through Alamo Heights, are all "in the loop" (410). The Medical Center area lies just outside it, but North Central, Far Northwest, and West are expanding beyond even Loop 1604.

**Downtown**　Site of San Antonio's three oldest Spanish settlements, this area includes the Alamo and other historic sites, along with the River Walk, the Alamodome, the convention center, the Rivercenter Mall, and many high-rise hotels, restaurants, and shops. It's also the center of commerce and government; many banks and offices, as well as most city buildings, are located here. Once seedy and largely deserted at night, it has rebounded with a vengeance—a proliferation of bars and clubs catering to younger crowds resulted in a city ordinance restraining the volume of outdoor noise.

**King William**　The city's first suburb, this historic district directly south of downtown was settled in the mid- to late 1800s by wealthy German merchants who built some of the most beautiful mansions in town. It began to be yuppified in the 1970s, and, at this point, you'd never guess it had ever been allowed to deteriorate. Only two of the area's many impeccably restored homes are generally open to the public, but a number have been turned into bed-and-breakfasts.

**Southtown**　Alamo Street marks a rough border between King William and Southtown, the adjoining commercial district. Long a depressed area, it's now becoming trendy, thanks to a Main Street refurbishing project and the opening of the Blue Star arts complex. You'll find a nice mix of Hispanic neighborhood shops and funky coffeehouses and galleries here.

**Monte Vista**　Immediately northwest of downtown, Monte Vista was established soon after King William by a conglomeration of wealthy cattlemen, politicos, and generals who moved "on to the hill" at the turn of the century. A number of the area's large houses have been split into apartments for students of nearby Trinity University and San Antonio Community College, but many lovely old homes have been restored in the past 20 years. It hasn't reached King William status yet, but this is already a highly desirable (read: pricey) place to live.

**Fort Sam Houston**　Built in 1876 to the northeast of downtown, Fort Sam Houston boasts a number of stunning officers' homes. Much of the working-class neighborhood surrounding Fort Sam is now run-down, but renewed interest in restoring San Antonio's older areas is beginning to have some impact here, too.

**Alamo Heights Area**    In the 1890s, when construction in the area began, Alamo Heights was at the far northern reaches of San Antonio. It has slowly evolved into one of the city's most exclusive neighborhoods, and is now home to wealthy families, expensive shops, and trendy restaurants. Terrell Hills to the east, Olmos Park to the west, and Lincoln Heights to the north are all offshoots of this moneyed area; the latter is home to the Quarry, once just that, but now a ritzy golf course and huge shopping mall. The greater portion of these neighborhoods share a single ZIP code ending in the numbers "09"—thus the local term "09ers," referring to the area's affluent residents.

**Medical Center**    The mostly characterless neighborhood surrounding the South Texas Medical Center—host to the majority of San Antonio's hospitals and medical facilities, including the University of Texas Health Science Center—is one of the city's more recently established areas. Many of the homes occupied by the young professionals who have been moving here are condominiums and apartments, and much of the shopping and dining is in strip malls. The farther north you go, the nicer the housing complexes get.

**Far Northwest**    The high-end Westin La Cantera resort, the exclusive La Cantera and Dominion residential enclave, and several tony new golf courses mark the direction that development in the far northwest part of town, just beyond Six Flags Fiesta Texas and near the public Friederich Park, is taking. It's becoming one of San Antonio's prime growth areas.

**North Central**    San Antonio is inching towards Bulverde and other Hill Country towns via this major corridor of development clustered around North Loop 1604, east of I-10 and west of I-35. It's a naturally beautiful area, hilly and dotted with small canyons, and recent city codes have motivated developers to retain trees and native plants in their residential communities.

**West**    Although SeaWorld has been out here since the late 1980s, and the Hyatt Regency Hill Country Resort settled here in the early 1990s, other development was comparatively slow in coming. Now the West is booming with new mid-price housing developments, strip malls, schools, and businesses. Road building hasn't kept pace with growth, however, so traffic can be a bear.

## 2  Getting Around

### BY PUBLIC TRANSPORTATION

**BY BUS**    San Antonio's public transportation system is visitor friendly; although prices have gone up in recent years, they're still very reasonable. The 104 **VIA Metropolitan Transit Service** bus routes cost 75¢ for regular lines, with an additional 5¢ charge for transfers, and $1.50 for express buses (5¢ for transfers). You'll need exact change. Call ☎ **210/362-2020** for transit information, check the Web site at **www.viainfo.net**, or stop in at VIA's downtown center, 112 N. Soledad; it's open Monday to Friday 7am to 6pm, Saturday 9am to 2pm. Among popular tourist routes, the no. 64 bus goes to SeaWorld when it is open; the no. 8 bus goes to the zoo and botanical gardens area.

**BY STREETCAR**    In addition to its bus lines, VIA offers five convenient downtown streetcar routes that cover all the most popular tourist stops. Designed to look like the turn-of-the-century trolleys used in San Antonio until 1933, the streetcars cost 50¢ (exact change). The trolleys, which have signs color-coded by route, note destinations.

A $2 day-tripper pass, good for an entire day of travel on all VIA transportation except express buses, can be purchased at VIA's downtown Information Center. Seniors (62 and over) can get a discount card at this office or at two other VIA offices: 1021 San Pedro (☎ **210/362-2000**), and the Crossroads Park and Ride in the Crossroads Mall parking lot (☎ **210/735-3317**). You have to go in person, with proof of age and a Social Security card; the picture ID that you receive on the spot will entitle you to half off all VIA fares, except the day-tripper pass.

## BY CAR

One word of advice about driving downtown: Unless you're familiar with the pattern of one-way streets and with the locations of the area's limited public parking—don't. It's not that the streets in downtown San Antonio are narrower or more crowded than those in most city centers; it's just that there's no need to bother when public transportation is so convenient. There's also the matter of the 3-second traffic light (I'm not making this up; I timed them) that many downtown streets seem to have. The continuous stop-and-go can get old pretty fast.

As for highway driving, because of the many convergences of major freeways here—described in the "Main Arteries & Streets" section, above—if you're not constantly vigilant, you'll find yourself in the express lane to somewhere you really don't want to go. Don't let your mind wander; watch the signs carefully and be prepared to make lots of quick lane changes.

Rush hour lasts from about 7:45 to 9am and 4:30 to 6pm Monday through Friday. The crush may not be bad compared with that of Houston or Dallas, but it's getting worse all the time. Because of San Antonio's rapid growth, you can also expect to find major highway construction or repairs going on somewhere in the city at any given time. Areas that will be particularly hard hit in the next few years are the Loop 410/I-10 and Loop 410/U.S. 281 links, where four-level interchanges, with ramps directly connecting the respective freeways with one another, are in the works. Construction is not scheduled to be completed until 2005 or 2006. For the gory details, log on to the Texas Department of Transportation's Web site at **www.dot.state.tx**.

**RENTALS** **Advantage** (☎ 800/777-5500; www.arac.com), **Alamo** (☎ 800/327-9633; www.freeways.com), **Avis** (☎ 800/831-2847; www.avis.com), **Budget** (☎ 800/527-0700; www.budgetrentacar.com), **Dollar** (☎ 800/800-4000; www.dollar.com), **Enterprise** (☎ 800/736-8222; www.pickenterprise.com), **Hertz** (☎ 800/654-3131; www.hertz.com), **National** (☎ 800/227-7368; www.nationalcar.com), and **Thrifty** (☎ 800/367-2277; www.thrifty.com) all have desks at both of the airport terminals. **Hertz** is also represented downtown at the Marriott Rivercenter at Bowie and Commerce (☎ 210/225-3676).

Almost all the major car-rental companies have their own discount programs. Your rate will often depend on the organizations to which you belong, the dates of travel, and the length of your stay. Some companies give discounts to AAA members, for example, and some have special deals in conjunction with various airlines or telephone companies. Off-season rates are likely to be lower, and prices are sometimes reduced on weekends (or midweek). Call as far in advance as possible to book a car, and always ask about specials.

On top of the standard rental prices, other optional charges apply to most car rentals. The Collision Damage Waiver (CDW), which requires you to pay for damage to the car in a collision, is illegal in some states but not Texas. It is, however, covered by many credit-card companies. Check with yours before you go so you can avoid paying this hefty fee (as much as $10/day).

The car-rental companies also offer additional liability insurance (if you harm others in an accident), personal accident insurance (if you harm yourself or your passengers), and personal effects insurance (if your luggage is stolen from your car). If you have insurance on your car at home, you are probably covered for most of these unlikelihoods. If your own insurance doesn't cover rentals, or if you don't have auto insurance, you should consider the additional coverage (the car-rental companies are liable for certain base amounts, depending on the state). But weigh the likelihood of getting into an accident or losing your luggage against the cost of these coverages (as much as $20/day combined), which can significantly add to the price of your rental.

There are Internet resources that can make comparison shopping easier. For example, Yahoo!'s travel site (**http://travel.yahoo.com**) allows you to look up rental prices for any size car at more than a dozen rental companies in hundreds of cities. Just enter the size car you want, the rental and return dates, and the city where you want to rent, and the server returns a price. It will even make your reservation for you.

In case you were wondering—yes, the Alamo car-rental company got its start in San Antonio.

**PARKING**   Parking meters are not plentiful in the heart of downtown, but you can find some on the streets near the River Walk and on Broadway. The cost is 75¢ per hour, which is also the time limit. There are some very inexpensive (2 hours for $1) meters at the outskirts of town; the trick is to find one. Although too few signs inform you of this, parking next to meters is free after 6pm Monday to Saturday and all day Sunday, except during Alamodome events when time meters are enforced. If you don't observe the laws, you'll be ticketed pretty quickly.

Except during Fiesta or other major events, you shouldn't have a problem finding a parking lot or garage for your car; rates run from $3 to $6 per day—the closer you get to the Alamo and the River Walk, the more expensive they become. Prices tend to go up during special events and summer weekends; a parking lot that ordinarily charges $3.50 a day is likely to charge $5.

**DRIVING RULES**   Right turns on red are permitted after a full stop. Left turns on red are also allowed, but only if you're going from a one-way street onto another one-way street. Seat belts and child restraint seats are mandatory.

## BY RIVER TAXI

Yanaguana Cruises (see "Organized Tours," in chapter 6) runs the **Rio Trans River Shuttle** (☎ **210/244-5700**), with nine ticket locations on the River Walk; they include Alamo Plaza, La Villita, the Hard Rock Cafe, the Holiday Inn Riverwalk, and the Adam's Mark Hotel (which will be closed while the river's north channel is drained for repairs). Shuttle stops on the River Walk are marked by Rio Trans signs, but you have to get your ticket before you board. At $3.50 one-way, $10 for an all-day pass, or $25 for a 3-day pass, it's more expensive than ground transport, but it's a treat.

### Free Parking

If you're staying for only a short time, consider leaving your car in the Rivercenter Mall garage and getting your ticket validated at one of the shops; you don't have to buy anything, and you'll have 2 hours of free parking. This is only a good idea, however, if you have an iron will or are allergic to shopping; otherwise, you could end up spending a lot more than at a parking garage.

## BY TAXI

Cabs are available outside the airport, near the Greyhound and Amtrak terminals, and at most major downtown hotels, but they're next to impossible to hail on the street; most of the time, you'll need to phone for one in advance. The best of the major taxi companies in town is **Checker Cab** (☎ **210/222-2222**), which has an excellent record of turning up when promised. **Yellow Cab** (☎ **210/226-4262**) is a reasonable alternative. See "By Plane" in the "Arriving" section above for rates. Most cabbies impose a minimum of $6 for trips from the airport, $3 for rides downtown.

## ON FOOT

Downtown San Antonio is a treat for walkers, who can perambulate from one tourist attraction to another, or stroll along a beautifully landscaped river. Traffic lights even stay green long enough for pedestrians to cross without putting their lives in peril. Jay-walking is a ticketed offense, but it's rarely enforced.

## Fast Facts: San Antonio

**Airport**    See "Arriving," earlier in this chapter.

**American Express**    The branch at 8103 Broadway (☎ **210/828-4809**) is open Monday to Friday 9am to 5:15pm.

**Area Code**    The telephone area code in San Antonio is **210.**

**Baby-Sitters**    Your hotel should be able to recommend a reliable service.

**Business Hours**    Banks are open Monday to Friday 9am to 4pm, Saturday 9am to 1pm. Drive-up windows are open 7am to 6pm Monday to Friday, and 9am to noon on Saturday. Office hours are generally weekdays 9am to 5pm. Shops tend to be open from 9 or 10am until 5:30 or 6pm Monday to Saturday, with shorter hours on Sunday. Most malls are open Monday to Saturday 10am to 9pm, Sunday noon to 6pm. The majority of bars and clubs boot their last customers out at 2am.

**Camera Repair**    Havel Camera Service, 1102 Basse Rd. (☎ **210/735-7412**), a reputable camera repair shop, is about 15 minutes north of downtown.

**Car Rentals**    See "Getting Around," earlier in this chapter.

**Climate**    See "When to Go," in chapter 2.

**Dentist**    To find a dentist near you in town, contact the San Antonio District Dental Society, 202 W. French Place (☎ **210/732-1264**).

**Doctor**    For a referral, contact the Bexar County Medical Society at 3355 Cherry Ridge, Suite 214 (☎ **210/734-6691**).

**Driving Rules**    See "Getting Around," earlier in this chapter.

**Drugstores**    See "Pharmacies," below.

**Embassies/Consulates**    See "Fast Facts: For the Foreign Traveler," in Appendix B.

**Emergencies**    For police, fire, or medical emergencies, dial ☎ **911.** The Sheriff's Department number is ☎ **210/270-6000,** and the Texas Department of Public Safety, including the Texas Highway Patrol, can be reached at ☎ **210/533-9171.**

**Eyeglass Repair**    North of the airport, Texas State Optical (TSO), 16111 San Pedro (☎ **210/545-5755**), is a trusted name for glasses. Also near the airport,

## When Nature Calls

You can use the restrooms downtown at the Rivercenter Mall or you can duck into any of the free tourist attractions. (Yes, you can go to the bathroom at the Alamo, gratis.) Most restaurants don't mind quick visits, either—they never know; you might come back for a meal later on.

---

Eye Mart, Hwy. 281 and Bitters (☎ 210/496-6549), offers quick and friendly service. You'll find many branches of LensCrafters around town, too.

**Hospitals**   The main downtown hospital is Baptist Medical Center, 111 Dallas St. (☎ 210/297-7000). Christus Santa Rosa Health Care Corp., 519 W. Houston (☎ 210/704-2011), is also downtown. Contact the San Antonio Medical Foundation (☎ 210/614-3724) for information on other facilities.

**Hot Lines**   Contact the National Youth Crisis Hotline at ☎ 800/448-4663; Rape Crisis Hotline at ☎ 210/349-7273; Child Abuse Hotline (☎ 800/252-5400); Mental Illness Crisis Hotline (☎ 210/227-4357); Bexar County Adult Abuse Hotline (☎ 800/252-5400); and Poison Control Center (☎ 800/764-7661).

**Information**   See "Visitor Information," earlier in this chapter.

**Laundry**   The only laundromat convenient to downtown is the coin-operated, self-service Kwik Wash, 1823 W. Commerce (☎ 210/222-8118), located west of I-35 near the UTSA Downtown campus.

**Libraries**   In 1995, San Antonio opened its magnificent new main library at 600 Soledad Plaza (☎ 210/207-2500); see "More Attractions," in chapter 6, for details.

**Liquor Laws**   The legal drinking age in Texas is 21. Under-age drinkers can legally imbibe as long as they stay within sight of their legal-age parents or spouses, but they need to be prepared to show proof of the relationship. Open containers are prohibited in public and in vehicles. Liquor laws are strictly enforced; if you're concerned, check www.tabc.state.tx.us for the entire Texas alcoholic beverage code.

**Lost Property**   For lost property at the bus station call ☎ 210/270-5826; at the airport, ☎ 210/207-3526 (after 4:30pm, call ☎ 210/207-3526). In addition, each airline operates its own Lost and Found.

**Luggage Storage/Lockers**   There are lockers at the Greyhound Bus Station and the Amtrak station; as we went to press, they hadn't been installed at the airport yet.

**Maps**   See "City Layout," earlier in this chapter.

**Newspapers/Magazines**   Since the early 1990s, when the Hearst Corporation, owner of the *San Antonio Express-News,* bought the competing *San Antonio Light* and shut it down, the *Express* has been the only mainstream source of news in town. See "Visitor Information," above, for magazine recommendations.

**Pharmacies (Late-Night)**   Most branches of Eckerd and Walgreens, the major chain pharmacies in San Antonio, are open late Monday to Saturday. There's an Eckerd downtown at 211 Losoya/River Walk (☎ 210/224-9293). Call ☎ 800/925-4733 to find the Walgreens nearest you; punch in the area code and the first three digits of the number you're phoning from and you'll be directed to the closest branch (or, if you choose, the closest one that has 24-hour service).

**Police**    The Sheriff's Department can be reached at ☎ **210/270-6000;** the Texas Highway Patrol, at ☎ **210/533-9171.** Call ☎ **911** in an emergency.

**Post Office**    The main post office is at the far northeast part of town at 10410 Perrin-Beitel, but the most convenient location is downtown at 615 E. Houston St., just across from the Alamo. For all postal service, including the location of the post office nearest to your hotel (be sure to know the ZIP code), call ☎ **800/275-8777.**

**Radio**    You should be able to find something to suit your radio tastes in San Antonio. KPAC at 88.3 FM plays classical music; KJ97 at 97.3 FM, country; KISS at 99.5 FM, rock; KONO at 101.1 FM, oldies; KSMG at 105.3 FM, easy listening; KCJZ at 106.7 FM, rhythm and blues. KSYM at 90.1 FM is the only college alternative station in south Texas. For Tejano music, tune in to KXTN at 107.5 FM. You'll find National Public Radio on KSTX at 89.1 FM, and classical music on sister station KPAC at 88.3 FM. KTSA 550 on the AM dial is a news/talk radio station.

**Safety**    The crime rate in San Antonio has gone down along with that of the rest of the country, and there are frequent police patrols downtown at night; as a result, muggings, pickpocketings, and purse snatchings in the area are rare. But use common sense, as you would anywhere else: Walk only in well-lit, well-populated streets. It's generally not a good idea to stroll south of Durango after dark.

**Taxes**    Sales tax is 7.875%; the city surcharge on hotel rooms comes to a whopping 16.75%.

**Taxis**    See "Getting Around," earlier in this chapter.

**Television**    The local television affiliates are KMOL on Channel 4, NBC; KENS on Channel 5, CBS; KSAT on Channel 12, ABC; KLRN on Channel 9, PBS. FOX on Channel 11 is the Fox network.

**Time Zone**    San Antonio is on central standard time and observes daylight saving time.

**Transit Information**    Call ☎ **210/362-2020.**

**Weather**    Call ☎ **210/226-3232.**

# San Antonio Accommodations

## 4

**Y**ou don't have to leave your lodgings to sightsee in San Antonio: The city has the highest concentration of historic hotels in Texas. Even low-end hotel chains are reclaiming old buildings—many are covered in this chapter—so don't judge a place on the basis of its name. Most of these, as well as other more recently built luxury accommodations, are in the downtown area, which is where you'll likely want to be whether you're here on pleasure or business. Prices in this prime location can be high, especially for hotels on the river, but you'll generally get your money's worth. You'll also economize by eliminating the need to rent a car: Most of the tourist attractions are within walking distance or easily accessible by public transportation, and many of the best restaurants are only an inexpensive cab ride from downtown.

In recent years, a number of the old mansions in the King William and Monte Vista historic districts have been converted into bed-and-breakfasts; several are reviewed in this chapter, too. Assume that your room will have a private bathroom unless I say otherwise. For information about additional bed-and-breakfasts in these areas and in other neighborhoods around the city, contact the **San Antonio Bed & Breakfast Association,** P.O. Box 830101, San Antonio, TX 78283, which offers a bed-and-breakfast hot line (☎ **800/210-8422**). Several of San Antonio's inns are also bookable via **Historic Accommodations of Texas,** P.O. Box 139, Fredericksburg, TX 78624 (☎ **800/HAT-0368;** www.hat.org; e-mail: info@hat.org).

San Antonio also has two top-notch destination resorts on the outskirts of town, the Hyatt Regency Hill Country Resort and the new Westin La Cantera Resort; a Radisson resort is also in the works on the west side. They're great places to hole up and relax, maybe play some golf, with sightseeing as a secondary goal.

Areas around town where moderately priced and inexpensive chain lodgings are concentrated are included in the listings that follow; the pricier or more distinctive properties in these sections are reviewed fully, while the more familiar standardized hotels or motels are noted in brief. For a full alphabetical listing of the accommodations in the city, mapped by area and including rate ranges as well as basic amenities, phone the **San Antonio Convention and Visitors Bureau** (☎ **800/447-3372**) and request a lodging guide; it's more user friendly than the one online at www.SanAntonioCVB.com, although the Web site has links to several of the hotels listed.

## Deal Well, Sleep Well

Don't eliminate a choice because of its price category alone; the prices listed here are the hotel's "rack rates"—the room rate charged without any discount—and you can almost always do better. The San Antonio Convention and Visitors Bureau's annual SAVE (San Antonio Vacation Experience) promotion features discounts on hotel rooms (more than 50 properties participate) as well as on dining and entertainment. Some bed-and-breakfasts and hotels offer better rates to those who book for at least 4 days, although a week is usually the minimum. Even though most leisure travelers visit in summer, rooms tend to be less expensive then; in general, rates are highest from November through April, when conventions converge on the town.

But even in peak season, hotel rates vary widely: Some hotels in San Antonio host business clients during the week, whereas others cater to tourists who come on the weekend, so you never know when a property is not fully booked and willing to give you a good deal. In addition, ask about any discounts you can think of—corporate, senior citizen, military, AAA—and about packages such as family, romance, or deals that include meals or sightseeing tours. Bottom line: *Always ask for the lowest-priced room with the most perks available.* Reservation agents are eager to sell rooms, so you shouldn't have a problem getting a good deal.

Wherever you decide to stay, but especially if it's downtown, try to book as far in advance as possible. And don't even think about coming to town during Fiesta (the third week in Apr) if you haven't reserved a room 6 months in advance.

In the following reviews, unless otherwise specified, you can assume that all the hotels in the "Very Expensive" and "Expensive" categories offer such standard amenities as room service, laundry and dry cleaning services, and cable TV with free movie channels. Accommodations in the "Moderate" category guarantee you basics like private bathrooms, TVs (except in some B&Bs), and air-conditioning; at many motels, you'll get a lot more. "Inexpensive" rooms are guaranteed clean and comfortable, if often no-frills.

In all cases, rates do not include the 16.75% room tax.

*Note:* This year I added a new feature: an indication of whether pets are accepted at the hotels (can you tell I'm thinking about getting a dog?). No reference at all means pets are not accepted. If it's noted that pets are allowed but no indication is given of size restriction, deposit amount, or additional room charge, assume that your well-behaved furry friend can stay with you, gratis, and that you're not required to put down any bucks in advance—but that the hotel has your credit card, and you will be responsible for any damage wreaked by Spot or Kitty.

## 1  Downtown

### VERY EXPENSIVE

✪ **Hilton Palacio del Rio.** 200 S. Alamo, San Antonio, TX 78205. ☎ **800/HILTONS** or 210/222-1400. Fax 210/270-0761. www.hilton.com. 491 units. A/C TV TEL. $225–$325 double; $700–$950 suite. Romance, bounce-back weekend specials. AE, CB, DC, DISC, MC, V. Self-parking $12.50; valet parking $23.50. Pets under 50 lbs. accepted.

Although relatively new, the Hilton has already earned a footnote in San Antonio history. To get it finished in time for the 1968 HemisFair, the hotel was built using precast concrete modules: 500 fully furnished, 35-ton rooms were hoisted into a steel frame. The whole thing was designed, completed, and occupied in a record 202 days.

Inside this miracle of modern construction, the decor is European elegant, with more-than-passing nods to the Southwest: Polished parquet floors, Oriental rugs, and a grand piano rub elbows in the hotel lobby with Mexican tile, sink-into-me leather couches, and a beautiful hand-tooled saddle. Spacious guest rooms feature tasteful French provincial furnishings with interesting abstract art. All cater to business travelers, offering oversized desks with laptop drawer pullouts, surge protectors, and two separate phone lines, as well as coffeemakers, hair dryers, irons, and ironing boards. The original large balconies in the standard rooms were narrowed a bit to make room for a sitting area, but you still get stunning river views from half of them (the city views from the rest aren't bad either).

**Dining/Diversions:** All the Hilton's dining and entertainment areas have plum locations either on or overlooking the river. The Rincón Alegre is your standard lobby piano lounge with a twist—the gleaming rosewood instrument plays itself. Ibiza, with its colorful Matisse-style cutouts, has a snazzy Mediterranean menu with some Tex-Mex dishes that regular visitors have insisted on. Tex's sports bar, with its multiple TV and local team memorabilia, was so successful at the Airport Hilton that a River Walk version was opened here. Most fun of all is Durty Nelly's Irish Pub, where you can throw your peanut shells on the floor and join in some seriously soppy singalongs (see chapter 8 for details).

**Amenities:** Kosher food available on request from room service, outdoor heated pool, hot tub, fitness room, airline and car-rental desks, complimentary washer/dryer.

**Hyatt Regency on the River Walk.** 123 Losoya St., San Antonio, TX 78205. ☎ **800/ 233-1234** or 210/222-1234. Fax 210/227-4925. www.hyatt.com. 631 units. A/C MINIBAR TV TEL. $259–$319 double; $328–$768 suite. AE, CB, DC, DISC, MC, V. Self-parking $10; valet parking $14.

There's something stimulating about all that glass and steel rising from this hotel's lobby, where the Hyatt's signature cage elevators ascend and descend the skylit atrium. Maybe the quality of openness determines the difference between a hotel that's bustling and one that just feels overcrowded. This one's definitely bustling, both with business travelers and families who enjoy its convenience to all the downtown attractions; you couldn't be closer to the river's hopping South Bank section. And having a bit of said river running through the lobby adds to the dramatic effect.

Guest rooms, done in light woods with southwest accents and featuring live plants, are very attractive. All have excellent standard amenities, including hair dryers, irons and ironing boards, and servibars—still fairly rare in this city.

**Dining/Diversions:** On the river level is the New Orleans–oriented The Landing, long-time home to the Dixieland jazz of Jim Cullum and his band (see chapter 8), plus Mad Dogs and Englishmen, a British-style pub. On the lobby level, the casual Chaps Restaurant, which serves breakfast, lunch, and dinner, has American and Mexican fare; there's a pasta bar at lunch. Just below it is the multilevel River Terrace lounge.

**Amenities:** 24-hour currency exchange, express checkout, business center, concierge, rooftop pool, Jacuzzi, sundeck, health club, river-level shopping arcade.

**✪ La Mansión del Rio.** 112 College St., San Antonio, TX 78205. ☎ **800/292-7300** or 210/518-1000. Fax 210/226-0389. www.lamansion.com. 337 units. A/C TV TEL. $258–$484 double; $549–$1,949 suite. AE, CB, DC, DISC, MC, V. Valet parking $15. Domesticated pets accepted, subject to room availability and manager's approval.

This lushly landscaped Spanish hacienda–style hotel—converted from a 19th-century seminary in 1968 to meet the city's room needs for the HemisFair exposition—fronts the Paseo del Rio and is down the block from the beautifully restored Majestic

# Downtown San Antonio Accommodations

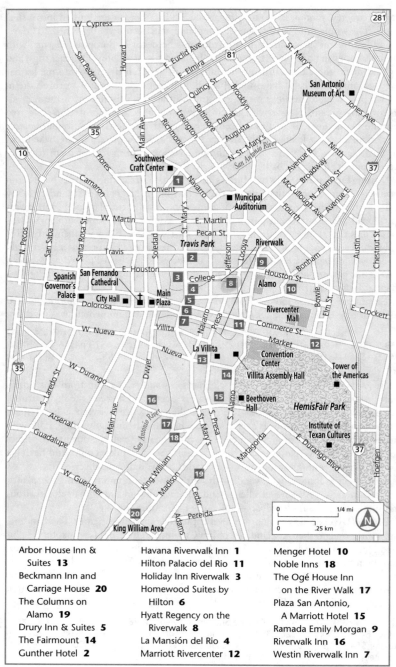

Arbor House Inn & Suites **13**

Beckmann Inn and Carriage House **20**

The Columns on Alamo **19**

Drury Inn & Suites **5**

The Fairmount **14**

Gunther Hotel **2**

Havana Riverwalk Inn **1**

Hilton Palacio del Rio **11**

Holiday Inn Riverwalk **3**

Homewood Suites by Hilton **6**

Hyatt Regency on the Riverwalk **8**

La Mansión del Rio **4**

Marriott Rivercenter **12**

Menger Hotel **10**

Noble Inns **18**

The Ogé House Inn on the River Walk **17**

Plaza San Antonio, A Marriott Hotel **15**

Ramada Emily Morgan **9**

Riverwalk Inn **16**

Westin Riverwalk Inn **7**

Theater. Moorish arches, Mexican tile, a central patio, wrought-iron balconies, and antique pieces in every nook and cranny combine to create a low-glitz, high-tone Mediterranean atmosphere. The layout can seem a bit mazelike, but staff discretion, a willingness to cater to special requests—say, a room just for shoes booked by a Middle Eastern sheik—and a location that's just slightly away from the action make this the hotel of choice for high-profile visitors.

Guest rooms all have rough-hewn beamed ceilings, brick walls, and soothing earth-tone furnishings; luxurious touches include cotton robes, hair dryers, and complimentary newspapers. The more expensive quarters boast balconies overlooking the River Walk, but the interior courtyard views are fine, too. A $10 million renovation in 2000 gave all the rooms and public areas a fresh look.

**Dining/Diversions:** The hotel's upscale dining room, Las Canarias, serves up a terrific river view with its excellent American regional cuisine (see chapter 5); you can enjoy cocktails in an adjoining garden courtyard. The more casual Watermark, which looks out on the pool and courtyard, is open for breakfast and lunch. The El Colegio piano bar, located in the lobby, boasts a cozy fireplace.

**Amenities:** Express checkout, concierge, outdoor pool, exercise room, gift shop.

✪ **Marriott Rivercenter.** 101 Bowie St., San Antonio, TX 78205. ☎ **800/228-9290** or 210/223-1000. Fax 210/223-4092. www.marriotthotels.com. 1,086 units. A/C TV TEL. $279 double; suites from $450. River barge packages available. AE, DC, DISC, MC, V. Self-parking $10; valet parking $14. Pets under 50 lbs. accepted with a nonrefundable $25 cleaning fee.

Serious retail hounds will find heaven in this glitzy high-rise; they can shop more than 100 Rivercenter emporiums until they're ready to drop, and then collapse back into their hotel rooms without ever leaving the mall. Sightseers will be happy here, too; a cruise along the River Walk departs from the mall's downstairs "dock," and the Alamo and HemisFair Park are just a few blocks away.

Convenience is definitely the goal here—facilities include transportation desks, a good range of dining-and-drinking areas, a large indoor/outdoor pool, and an extremely well-equipped exercise center. Free washers and dryers on the same floor as the health club let you bicycle while your clothes cycle. Guest rooms, all updated during a $5 million hotel renovation in 2000, have an earth-toned, simple elegance. In addition to the standard upscale business features, including irons, hair dryers, and coffeemakers, the rooms now feature high-speed Internet access—a rarity in this comparatively low-tech city. Many also afford spectacular River Walk or city views. If you find all this convenience—and the bustle that goes along with it—a bit overwhelming, an option is to stay at the smaller Marriott Riverwalk across the street. This slightly older and slightly less expensive sister hotel has equally comfortable, recently refreshed Southwest-style rooms, and its guests have access to all the facilities of the Rivercenter.

**Dining:** The casual, plant-filled Garden Cafe is open for breakfast (including a buffet), lunch, and dinner; it's adjacent to J. W. Steakhouse, the hotel's fine dining room, where surf and turf rule (closed Sun and Mon). The Lobby Bar serves drinks and light fare. Guests at the Rivercenter can also charge any meals and drinks they have at the restaurants and lounges in the Marriott Riverwalk to their rooms.

**Amenities:** Secretarial services, concierge, baby-sitting, doctor (24-hour availability), gift shops, car-rental desk, separate men's and women's saunas, Jacuzzi.

**Plaza San Antonio, A Marriott Hotel.** 555 S. Alamo St., San Antonio, TX 78205. ☎ **800/727-3239** or 210/229-1000. Fax 210/223-6650. www.plazasa.com. 252 units. A/C TV TEL. $249–$269 double; suites from $420. AE, CB, DC, DISC, MC, V. Self-parking $8; valet parking $14. Pets under 20 lbs. accepted.

Pheasants stroll the beautifully landscaped grounds of this gracious hotel, located across from HemisFair Park, close to La Villita, and just north of the King William district. Four 19th-century buildings that were saved from HemisFair's bulldozer in 1968 were later incorporated into the Plaza complex. Three are used for intimate conference centers—the initialing ceremony for the North American Free Trade Agreement was held in one of them—and the fourth houses the hotel's health club and spa.

Service is excellent at this top-notch property; this is a place to come and feel pampered. Elegant rooms are decorated in muted colors and floral patterns, with antique-style furnishings that include gleaming cherry headboards. Each accommodation offers a plush terry robe, full-length mirror, snack drawer, hair dryer, coffeemaker, iron, and ironing board. Bottled water and filled ice buckets are left at evening turndown service. This is one of the few hotels in town that has lit tennis courts—not to mention a croquet lawn.

**Dining/Diversions:** You can order drinks or snacks at the pool, or enjoy afternoon tea at the Palm Terrace, overlooking the hotel's lovely gardens (light meals are available here during the entire day). The adjacent Lobby Bar offers cappuccino and espresso in addition to cocktails. The full-service Anaqua Grill is known for its innovative Southwestern cuisine.

**Amenities:** Complimentary shoeshine, newspapers, use of bicycles, limousine to downtown business district Monday to Friday 7:30 to 9:30am, 24-hour room service, concierge, health club with men's and women's saunas, spa, outdoor swimming pool, whirlpool, two night-lit tennis courts (free for guests), croquet lawn.

✪ **The Fairmount, A Wyndham Grand Heritage Hotel.** 401 S. Alamo St., San Antonio, TX 78205. ☎ **800/WYNDHAM** or 210/224-8800. Fax 210/475-0082. www.wyndham. com. 37 units. A/C TV TEL. $215–$235 double; $269–$550 suite. Weekend, seasonal specials. AE, DC, MC, V. Valet parking $15.

This lovely boutique hotel, built in an ornate Italianate-Victorian style in 1906, is across the street from HemisFair Park, adjacent to La Villita, and within walking distance of the King William historic district—but it wasn't always. In 1985, it was hoisted 6 blocks across town, earning it a place in the *Guinness Book of World Records* as the heaviest building ever moved. Excavations of the site on which it now sits uncovered artifacts from the battle at the Alamo, some of which are showcased in the building's lobby.

The Fairmount once lodged railway travelers, but today's clientele is more likely to jet in; the hotel is sought out by film stars and other celebrities looking for low-key but luxurious digs. The hotel's intimate size, along with richly carpeted corridors and small parlors, makes it seem like the home of a wealthy—and very attentive—friend. The suites are naturally the largest rooms—some have hardwood floors, wet bars, skylights, Jacuzzi tubs, or combinations thereof—but even the double rooms are outstanding. All are individually decorated in muted Southwestern tones, with rich wood furniture (some in Craftsman style), plants, and original artwork, and all have balconies overlooking the city or a small central courtyard. Irons, coffeemakers, VCRs, and phones with data ports and voice messaging are standard features. Italian marble and brass gleam in the bathrooms, which have Bath & Body Works toiletries along with makeup mirrors, hair dryers, monogrammed terry robes, and phones (hey, you never know when you're going to get that important business call).

**Dining/Diversions:** You can enjoy the soft strains of a jazz piano at Polo's lounge, a cushy, dim-lit room where deals are closed over single-malt scotches, and romantic liaisons are celebrated with champagne (see chapter 8 for a full listing). Warm smells wafting from the brick oven may lure folks next door to the elegant Polo's restaurant, which serves beautifully presented nouvelle continental cuisine.

**Amenities:** Complimentary newspaper (Mon to Fri), 24-hour room service, shoeshine service, film library (free movie rentals), baby-sitting available.

✪ **Westin Riverwalk Inn.** 420 W. Market St., San Antonio, TX 78205. ☎ **800/WESTIN**-1 or 210/224-6500. Fax 210/224-6000. www.westin.com. 474 units. A/C MINIBAR TV TEL. $305–$335 double (guest office rooms $20 additional); $365–$395 suite. AE, CB, DC, DISC, MC, V. Self-parking $10; valet parking $20.

The recycling of downtown historic buildings into hotels is an admirable trend, but there's also something to be said for new construction—at least when it's done right. Opened in late 1999, this ultraluxe property was designed to blend in architecturally with the older structures that flank it on this (relatively) quiet section of the river bend, but its clean, elegant lines are attuned to 21st-century sensibilities.

From the lobby to the rooms, earth tones balance with Spanish colonial accents to create an atmosphere that's soothing without being bland. Built-from-scratch also means incorporating the latest amenities, including Westin's new signature "Heavenly Beds"—layers and layers of bedding, a guest's dream but a housekeeper's nightmare— hypoallergenic pillows, coffeemakers complete with Starbucks, and minibars. The Guest Office units also feature ergonomically designed chairs, halogen lamps, fax/ printer/copier machines, and all the paperclips and Post-Its you might need. A large number of rooms boast river-view balconies.

**Dining/Diversions:** You'll be heading down to the river when you visit the chic Rincon de Maria bar, where guests constantly try to buy the darling individual martini shakers from the barkeep. The Caliza Grille has a superb riverside setting and the buzz around town is that the Mediterranean fare is very good.

**Amenities:** 24-hour room service, concierge, business center, outdoor pool, men's and women's saunas, exercise room, Kids Club (including special services and amenities).

## EXPENSIVE

**Arbor House Inn & Suites.** 540 S. St. Mary's St., San Antonio, TX 78205. ☎ **888/ 272-6700** or 210/472-2005. Fax 210/472-2007. www.arborhouse.com. E-mail: arborhaus@ aol.com. 17 units. A/C TV TEL. $140–$175 double. Rates include continental breakfast. AE, DISC, MC, V. Free parking. Housebroken pets under 25 lbs. accepted with carrier.

This is not exactly your standard hotel: Eleven suites and six rooms occupy five adjacent cottages that share a restful backyard with a grape arbor. (The restoration of these homes garnered an award from the San Antonio Conservation Society.) But it's not a bed-and-breakfast either, although a repast of croissants, muffins, and juice arrives outside your door each morning. The personable owners clearly had fun designing the rooms, which include leopard rugs, colorful artwork, and lots of interesting antiques that they've collected over the years. All the units have coffeemakers, some have refrigerators, and four have full kitchenettes. Leisure travelers will like the proximity to the River Walk and La Villita, while business travelers who aren't overly buttoned down will appreciate the closeness to the Convention Center and the 40-seat conference room.

**Gunter Hotel.** 205 E. Houston St., San Antonio, TX 78205. ☎ **888/999-2089** or 210/227-3241. Fax 210/227-3299. www.gunterhotel.com. 333 units. A/C TV TEL. $165 double; $250–$350 suite. Various promotional rates available. AE, CB, DC, DISC, JCB, MC, V. Valet parking $12.

Western stars Will Rogers, John Wayne, and Tom Mix all trod the polished marble halls of this opulent hotel—in dusty, beat-up cowboy boots, one likes to imagine. The first steel structure in San Antonio when it was built in 1909, the Gunter had its posh tone restored in the early 1980s with crystal chandeliers, potted palms, ornate plaster ceiling casts, and rich mahogany fittings. Resting on the site of an even earlier series of hotels and military headquarters, the first one established in 1837 (ask at the front desk for a historical pamphlet), the hotel is a stone's throw from the Majestic Theater and close to the River Walk.

Guest rooms are done in a "cattleman" motif with rich Southwestern reds and golds; all have a photo of the hotel or neighborhood in the old days. Standard amenities include data-port phones with voice mail, in-room coffeemakers, and irons, as well as video-game capacity on the TV. When I last stayed here, in late 2000, this property was undergoing a management change, and the service was abysmal. It's an attractive, convenient place with relatively reasonable rates, so I hope by the time you read this, things will be running smoothly again.

**Dining/Diversions:** Breakfast, lunch, and dinner are served at the turn-of-the-century-style Cafe, which also includes a deli and wonderful European bakery. The men's club–looking Padre Muldoon's bar, open daily at 4pm, is a popular after-work watering hole for local businesspeople.

**Amenities:** Outdoor pool, whirlpool, sundeck, exercise room, gift shop, barber shop, video arcade.

**Homewood Suites by Hilton.** 432 Market St., San Antonio, TX 78205. ☎ **800/CALL-HOME** or 210/222-1515. Fax 210/222-1575. www.homewood-suites.com. 146 suites. A/C TV TEL. $139–$199 suite. Rates lower during the week. AE, CB, DC, DISC, MC, V. Valet parking $14.

Opened in the mid-1990s in the former San Antonio Drug Company building (1919), this all-suites hotel is a nice addition to downtown's accommodations. Located on a quiet stretch of the river, it's convenient to west side attractions such as Market Square and only a few extra blocks from the Alamo. In-room amenities such as hair dryers, microwave ovens, refrigerators with icemakers, dishwashers, and coffeemakers appeal to business travelers and families alike; the dining area can double as a workspace, and there's a sleeper sofa in each suite as well as two TVs equipped with VCRs. The decor is a cut above that of most chains, with Lone Star–design headboards, light wood desks and bureaus, and attractive Southwestern bedspreads and drapes. Two suites have river views.

**Dining/Diversions:** Free continental breakfast, afternoon manager's social with complimentary drinks.

**Amenities:** Grocery shopping service, heated rooftop pool and whirlpool, exercise room, self-service guest laundry, 24-hour business center, tour desk.

**✪ Menger Hotel.** 204 Alamo Plaza, San Antonio, TX 78205. ☎ **800/345-9285** or 210/223-4361. Fax 210/228-0022. www.mengerhotel.com. 345 units. A/C TV TEL. $165 double; $350–$510 suite. Honeymoon packages available. AE, CB, DC, DISC, MC, V. Self-parking $10; valet parking $14.

Its location, smack between the Alamo and the Rivercenter Mall and a block from the River Walk, is perfect. Its history is fascinating. Its public areas, particularly the Victorian Lobby, are gorgeous. Its guest rooms are charming. And its rates are quite reasonable. Why would anyone visiting San Antonio want to stay anywhere else?

Indeed, in the late 19th century, no one who was anyone would consider staying anywhere but the Menger. A self-guided tour pamphlet of the hotel will take you to halls, ballrooms, and gardens through which Ulysses S. Grant, Sarah Bernhardt, and Oscar Wilde walked. Robert E. Lee even rode a horse through the hotel. Established in 1859, the Menger is the only hotel west of the Mississippi that's never closed its doors since. Successfully combining the original, restored building with myriad additions, it now takes up an entire city block.

Decor in the guest rooms ranges from ornate 19th-century to modern but still colorful styles—some of the newer rooms have Asian touches, others tasteful Western motifs. Some in the rather plain central section built in 1944 offer kitchenettes and balconies. All have modern amenities, including hair dryers. If you want to stay in one of the antiques-filled Victorian rooms, be sure to request this when you book.

**Dining/Diversions:** The Menger Bar is one of San Antonio's great historic taverns. The pretty Colonial Room Restaurant offers breakfast-and-lunch buffets and a Southwestern-style menu that includes a number of game specials for dinner. Be sure to try the mango ice cream: President Clinton liked it so much that he had hundreds of gallons shipped in for his inauguration.

**Amenities:** Free morning coffee in the lobby, limousine service, heated outdoor pool, hot tub, exercise room, Alamo Plaza Spa (facials, wraps, massage), shopping arcade, tourist information center, game room, gift shop.

## MODERATE

Other hotels in the moderate category that are not quite as well located or as loaded with character as those listed below include the **Holiday Inn Express,** 524 S. St. Mary's St. (☎ **800/959-3239** or 210/354-1333), and the **AmeriSuites River Walk,** 601 S. St. Mary's (☎ **800/833-1516** or 210/227-6854), near the convention center. Both are well equipped with kitchenettes, hair dryers, and irons in the rooms, outdoor pool and exercise room, and complimentary continental breakfast. The Holiday Inn also offers a cocktail reception and guest laundry, while AmeriSuites has free parking and free popcorn in the afternoon. Of the clump of Moderate properties on the west side of downtown, the closest to Market Square and other tourist attractions is **La Quinta Market Square,** 900 Dolorosa (☎ **800/687-6667** or 210/271-0001), with an outdoor pool. A little farther south and a bit more expensive, but with more facilities, are the **Holiday Inn Market Square,** 318 W. Durango (☎ **800/HOLIDAY** or 210/225-3211), and the **Residence Inn Marriott Market Square** (☎ **800/ 331-3131** or 210/231-6000). Both have an outdoor pool and exercise room. The Holiday Inn also features a restaurant and room service, while you get kitchenettes and a few tennis courts at the Marriott.

⭘ **Drury Inn & Suites San Antonio Riverwalk.** 201 N. St. Mary's St., San Antonio TX 78205. ☎ **800/DRURY-INN** or 210/212-5200. Fax 210/352-9939. www.druryinn.com. $129–$154 double; $170–$185 suite. AE, CB, DC, DISC, MC, V. Self-parking $7. One pet permitted per room.

San Antonio's most recent (2000) historic conversion on the River Walk, the one-time Petroleum Commerce Building is now a comfortable modern lodging, although the polished marble floors and chandeliers in the lobby and the high ceilings and ornate window treatments in the guest rooms hearken back to a grander era. Then again, the Petroleum Commerce folks would probably have considered such business traveler perks as free hot breakfasts, free evening cocktails and snacks, and free local phone calls to be pretty grand. The attractive Southwest-style rooms are all equipped with coffeemakers, refrigerators, and microwaves. There's a rooftop pool and whirlpool and small exercise room. Businesspeople will appreciate the Texas Land & Cattle Steakhouse (see chapter 5) on the hotel's River Walk level, a nice, reasonably priced place to schmooze clients, as well as the 24-hour business center.

⭘ **Havana Riverwalk Inn.** 1015 Navarro, San Antonio, TX 78205. ☎ **888/224-2008** or 210/222-2008. Fax 210/222-2717. E-mail: hhinfo@havanahotel.com. 37 units. A/C TV TEL. $110–$155 double; $185–$600 suite. Rates include continental breakfast. AE, CB, DC, DISC, MC, V. Self-parking $10. Ages 15 and over only.

Decked out to suggest travelers' lodgings circa the 1920s, this intimate inn, built in 1914 in Mediterranean Revival style, oozes character. All the rooms are delightfully different, with a safari hat covering a temperature control gauge here, an old photograph perched over a toilet paper roll there, gauzy curtains draped on a canopy bed, wooden louvres on the windows, brick walls, and so on. Touches like fresh flowers and bottled water add to the charm, and modern amenities have not been ignored: All the rooms have large desks, data-port phones, irons and ironing boards, and hair dryers. They do not, however, all have closets, so be prepared to have your clothes hanging in public view if you plan to invite anyone to your room.

There's enough action at the hotel's superhip cigar bar, Club Cohiba, to keep you on the premises at night. Wake up the next morning to coffee and baked goods laid out for guests in the dining room. Siboney, the hotel's industrial chic but romantic dining room, has been through a variety of chefs. The New American cuisine was terrific when I last visited, but best peer into the restaurant the night you arrive to see if it's thriving before booking what can be an expensive meal.

*Note:* The inn is near a section of the River Walk that's being drained for repairs starting in late 2000; guests here usually have easy access to a quiet stretch of water, but, until late 2001, you'll have to walk a bit farther to see the river.

**Holiday Inn Riverwalk.** 217 N. St. Mary's St., San Antonio, TX 78205. ☎ **800/465-4329** or 210/224-2500. Fax 210/223-1302. www.holidayinn.com. 313 units. A/C TV TEL. $139–$179 double; $185–$285 suite. AE, CB, DC, DISC, MC, V. Self- or valet parking $10. Pets accepted.

This luxurious link in the Holiday Inn chain may not have the name-drop cachet of some of the historic hotels nearby, but it does offer a River Walk location and many of the same amenities at a lower price. The hotel looks out on a quiet stretch of the river, but it's just a few minutes' walk from all the action.

Fairly standard and boxy from the outside, this high-rise opens into a plush lobby with lots of plants, comfortable chairs, and polished tile. Guest rooms are done in attractive contemporary style, and almost all of them have balconies; those looking out onto the river are slightly more expensive than those that overlook the city, although the urban vistas can be stunning at night, especially from the higher floors. All rooms have hair dryers, and suites add coffeemakers and mini-refrigerators. The hotel features an outdoor heated pool, a whirlpool, an exercise room, a game room, and a gift shop.

The three-level Fandangos Restaurant serves up a spectacular view of the river with its fairly standard American/Tex-Mex fare. It's open for three meals daily and offers breakfast-and-lunch buffets during the week. A few of the tables at the lively Ripples lounge also peek out over the water.

○ **Ramada Emily Morgan.** 705 E. Houston St., San Antonio, TX 78205. ☎ **800/824-6674** or 210/225-8486. Fax 210/225-7227. http://pw1.netcom.com/~ramadaem. 177 units. A/C TV TEL. $129–$179 double. Various discounts, romance packages. AE, CB, DC, DISC, MC, V. Self-parking $9.

Converted to a hotel in the mid-1980s, the Ramada Emily Morgan is in a beautiful 1926 Gothic revival building, the first documented skyscraper built west of the Mississippi. It was originally designed as a medical arts center; be sure to look up at the gargoyles, said to have been placed there to help the doctors ward off disease.

The hotel is centrally located, a musket shot from the Alamo, and convenient to all the other downtown attractions. Guest rooms are modern, bright, and immaculate; each has a remote-control TV with HBO and pay-per-view movies as well as a hair dryer, coffeemaker, and iron—amenities frequently missing from far more expensive accommodations (frequent specials almost always keep this hotel in the low end of the Moderate category). In addition, pricier Executive and Plaza rooms offer mini-refrigerators and double or single Jacuzzi tubs. Amenities include an outdoor pool and whirlpool, an exercise room, his-and-her saunas, room service, free coffee in the lobby, and concierge service.

The lobby hosts the cheerful Yellow Rose Cafe, which serves breakfast and lunch (including an all-you-can-eat buffet), and Emily's Oasis Cocktail Lounge, where dinner is served and complimentary hors d'oeuvres are offered during happy hour. In case you were wondering—Emily Morgan, called the "Yellow Rose of Texas," was the mulatto slave mistress of Mexican general Santa Anna; she was reputed to have spied on him for the Texas independence fighters.

**Riverwalk Inn.** 329 Old Guilbeau, San Antonio, TX 78204. ☎ **800/254-4440** or 210/212-8300. Fax 210/229-9422. www.riverwalkinn.com. E-mail: Innkeeper@riverwalkinn. com. 11 units. A/C TV TEL. $115–$180 double. Rates include breakfast. Specials offered. AE, DISC, MC, V. Free off-street parking.

If you've ever had a hankering to stay in an old log cabin but don't really care to go rustic, consider this unusual bed-and-breakfast. Native Texans Jan and Tracy Hammer had eight 1840s Tennessee cabins taken apart log by log and put back together again near the banks of the San Antonio River, a few blocks south of HemisFair Park and north of the King William area.

Except for a few anachronistic but welcome details—indoor plumbing, individual air-conditioning and heating units, refrigerators, TVs, phones with voice mail, coffeemakers, and digital alarm clocks—everything in the cabins is authentic. Each room has a fireplace, quilt, braided rug, and many fascinating primitive antiques. Most rooms also have balconies or porches fronting the river. Fresh-made desserts are served in the parlor every evening. The wooden plank breakfast table can get a bit crowded on weekend mornings, but that's in keeping with the inn's pioneer spirit—and at least guests don't have to sleep together in one room.

## INEXPENSIVE

For the most part, you'll have to go out of the way to get any kind of bargains downtown. The exception is the **Fairfield Inn by Marriott,** 620 S. Santa Rosa (☎ **800/ 229-2800** or 210/299-1000), part of, but a bit less expensive than, the abovementioned group of motels near Market Square that fall into the Moderate range. On the northwest side of downtown, the aptly named **Rodeway Inn,** 900 N. Main (☎ **800/ 635-4451** or 210/223-2951), looks out on I-35, but it has a restaurant and pool, and it's on the trolley line. On the east side, near the Rivercenter Mall and the Alamo but on the wrong side of the tracks (i.e., I-37), the **Red Roof Inn,** 1001 E. Houston (☎ **800/843-7663** or 210/229-9983), gives you a decent place to lay your head—and to take a swim.

## 2 King William Historic District

### EXPENSIVE

✪ **Noble Inns.** 102 Turner St., San Antonio, TX 78204. ☎ **800/221-4045** or 210/ 225-4045. Fax 210/227-0877. www.nobleinns.com. E-mail: innkeeper@nobleinns.com. 9 units. A/C TV TEL. $130–$180 double in the Jackson House; $140–$190 Pancoast House suites. Rates include breakfast. AE, DISC, MC, V. Free off-street parking.

It's hard to imagine that Donald and Liesl Noble, both descended from King William founding families, grew up in the neighborhood when it was run-down; the area has undergone an amazing metamorphosis in the short span of the young couple's life. Indeed their gracious lodgings—the 1894 Jackson House, a traditional-style B&B and, a few blocks away, the 1896 Pancoast Carriage House, offering three suites with kitchens—are a tribute to just how far it has come.

The decor in both houses hearkens back to the period in which they were built, but manages to do so without being fussy. Rooms, individually decorated with fine antiques, are ideal for both business and leisure travelers. All have gas fireplaces and telephones with voice mail and data ports; three in the Jackson House feature two-person Jacuzzi tubs. Other luxurious touches include bathrobes, Godiva chocolate at turndown, and fresh flowers.

**Dining:** Guests at the Jackson House come downstairs to the dining room for a full breakfast, while those at the Pancoast Carriage House enjoy fresh baked goods, fruit, cereal, and other goodies at leisure in their own dining areas.

**Amenities:** The Pancoast House boasts a swimming pool and heated spa, while the Jackson House features a lovely conservatory with a 14-foot swimmable spa. A silver-gray classic Rolls Royce is available for airport transportation or downtown drop-off.

✪ **Ogé House Inn on the River Walk.** 209 Washington St., San Antonio, TX 78204. ☎ **800/242-2770** or 210/223-2353. Fax 210/226-5812. www.ogeinn.com. E-mail: ogeinn@swbell.net. 10 units. A/C TV TEL. $155 double; $185–$225 suite. Rates include breakfast. Corporate rates available for single business travelers (Sun–Thurs). 2-night minimum stay on weekends; 3 nights during Fiesta, holidays, and other special events. AE, CB, DC, DISC, MC, V. Free off-street parking.

One of the most glorious of the mansions that grace the King William district, the 1867 Greek revival–style Ogé House is more boutique inn than folksy bed-and-breakfast. You'll still get the personalized attention you would expect from a host home, but it's combined here with the luxury of a sophisticated small hotel. Impeccably decorated in high Victorian style, all the accommodations offer private phone lines, cable TV, and refrigerators; many have fireplaces and views of the manicured, pecan-shaded grounds, and one looks out on the river from its own wrought-iron balcony.

**Dining:** A bountiful gourmet breakfast is served on individual white-clothed tables set with the finest of crystal and china. Single travelers who don't take to talking to strangers in the morning can bury themselves in one of the daily newspapers laid out on the bureau just beyond the dining room. More social-minded folks might be seen lounging on the downstairs porch in the late afternoon, perhaps enjoying a drink with hosts Patrick and Sharrie Magatagan; they know all the best places to eat in town and can help you get a reservation.

## MODERATE

**Beckmann Inn and Carriage House.** 222 E. Guenther St., San Antonio, TX 78204. ☎ **800/945-1449** or 210/229-1449. Fax 210/229-1061. www.beckmanninn.com. E-mail: beckinn@swbell.net. 5 units. A/C TV TEL. $99–$119 double; $130–$150 suite. Rates include breakfast. AE, DC, DISC, MC, V.

Sitting on the lovely wraparound porch of this 1886 Queen Anne home, surrounded by quiet, tree-lined streets on an uncommercialized stretch of the San Antonio River, you can easily imagine yourself in a kinder, gentler era. In fact, you can still see the flour mill on whose property the Beckmann Inn was originally built. Nor will the illusion of time travel be dispelled when you step through the rare Texas red-pine door into the high-ceilinged parlor.

Innkeepers Betty Jo and Don Schwartz filled the house with antique pieces that do justice to the setting, such as the ornately carved Victorian beds in each of the guest

---

**ⓘ Family-Friendly Lodgings**

**Hyatt Regency Hill Country Resort** (*p. 45*)   In addition to its many great play areas (including a beach with a shallow swimming area), this hotel has Camp Hyatt, a special program of excursions, sports, and social activities for children 3 to 12. Rates are $35 for the morning or afternoon program ($45 with lunch for either), and $40 (including dinner) for the evening program (6 to 10pm). This program fills up fast during school breaks and other holidays, when reservations are mandatory.

**Homewood Suites** (*p. 34*)   Downtown's addition of a reasonably priced all-suites hotel, with in-room kitchen facilities and two TVs (each with its own VCR), not to mention a guest laundry, is welcome news for families.

**O'Casey's** (*p. 40*)   Usually B&Bs and family vacations are a contradiction in terms, but O'Casey's is happy to host well-behaved kids (they accept the other kind too, but you can't expect happiness). Best bet: Stay in the separate guesthouse with the fold-out bed, and join the main-house guests for breakfast in the morning.

---

rooms. Two of the rooms have private entrances, as does the separate Carriage House, decorated in a somewhat lighter fashion. A full breakfast—perhaps stuffed cinnamon French toast with light cream cheese and pecans—is served in the formal dining room, but you can enjoy your coffee on a flower-filled sun porch.

**The Columns on Alamo.** 1037 S. Alamo, San Antonio, TX 78210. ☎ **800/233-3364** or 210/271-3245. www.bbonline.com/tx/columns. E-mail: artlink@flash.net. 13 units. A/C TV TEL. $92–$162 double; $162–$255 cottage. Rates include breakfast. Extended-stay discounts. AE, CB, DC, DISC, MC, V. Free off-street parking.

Guests at this B&B can stay in the 1892 Greek revival mansion from which the inn derives its name; the adjacent guesthouse, built 9 years later; or a separate limestone cottage that's new but built in rustic early 1880s style. The mansion, where the innkeepers live, is the most opulent and offers unusual walk-through windows leading to a veranda, but the guesthouse, which houses most of the guest rooms, affords more privacy if you're uncomfortable with the idea of staying in someone else's home. Those who really want to hole up on their own should book the Honeymoon and Anniversary cottage, attached to the guesthouse, or the separate Rock House cottage in the back, large enough for four.

All the rooms are light, airy, and very pretty, although this is not the place for those allergic to pastels and frills; pink dominates many of the accommodations, and even the darker-toned Imari Room has lace curtains. (The Rock House, done in more casual country style, is the exception.) Several of the units boast two-person Jacuzzis and gas-log fireplaces. The inn straddles the boundary between King William and the livelier Southtown. Hosts Ellenor and Arthur Link are extremely helpful, and breakfasts are all you could ask for in morning indulgence.

## 3 Monte Vista Historic District

### MODERATE

**Bonner Garden.** 145 E. Agarita, San Antonio, TX 78212. ☎ **800/396-4222** or 210/733-4222. Fax 210/733-6129. www.bonnergarden.com. 5 units. A/C TV TEL. $85–$105 double; $115–$125 suite. Rates include full breakfast. Extended stay (minimum 3 nights) and corporate rates (Sun–Thurs) available. AE, CB, DISC, MC, V. Free off-street parking.

Those who like the intimacy of the bed-and-breakfast experience but aren't keen on Victorian froufrou should consider the Bonner Garden, located in the Monte Vista Historic District, about a mile north of downtown. Built in 1910 for Louisiana artist Mary Bonner, this large, Italianate villa has a beautiful, classical simplicity and lots of gorgeous antiques—not to mention a 50-foot sunken swimming pool.

The Portico Room, in which guests can gaze up at a painted blue sky with billowing clouds, offers a private poolside entrance. You don't have to be honeymooners to enjoy the large Jacuzzi tub in the Bridal Suite, perhaps the prettiest room, with its Battenburg lace drapes and blue porcelain fireplace. Most of the rooms feature European-style decor, but Mary Bonner's former studio, separate from the main house, is done in tasteful Santa Fe style. In addition to phones and TVs, all the rooms have VCRs—the better to take advantage of the excellent film library. Generous breakfasts are enjoyed around a long, gleaming wood table that once hosted diplomats in Denmark's British Embassy. A rooftop deck with a wet bar affords a sparkling nighttime view of downtown.

**The Inn at Craig Place.** 117 W. Craig Place, San Antonio TX 78212. ☎ **877/427-2447** or 210/736-1017. Fax 210/737-1562. www.craigplace.com. E-mail: stay@craigplace.com. 3 units. A/C TV TEL. $125–$150 room. Corporate rates, various packages available. AE, DC, MC, V. Free parking.

Monte Vista's newest old thing, this 1891 mansion, turned 1999 B&B, will appeal to history, art, and architecture buffs alike. It was built by one of Texas's preeminent architects, Alfred Giles, for H.H. Hildebrand, one of San Antonio's movers and shakers, and the living room boasts a mural by Julian Onderbronk, an influential Texas landscape artist.

But that's all academic. More to the point, this place is gorgeous, with forests of gleaming wood and clean Arts-and-Crafts lines, as well as cushy couches and a wrap-around porch. Rooms are at once luxurious—all have working fireplaces, hardwood floors, and come with robes, slippers, and down comforters—and equipped for modern needs, featuring phones with private lines and data ports, cable TV, and CD players. To gild the lily, one of the innkeepers, Tamra Black, worked as a professional chef, so you can expect the three-course breakfasts to be outstanding.

## INEXPENSIVE

✪ **O'Casey's Bed & Breakfast.** 225 W. Craig Place, San Antonio, TX 78212. ☎ **800/ 738-1378** or 210/738-1378. www.ocaseybnb.com. E-mail: info@ocaseybnb.com. 7 units. A/C TV. $79–$99 double; $89–$99 suite; $109 apt. Rates include full breakfast. Lower week-day rates; discounts on stays of 5 days or more. AE, DISC, MC, V. Free parking. Pets allowed in apartments ($5 extra per night).

If there is a twinkle in John Casey's eye when he puts on a brogue, it's because he was born on U.S. soil, not the auld sod. But his and his wife Linda Fay's down-home friendliness is no blarney. This Irish-themed B&B is one of the few around that welcomes families, and it's well equipped to handle them. One suite in the main house has a sitting area with a futon large enough for a couple of youngsters; another has a trundle bed for two kids in a separate bedroom. And the studio apartments in the carriage house both offer full kitchens.

Which is not to suggest that accommodations are utilitarian—far from it. Rooms in the main house—a gracious structure built in 1904—feature hardwood floors and fine antiques, and many bathrooms have clawfoot tubs. There's also a wraparound balcony upstairs. For a treat, ask Linda Fay, a professional pianist, and John, a choir director and singer, to perform a few numbers for you. (But don't ask *too* often; they work hard to run their B&B smoothly.)

## 4  Fort Sam Houston/Northeast I-35

### MODERATE

**Terrell Castle.** 950 E. Grayson St., San Antonio, TX 78208. ☎ **800/481-9732** or 210/271-9145. Fax 210/527-1455. www.terrellcastle.com. E-mail: smilgin@aol.com. 8 units. A/C TV. $105–$115 double; $135–$235 suite. Rates include full breakfast. $10 less during the week. Children under 6 stay free. AE, DISC, MC, V. Free parking.

Unless a trip to Scotland is in the cards, this could be your best chance to spend a night in a castle. Built in 1894 by English-born architect Alfred Giles, this massive limestone structure was commissioned by Edwin Terrell, a statesman who fell in love with the European grand style while serving as U.S. ambassador to Belgium. Turned into a bed-and-breakfast in 1986, it's an anomaly in the working-class area near the Fort Sam Houston quadrangle. Guest rooms don't feature as many antiques as you'll see in the glorious public areas, but they're comfortable and clean; several offer fireplaces and all have TVs, but they're all phoneless. A variety of suites, some with kitchen facilities, as well as free lodging for children under 6 and the free use of a crib, make this B&B uncharacteristically family-friendly. Breakfasts, served in the formal dining room, are copious and elaborate.

### INEXPENSIVE

A few chain hotels along the section of I-35 just northeast of downtown and south of Fort Sam Houston offer rooms in the "Inexpensive" price category: **Days Inn Northeast,** 3443 I-35 North (☎ **800/548-2626** or 210/225-4040); **Super 8 Motel,** 3617 I-35 North (☎ **800/800-8000** or 210/227-8888); and **Quality Inn & Suites,** 3817 I-35 North (☎ **800/942-8913** or 210/224-3030). All have swimming pools. Scenic this area is not, but it's convenient if you have a car.

✪ **Bullis House Inn.** 621 Pierce St., San Antonio, TX 78208. ☎ **210/223-9426.** Fax 210/299-1479. E-mail: HISanAnton@aol.com. 7 units in Bullis House, separate cottage. A/C TV. $59–$69 double with shared bathroom, $79 double with private bathroom; $150 3-bedroom cottage. Weekly rates available; rates in most rooms include continental breakfast. AE, DISC, MC, V. Free off-street parking.

This graceful neoclassical mansion, just down the street from the Fort Sam Houston quadrangle and easily accessible from the airport and downtown by car, is an excellent bed-and-breakfast bargain, especially for those who don't mind sharing bathrooms. Beautifully restored in the 1980s, it was built from 1906 to 1909 for General John Lapham Bullis, a frontier Indian fighter who played a key role in capturing Geronimo (some claim the Apache chief's spirit still roams the mansion). More concerned with creature comforts when he retired, the general had oak paneling, parquet floors, crystal chandeliers, and marble fireplaces installed in his home, which is now often used for wedding receptions. Guest rooms all have 14-foot ceilings and are furnished with some period antiques along with good reproductions; three of them feature fireplaces, and one offers a private bathroom. The family room, which sleeps up to six, has a refrigerator. A large swimming pool, movie nights, and VCR/video rentals are among the perks.

The owners also rent out a three-bedroom, two-bathroom cottage on the other side of Fort Sam Houston, near Breckenridge Park and the San Antonio Botanical Gardens. Built in the 1940s, it features a full kitchen (including washer/dryer), fireplace, cable TV, hardwood floors, attractive art deco–style period pieces, and a lovely wraparound deck.

**Hostelling International—San Antonio.** 621 Pierce St., San Antonio, TX 78208. ☎ **210/223-9426.** Fax 210/299-1479. E-mail: HISanAnton@aol.com. 38 beds. $15.35—$16.95 for members; $3 additional for nonmembers. AE, DISC, MC, V.

# Greater San Antonio Accommodations & Dining

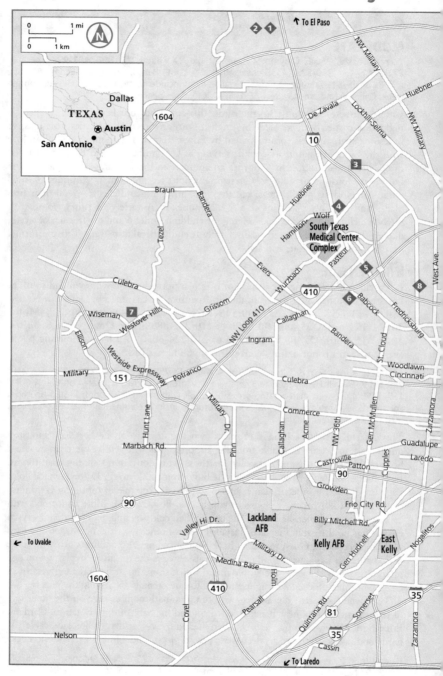

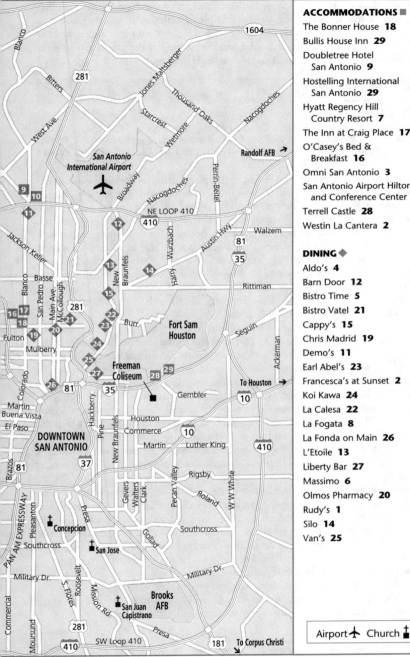

43

Right next door to the Bullis House Inn (see above), this youth hostel has a reading room, small kitchen, dining area, lockers, and picnic tables, in addition to male and female dorms. Hostelers are welcome at the Bullis House Inn on film nights, and the two lodgings share a pool. A continental breakfast, served at the inn, is available for an additional $5. Bus no. 15 from downtown stops close by.

## 5 Medical Center/Northwest

### VERY EXPENSIVE

✪ **Westin La Cantera.** 16641 La Cantera Parkway, San Antonio, TX 78256. ☎ **800/ WESTIN-1** or 210/558-6500. Fax 210/641-0721. www.westin.com. 508 units. A/C TV TEL. $199–$330 double; $380–$1,800 suite; $350–$1,200 casita. AE, CB, DISC, JCB, MC, V. Free self-parking; valet parking $10.

Locals like to joke that the 1999 opening of this posh northwest property doubled the number of resorts in San Antonio. No doubt about it: This lovely retreat is giving the Hyatt Regency Hill Country Resort (see under "West," below) a run for the high-end visitor money. They're similar in many ways, offering knockout facilities, sprawling, gorgeous grounds, and loads of Texas character. Both are family-friendly, with theme parks in their backyards (the Westin is right next door to Six Flags Fiesta Texas) and excellent children's programs. But the Westin has the edge when it comes to golf, boasting two championship courses (in addition to the much-praised La Cantera, a new Arnold Palmer–designed course) plus a professional golf school. It's a tad more romantic, too, with dramatic rocky outcroppings and drop-dead views from its perch on one of the highest points in San Antonio.

The resort is elaborately designed around state historical motifs. The Texas colonial architecture is definitely impressive and the tales and legends detailed in plaques in the various rooms are interesting, but I suspect most guests are too busy having fun to pay them much mind. Likewise, the casual elegant rooms—beautifully decorated in muted earth tones and subtle florals and equipped with all the business amenities conference attendees need—are likely to be abandoned for the resort's various recreation areas, or at least for the balconies (terraces in the case of the secluded Casita Villas) that many of the guest quarters offer. Remnants of the limestone quarry on which the resort was built were incorporated into the five swimming pools interconnected with bridges and channels and a dramatic waterfall. And the indigenous plant life and animal life—deer, rabbits, and wild turkeys come out at dusk—should have you oohing and cooing.

**Dining/Diversions:** The resort's full-service restaurant, Brannon's, has a Tex-American menu with something for everyone. For dinner, La Cantera Grille, in the clubhouse, with great vistas and excellent steaks and Southwest specialties, would shine even brighter if it weren't for the resort's star dining room, Francesca's at Sunset (see chapter 5). Other dining and drinking areas include Steinheimer's clubby lounge and cigar bar, with a fun skee-ball/hockey game, and a poolside refreshment spot.

**Amenities:** Two 18-hole golf courses, five outdoor pools, two outdoor hot tubs, two tennis courts, health club with exercise and weight rooms, beauty salon, spa services, children's activity center, Westin Kids Club, 24-hour room service, gift shop, multilingual concierge desk, business center, newsstand, car-rental desk.

### EXPENSIVE

**Omni San Antonio.** 9821 Colonnade Blvd., San Antonio, TX 78230. ☎ **800/843-6664** or 210/691-8888. Fax 210/691-1128. www.omnihotels.com. 326 units. A/C TV TEL. $199 double; $300–$600 suite. Romance and other packages available. AE, CB, DC, DISC, JCB, MC, V. Free self-parking; valet parking $5. Pets 25 lbs. or under permitted with $25 deposit.

This polished granite high-rise off I-10 west is convenient to SeaWorld, Six Flags Fiesta Texas, the airport, and the Hill Country, and the shops and restaurants of the 66-acre Colonnade complex are within easy walking distance. The lobby is soaring and luxurious, and guest rooms, updated in early 2001, are well appointed in a traditional European style. All offer coffeemakers, hair dryers, and minibars—and Nintendo, which fits in with the free Omni Kids features. Although the hotel sees a lot of tourist and Medical Center traffic, service here is always prompt and courteous.

**Dining/Diversions:** At a clubby lobby lounge, you can settle into plush leather chairs and listen to live piano music (Tues to Sat). The hotel's full-service restaurant is the Southwestern-style Bolo's, a rotisserie grill with lots of interesting game entrees and a nice selection of wines by the glass; breakfast buffets and pasta bars are laid on during the week, and there's a good Sunday brunch.

**Amenities:** A health complex offers indoor-and-outdoor pools (the latter large enough for laps) and two Jacuzzis, along with a well-equipped exercise room and sauna; racquetball facilities are adjacent to the hotel. Complimentary airport shuttle, gift shop, concierge, business center.

## MODERATE

A number of lower-end properties are concentrated around the area where NW Loop 410 meets I-10 west. This northwest section of San Antonio, home to the huge South Texas Medical Center, is one of the newer parts of town to be developed. It doesn't have much character, but it affords easy access to Six Flags Fiesta Texas and SeaWorld. Moderately priced hotels that offer the most extras for your money include **Courtyard by Marriott/Medical Center,** 8585 Marriott Dr. (☎ **800/321-2211** or 210/614-7100), with exercise room, restaurant, and pool; **Hawthorn Suites,** 4041 Bluemel Rd. (☎ **800/527-1133** or 210/561-9660), featuring an exercise room, pool, kitchenettes, and tennis courts; and **Homewood Suites,** 4323 Spectrum One (☎ **800/225-5466** or 210/696-5400), with exercise room, pool, and kitchenettes.

## INEXPENSIVE

Lodgings in the area that fall into the "Inexpensive" category (most at the high end of it) include the **Hampton Inn Northwest,** 4803 Manitou, 78228 (☎ **800/HAMPTON** or 210/684-9966); **Holiday Inn Express/Northwest,** 9411 Wurzbach, 78240 (☎ **800/HOLIDAY** or 210/561-9300); **La Quinta Wurzbach,** 9542 I-10 West, 78230 (☎ **800/531-5900** or 210/593-0338); and **Ramada Limited Six Flags,** 9447 I-10 West, 78320 (☎ **800/757-4707** or 210/558-9070). All offer a pool but no other facilities.

## 6 West

### VERY EXPENSIVE

✪ **Hyatt Regency Hill Country Resort.** 9800 Hyatt Resort Dr., San Antonio, TX 78251. ☎ **800/233-1234** or 210/647-1234. Fax 210/681-9681. www.sanantoniohyatt.com. 501 units. A/C TV TEL. $275 double; $365 Regency Club; $450–$1,550 suite. Rates lower late Nov to early Mar; many packages available. AE, CB, DC, DISC, JCB, MC, V. Free self-parking; valet parking $8.

The setting, on 200 acres of former ranchland on the far west side of San Antonio, is idyllic. The on-site activities, ranging from golf to tubing on a man-made river, are endless, and SeaWorld of Texas sits at your doorstep. The rooms are beautifully appointed, and there are even free laundry facilities and a country store for supplies. In short, the Hyatt will fulfill all your needs.

The best of Texas design is showcased here. The resort's low-slung buildings, made of native limestone, are inspired by the architecture of the nearby Hill Country. The light-filled lobby is rustic elegant—sort of Ralph Lauren with antlers—and the guest quarters are done in updated country style: Carved maple beds are topped with quilt-style covers, and walls have stenciled borders, but the lines are clean and unfussy. Most rooms feature French doors that open out onto wood-trimmed porches, and all have in-room refrigerators.

The recreation facilities are top-notch. Along with an 18-hole championship golf course, the Hyatt boasts tennis courts; a well-equipped health club with Jacuzzi, sauna, and massage room; two swimming pools (one for adults only) and two outdoor whirlpools; volleyball and basketball courts; and jogging and bike paths. Above all, there's the 950-foot-long Ramblin' River, a lushly landscaped 4-acre park where you can grab an inner tube and float your cares away.

**Dining/Diversions:** Sit out on Aunt Mary's Porch and down a good local brew, or stop in at Charlie's to see the 56-foot, carved-wood and copper bar; you might be inspired to shoot a few rounds of pool. Golfers tend to guzzle at the Cactus Oak Tavern, the clubhouse bar and grill with a great view, of the course. The Springhouse Cafe, serving three meals a day in the hotel's main building, is country casual, offering both an à la carte menu and buffet service. The hotel's fine dining room features upscale Southwestern cuisine and boasts the world's largest antler chandelier, 9 feet high and made of 506 naturally shed horns.

**Amenities:** Shuttle service to airport and to downtown (fee), concierge service, gift shop, golf pro shop, car-rental agency, Regency Club lounge, business center, game room, Camp Hyatt (see "Family-Friendly Lodgings," earlier in this chapter, for details).

## 7 Near the Airport

### EXPENSIVE

✪ **San Antonio Airport Hilton and Conference Center.** 611 NW Loop 410, San Antonio, TX 78216. ☎ **800/HILTONS** or 210/340-6060. Fax 210/377-4674. www.hilton.com. 386 units. A/C TV TEL. $165–$175 double; $425–$550 suite. Romance, weekend packages available. AE, CB, DC, DISC, MC, V. Free covered parking. Pets up to 20 lbs. accepted.

You'll go straight from the airport to the heart of Texas if you stay at this friendly hotel, where the cheerful lobby has a bull-rider mural and the guest quarters feature Lone Star–pattern chairs and cowboy lamps. The decor may be fun, but the rooms also get down to business: All offer coffeemakers, large desks, and two-line phones equipped with data ports and voice mail capability. Free newspapers are delivered Monday to Friday. Guests on the 14th-floor Executive Level get bathrobes, daily newspaper delivery, and free continental breakfast.

**Dining/Diversions:** Jocks will like the Hilton's sports bar, with Texas sports memorabilia and enough TVs to let patrons tune in to their favorite home games (see chapter 8 for details). The wood-burning grill and rotisserie of Tex's, serving three meals a day, turns out updated ranch-style food to match its updated ranch-style decor; prices are reasonable and preparations sophisticated.

**Amenities:** Complimentary shuttle to the airport and nearby businesses and Quarry golf course, 24-hour security guards, outdoor heated pool, men's and women's saunas, Jacuzzi, exercise room, video-game room, putting green, business center.

### MODERATE

A number of less distinctive and/or less well-outfitted chain properties in the airport area fall into the "Moderate" price range. The ones that give you the most facilities for the money include (in descending range of price and services): **Embassy Suites Airport,** 10110 Hwy. 281 North (☎ **800/EMBASSY** or 210/525-9999); **Holiday Inn Select Airport,** 77 NE Loop 410 (☎ **800/445-8475** or 210/349-9900); and **Comfort Suites Airport,** 14202 Hwy. 281 North (☎ **888/727-8483** or 210/494-9000). All offer a pool and an exercise room and provide free airport transfers; the Embassy Suites and Holiday Inn have a restaurant and room service, while Comfort Suites has kitchenettes.

**Doubletree Hotel San Antonio Airport.** 37 NE Loop 410, San Antonio, TX 78216. ☎ **800/535-1980** or 210/366-2424. Fax 210/341-0410. www.sanantonio.doubletreehotels. com. 291 units. A/C TV TEL. $125–$165 double; $225–$295 suite. Various packages and discounts available. AE, CB, DC, DISC, MC, V. Free parking.

For an airport hotel, the Doubletree is surprisingly serene. The same developer who converted a downtown seminary into the posh La Mansión del Rio hotel (see "Downtown," above) was responsible for this hotel's design. Moorish arches, potted plants, stone fountains, and colorful Mexican tile create a Mediterranean mood in the public areas; intricate wrought-iron elevators descend from the guest floors to the pool patio, eliminating the need to tromp through the lobby in a swimsuit. Guest rooms are equally appealing, with brick walls painted in peach or beige, wood-beamed ceilings, draped French doors, and colorful contemporary art. In-room irons, hair dryers, coffeemakers, and two-line speakerphones with voice mail and data ports remind you that the hotel has a large business clientele, much of it from Mexico.

The hotel's contemporary-style fine dining room, Cascabel, serves Southwest cuisine with Mediterranean touches. Next door, you can sink down into one of the plush leather chairs of the Spanish colonial-style Cascabel Bar. From 5 to 9pm Monday through Friday, there's live music at the Lobby Bar.

Amenities include complimentary newspaper, Executive (concierge) level, business services, complimentary van service to airport and North Star and Central Malls, express checkout, chocolate chip cookies on check-in, outdoor swimming pool and Jacuzzi, sauna, exercise room, and gift shop.

## INEXPENSIVE

Reliable lodgings near the airport that fall into the "Inexpensive" price range include **Homegate Studios and Suites,** 11221 San Pedro (☎ **888/456-GATE** or 210/ 342-4800), with exercise room and kitchenettes; and **Pear Tree Inn by Drury,** 143 NE Loop 410 (☎ **800/282-8733** or 210/366-9300), with kitchenettes. Two links in the appealing San Antonio–based La Quinta chain are **La Quinta Airport East,** 333 NE Loop 410 (☎ **800/531-5900** or 210/828-0781), and **La Quinta Airport West,** 219 NE Loop 410 (☎ **800/531-5900** or 210/342-4291). There's also the **Super 8 Airport,** 11355 San Pedro (☎ **800/800-8000** or 210/342-8488). In addition to the features noted, all have pools and all except Homegate provide free airport transfers.

# 5 San Antonio Dining

It's easy to eat well in San Antonio, especially if you enjoy Mexican food—or are willing to give it a try. You can get great Tex-Mex standards here, but you'll find less familiar, often sophisticated, dishes from the interior of Mexico, too. New American cuisine, emphasizing fresh regional ingredients and spices combined in exciting ways, is served in some of the most chic dining rooms in town, as well as in some unlikely dives. Then there's high-class French, chicken-fried steak, burgers, barbecue . . . in short, something to satisfy every taste and wallet. The national chains are represented here, naturally—everything from Mickey D's to Morton's of Chicago—but I've concentrated on eateries that are unique to San Antonio, or at least Texas.

The downtown dining scene is burgeoning. Entertainment complexes around the River Walk include South Bank, which hosts a Hard Rock Cafe, Starbucks, and other trendy refueling spots, and Presidio Plaza, anchored by Planet Hollywood. But although dining on the river is a unique, not-to-be-missed experience, many of the restaurants that overlook the water are overpriced and overcrowded. Several hotel restaurants have excellent, if sometimes pricey, menus but in general, even if you're willing to pass up a river view, downtown is not the best place for fine dining.

Most locals chow down a bit north of downtown. The two closest concentrations of restaurants are the San Antonio College/Monte Vista area, north of I-35 and west of Hwy. 281, and the section around North St. Mary's (the Strip), where you can get live entertainment dished up with your food on the weekends. There are also some good restaurants in Beacon Hill, a working-class neighborhood just northwest of downtown off I-10, and a dining scene is beginning to evolve at Southtown, the aptly named area just below downtown. But by far the best eating area in San Antonio is still on and around Broadway, starting a few blocks south of Hildebrand, extending north to Loop 410, and comprising much of the posh area known as Alamo Heights. Brackenridge Park, the zoo, the botanical gardens, and the Witte and McNay museums are in this part of town, so you can combine your sightseeing with some serious eating.

A number of popular places don't take reservations; if you arrive around 8pm when everyone else does, you can expect to wait up to an hour for a table. Make reservations wherever you can.

## The Early Bird

If you're budget conscious, consider eating early, when some restaurants have early-bird specials, or hitting the expensive restaurants at lunch; some of the most upscale eateries in town have good lunch specials.

## RESTAURANT CATEGORIES

Rather than trying to make sharp distinctions between Regional American, New Texan, and American Fusion cuisine, I defined any menu likely to include mashed potatoes, feta cheese, pesto, and chorizo among its staples (although not necessarily in the same dish) as **New American. Southwestern,** on the other hand, is a contemporary cooking style that tends to confine itself to ingredients from, well, the American Southwest (blue corn and jicama, say). Tex-Mex and northern Mexican, which are inextricably intertwined, were merged into a single **Mexican** category. And **Regional Mexican** encompasses Mexican cuisine from other parts of the country.

The price categories into which the restaurants have been divided are only rough approximations; by ordering carefully or by splurging, you can eat more or less expensively at almost any place you choose.

## 1 Restaurants by Cuisine

### AMERICAN
Barn Door (p. 59)
Cappy's (p. 60)
Chris Madrid (p. 58)
Earl Abel's (p. 61)
Guenther House (p. 57)
Little Rhein Steak House (p. 51)
Olmos Pharmacy (p. 59)
Texas Land & Cattle Co. (p. 54)

### BARBECUE
See also "Only in San Antonio," below
Carranza's Grocery & Market (p. 52)
County Line (p. 54)
Rudy's (p. 63)

### CHINESE
Van's (p. 61)

### CONTINENTAL
Bistro Time (p. 62)

### DELI
Pecan Street Market (p. 55)
Schilo's (p. 55)
Twin Sisters (p. 56)

### ECLECTIC
Carranza's Grocery & Market (p. 52)

### FRENCH
Bistro Vatel (p. 58)
Le Rêve (p. 51)
L'Etoile (p. 59)

### GERMAN
Schilo's (p. 55)

### GREEK
Demo's (p. 63)

### HEALTH FOOD
Twin Sisters (p. 56)

### ITALIAN
Aldo's (p. 62)
La Focaccia (p. 56)
Massimo (p. 63)
Paesano's Riverwalk (p. 52)

### JAPANESE
Koi Kawa (p. 60)
Van's (p. 61)

### MEXICAN (NORTHERN & TEX-MEX)
See also "Only in San Antonio," below
El Mirador (p. 56)
La Fogata (p. 61)
La Fonda on Main (p. 58)

La Margarita (p. 54)
Mi Tierra (p. 54)
Rosario's (p. 57)

### NEW AMERICAN
Biga on the Banks (p. 50)
Boudro's (p. 51)
Las Canarias (p. 50)
Liberty Bar (p. 57)
Silo (p. 60)

### REGIONAL MEXICAN
El Mirador (p. 56)
La Calesa (p. 60)
Rosario's (p. 57)

### SOUTHWESTERN
Francesca's at Sunset (p. 62)
Zuni Grill (p. 52)

### STEAKS
Barn Door (p. 59)
Little Rhein Steakhouse (p. 51)
Texas Land & Cattle Co. (p. 54)

### VIETNAMESE
Van's (p. 61)

## 2  The River Walk & Downtown

### VERY EXPENSIVE

**Biga on the Banks.** International Center, 203 S. St. Mary's St. at Market. ☎ **210/225-0722.** Reservations recommended. Main courses $17–$31. AE, CB, DC, DISC, MC, V. Mon–Thur 5:30–10pm; Fri–Sat 5:30–11pm; Sun 11am–3pm (brunch) and 5:30–10pm. NEW AMERICAN.

With its move to the Riverwalk in 2000, one of San Antonio's earliest culinary innovators got a venue to match its menu: elegant, bold, and contemporary. Clean lines, high ceilings, gleaming wood floors, and lots of seraglio-sexy white draperies—plus a balcony with dramatic river views—set the scene for chef Bruce Auden's consistently interesting food. The game packet starters, for example, cross a few continents, combining Texas and Asia in spring-style rolls filled with minced venison, buffalo, ostrich, and pheasant accompanied by two spicy dipping sauces. A different Asian influence is evident in the apple-smoked pork chop Calcutta, which comes with okra, pearl onions, tomatoes, and curried cranberry sauce. The variations on a theme in the Paseo de Chocolate dessert will send you happily into sugar shock, international style.

It's hard to say whether increased tourist volume will affect the service or cooking adversely; all was fine the evening we visited but that was off-season, and I've heard rumblings of both going awry. The move to the river has definitely affected parking, which is now tough to find or expensive.

✪ **Las Canarias.** La Mansión del Rio, 112 College St. ☎ **210/518-1063.** Reservations recommended. Main courses $19–$33; 3-course tasting menu $40 ($55 paired with wine); champagne brunch $28.95. AE, DC, DISC, MC, V. Sun–Thurs 5:30–10:30pm; Fri–Sat 5:30–11pm; Sun brunch 10:30am–2:30pm. NEW AMERICAN.

The fine dining room at La Mansión del Rio has a couple of things going for it. For one, there are the romantic, candlelit settings: a lovely riverside veranda; a palm-decked, Mexican-tiled patio; or one of several cozy, antiques-filled interior rooms, enlivened by the soft music of a grand piano.

For another, there's the food: It's inventive and beautifully presented. Menus change seasonally, but you might encounter delicate crispy-skin salmon topped with Texas sweet onion rings, and dishes such as grilled rack of local venison with braised cabbage and fig demi-glace, which demonstrate the chef's ability to balance unusual textures and flavors. Appetizers are equally exciting, but you'll want to share to leave room for dazzling desserts like the phyllo-crusted banana cream pie with chocolate pecan ice cream on the side.

✪ **Le Rêve.** 152 E. Pecan St. ☎ **210/212-2221.** Reservations required. Main courses $25–$31. AE, CB, DC, DISC, MC, V. Tues–Sat 5:30–11pm (last reservation taken for 8:30 seating). FRENCH.

San Antonio doesn't have many celebrity chefs, but Le Rêve's Andrew Weissman definitely qualifies as one—especially since the prestigious *Texas Monthly* magazine dubbed his restaurant tops for Francophile fare in the state. Weissman, a local boy made good who studied in France and did a stint at New York's famed Le Cirque, is very serious about his food—and it shows (and tastes). Presentations are lovely, and everything's made from scratch with the freshest of ingredients, so such dishes as the caramelized onion tart appetizer, pigeon stuffed with veal and sage, or the light but rich sour cream cheesecake are sensual delights.

Don't even think about coming here for a quick pre-theater bite. Weissman expects diners to take his food as seriously as he does. Everyone who phones to reserve is told that dining here is an experience that will take at least 2½ hours; the staff has been known to give tables away when diners don't show up in time for their reservations, and although there's no actual dress code, sloppy tourist attire is most definitely frowned upon. As a result, this tiny, chic dining room with a peek-a-boo view of the river is one of the prime see-and-be-seen spots in town, a place where local foodies get fancied up and indulge in the yuppie urges that San Antonians usually disdain.

**Little Rhein Steak House.** 231 S. Alamo. ☎ **210/225-2111.** Reservations recommended. Main courses $18.95–$30.95. AE, CB DC, DISC, MC, V. Sun–Thurs 5–10pm; Fri–Sat 5–11pm. AMERICAN/STEAKS.

Built in 1847 in what was then the Rhein district, the oldest two-story structure in San Antonio has hosted an elegant steakhouse abutting the river and La Villita since 1967. Antique memorabilia decks the indoor main dining room, and a miniature train surrounded by historic replicas runs overhead. Leafy branches overhanging the River Walk patio—elevated slightly and railed off for privacy—are draped in little sparkling lights.

The setting is pretty as ever, and the choice USDA Prime steaks from the restaurant's own meat plant are tasty, but recent competition from chains such as Morton's, nearby, have resulted in a price hike. Now everything here is à la carte: You'll shell out $4.50 for a baked potato, another $6.95 for steamed asparagus (you do still get a loaf of fresh wheat bread, gratis). The restaurant can also get quite noisy. That said, this is still one of the few family-owned steakhouses around, and it offers a unique River Walk dining experience.

## EXPENSIVE

✪ **Boudro's.** 421 E. Commerce St./River Walk. ☎ **210/224-8484.** Reservations strongly recommended. Main courses $13.50–$26.50. AE, DC, DISC, MC, V. Sun–Thurs 11am–11pm; Fri–Sat 11am–midnight. NEW AMERICAN. *Nov 5 - dinner*

Locals tend to look down their noses at River Walk restaurants—that is, with the long-running exception of Boudro's. And with good reason. The kitchen uses fresh local ingredients—Gulf Coast seafood, Texas beef, Hill Country produce—and the preparations and presentations do them justice. The setting is also out of the ordinary: a turn-of-the-century limestone building with hardwood floors and a handmade mesquite bar.

You might start with the guacamole, prepared tableside and served with tostadas, or the crab quesadillas topped with papaya salsa. The prime rib, blackened on a pecan-wood grill, is deservedly popular, as are the lamb chops with peach chutney and garlic mashed potatoes. The food may be innovative, but the portions are not nou-velle. Lighter alternatives include the coconut shrimp with orange horseradish and the grilled yellowfin tuna. For dessert, the whisky-soaked bread pudding is fine, but the lime chess pie with a butter pastry crust . . . divine. Service is very good, especially con-sidering the volume of business and the time the servers spend mixing up guacamole.

✪ **Paesano's Riverwalk.** 111 W. Crockett, Suite 101. ☎ **210/22-PASTA.** Reservations accepted for 10 or more only. Pizzas $11.95–$13.95; main courses $15.95–$26.95. AE, DISC, MC, V. Mon–Thurs 11am–10pm; Fri–Sat 11am–11pm. ITALIAN.

This River Walk incarnation of a longtime San Antonio favorite relinquished its old Chianti bottle–kitsch decor for a soaring ceiling, lots of inscrutable contemporary art, and a much more up-to-date menu. But the one thing they couldn't give up, at the risk of a local insurrection, was the signature shrimp Paesano's. The crispy crustaceans are as good as their devotees claim, as are the reasonably priced pizzas, including the one topped with grilled chicken, artichokes, basil pesto, and feta cheese. Other stand-outs: the grilled pork chops with potato gnocchi, and pan-seared trout with almonds on linguini. The newest version of Paesano's, across from the Quarry Golf Club at 555 Basse Rd., Suite 100 (☎ **210/828-5191**), has a larger menu, with more South-ern Italian staples.

**Zuni Grill.** 511 River Walk/223 Losoya St. ☎ **210/227-0864.** Reservations accepted only for parties of 6 or more. Main courses $13.95–$24.95. AE, DC, DISC, MC, V. Daily 8am–10pm. SOUTHWESTERN.

*[handwritten margin note: Nov 5 lunch]*

With its chile strings, stylized steers, and chic Southwestern menu, this popular River Walk cafe is a little bit of Santa Fe-on-the-San Antonio. If you've never had a prickly pear margarita (and how many of us have?), this is the place to try one: Pureed cactus fruit, marinated overnight in tequila and cactus-juice schnapps, turns the potent, deli-cious drink a shade ranging from pink to startling purple, depending on the ripeness of the fruit.

This is a good place to come from morning 'til dark. Kick-start your day with a breakfast taco, or take a mid-afternoon break with a grilled salmon sandwich with black bean and corn relish. At night, vegetarians will appreciate the gardener and gath-erer platter (grilled vegetables accompanied by roasted garlic mashed potatoes and wilted spinach). For something more substantial, try the honey-coriander pork loin with adobo sauce or seared ahi with polenta. You might want to finish with another culinary dazzler, a bourbon pecan crème brûlée that tastes every bit as good as it sounds.

## MODERATE

**Carranza's Grocery & Market.** 701 Austin St. ☎ **210/223-0903.** Reservations accepted only for large parties. Main courses $7.50–$28.50. AE. Mon–Fri 11am–2pm; Mon–Thurs 5–10pm; Fri–Sat 5–11pm. ECLECTIC/BARBECUE.

If you and your dining companion can't agree on what you want to eat or how much you want to spend, you could: (1) reconsider the relationship, or (2) come to Car-ranza's. The combined lunch-and-dinner menu is broken down into categories for sandwiches, Italian, Mexican, seafood, and meats: You can get a hearty brisket sand-wich on a Mexican roll for $5.50, or a delicious seafood platter, including red snap-per, scallops, shrimp, and a soft-shell crab cake, for $28.50. But most people order the succulent mesquite-smoked meats: brisket, chicken, sausage, pork ribs, or chopped barbecue. Get a combination plate if you can't decide between them.

You can also order your barbecue to go, by the pound; Carranza's has been around as a grocery and market since 1920—when the current owners' grandfather, a cousin

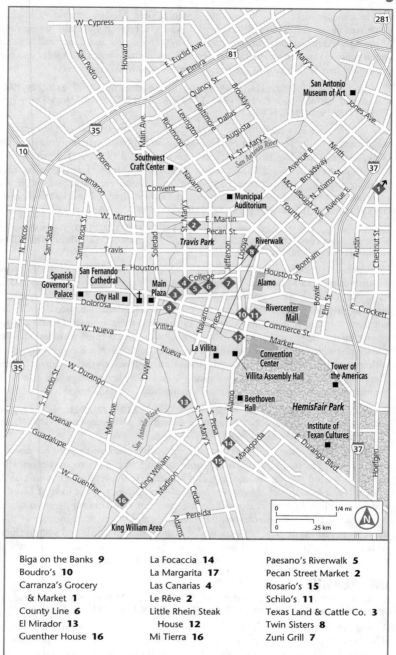

Biga on the Banks **9**
Boudro's **10**
Carranza's Grocery
  & Market **1**
County Line **6**
El Mirador **13**
Guenther House **16**

La Focaccia **14**
La Margarita **17**
Las Canarias **4**
Le Rêve **2**
Little Rhein Steak
  House **12**
Mi Tierra **16**

Paesano's Riverwalk **5**
Pecan Street Market **2**
Rosario's **15**
Schilo's **11**
Texas Land & Cattle Co. **3**
Twin Sisters **8**
Zuni Grill **7**

of Mexican president Don Venustiano Carranza, fled Mexico because of his kin's assassination—and still has a deli counter downstairs. From the upstairs dining room of the restored limestone structure, built in 1870 as a saloon and dance hall, you can watch trains go by during the day or view the city lights at night. Consider combining a meal here with a visit to the nearby San Antonio Museum of Art.

*Nov 4*

✪ **County Line.** 111 W. Crockett St., Suite 104 (Southbank complex). ☎ **210/229-1941.** Reservations not accepted. Platters $8.95–$18.95. AE, DC, MC, V. Sun–Thurs 11am–9pm; Fri–Sat 11am–10pm. BARBECUE.

A roadhouse on the river? Why not? The County Line has transplanted the menu and the signature 1940s Texas decor of this popular Austin-based restaurant to the River Walk, where it's thriving. Even locals come downtown to dig into the fall-off-the-bone beef ribs or the tender pork. The restaurant's claim to fame is that it smokes all its meat for more than 18 hours. Barbecued chicken, turkey, and even some salads are also available. You can find the same good eats at County Line's second location on the city's north side, 10101 West I-10 (☎ **210/641-1998**).

**La Margarita.** 120 Produce Row (Market Sq.). ☎ **210/227-7140.** Reservations not accepted. Main courses $7.25–$16.25. AE, CB, DC, DISC, MC, V. Sun–Thurs 11am–10pm; Fri–Sat 11am–midnight. MEXICAN.

Worked up an appetite with all that Market Square shopping? There's no better place to satisfy it than La Margarita. This lively restaurant is renowned for its fajitas and for its *parilla* platters: huge mounds of charbroiled sausage, chicken, and beef accompanied by *queso flameado* (melted cheese), fried potatoes, beans, guacamole, pico de gallo, and hot flour tortillas. If you're not quite up to the task, there are many smaller, if not exactly lighter, dishes to consider—the enchiladas Acapulco filled with seafood stew and topped with shrimp, scallops, and cheese, for example. Or you can just sit outdoors with an order of nachos and sip a margarita; they do credit to the restaurant's name. The people-watching is great, and who knows—after a margarita *magnífica,* you might be inspired to call over one of the strolling mariachis. (Just don't forget to tip.)

**Texas Land & Cattle Co.** 201 N. St. Mary's St. ☎ **210/222-2263.** No reservations accepted, but you can call ahead to get on a waiting list. Main courses $10–$19. AE, DC, DISC, MC, V. Daily 11am–11pm. AMERICAN/STEAKS.

If you're hankering for a big meat fix, slip into some jeans and mosey on down to this dining room that shouts "Texas" from its branding irons to its wagon-wheel chandeliers—and its huge mesquite-grilled steaks. Located on a quiet stretch of the river, this is a kicked-back downtown bargain—not as fancy as the likes of Morton's and Ruth's Chris, but not nearly as pricey, either. Nor will you find Mexican charro-style steaks served with guacamole, pico de gallo, and warm flour tortillas at those haute steak chains, or great baby-back ribs, or sides such as salads and soup included with the meal, or desserts like the outrageous brownie/ice cream sundae . . . Come to think of it, better slip on those reserve "fat" jeans for this trip.

## INEXPENSIVE

**Mi Tierra.** 218 Produce Row (Market Sq.). ☎ **210/225-1262.** Reservations accepted for large groups only. Main courses $5.75–$16.75. AE, MC, V. Open 24 hours. MEXICAN.

Almost anyone who's ever been within striking distance of San Antonio has heard of this Market Square restaurant, open since 1946. Much expanded and gussied up since then, it still draws a faithful clientele of Latino families and businesspeople along with busloads of tourists. Where else could you come at 2am and order anything from chorizo and eggs to an 8-ounce charbroiled rib eye—and be serenaded by mariachis?

# It's Always Chili in San Antonio

It ranks up there with apple pie in the American culinary pantheon, but nobody's mom invented chili: The stew, which contains chiles, onions, and a variety of spices, was likely conceived around the 1840s by Texas cowboys who needed to make tough meat palatable and to cover up its taste when it began to go bad. The name is a Texas corruption of the Spanish "chile" ("chee-lay"), the peppers—which are not really peppers, but that's another long story—most conventionally used in the stew.

The appellation chili *con carne* is really redundant in Texas, where chili without meat isn't considered chili at all; indeed, most Texans think that adding beans is only for wusses. Beef is the most common base, but everything from armadillo to venison is acceptable.

No one really knows exactly where chili originated, but San Antonio is the prime candidate for the distinction: In the mid–19th century, accounts were widespread of the town's "chili queens," women who ladled steaming bowls of the concoction in open-air markets and street corners. It wasn't until the 1940s that they stopped dishing out chili in front of the Alamo.

William Gebhardt helped strengthen San Antonio's claim to chili fame when he began producing chili powder in the city in 1896. His Original Mexican Dinner package, which came out around 20 years later, included a can each of chili con carne, beans, and tamales, among other things; it fed five for $1. This precursor of the TV dinner proved so popular that it earned San Antonio the nickname "Tamaleville."

Oddly enough, chili isn't generally found on San Antonio restaurant menus. But modern-day chili queens come out in force for special events at Market Square, as well as for Nights in Old San Antonio, one of the most popular bashes of the city's huge Fiesta celebration. And there's not a weekend that goes by without a chili cook-off somewhere in the city. For the king of all chili competitions, however, you need to go to Terlingua, Texas, where the World Championship Chili Cook-off is held each November.

A full menu is available all night, but you needn't have anything heavy. Mi Tierra is justly renowned for its *panadería* (bakery), and you can get all kinds of delicious *pan dulces* to go along with a cup of coffee or Mexican hot chocolate.

**Pecan Street Market.** 152 E. Pecan St., no. 102 (across from the Greyhound Station). ☎ **210/227-3226.** Sandwiches $4.25–$6. AE, DC, DISC, MC, V. Mon–Fri 10am–3pm. DELI.

Choosing a sandwich can be difficult at this downtown deli and gourmet mini-market on the ground floor of the historic Exchange Building. Picking the condiment alone is a challenge—will it be chipotle mayonnaise, cranberry Dijon, or sun-dried tomato spread? Area businesses, long stuck with the same old, same old, have welcomed this little industrial chic spot and its fresh soups, salads, specialty sandwiches (say, focaccia with veggies and smoked gouda cheese), and tempting desserts. Heart-healthy items—sorry, no desserts among 'em—are noted. If you want to hole up in your hotel room during lunch and don't like the room service, you can order in from here.

**Schilo's.** 424 E. Commerce St. ☎ **210/223-6692.** Sandwiches $2.85–$4.95; hot or cold plates $4.45–$5.25; main dishes (served after 5pm) $6.75–$8.95. AE, CB, DC, DISC, MC, V. Mon–Sat 7am–8:30pm (9pm Fri–Sat in summer). GERMAN/DELI.

You can't leave town without stopping in at this San Antonio institution, if only for a hearty bowl of split-pea soup or a piece of the signature cherry cheesecake. The large, open room with its worn wooden booths is a door into the city's German past. The waitresses—definitely not "servers"—wear dirndl-type outfits, and live German bands play on Saturday from 5 to 8pm. It's a great place to refuel while sightseeing near Alamo Plaza; for under $5, a good, greasy Reuben or a bratwurst plate should keep you going for the rest of the day.

**Twin Sisters.** 124 Broadway at Travis. ☎ **210/354-1559.** No reservations. $1.65–$5.50 breakfast; $3.50–$8.50 lunch. MC, V. Mon–Fri 9am–3pm. HEALTH FOOD/DELI.

If you want to avoid overpriced sandwiches and junk food while sightseeing, join the downtown working crowd at this bakery and health food cafe just a few blocks from the Alamo. Eggless and meatless doesn't mean tasteless here—you can get great Greek salads, spicy tofu scrambles, and salsa-topped veggie burgers—but carnivores can also indulge in the likes of ham, pastrami, and salami sandwiches on the excellent bread made on the premises. This popular place fills up by 11:30am but empties after 12:45pm, so gauge your visit accordingly. A branch in Alamo Heights, 6322 N. New Braunfels (☎ **210/822-2265**), has longer hours (7am to 9pm Mon to Sat and 9am to 2pm on Sun), but then, it's not near the Alamo.

## 3  Southtown

### MODERATE

**El Mirador.** 722 S. St. Mary's St. ☎ **210/225-9444.** Reservations accepted, but not generally needed. Main courses $7–$19. MC, V. Mon 6:30am–3pm; Tues–Thurs 6:30am–9pm; Fri–Sat 6:30am–10pm; Sun brunch 9am–3pm. MEXICAN/REGIONAL MEXICAN.

It's not the decor that draws locals of all stripes to this family-owned restaurant near the King William area, but Saltillo tile floors and a few art prints provide a bit of character to two otherwise nondescript rooms. At breakfast, it's the huge plates of eggs scrambled with spicy *machacado* (dried beef) or cooked ranchero style. At lunchtime, it's such specials as enchiladas *suizas* with rice, refried beans, and salad for $4.50. And at dinner, when the menu ranges over different tastes and regions in Mexico, well, everyone has their favorite. . . . The Monterrey-style *cabrito* (grilled goat) and grilled chicken with roasted poblano salsa are among mine, and it's hard to go wrong with the shrimp diablo—not quite as devilishly hot as its name suggests, but wonderfully redolent with garlic. The fresh catch of the day is also usually a winner, and lots of people just come in for the tortilla soup, a meal in itself. Save room for the fruit tacos, served with a variety of sorbets and fresh berries and topped with chocolate sauce.

**La Focaccia.** 800 S. Alamo. ☎ **210/223-5353.** Reservations required for 5 or more only. Pizzas $6.45–$8.95; pastas $5.95–$9.95; main courses $7.95–$15.95 (lobster higher). AE, CB, DC, DISC, MC, V. Mon–Thurs 11am–2:30pm and 5–10pm; Fri 11am–2:30pm and 5–11pm; Sat noon–11pm; Sun noon–10pm. ITALIAN.

In spite of its trendy name and its funky former gas-station setting, this restaurant is about as traditional as they come. Owner/chef Luigi Ciccarelli was born and raised in Rome; his recipes were handed down from his grandfather, who used to be a chef for the royal house. The same large menu is offered at lunch and dinner, making this place a particular bargain after dark. You can opt for well-prepared versions of lasagna or spaghetti and meatballs; the seafood dishes are especially good. The salad bar, which includes such unusual dishes as marinated grilled eggplant and mushrooms, is well worth the $3.50 investment (if you get it without an entree). Portions are large, so try to resist scarfing down the basket of focaccia, made in the wood-burning pizza oven.

> ### ⊕ Family-Friendly Restaurants
>
> **La Calesa** (*see p. 60*)    Here you'll find an inexpensive "chiquitos" menu ($3.50) and a staff that loves youngsters. It's a great place to introduce your kids to Mexican food.
>
> **Olmos Pharmacy** (*see p. 59*)    Kids entertain themselves by swiveling in the seats at this classic soda fountain, where the food is as reasonable as it comes. They won't even mind too much when you go on and on about how this is ice cream the way it's supposed be.
>
> **Schilo's** (*see p. 55*)    A high noise level, a convenient location near the River Walk (but with prices far lower than anything you'll find there), and a wide selection of familiar food make this German deli a good choice.

✪ **Rosario's.** 910 S. Alamo. ☎ **210/223-1806.** Reservations not accepted. Main courses $7.25–$12.95. AE, DC, DISC, MC, V. Mon 11am–3pm; Tues–Thurs 11am–10pm; Fri and Sat 11am–11pm (bar until 2am). MEXICAN/REGIONAL MEXICAN.

When it relocated to a new, much larger space, this long-time Southtown favorite lost some of its coziness, but it's hipper and more colorful than ever, with witty Frida Kahlo and Botero knock-offs, abundant neon—and knockout margaritas.

This is the place to sample tasty versions of such adventurous regional dishes as *camote y pollo adobado*—sweet potato and chicken casserole in a sweet and spicy ancho chile sauce—or *nopalito* (cactus pad) tacos, as well as Tex-Mex standards, all prepared with fresh ingredients. You might start with the shrimp nachos with all the fixin's or the more restrained seafood ceviche (scallop, shrimp, and fish marinated in lime juice), and then go on to the delicious chile relleno, with raisins and potatoes added to the chopped beef stuffing. The noise level can make conversation difficult; fortunately, the food and drink are worth concentrating on.

## INEXPENSIVE

✪ **Guenther House.** 205 E. Guenther St. ☎ **210/227-1061.** Reservations not accepted. Breakfast $3.25–$6.25; lunch $4.75–$6.95. AE, DC, DISC, MC, V. Mon–Sat 7am–3pm; Sun 8am–2pm (the house and mill store are open Mon–Sat 9am–5pm, Sun 8am–2pm). AMERICAN.

The Guenther House offers good food inside one of King William's historic homes. Hearty breakfasts and light lunches are served indoors in a pretty art nouveau–style dining room added on to the Guenther family residence (built in 1860) or outdoors on a trellised patio. The biscuits and gravy are a morning specialty, and the chicken salad (made with black olives) at lunch is excellent, but you can't go wrong with any of wonderful baked goods made on the premises. Adjoining the restaurant are a small museum, a Victorian parlor, and a mill store featuring baking-related items, including mixes for lots of the Guenther House goodies. The house fronts a lovely stretch of the San Antonio River; in the back, you can still see the Pioneer Flour Mill that earned the family its fortune.

# 4 North St. Mary's (The Strip)

## MODERATE

✪ **Liberty Bar.** 328 E. Josephine St. ☎ **210/227-1187.** Reservations recommended. Main courses $6.95–$16.50. AE, MC, V. Sun–Thurs 11:30am–10:30pm; Fri–Sat 11:30am–midnight; Sun brunch 10:30am–2pm; bar until midnight Sun–Thurs, 2am Fri–Sat. NEW AMERICAN.

You'd be hard-pressed to guess that this ramshackle former brothel (opened 1890) near the Hwy. 281 underpass hosts one of the hippest haunts in San Antonio. But as every foodie in town can tell you, it's bright and inviting inside, and you'll find everything here from comfort food (pot roast, say, or a ham-and-Swiss sandwich) to regional Mexican cuisine (the chiles rellenos *en nogada* are super). The toasted French bread with roast garlic spread or eggplant puree goes great with many of the fine—and generally affordable—wines available by the glass; there's a good beer selection, too. And don't worry—even if you've had a few too many, you're not imagining it: The house really *is* leaning.

## 5  Monte Vista/Olmos Park
### EXPENSIVE

✪ **Bistro Vatel.** 218 E. Olmos Ave. ☎ **210/828-3141.** Reservations recommended on the weekends. Main courses $12.50–$24; prix-fixe $24 dinner, $12.95 lunch. Tues–Fri 11:30am–1:30pm; Tues–Sat 5:30–10pm. AE, MC, V. FRENCH.

Talk about a pressure cooker. In 1671, the great French chef Vatel killed himself out of shame because the fish for a banquet he was preparing for Louis XIV wasn't delivered on time. Fortunately his descendent, Damian Watel, has less stress to contend with in San Antonio, where diners are very appreciative of the chef's efforts to bring them classic French cooking at reasonable prices.

The restaurant's strip mall location isn't exactly inspiring, and the dining room has a low, acoustic-tile ceiling, but copper pots, wine racks, and white tablecloths help create a charming, intimate atmosphere. You can't go wrong with the rich seafood cassoulet, and fans of sweetbreads will be pleased to find them here beautifully prepared in duxelle sauce. But your best bet is the bargain prix-fixe meal, where you can choose one each from a trio of appetizers, entrees, and desserts of the day.

### INEXPENSIVE

**Chris Madrid.** 1900 Blanco. ☎ **210/735-3552.** Reservations not accepted. Main courses $3–$6. AE, CB, DC, DISC, MC, V. Mon–Sat 11am–10pm. AMERICAN.

It's hard to drop much money at this funky gas station turned burger joint, but you might lose your shirt—over the years, folks have taken to signing their tees and hanging them on the walls. An even more popular tradition is trying to eat the macho burger, as huge as its name and topped with cheese and jalapeños. The menu is pretty much limited to burgers, nachos, fries, and various combinations thereof, but the casual atmosphere and down-home cooking keep the large outdoor patio filled.

**La Fonda on Main.** 2415 N. Main. ☎ **210/733-0621.** Reservations recommended for 6 or more. Main courses $5.95–$10.95. AE, DC, MC, V. Mon–Thurs 11am–3pm and 5–9:30pm; Fri–Sat 11am–3pm and 5–10:30pm; Sun brunch 11am–3pm. MEXICAN.

One of San Antonio's oldest continually operating restaurants, established in 1932, has revamped both its premises and menu, thanks to Cappy Lawton of Cappy's fame (see "Broadway/Alamo Heights," below), who acquired it a few years ago. The lovely red-tile-roof residence was spiffed up, rendering the dining rooms cheerful and bright—almost as inviting as the garden-fringed outdoor patio. The food is still mainly classic Tex-Mex, featuring giant combination plates—say, *carne asada a la tampiqueña,* strips of beef tenderloin served with a green enchilada, guacamole, Spanish rice, and charro beans—but some lighter selections, including a grilled chicken breast with black beans, are offered too, and "gourmet" touches such as cilantro cream and mole sauces are in evidence. This is still not a place to come if you're seeking culinary adventure (or if you're on a diet), but if you want lots of good food in a pretty setting, you'll be well satisfied.

**Olmos Pharmacy.** 3902 McCullough. ☎ **210/822-3361.** Sandwiches, burgers, platters $1.50–$5.50. AE, MC, V. Mon–Fri 7am–6pm (fountain until 6:30pm); Sat 8am–5:30pm; Sun 9am–1:30pm. AMERICAN.

When was the last time you had a rich chocolate malt served in a large metal container with a glass of whipped cream on the side? Grab a stool at Olmos' Formica counter and reclaim your childhood. Olmos Pharmacy, opened in 1938 (one of the waitresses has been around since the early '60s), also scoops up old-fashioned ice-cream sodas, Coke or root beer floats, sundaes, banana splits . . . if it's cold, sweet, and nostalgia inducing, they've got it. This is also the place to come for filling American and Mexican breakfasts, a vast array of tacos, and classic burgers and sandwiches, all at seriously retro prices.

## 6  Broadway/Alamo Heights

### VERY EXPENSIVE

**L'Etoile.** 6106 Broadway. ☎ **210/826-4551.** Reservations recommended. Main courses $18.95–$33.95 (lobster may be higher); early-bird menu (Mon–Sat 5:30–6:30pm) $13.95. AE, DC, DISC, MC, V. Mon–Thurs 11:30am–2:30pm and 5:30–10pm; Fri–Sat 11:30am–2:30pm and 5:30–11pm. FRENCH.

Knowing some attitude adjustment might be required, the French owners of this appealing bistro set out to convince a kicked-back Texas town that French dining need not be overly formal. Over the years, they've managed to combine top-notch service and excellent food with a relaxed atmosphere, while offering a sufficient number of specials—especially at lunch—to demonstrate that you need not spend half the plane fare to France to eat like a Parisian.

Moorish archways, dun-colored brick walls, and an enclosed patio create a Mediterranean mood; upstairs, there's an intimate skylit dining nook. The menu changes regularly, but the focus is always on seafood, as the lobster tank attests; you might order your favorite crustacean poached, flamed in cognac, or stuffed with crabmeat. The fresh red snapper in potato crust is another good choice. For dessert, the black-and-white chocolate mousse on a raspberry coulis looks almost too gorgeous to eat. Almost. Portions are large, the French bread rolls are warm and crusty, and the accompanying salad is dressed in a nice mustardy vinaigrette. It's tough to find wine bargains, however, on an otherwise impressive list.

### EXPENSIVE

**Barn Door.** 8400 N. New Braunfels Ave. ☎ **210/824-0116.** Reservations recommended for dinner. Main courses $7.95–$37.95. AE, DC, DISC, MC, V. Mon–Fri 10am–2pm and 5–10pm (Fri until 10:30pm); Sat 5–10:30pm; Sun 4–9pm. AMERICAN/STEAKS.

Photographs on the walls of this sprawling, down-home Texas steakhouse show San Antonio in 1955, when the restaurant first opened its doors. Hundreds of business cards attached to every possible space attest to the number of folks who continue to come from all over to enjoy good cuts of charcoal-broiled beef.

Not all of them scarf down steaks the size of the 24-ounce T-bone in the display case at the entryway; most opt for the 6-, 8-, or 12-ounce filets. However, if you've been feeling overly underindulgent, consider the chopped sirloin topped with spicy cheese and sliced avocado, or the chicken-fried steak. The usual versions of the latter dish use pounded-thin, tenderized beef, but here a regular rib-eye gets the Kentucky colonel treatment.

Call ahead if you're celebrating an anniversary or a birthday; the event will be announced on a billboard above the front door.

**Cappy's.** 5011 Broadway (behind the Twig Book Store). ☎ **210/828-9669.** Reservations recommended. Main courses $14–$23; prix-fixe $30. AE, MC, V. Mon–Thurs 11am–3pm and 5–10pm; Fri–Sat 11am–3pm and 5–11pm; Sun 10:30am–3pm and 5–10pm. AMERICAN.

One of the earliest businesses to open in the now-burgeoning Alamo Heights neighborhood, Cappy's is set in an unusual broken-brick structure dating back to the late 1930s. But there's nothing outdated about this cheerful, light-filled place—high, wood-beam ceilings, hanging plants, colorful work by local artists—or its romantic, tree-shaded outdoor patio.

The enticing smell of a wood-burning grill (no, not mesquite, but the somewhat milder live oak) gives a hint of some of the house specialties: the prime rib-eye or slow-roasted Italian chicken with risotto. Lighter fare includes snapper with shrimp and artichoke hearts over bow-tie pasta. A chef's prix-fixe lets you choose an appetizer, salad, and entree.

**☉ Silo.** 1133 Austin Hwy. ☎ **210/824-8686.** Reservations recommended. Main courses $12–$26. AE, DC, DISC, MC, V. Mon–Thurs 11:30am–2:30pm and 5:30–10pm; Fri–Sat 5:30–11pm. NEW AMERICAN.

Silo is consistently top-listed by San Antonio foodies, and deservedly so. Chef Mark Bliss, formerly of Biga, has poured his considerable talents into a small but well-balanced menu that uses fresh ingredients in fresh combinations. Starters such as the seared sea scallop on a roasted garlic potato blini or a salad of endive, frisee, pears, walnuts, and blue cheese get the mix of textures and tastes just right, as do entrees like Chilean sea bass wrapped with Parma ham, or pork tenderloin on a bacon, corn, and potato hash. Desserts are divine, too, and change nightly. Although the chic, industrial-design perch (the "Elevated Cuisine" alluded to in the restaurant's logo) makes for a somewhat cold setting, service is warm and superefficient to boot. You won't be the only one making the trip to this slightly off-the-beaten-path location, on the edge of Alamo Heights; play it safe and reserve for dinner, even if you're going during the week.

## MODERATE

**☉ Koi Kawa.** 4051 Broadway (in the back corner of the Boardwalk Complex, closest to the Witte Museum). ☎ **210/805-8111.** Reservations recommended on weekends. Main courses $10–$22. AE, DISC, DC, MC, V. Mon–Fri 11:30am–2pm and 5:30–10pm; Sat 5:30–10pm. JAPANESE.

David Mukai is the sushi dude. At least that's what he's called by some of his devoted fans, who sit around Koi Kawa's sushi bar and watch him perform his magic. Among the secrets of his success is the use of high-quality ingredients, such as real crabmeat and hothouse-grown cucumbers. But if you don't want to put yourself in the amicable Mukai's hands, there are plenty of other options. The crispy vegetable, seafood, and shrimp tempuras get a lot of attention, as do the various *udon* (wheat noodle) and *soba* (cold buckwheat noodle) soups, meals in themselves. In the back of the Boardwalk complex, with a view of the tree-shaded banks of the San Antonio River (admittedly, a generally stagnant section), Koi Kawa is a bit hard to locate, but by all means persevere if you're a Japanese food fan.

A newer, smaller version in the Quarry shopping complex, 255 E. Basse Rd. (☎ **210/930-6042**), dazzles with a sushi conveyor belt, but most locals remain loyal to the less gimmicky original.

**☉ La Calesa.** 2103 E. Hildebrand (just off Broadway). ☎ **210/822-4475.** Reservations not accepted. Main courses $5.95–$14.95. AE, CB, DC, DISC, MC, V. Mon–Thurs 11am–9:30pm; Fri 11am–10:30pm; Sat 11:30am–10:30pm; Sun 11:30am–9pm. REGIONAL MEXICAN.

Tucked away in a small house just off Broadway—look for Earl Abel's large sign across the street—this family-run restaurant features several dishes from the southern Yucatán region, as well as many from northern Mexico. The difference is mainly in the sauces, and they're done to perfection here. The mole, for example, strikes a fine balance between its rich chocolate base and the picante spices. The *conchinita pibil,* a classic Yucatecan pork dish—the meat is marinated and served in an achiote sauce—also has a marvelous texture and taste. Rice and black beans (richer than the usual pintos) accompany many of the meals. Everything is cooked up fresh, including the tortilla chips; even the coffee is good. You can eat indoors in one of three cozy dining rooms, decorated with Mexican art prints and tile work, or outside on the small flower-decked wooden porch.

**Van's.** 3214 Broadway. ☎ **210/828-8449.** Reservations for large parties only. Main courses $8.95–$19.95. AE, DC, DISC, MC, V. Daily 11am–10pm. CHINESE/JAPANESE/VIETNAMESE.

The sign outside announces that Van's is a "Chinese Seafood Restaurant and Sushi Bar," but the cuisine also has a Vietnamese influence. The dining room is low-key but appealing, with crisp green and white tablecloths, and the menu is, not surprisingly, huge. If you like seafood, go for the shrimp in a creamy curry sauce or the restaurant's touted specialty, fresh crab with black-bean sauce (market prices). You might also consider one of the meal-size soups—beef brisket with rice noodles, say, or a vegetable clay pot preparation—or tasty versions of such Szechuan standards as spicy kung pao chicken with carrots and peanuts.

## INEXPENSIVE

**Earl Abel's.** 4200 Broadway. ☎ **210/822-3358.** Reservations accepted for parties of 8 or more. Sandwiches $5–$6.75; main courses $5.25–$19.95. AE, CB, DC, DISC, MC, V. Daily 6:30am–1am. AMERICAN.

Earl Abel opened his first restaurant on Main Street in 1933; an organist for silent-film theaters in the 1920s, he had to find something else to do when the talkies took over. But his old Hollywood pals didn't forget him; Bing Crosby and Gloria Swanson always dropped in to Earl's place when they blew through San Antone.

His granddaughter now runs the restaurant, which moved to Broadway in 1940, and the menu is much like it was more than 50 years ago, when what's now called comfort food was simply chow. The restaurant is no longer open 24 hours, but you can still come in after midnight for a cup of coffee and a thick slice of lemon meringue pie. The bargain daily specials and fried chicken are the all-time favorites, but lots of folks come around for a hearty breakfast of eggs, biscuits and gravy, and grits.

## 7 Balcones Heights

## INEXPENSIVE

**La Fogata.** 2427 Vance Jackson. ☎ **210/340-0636.** Reservations recommended on weekends. Main courses $5.75–$11. AE, DC, DISC, MC, V. Mon–Thurs 11am–10pm; Fri 11am–11pm; Sat 8am–11pm; Sun 8am–10pm. MEXICAN.

A massive carved wooden door opens into the fountain-splashed courtyard of this northside Mexican restaurant, reminiscent of a sprawling Spanish villa. (If you get lost, as I did, you can also enter through one of the many parking lots.) This place is huge: What started out in 1978 as a single room in a former diner just kept growing and growing. Plant-draped trellises divide a number of smaller outdoor eating areas, all with Mexican tile floors, wrought-iron tables, and loads of greenery. The newest indoor dining room, done in light wood and hung with Frida Kahlo prints, is the best place to beat the heat.

The menu is as large as the restaurant. Along with the familiar tacos and tamales, you'll find such dishes as *queso flameado* (Mexican sausage mixed with melted Oaxaca cheese and served with tortillas) or *chile poblano al carbon* (pepper stuffed with chicken and cheese, and then charcoal flamed). The margaritas are so potent, they've earned the restaurant the nickname "I Fogata." Mariachi serenades are 10 bucks a pop, but for less expensive entertainment, check out the celebrity wall with photos of diners from Bill Clinton to Shaquille O'Neal.

## 8 Northwest/Medical Center

### VERY EXPENSIVE

**Francesca's at Sunset.** Westin La Cantera, 16641 La Cantera Parkway. ☎ **210/558-6500.** Reservations strongly suggested. Main courses $18–$30. AE, CB, DC, DISC, MC, V. Tues–Sat 6–10pm. SOUTHWESTERN.

A menu created by celebrity chef Mark Miller of Coyote Café fame and expertly executed by Jared Hunter, an excellent wine list (150 bottles and 30 by the glass), fine service, and idyllic Hill Country views from an ultra-romantic terrace—what's not to like about Francesca's at Sunset? Starters such as the wild mushroom tamale or quail on a smoked cheddar potato cake were unqualified sensations. The wild boar chops with fig mole also won raves from my dining companions, and I was pleased by the sea bass with smoked mussel hash. However, both the ancho honey–glazed chicken and the pepper mustard–rubbed rib eye were reported as too hot to handle by usually stout friends, so best inquire about the heat level when ordering. Of course, you can always placate your palate with the excellent house-made sorbets or perhaps a Jack Daniel's pecan tart.

### EXPENSIVE

**Aldo's.** 8539 Fredericksburg Rd. ☎ **210/696-2536.** Reservations recommended, especially on weekends. Main courses $12–$26. AE, CB, DC, DISC, MC, V. Mon–Thurs 11am–10pm; Fri 11am–11pm; Sat 5–11pm; Sun 5–10pm. ITALIAN.

A northwest San Antonio favorite, Aldo's offers good, old-fashioned Italian food in a pretty, old-fashioned setting. You can enjoy your meal outside on a tree-shaded patio or inside a 100-year-old former ranch house in one of a series of Victorian-style dining rooms. The scampi Valentino, sautéed shrimp with a basil cream sauce, is a nice starter, as is the lighter steamed mussels in marinara sauce (available seasonally). A house specialty, the sautéed snapper di Aldo comes topped with fresh lump crabmeat, artichoke hearts, mushrooms, and tomatoes in a white-wine sauce.

### MODERATE

✪ **Bistro Time.** 5137 Fredericksburg Rd. ☎ **210/344-6626.** Reservations recommended. Main courses $9–$24. AE, DC, MC, V. Mon–Thurs 5–9pm; Fri–Sat 5–10pm. CONTINENTAL.

In a nondescript mall in a nondescript northwest neighborhood hides a gem of a restaurant. This elegant eatery, with a central fountain and candlelit tables, features a series of weekly alternating menus, highlighting French, Asian, American, and northern European dishes. Whatever part of the globe you visit, you can depend on being satisfied (and, when in doubt, you won't go wrong with the signature rack of lamb with blackberry–red wine sauce). This is not a place to watch your weight; portions are huge and rich sauces are a specialty. Desserts are particularly hard to resist; if you're lucky, a supremely chocolaty Sacher torte might be in your stars. The pre-6pm early-bird specials include soup, salad, and dessert with any entree for no additional charge.

## 9  The Airport Area

### EXPENSIVE

**Massimo.** 4263 NW Loop 410 (just off the Babcock exit of Loop 410). ☎ **210/342-8556.** Reservations recommended on weekends. Main courses $12–$22. AE, DC, DISC, MC, V. Mon–Sat 11:30am–2:30pm and 5:30–11pm. ITALIAN.

There's lots of good Americanized Italian fare in San Antonio, but for authentic *cucina italiana*, prepared by a chef from Milan, this is the place. The kitchen is particularly strong in pastas and risottos, all made fresh on the premises; the tasty potato gnocchi are a special treat. Which is not to downplay such successful entrees as the moist pan-roasted salmon in potato crust, or the tender veal with porcini mushrooms, prosciutto, and fontina cheese in a white truffle sauce. Desserts are not quite as exciting. The servers are knowledgeable about the appealing wine list, and the setting is elegant but low-key. The location is a bit offbeat, but if you're staying near the airport, you're less than 10 minutes away.

### INEXPENSIVE

**Demo's.** 7115 Blanco Rd. ☎ **210/342-2772.** Reservations not accepted. Main courses $3.50–$6.95. AE, DC, DISC, MC, V. Mon–Thurs 11am–9pm; Fri–Sat 11am–10pm; Sun noon–8pm. GREEK.

The area around Loop 410 across from Central Park Mall is pretty soulless, which makes this little bit of Greece doubly welcome. In a two-tiered dining room with a trompe l'oeil painting of a white stucco fishing village, you can enjoy gyros, Greek burgers, dolmas, spanakopita, and other Mediterranean specialties; if you go for the Dieter's Special, a Greek salad with your choice of gyros or souvlaki (beef or chicken), you might be able to justify the baklava. In addition to this original location, opened in 1979, there's another Demo's on St. Mary's strip at 2501 N. St. Mary's St. (☎ **210/ 732-7777**), across from a Greek Orthodox church. A belly dancer gyrates at the Blanco location on Monday night, at St. Mary's on Wednesday.

## 10  Leon Springs

### INEXPENSIVE

✪ **Rudy's.** 24152 I-10 West (Leon Springs/Boerne Stage Rd. exit). ☎ **210/698-2141.** Reservations not accepted. $5.25–$9.45/lb. for barbecue; $10.95 rack of baby-back ribs. AE, DC, DISC, MC, V. Sun–Thurs 10am–10pm; Fri–Sat 10am–11pm. BARBECUE.

You've got to know the drill at Rudy's. Wait in one line (just follow the crowd) for the meat—pork ribs, beef short ribs, brisket, sausage, huge turkey legs, you name it. It'll come wrapped up in butcher paper, with lots and lots of white bread. Then, if you want a side dish—beans, creamed corn, potato salad, coleslaw—or some peach cobbler, go next door to the country store. Now plunk it all down on one of the red-and-white checked vinyl tablecloths or bring it outside to the wooden picnic tables, and enjoy. You'll be rubbing elbows here with cowboys, bicyclists, and other city folk who come from miles around for what they insist is the best barbecue in town. Just beware of the sauce: It's seriously spicy. There's a newer location right across from SeaWorld at 10623 Westover Hills, corner of Hwy. 151 (☎ **210/520-5552**).

## 11  Only in San Antonio

Some of the best and most popular places to eat Mexican have been reviewed above, but you can be sure you'll run into San Antonians who are passionate about their

# Coffee or Tea?

San Antonio isn't known for its bohemian coffeehouse scene, but it does have some winners in the caffeine and herbal brew department.

**Berings** (formerly Scrivener's), 8502 Broadway (☎ **210/824-2353**), has a wonderfully retro tearoom, but its longstanding patrons, who are often a tad blue-haired, aren't likely to describe it that way. Order anything—say, the crunchy chicken salad—and you'll also get a small cup of bouillon, cheese cookies, fresh-baked cinnamon rolls, and nut bread. So much for that diet.

**Candlelight Coffee House,** 3011 N. St. Mary's St. (☎ **210/738-0099**), on the northern end of St. Mary's strip, has mismatched antiques, overstuffed chairs, subdued lighting, and a piano that gets frequent play. You can drink your espresso, latte, or other jump-start concoction inside or underneath the pecan trees on an outdoor patio, complete with soothing fountain and goldfish pond.

**Espuma Coffee and Tea Emporium,** 928 S. Alamo (☎ **210/226-1912**), a converted house in Southtown, is the favorite daytime gathering spot for neighborhood artists and writers. Good local art, a cozy front porch, and above-average versions of the usual coffee and tea variations are all part of the draw.

**Madhatter's Tea,** 3606 Ave. B (☎ **210/821-6555**), tucked away behind the east side of Brackenridge Park, and a stone's throw from the Witte Museum, plays up an Alice in Wonderland theme with THIS WAY DOWN signs outside, tilted bookshelves stacked with teacups, and a menu with items like "woofles" and "try me, have me, eat me" breakfast burritos. There are a dizzying number of teas—41 to be exact—as well as coffees, juices, and (would Lewis Carroll approve?) wine and beer.

---

personal favorite tacquerias. Three high-ranking ones near downtown include **Estela's,** 2200 W. Martin St. (☎ **210/226-2979**), which has mariachi breakfasts (with an all-female mariachi band) on Saturday and Sunday 9:30 to 11:30am, as well as a great conjunto/Tejano jukebox; **Piedras Negras de Noche,** 1312 S. Laredo St. (☎ **210/227-7777**), renowned for, among other dishes, its carne asada tacos; and **Taco Haven,** 1032 S. Presa St. (☎ **210/533-2171**), where the breakfast *migas* or *chilaquiles* will kick-start your day. In Olmos Park, **Panchito's,** 4100 McCullough (☎ **210/821-5338**), has 'em lining up on weekend mornings for *barbacoa* plates, heaped with two eggs, potatoes, beans, and homemade tortillas, along with the Mexican-style barbecue. The tropical shack–style **Beto's,** 7325 Broadway (☎ **210/930-9393**), is a hot, hot, hot Alamo Heights spot to listen to Latin music and drink sangria while munching *tacos al pastor*—slow-roasted pork basted with an spicy *adobado* pineapple sauce.

You'll also find emotions rising when the talk runs to barbecue, with many locals insisting that their favorite is the best and most authentic—because the meat has been smoked the longest, because the place uses the best smoking technique, because the sauce is the tangiest—the criteria are endless and often completely arcane to outsiders. Of San Antonio's more than 90 barbecue joints, Rudy's and the County Line are reviewed above; a few other possibilities in town for a smoked-meat fix include **Fay Willie's Bar-B-Q,** 119 Heiman, in the Sunset Station complex (☎ **210/222-0887**), where lamb chops and brisket get eaten with your hands; **Barbecue Station,** 1610 NE Loop 410 (☎ **210/824-9191**), a remodeled service station in

Alamo Heights that serves super ribs; and **Bob's Smokehouse,** 5145 Fredericksburg Rd. (☎ **210/344-8401**) and 3306 Roland Ave. (☎ **210/333-9338**), not on the regular tourist route but eliciting die-hard local testimonials.

San Antonians have been coming to **Bun 'N' Barrel,** 1150 Austin Hwy. (☎ **210/828-2829**), for 50 years to eat barbecue and to check out each other's cool Chevies. Hang around on Friday night and you might even see the occasional drag race down Austin Highway; winner gets the other guy's car. This place is near Silo (see above), but there's not much other reason to detour to this generally featureless part of town; if you're short on time, save a trip and catch this retro classic in the film *Selena*.

# 6

# Exploring San Antonio

San Antonio's dogged preservation of its past and avid development of its future guarantee that there's something in town to suit every visitor's taste. The biggest problem with sightseeing here is figuring out how to get it all in; you can spend days in the downtown area alone and still not cover everything. The itineraries below give some suggestions on how to organize your time. Walkers will love being able to hoof it from one downtown attraction to another, but the sedentary needn't despair—or drive. One of the most visitor-friendly cities imaginable, San Antonio has excellent and inexpensive tourist transportation lines, extending to such far-flung sights as SeaWorld San Antonio and Six Flags Fiesta Texas.

Before you visit any of the paid attractions, stop in at the **San Antonio Visitor Information Center,** 317 Alamo Plaza (☎ **210/ 207-6748**), across the street from the Alamo, and ask for their SAVE San Antonio discount book, including everything from the large theme parks to some city tours and museums. Many hotels also have a stash of discount coupons for their guests.

## Suggested Itineraries

### If You Have 1 Day

If your time is very limited, it makes sense to stay downtown, where many of the prime attractions are concentrated. Start your day at the **Alamo,** which tends to get more crowded as the day goes on. When you finish touring the complex, take a streetcar from Alamo Square to **HemisFair Park;** from the observation deck at the Tower of the Americas, you can see everything there is to see in town from a bird's-eye view. Then board the streetcar again and head to the nearby **King William Historic District,** where you can pick up a self-guided walking tour at the office of the San Antonio Conservation Society. If you're really hungry by now, have lunch at the historic Guenther House; if you can hold out, and have a hankering for Mexican food, wait until you get to **Market Square** (via another streetcar) and eat at Mi Tierra or La Margarita, both owned by the same family. Spend a few hours poking around the 2 square blocks of shops and stalls and then head over to the **River Walk,** where you might catch a riverboat tour before eating at one of the riverside restaurants (I'd vote for Boudro's). Or, if you can manage to get tickets to anything at either the Majestic or the Arneson River theaters, eat early (again, you'll have beaten the crowds) and enjoy the show.

### If You Have 2 Days

**Day 1**   Follow the same itinerary outlined above.

**Day 2**   See the San Antonio **missions** in the morning (at the least, Mission San José). In the afternoon, go to **San Antonio Museum of Art,** or, if you're using public transportation, the **McNay** or **Witte Museum.** If you're traveling with kids, you might want to visit the **Children's Museum** first thing in the morning, then go to **SeaWorld** or **Six Flags Fiesta Texas** in the afternoon (although the Witte is terrific for kids, too).

### If You Have 3 Days

**Day 1**   Start at the **Alamo** and then tour the rest of the **missions;** that way, you'll see the military shrine in its historic context. Spend the late afternoon at one of the **theme parks** or at one of the **museums** (the San Antonio Museum of Art, the McNay, or the Witte).

**Day 2**   Go to **HemisFair Park** and visit the Tower of the Americas and the Institute of Texan Cultures, then stroll around nearby **La Villita.** Afterward, head down to the **King William district** and take the tour of the **Steves Homestead.** In the afternoon, enjoy a **riverboat tour** and visit the **Southwest Center of Art and Craft** and, if you like contemporary work, **ArtPace.**

**Day 3**   See the **Spanish Governor's Palace** and the **Navarro Cathedral,** then shop and have lunch at **Market Square.** In the afternoon, go to one of the **museums** you haven't yet visited or to the **San Antonio Botanical Gardens.**

### If You Have 4 Days

**Days 1–3**   Follow the itinerary outlined in "If You Have 3 Days," but eliminate the attractions in the Brackenridge Park area (the Witte and the McNay Museums), substituting another downtown sight or a theme park.

**Day 4**   Visit the attractions in the **Brackenridge Park area,** including the Japanese Tea Garden, the Witte Museum, the McNay Museum, the zoo, and the San Antonio Botanical Gardens. Some of the best restaurants in San Antonio are in this part of town.

### If You Have 5 Days or More

**Days 1–4**   Follow the above 4-day itinerary, but break it up with:

**Day 5**   A day trip through scenic ranch country to **Bandera,** a sleepy cowboy town that will remind you you're in the Wild West. An afternoon trail ride is great, but if you have more time, book a room at one of Bandera's many dude ranches; a 2-night minimum stay is usually required.

## 1  The Top Attractions

✪ **The Alamo.** 300 Alamo Plaza. ☎ **210/281-0710.** www.thealamo.org. Free admission (donations welcome). Mon–Sat 9am–5:30pm; Sun 10am–5:30pm. Closed Christmas Eve and Christmas Day. Streetcar: Red, Brown, and Blue lines.

Many people, expecting something more dramatic and remote, are taken aback to discover that Texas's most visited site is not only rather small, but it sits smack in the heart of downtown San Antonio. But you'll immediately recognize the graceful mission church, a ubiquitous symbol of the state. It was here that 188 Texas volunteers defied the much larger army—its numbers depending on the Texas chauvinism of the teller—of Mexican dictator Santa Anna for 13 days in March 1836. Although all the men, including pioneers Davy Crockett and Jim Bowie, were killed, their deaths were used by Sam Houston in the cry "Remember the Alamo!" to rally his troops and defeat the Mexican army at the Battle of San Jacinto a month later, securing Texas's independence.

The Daughters of the Republic of Texas, who saved the crumbling complex from being turned into a hotel by a New York syndicate in 1905, has long maintained it as a shrine to these fighters. More recently, however, additional emphasis has been placed on the Alamo's other historic roles, including as a Native American burial ground when it was founded on a nearby site in 1718 as the Mission San Antonio de Valero. The complex was secularized by the end of the 18th century and leased out to a Spanish cavalry unit; by the time the famous battle took place, it had been abandoned. A Wall of History, erected in the late 1990s, provides a good chronology of these events.

Little remains of the original mission today; only the Long Barrack (formerly the *convento,* or living quarters for the missionaries) and the mission church are still here. The former houses a museum detailing the history of Texas in general and the battle in particular; the latter includes artifacts of the Alamo fighters, along with an information desk and small gift shop. A larger museum and gift shop are at the back of the complex. There's also a peaceful garden and an excellent research library (closed Sun) on the grounds. Interesting historical presentations are given every half hour by Alamo staffers; for private, after-hour tours, phone ☎ **210/225-1391.**

✪ **Six Flags Fiesta Texas.** 17000 I-10 West (corner of I-10 West and Loop 1604). ☎ **800/ 473-4378** or 210/697-5050. www.sixflags.com. Admission $38.80 adults, $25 seniors, $19.40 children under 48 in.; children 2 and under free. Discounted 2-day and season passes available. Parking $6 per day. Opening hours are 8–10am to 10pm, depending on the season. The park is generally open daily late May to late Aug; Fri–Sun from Mar–May and Sept–Nov; closed Nov–Feb. Call ahead or visit the Web site for current information. Bus: 94. Take exit 555 on I-10 West.

Every year seems to bring another major thrill ride or two to this 200-acre amusement park, set in an abandoned limestone quarry and surrounded by 100-foot cliffs on the northwest side of town. In 2000, the huge, floorless Superman Krypton Coaster, nearly a mile of twisted steel with six inversions and a unique design, and Boardwalk Canyon Blaster, a steam train–themed coaster, were added to the Rattler, the world's highest and fastest wooden roller coaster; the Joker's Revenge, with a funhouse entryway and a reverse start; the 60-m.p.h.-plus Poltergeist roller coaster; the forward-and-backward Boomerang; and Scream!, a 20-story space shot and turbo drop. Laser games and virtual reality simulators complete the technophile picture. Feeling more primal? Wet 'n' wild attractions include the Lone Star Lagoon, the state's largest wave pool; the Texas Treehouse, a five-story drenchfest whose surprises include a 1,000-gallon cowboy hat that tips over periodically to soak the unsuspecting; and Bugs' White Water Rapids.

For those wishing to avoid both sogginess and adrenaline overload, myriad alternatives include a vast variety of food booths, shops, crafts demonstrations, and live shows—everything from 1950s musical revues to big-name (Trisha Yearwood, Alabama, and the Beach Boys, to name a few) live concerts in summer. Because Six Flags is a Time Warner company, such Looney Tunes cartoon characters as Tweety Bird are ubiquitous, especially in the souvenir shops.

**La Villita National Historic District.** Bounded by Durango, Navarro, and Alamo sts. and the River Walk. ☎ **210/207-8610.** www.lavillita.com. Free admission. Shops, daily 10am–6pm. Closed Thanksgiving, Christmas, New Year's Day. Bus: 40. Streetcar: Red, Purple, Brown, and Blue lines.

Developed by European settlers along the higher east bank of the San Antonio River in the late 18th and early 19th centuries, La Villita (the Little Village) was on the

# Downtown San Antonio Attractions & Shopping

**SHOPPING**
Boot Hill **20**
Chamade Jewelers **23**
Dillard's **20**
Finesilver Gallery **2**
Galena Ortiz **8**
NanEtte Richardson Fine Art **21**
Papa Jim's Botanica **29**

Paris Hatters **15**
The Red Iguana **25**
Rivercenter Mall **20**
San Angel Folk Art **30**
Southwest School of Art
& Craft **3**
Tienda Guadalupe Folk Art
& Gifts **27**

**ATTRACTIONS**
The Alamo **17**
Alamo IMAX Theatre **19**
ArtPace **6**
Blue Star Arts Complex **30**
Buckhorn Saloon & Museum **14**
Casa Navarro State Historical Park **10**
Hertzberg Circus Collection and Museum **22**
Institute of Texan Cultures **26**
Majestic Theatre **13**
Plaza Wax Museum &
Ripley's Believe It or Not **18**

San Antonio Children's Museum **12**
San Antonio Central Library **4**
San Antonio Museum of Art **1**
San Fernando Cathedral **11**
Southwest School of Art & Craft **3**
Spanish Governor's Palace **9**
Spirit of Healing Mural **7**
Steves Homestead Museum **28**
The Texas Adventure **16**
Tower of the Americas **24**
Vietnam War Memorial **5**

proverbial wrong side of the tracks until flooding of the west bank settlements made it the fashionable place to live. It fell back into poverty by the beginning of the 20th century, only to be revitalized in the late 1930s by artists and craftspeople and the San Antonio Conservation Society. Now boutiques, crafts shops, and restaurants occupy this historic district, which resembles a Spanish/Mexican village, replete with shaded patios, plazas, brick-and-tile streets, and some of the settlement's original adobe structures. You can see (but not enter) the house of General Cós, the Mexican military leader who surrendered to the Texas revolutionary army in 1835, or attend a performance at the Arneson River Theatre (see "The Performing Arts," in chapter 8).

✪ **Market Square.** Bounded by Commerce, Santa Rosa, Dolorosa, and I-35. ☎ **210/ 207-8600.** Free admission. El Mercado and Farmer's Market Plaza, June–Aug daily 10am–8pm; Sept–May daily 10am–6pm; restaurants and some of the shops open later. Closed Thanksgiving, Christmas, New Year's Day, Easter. Streetcar: Red and Yellow lines.

It may not be quite as colorful as it was when live chickens squawked around overflowing, makeshift vegetable stands, but Market Square will still transport you south of the border. Stalls in the indoor El Mercado sell everything from onyx paperweights and manufactured serapes to high-quality crafts from the interior of Mexico. Across the street, the Farmer's Market, which formerly housed the produce market, has carts with more modern goods. If you can tear yourself away from the merchandise, take a look around at the buildings in the complex; some date back to the late 1800s.

Bring your appetite along with your wallet: In addition to two good Mexican restaurants (one open 24 hours a day), almost every weekend sees the emergence of food stalls selling specialties such as gorditas (chubby corn cakes topped with a variety of goodies) or funnel cakes (fried dough sprinkled with powdered sugar). Most of the city's Hispanic festivals are held here, and mariachis usually stroll the square. The Alameda National Center for Latino Arts and Culture, a Smithsonian Institution affiliate scheduled to open in Market Square's Centro des Artes building in 2002, should provide a historic context to an area that sometimes seems touristy.

**King William Historic District.** East bank of the river just south of downtown. Streetcar: Blue line.

San Antonio's first suburb, King William was settled in the late 19th century by prosperous German merchants who displayed their wealth through extravagant homes and named the 25-block area after Kaiser Wilhelm of Prussia. (The other residents of San Antonio were less complimentary about this German area, which they dubbed "sauerkraut bend.")

The neighborhood fell into disrepair for a few decades, but you'd never know it from the pristine condition of most of the houses here today. The area has gotten so popular that tour buses have been restricted after certain hours. But it's much more pleasant to stroll up and down tree-shaded King William Street, gawking at the beautifully landscaped, magnificent mansions. Stop at the headquarters of the San Antonio Conservation Society, 107 King William St. (☎ **210/224-6163;** www. saconservation.org), and pick up a self-guided walking tour booklet outside the gate. Only the Steves Homestead Museum (see "More Attractions," below) and the Guenther House (see chapter 5) are open to the public. The neighborhood is within walking distance of the Convention Center.

✪ **Paseo Del Rio/The River Walk.** Downtown, from the Municipal Auditorium on the north end to the King William Historic District on the south end. All streetcar lines.

Just a few steps below the streets of downtown San Antonio is another world, alternately soothing and exhilarating, depending on where you venture. The quieter areas of the 2½ paved miles of winding riverbank, shaded by cypresses, oaks, and willows,

# It's Not Easy Being Purple

In addition to being plagued by tour buses, in the late 1990s, the staid King William neighborhood (see above) was subjected to something else it intensely dislikes: controversy. It began in 1997, when acclaimed Chicana writer Sandra Cisneros—author of *House on Mango Street* and *Women Hollering Creek*—bought a Victorian house in the area and decided to paint it purple, thus butting heads with what some have termed the "authenticity police" (officially, the San Antonio Historic Design and Review Commission). Cisneros contended that purple was a typical Mexican color and that the commission's request to have her repaint the house was a slight to the city's Hispanic history. The commission argued that this particular neighborhood was German, and that purple was not used during the era in which the house was built. Finally, after 2 years of controversy, the house faded on its own to what was deemed a "historically appropriate" lavender. If you want to see what all the fuss is about, go to 795 E. Guenther St., corner of Barbe.

exude a tropical, exotic aura; the River Square and South Bank sections, chock-a-block with sidewalk cafes, tony restaurants, bustling bars, high-rise hotels, and even a huge shopping mall, have a festive, sometimes frenetic feel. Tour boats, water taxis, and floating picnic barges regularly ply the river, and local parades and festivals fill its banks with revelers.

Although plans to cement over the river after a disastrous flood in 1921 were stymied, it wasn't until the late 1930s that the federal Works Project Administration (WPA) carried out architect Robert Hugman's designs for the waterway, installing cobblestone walks, arched bridges, and entrance steps from various street-level locations. And it wasn't until the late 1960s, when the River Walk proved to be one of the most popular attractions of the HemisFair exposition, that its commercial development began in earnest.

There's a real danger of the River Walk becoming overdeveloped—new restaurants, hotels, and entertainment complexes are opening at an alarming pace, and the crush of bodies along the busiest sections can be claustrophobic in the summer heat—but plenty of quieter spots still exist. And if you're caught up in the sparkling lights reflected on the water on a breeze-swept night, you might forget there was anyone else around.

✪ **San Antonio Missions National Historic Park.** Headquarters: 2202 Roosevelt Ave. ☎ **210/534-8833.** Visitors Center: 6701 San José Dr. at Mission Rd. ☎ **210/932-1001.** www.nps.gov/saan. Free admission, donations accepted. All the missions open daily 9am–5pm. Closed Thanksgiving, Christmas, New Year's Day. National Park Ranger tours daily.

Remember the Alamo? Well, it was originally just the first of five missions established by the Franciscans along the San Antonio River to Christianize the native population. The four missions that now fall under the aegis of the National Parks Department are still active parishes, run in cooperation with the Archdiocese of San Antonio. In 1996, a $9.5 million visitor center opened just outside Mission San José. The handsome building, made of Texas Hill Country sandstone to match the mission walls, offers an excellent introduction to the park via a variety of displays, including a touch-screen itinerary planner, a three-dimensional fiber-optic map, interactive slide displays of the northern Mexico/southwestern U.S. mission system, and a theater with an advanced audio system that screens a beautifully produced, award-winning short film. There's also a good bookstore.

The missions were more than churches; they were complex communities. The Parks Department has assigned each of the four missions an interpretive theme to educate visitors about the roles they played in early San Antonio society. The missions may be visited separately, but if you have the time, see all of them—they were built uncharacteristically close to each other and the cumulative experience is hard to match. Currently, visitors must follow brown signs that direct them from the Alamo to the 5½-mile mission trail that begins at Mission Concepción and winds its way south through the city streets to Mission Espada. In 1998, however, ground was broken for the $17.7 million Mission Trails Project, which will create a 12-mile hike-and-bike route along the San Antonio River and improve signage and linkage along the driving route. Parts of it are already operational, but the entire project is not expected to be completed until late 2002.

**Concepción,** 807 Mission Rd. at Felisa, was built in 1731. The oldest unrestored Texas mission, Concepción looks much as it did 200 years ago. Many of us tend to think of religious sites as somber and austere, but traces of color on the facade and restored wall paintings inside show how cheerful this one originally was.

**San José,** 6539 San José Dr. at Mission Road, established in 1720, was the largest, best known, and most beautiful of the Texas missions. It was reconstructed to give visitors a complete picture of life in a mission community—right down to the granary, mill, and Indian pueblo. The beautiful Rose Window is a big attraction, and popular mariachi masses are held here every Sunday at noon (come early if you want a seat).

Moved from an earlier site in east Texas to its present location in 1731, **San Juan Capistrano,** 9102 Graf at Ashley, doesn't have the grandeur of the missions to the north—the larger church intended for it was never completed—but the original simple chapel and the wilder setting give it a peaceful, spiritual aura. A short (three-tenths of a mile) interpretive trail, with a number of overlook platforms, winds through the woods to the banks of the old river channel.

The southernmost mission in the San Antonio chain, **San Francisco de la Espada,** 10040 Espada Rd., also has an ancient, isolated feel, although the beautifully maintained church shows just how vital it still is to the local community. Be sure to visit the Espada Aqueduct, part of the mission's original *acequia* (irrigation ditch) system, about 1 mile north of the mission. Dating from 1740, it's one of the oldest Spanish aqueducts in the United States.

✪ **San Antonio Museum of Art.** 200 W. Jones Ave. ☎ **210/978-8100.** www. sa-museum.org. Admission $5 adults, $4 seniors and students with ID, $1.75 children 4–11; children 3 and under free. Free on Tues 3–9pm. Tues 10am–9pm; Wed–Sat 10am–5pm; Sun noon–5pm. Bus: 7.

Almost as impressive for its architecture as for its art collection, this museum consists of several castlelike buildings of the 1904 Lone Star Brewery, which were gutted, connected, and turned into a visually exciting exhibition space in 1981. The spare and, in some sections, skylit interiors contrast strikingly with the more intricately detailed brick exterior, while the multi-windowed crosswalk between the buildings affords fine views of downtown.

Holdings range from early Egyptian, Greek, and Asian to 19th- and 20th-century American and (added in 2000) Oceanic, but the prime reason to come is the $11 million Nelson A. Rockefeller Center for Latin American Art, opened in 1998. This 30,000-square-foot wing hosts the most comprehensive collection of Latin American art in the United States, with pre-Columbian, folk, Spanish colonial, and contemporary works. You'll see everything here from magnificently ornate altarpieces to a whimsical Day of the Dead tableau. A variety of computer stations adds historical perspective to the collection, which is a nationwide resource for Latino culture.

**SeaWorld San Antonio.** 10500 SeaWorld Dr., 16 miles northwest of downtown San Antonio at Ellison Dr. and Westover Hills Blvd. ☎ **800/4-ADVENTURE** or 210/523-3611. www. seaworld.com. 1-day pass $33.95 adults, 10% discount for seniors (55 and over), $23.95 children 3–11; children 2 and under free. Discounted 2-day and season passes available. Parking $5 per day. Hours 10am–6pm, 8pm, or 10pm, depending on the season. Schedule varies with season; generally open weekends and some weekdays in spring and fall, daily during summer (through mid-Aug). Closed late Nov to early Mar. Call ahead or check Web site for current information. Bus: 64. From Loop 410 or from Hwy. 90 West, exit Hwy. 151 West to the park.

Leave it to Texas to provide Shamu, the performing killer whale, with his most spacious digs: At 250 acres, this SeaWorld is the largest of the Anheuser Busch–owned parks, which also makes it the largest marine theme park in the world. The walk-through habitats where you can watch penguins, sea lions, sharks, tropical fish, and flamingos do their thing are endlessly fascinating, but the aquatic acrobatics at the stadium shows might be even more fun. Shamu Visions, introduced in 2000, combines live action and close-ups (above and below water) on a giant video screen. The humans hold their own with an impressive water-skiing exhibition on a 12½-acre lake.

One needn't get frustrated just looking at all that water: There are loads of places here to get wet. The Lost Lagoon has a huge wave pool and water slides aplenty, and the Texas Splashdown flume ride and the Rio Loco river-rapids ride also offer splashy fun. Younger children can cavort in Shamu's Happy Harbor and the "L'il Gators" section of the Lost Lagoon.

Nonaquatic activities abound, too. SeaWorld's latest addition is the multimillion-dollar Steel Eel, a huge "hypercoaster" that starts out with a 150-foot dive at 65 m.p.h., followed by several bouts of weightlessness. It's a follow-up to The Great White, the Southwest's first inverted coaster—which means riders will go head-over-heels during 2,500 feet of loops (don't eat before either of them). Whatever you do during the day, stick around for the Summer Night Magic multimedia laser shows or one of the special high-season concerts.

## 2 More Attractions

### A CHURCH

**San Fernando Cathedral.** 115 Main Plaza. ☎ **210/227-1297.** Free admission. Daily 6am–7pm; gift shop Mon–Fri 9am–4:30pm (Sat until 5pm). Streetcar: Red and Yellow lines.

Construction of a church on this site, overlooking what was once the town's central plaza, was begun in 1738 by San Antonio's original Canary Island settlers, and completed in 1749. Part of the early structure—the oldest cathedral sanctuary in the United States and the oldest parish church in Texas—is incorporated into the magnificent Gothic revival–style cathedral built in 1868. Jim Bowie got married here, and General Santa Anna raised the flag of "no quarter" from the roof during the siege of the Alamo in 1836. A bronze plaque outside directs visitors to the chapel where, it says, the bones of the Alamo heroes are entombed, but that claim is widely disputed.

### HISTORIC BUILDINGS & COMPLEXES

**Fort Sam Houston.** Grayson St. and New Braunfels Ave., about 2½ miles northeast of downtown. ☎ **210/221-1151** (public affairs). Bus: 15 (Ft. Sam Houston).

Since 1718, when the armed Presidio de Béxar was established to defend the Spanish missions, the military has played a key role in San Antonio's development; it remains one of the largest employers in town today. The 3,434-acre Fort Sam Houston affords visitors an unusual opportunity to view the city's military past (the first military flight in history took off from the fort's spacious parade grounds) in the context of its military present—the fort currently hosts the Army Medical Command and the headquarters of

# Greater San Antonio Attractions & Shopping

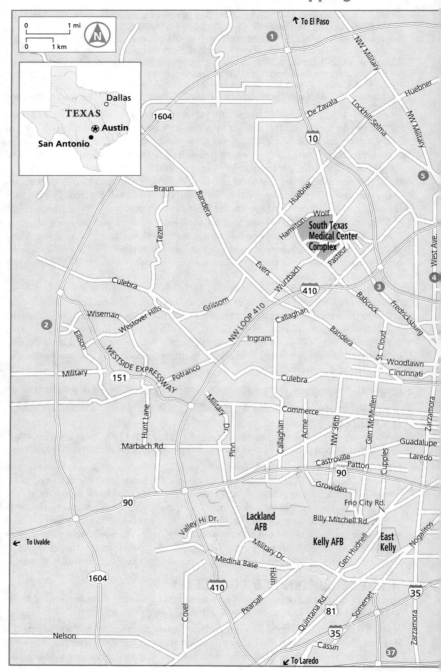

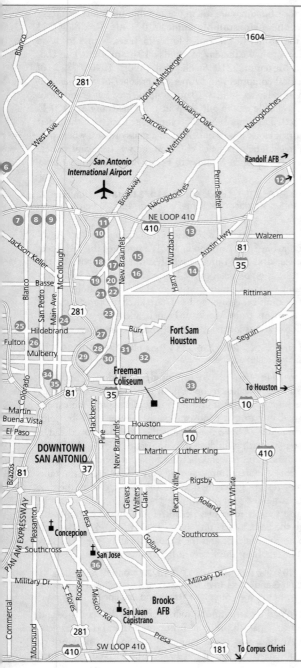

## ATTRACTIONS

Brackenridge Park **29**
Fort Sam Houston **32**
Marion Koogler McNay
  Art Museum **16**
San Antonio Missions
  National Historic Park **36**
San Antonio Botanical
  Gardens **31**
San Antonio Zoological
  Gardens and Aquarium **27**
SeaWorld San Antonio **2**
Six Flags Fiesta Texas **1**
Splashtown **33**
Witte Museum **28**

## SHOPPING

Adelante Boutique **15**
Alamo Fiesta **35**
Alamo Quarry Market **4**
Bambino's **17**
Burlington Coat Factory **3**
Bussey's Flea Market **12**
Center for Antiques **11**
Central Market **23**
Central Park Mall **8**
Cheever Books **30**
Crossroads Mall **3**
Eisenhauer Road
  Flea Market **14**
Flea Mart **37**
Gabriel's **25**
Gavin Metalsmith **24**
Kathleen Sommers **34**
The Land of Was **26**
Los Patios **13**
Lucchese Gallery **4**
Marshall's **7**
Mirabella **20**
Monarch Collectibles **5**
North Star Mall **9**
Playworks **10**
Remember the Alibi **6**
Saks Fifth Avenue **9**
Satel's **22**
SeaZar's Fine Wine
  & Spirits **15**
Sloan/Hall **19**
Stein Mart **18**
Todd's Inc. **9**
The Twig & Red Balloon **21**

Airport ✈   Church ⛪

the Fifth Army. Most of its historic buildings are still in use and thus off-limits, but three are open to the public. The **Fort Sam Houston Museum,** 1210 Stanley Rd., Bldg. 123 (☎ 210/221-1886), details the history of the armed forces in Texas, with a focus on San Antonio. Admission is free; open Wednesday to Sunday 10am to 4pm. The **U.S. Army Medical Department Museum,** 2310 Stanley Rd., Bldg. 1046 (☎ 210/221-6277), displays army medical equipment and American prisoner-of-war memorabilia. Admission is free; open Tuesday to Sunday 10am to 4pm. Free self-guided tour maps of the historic sites are available at the gift shop in the **Quadrangle,** 1400 E. Grayson St. (☎ 210/221-1232). This impressive 1876 limestone structure, the oldest on the post, is centered on a brick clock tower and encloses a grassy square where peacocks, deer, and rabbits roam freely. The Apache chief Geronimo was held captive here for 40 days in 1886. Admission is free; open Monday to Friday 8am to 4pm, Saturday and Sunday noon to 5pm.

**Casa Navarro State Historical Park.** 228 S. Laredo St. ☎ **210/226-4801.** Admission $2 adults, $1 children 6–12; children 5 and under free. Wed–Sun 10am–4pm. Streetcar: Yellow line.

A key player in Texas's transition from Spanish territory to American state, José Antonio Navarro was the Mexican mayor of San Antonio in 1821, a signer of the 1836 declaration of Texas independence, and the only native Texan to take part in the convention that ratified the annexation of Texas to the United States in 1845. His former living quarters, built around 1850, are an interesting amalgam of the architectural fashions of his time: The restored office, house, and separate kitchen, constructed of adobe and limestone, blend elements from Mexican, French, German, and pioneer styles. Guided tours and demonstrations are available; call ahead to inquire.

Nov
10

**Majestic Theatre.** 224 E. Houston St. ☎ **210/226-3333** (box office) or 210/226-5700 (administration). Tour $5 adults. Streetcar: Red line.

Everyone from Jack Benny to Mae West played this opulent vaudeville and film palace, one of the last "atmospheric" theaters to be built in America: The stock market crashed 4 months after its June 1929 debut and no one could afford such expensive showplaces again. Designed in baroque Moorish/Spanish revival style by John Eberson, it features an elaborate village above the sides of the stage and, overhead, a magnificent night sky dome, replete with twinkling stars and scudding clouds. Designated a National Historic Landmark and painstakingly and magnificently restored in 1988 to 1989, the Majestic affords a rare glimpse at a literally gilded era (we're talking genuine gold leaf detailing). It's not generally open to the public during the day, but you may be able to get on a guided group tour; they're offered for 10 people or more Tuesday through Friday, if theater schedules permit. Tours must be arranged 3 or 4 weeks in advance through the Las Casas Foundation (☎ 210/223-4343), which raised the money to restore both the Majestic and the Empire theaters (see "The Performing Arts," in chapter 8, for details on the shows at both).

**Spanish Governor's Palace.** 105 Plaza de Armas. ☎ **210/224-0601.** Admission $1 adults, 50¢ children 7–13; children 6 and under free. Mon–Sat 9am–5pm; Sun 10am–5pm. Closed Christmas, New Year's Day, Fiesta week. Streetcar: Yellow and Red lines.

Never actually a palace, this 1749 adobe structure formerly served as the residence and headquarters for the captain of the Spanish presidio. It became the seat of Texas government in 1772, when San Antonio was made capital of the Spanish province of Texas and, by the time it was purchased by the city in 1928, it had served as a tailor's shop, barroom, and schoolhouse. The building, with high ceilings crossed by protruding viga beams, is beautiful in its simplicity, and the 10 rooms crowded with

*We have no city, except, perhaps, New Orleans, that can vie, in point of picturesque interest that attaches to odd and antiquated foreignness, with San Antonio.*
—Frederick Law Olmsted, *A Journey Through Texas* (1853)

period furnishings paint a vivid portrait of upper-class life in a rough-hewn society. Consider taking a picnic lunch and eating on the tree-shaded, cobblestoned patio, overlooking a flowing stone fountain.

**Steves Homestead Museum.** 509 King William St. ☎ **210/225-5924** or 210/227-9160. www.saconservation.org. Admission $3 adults; children under 12 free. Daily 10am–4:15pm (last tour at 3:30). Streetcar: Blue line.

Built in 1876 for lumber magnate Edward Steves by prominent San Antonio architect Alfred Giles, this Victorian mansion was restored by the San Antonio Conservation Society, to whom it was willed by Steves's granddaughter. One of the only houses in the King William Historic District open to the public, it gives a fascinating glimpse into the lifestyle of the rich and locally famous of the late 19th century. You can't enter without taking a docent-led tour, which is fine: You wouldn't want to miss the great gossip about the Steves family that the Society's very knowledgeable volunteers pass along. The 30- to 45-minute tours are given when enough visitors arrive.

## A LIBRARY

**San Antonio Central Library.** 600 Soledad. ☎ **210/207-2500.** Free admission. Mon–Thurs 9am–9pm; Fri–Sat 9am–5pm; Sun 11am–5pm. Streetcar: Brown line.

San Antonio's main library, opened in the mid-1990s at a cost of $38 million, has a number of important collections, but it is most notable for its architecture. Ricardo Legorreta, renowned for his buildings throughout Mexico, has designed a wildly colorful and whimsical public space that people apparently love to enter—by the second month after the library opened, circulation had gone up 95%. The boxy building, painted what has been called "enchilada red," is designed like a hacienda around an internal courtyard. A variety of skylights, windows, and wall colors (including bright purples and yellows) affords a different perspective from each of the six floors.

## MUSEUMS & GALLERIES

**ArtPace.** 445 N. Main Ave. ☎ **210/212-4900.** www.artpace.org. Free admission. Wed and Fri–Sun noon–5pm; Thurs noon–8pm. Check local listings or call for lectures and other special events. Streetcar: Brown line.

San Antonio's cutting-edge contemporary art gallery features rotating shows displaying the work of artists selected by a prestigious international panel for 3-month residencies at the facility. One artist must be from Texas, one from anywhere else in the United States, and one from anywhere else in the world. The result has been a fascinating mélange, including everything from conceptual pieces like a roof terrace covered with 600 sunflowers, a gallery piled with 5 tons of salt, and a refrigerator stocked with frozen snakes, to more or less representational photographs, paintings, and sculptures. Lecture series by the artists and public forums to discuss the work have also helped make this a very stimulating art space.

**Blue Star Arts Complex.** Bordered by Probandt, Blue Star, and South Alamo sts. and the San Antonio River. ☎ **210/227-6960.** www.bluestarartspace.org. Free admission ($2 suggested donation). Hours vary from gallery to gallery; most are open Wed–Sun noon–6pm, with some opening at 10am. Streetcar: Blue line.

This huge former warehouse in Southtown hosts a collection of working studios and galleries, along with a performance space for the Jump-Start theater company. The 11,000-square-foot artist-run Contemporary Art Museum is its anchor. The style of work varies from gallery to gallery—you'll see everything from primitive-style folk art to feminist photography—but the level of professionalism is generally high. One of the most interesting spaces is SAY Sí, featuring exhibitions by talented neighborhood high school students that might include collages or book art. A number of galleries are devoted to (or have sections purveying) arty gift items such as jewelry, picture frames, and crafts.

**Buckhorn Saloon & Museum.** 318 E. Houston St. ☎ **210/247-4000.** www. buckhornmuseum.com. Admission $8 adults, $7 seniors (55 and up), $5 military, $4.50 children 4–13. Sun–Thurs 10am–5pm; Fri–Sat 10am–6pm (later hours in summer). Streetcar: Red and Blue lines.

If you like your educational experiences accompanied by a cold one, this is the place for you. With its huge stuffed animals, mounted fish, and wax museum version of history, this collection fulfills every out-of-stater's stereotype of what a Texas museum might be like. It's not nearly as funky as it was when it was in the old Lone Star brewery—all those dead animals seem out of place in this modern, new space—but it's still hard to resist exhibits like the church made out of 50,000 matchsticks or pictures designed from rattlesnake rattles. The facility includes a re-creation of the turn-of-the-century Buckhorn saloon, a curio shop, and a transported historic bar.

**Hertzberg Circus Collection and Museum.** 210 W. Market St. ☎ **210/207-7810.** Admission $2.50 adults, $2 seniors, $1 children 3–12. Mon–Sat 10am–5pm; Sun and holidays 1–5pm June–Aug only. Streetcar: Red, Yellow, and Purple lines.

They're not as large as the ones at the circus, but colorful elephants posted as sentries beside the front steps of this nostalgia-inducing museum hint at what's inside. Displays chosen from the massive collection of "circusana" that Harry Hertzberg bequeathed to the San Antonio Public Library (of which this is a branch) include Tom Thumb's carriage, a flea circus, and photographs of Buffalo Bill's Wild West show. A unique permanent exhibition details the *carpas*, Mexican tent shows that traveled the Southwest. On weekends, kids are entertained by jugglers, mimes, face-painting workshops, and the like, but when there are no such special events on, adults will probably get the most out of this history-oriented place.

**Institute of Texan Cultures.** 801 S. Bowie St. (at Durango St. in HemisFair Park). ☎ **210/ 458-2300.** www.texancultures.utsa.edu. Admission $4 adults, $2 seniors and children 3–12. Tues–Sun 9am–5pm. Dome shows presented at 10:15am, noon, 2pm, and 3:30pm. Closed Thanksgiving, Christmas. Streetcar: Purple line.

It's the rare visitor who won't discover here that his or her ethnic group has contributed to the history of Texas: Some 30 different ethnic and cultural groups are represented in the imaginative, hands-on displays of this educational center, which is one of three campuses of the University of Texas at San Antonio. Outbuildings include a one-room schoolhouse and a windmill, and the multimedia Dome Theater presents images of Texas on 36 screens. Volunteer docents lead tours and frequently put on puppet shows; call ahead to see if one is scheduled for the day you plan to visit. There's a great photo archive with more than 3 million images (call ☎ **210/458-2298** for information on using it) and an excellent bookstore and gift shop.

**◯ Marion Koogler McNay Art Museum.** 6000 N. New Braunfels Ave. ☎ **210/ 824-5368.** www.mcnayart.org. Free admission (fee for special exhibits). Tues–Sat 10am–5pm; Sun noon–5pm. Docent tours Sun at 2pm Oct–May. Closed New Year's Day, Fourth of July, Thanksgiving, Christmas. Bus: 7.

Set on a hill north of Brackenridge Park, with a striking view of downtown, the sprawling Spanish Mediterranean–style mansion of oil heiress and artist Marion Koogler McNay has been an art museum since 1954. A major refurbishing in 2000 to 2001 rendered the home more impressive than ever. The museum's main strength is French post-Impressionist and early 20th-century European painting, but there are also fine theater arts (costumes, set designs, etc.) and Mexican lithograph collections, as well as some excellent special exhibits—for example, a recent one on the Taos artists and their patrons. A well-stocked gift shop adjoins a shaded central patio. The graciousness of the setting, used for numerous weddings and photo shoots, combined with the intimacy of the collection make this a most appealing place to view art.

**Southwest School of Art and Craft.** 300 Augusta. ☎ **210/224-1848.** www.swschool. org. Free admission. Mon–Sat 9am–5pm (galleries); Mon–Sat 10–5 (gift shop). Streetcar: Blue line.

A stroll along the River Walk to the northern corner of downtown will lead you into another world: a rare French-designed cloister where contemporary crafts are now being created. An exhibition gallery and artist studios-cum-classrooms (not open to visitors) occupy the garden-filled grounds of the first girl's school in San Antonio, established by the Ursuline order in the mid–19th century. Stop in at the visitors center (open weekdays 10am to 3pm) if you'd like a volunteer to give you a tour around such structures as the First Academy Building, made by an unusual rammed-earth process, and the wood-and-native limestone Gothic church. You can also wander around yourself and then relax in one of many oak-shaded nooks. The Ursuline Sales Gallery carries unique crafts items, most made by the school's artists. You can enjoy a nice, light lunch in the Copper Kitchen Restaurant (weekdays 11:30am to 2pm, closed national holidays). The adjacent Navarro Campus, built in the late 1990s, is not as architecturally interesting, but it's worth stopping there for its large contemporary art gallery. In September 2001, a space for permanent historic exhibitions about the school and craft center is scheduled to open in the First Academy Building.

✪ **Witte Museum.** 3801 Broadway (at the edge of Brackenridge Park). ☎ **210/357-1900.** www.wittemuseum.org. Admission $5.95 adults, $4.95 seniors, $3.95 children 4–11; children 3 and under free. Free on Tues 3–9pm. Mon and Wed–Sat 10am–5pm (until 6pm June–Aug); Tues 10am–9pm; Sun noon–5pm (until 6pm June–Aug). Closed Thanksgiving, Christmas. Bus: 9 and 14.

A family museum that adults will enjoy as much as kids, the Witte focuses on Texas history, natural science, and anthropology, but often ranges as far afield as the Berlin Wall or the history of bridal gowns in the United States. Your senses will be engaged along with your intellect: You might hear animal cries as you crouch through south Texas thorn brush, or feel rough-hewn stone carved with Native American pictographs under your feet. Children especially like the exhibits devoted to mummies and dinosaurs, as well as the EcoLab, where the live Texas critters range from tarantulas to tortoises. But the biggest draw for kids is the terrific HEB Science Treehouse, a four-level, 15,000-square-foot science center that sits behind the museum on the banks of the San Antonio River. Its hands-on activities are geared to all ages. Also on the grounds are a butterfly and hummingbird garden and three restored historic homes. Excellent film, concert, and performing arts series draw folks back here on weekend afternoons and weekday evenings; check the Web site for the latest schedules.

# SAN ANTONIO OUTDOORS
## OUTDOOR ART

**Spirit of Healing Mural.** Santa Rosa Children's Hospital, facing Milam Park and across from Market Square. Streetcar: Yellow and Red lines.

This 40-by-90-foot tile mural by renowned local artist Jesse Treviño, one of the largest of its kind in North America, depicts a child holding a dove and protected by a guardian angel. It took 18 months to create and 3 months to install the mural's 150,000 tiles on the side of the children's hospital. It was a family affair—the child was modeled on Treviño's 10-year-old son, and brothers Jesse and Alex Villareal helped develop the techniques to create and install the mural. Because it's so big, it's best seen from a distance—but be careful of a too-long viewing from the freeway.

**Vietnam War Memorial.** Veterans Memorial Plaza, 1 block north of Travis Park at East Martin and Jefferson sts. Bus: 3, 4, 84, 86, 87, 90, or 92.

*Hill 881 S,* a moving bronze monument created by combat artist Austin Deuel and dedicated to the veterans of the Vietnam War, depicts a Marine holding a wounded comrade while looking skyward for an Evac helicopter.

## PARKS & GARDENS

**Brackenridge Park.** Main entrance 2800 block of N. Broadway. ☎ **210/207-3000.** Open daily dawn–dusk. Bus: 7.

With its rustic stone bridges and winding walkways, the city's main park, opened in 1899, has a charming, old-fashioned feel, and serves as a popular center for recreational activities, including golf, polo, biking, and picnicking. Particularly appealing is the Japanese Tea Garden—also called the Japanese Sunken Garden—located next to the zoo. It was created in 1917 by prison labor to beautify an abandoned cement quarry, one of the largest in the world in the 1880s and 1890s. (The same quarry furnished cement rock for the state capitol in Austin.) You can still glimpse a brick smokestack and a number of the old lime kilns among the beautiful flower arrangements, which are less austere than those in many Japanese gardens. After Pearl Harbor, the site was officially renamed the Chinese Sunken Garden, with a Chinese-style entryway added on; not until 1983 was the original name restored. Just to the southwest, a bowl of limestone cliffs found to have natural acoustic properties was turned into the Sunken Garden Theater (see "The Performing Arts," in chapter 8, for details). A 60-foot-high waterfall and water lily–laced ponds are among the lures. See also the entry for the San Antonio Zoological Gardens in this section.

**HemisFair Park.** Bounded by Alamo, Bowie, Market, and Durango sts. No main park telephone number. Bus: 40. Streetcar: Red, Purple, Brown, and Blue lines.

Built for the 1968 HemisFair, an exposition celebrating the 250th anniversary of the founding of San Antonio, this urban oasis boasts water gardens and a wood-and-sand playground constructed by children. Among its indoor diversions are the Institute of Texan Cultures (described above) and the Tower of the Americas (detailed below). Be sure to walk over to the Henry B. Gonzales Convention Center and take a look at the striking mosaic mural by Mexican artist Juan O'Gorman. The Schultze House Cottage Garden, created and maintained by Master Gardeners of Bexar County, is also worth checking out for its heirloom plants, varietals, tropicals, and xeriscape area; it's located at 514 HemisFair Park, behind the Federal Building.

**⊙ San Antonio Botanical Gardens.** 555 Funston. ☎ **210/207-3255.** www.sabot.org. Admission $4 adults, $2 seniors and military, $1 children 3–13; children under 3 free. Daily 9am–6pm Mar–Oct; 8am–5pm Nov–Feb. Closed Christmas, New Year's Day. Bus: 8.

Take a horticultural tour of Texas at this gracious 38-acre garden, encompassing everything from south Texas scrub to Hill Country wildflowers. Fountains, pools, paved paths, and examples of Texas architecture provide visual contrast to the flora. The

> **❷ Did You Know?**
>
> - The world's largest bowling-ball manufacturer, Columbia 300 Inc., is in San Antonio.
> - Elmer Doolin, the original manufacturer of Fritos corn chips, bought the original recipe from a San Antonio restaurant in 1932 for $100. He sold the first batch from the back of his Model-T Ford.
> - *Wings,* a silent World War I epic that won the first Academy Award for best picture in 1927, was filmed in San Antonio. The film marked the debut of Gary Cooper, who was on screen for a total of 102 seconds.
> - Lyndon and Lady Bird Johnson were married in San Antonio's St. Mark's Episcopal Church.
> - The building that currently houses the Ramada Emily Morgan hotel was the first skyscraper built west of the Mississippi.

formal gardens include a garden for the blind, a Japanese garden, an herb garden, a biblical garden, and a children's garden. Perhaps most outstanding is the $6.9 million Lucile Halsell Conservatory complex, a below-ground greenhouse replicating a variety of tropical and desert environments. The 1896 Sullivan Carriage House, built by Alfred Giles and moved stone-by-stone from its original downtown site, serves as the entryway to the gardens. It hosts a gift shop (☎ **210/829-1227;** open daily 9am to 4:30pm in winter, until 5pm in summer) and restaurant offering salads, quiches, and sandwiches (open Tues to Sun 11am to 1:45pm).

## A VIEW

**❂ Tower of the Americas.** 600 HemisFair Park. ☎ **210/207-8616.** Admission $3 adults, $2 seniors 55 and over, $1 children 4–11; children 3 and under free. Sun–Thurs 9am–9pm; Fri–Sat 9am–10pm. Streetcar: Purple line.

For a quick take on the lay of the land, just circle the eight panoramic panels on the observation level of the Tower of the Americas. The 750-foot-high tower was built for the HemisFair in 1968; the deck sits at the equivalent of 59 stories and is lit for spectacular night viewing. The tower also hosts a rotating restaurant with surprisingly decent food, for the revolving genre, as well as a thankfully stationary cocktail lounge.

## A ZOO

**San Antonio Zoological Gardens and Aquarium.** 3903 N. St. Mary's St. in Brackenridge Park. ☎ **210/734-7183.** www.sazoo-aq.org. Admission $7 adults, $5 seniors 62 and over and children 3–11; children 2 and under free. Boat rides $1. Daily 9am–5pm (until 6pm in summer). Bus: 7 or 8.

Home to more than 700 different species, this zoo in Brackenridge Park hosts one of the largest animal collections in the United States. It's also considered one of the top facilities in the country because of its conservation efforts and its successful breeding programs—it produced the first white rhino in the United States. A children's zoo features a Tropical Tour boat ride (weekends only, except in summer) that visits miniature exhibits of animals from many countries. The zoo has expanded and upgraded its exhibits since it opened in 1914, but it's likely to strike those who have visited newer and glitzier zoos as pretty old-fashioned.

## 3 Especially for Kids

Without a doubt, the prime spots for kids in San Antonio are **SeaWorld** and **Six Flags Fiesta Texas.** They'll also like the hands-on, interactive **Witte Museum** and the various ethnic pride kids' programs at the **Institute of Texas Cultures,** as well as the weekend activities at the **Herzberg Circus Collection and Museum.** There's a children's area in the **zoo,** which vends food packets so people of all ages can feed the animals. Youngsters will also get a kick out of petting the critters roaming around the Quadrangle at **Fort Sam Houston.** The third floor of the main branch of the **San Antonio Public Library** is devoted to children, who get to use their own catalogs and search tools. Story hours are offered regularly, and there are occasional puppet shows.

In addition to these sights, detailed in "The Top Attractions" and "More Attractions" sections, above, and the **Magik Theatre,** covered in chapter 8, the following should also appeal to the sandbox set and up. Look out, too, for the **Aztec Theater,** scheduled to open on the River Walk by the end of 2001; its large-screen Iwerks movie theater is bound to give the IMAX some competition.

**Alamo IMAX Theater.** 849 E. Commerce St., in the Rivercenter Mall. ☎ **800/354-4629** (recorded schedule information) or 210/247-4629. www.imax-sa.com. Admission $8.50 adults, $7.50 seniors, $5.50 children 3–11. Daily 8:30am–10:30pm. Streetcar: All lines.

Having kids view "Alamo–The Price of Freedom" on a six-story-high screen with a stereo sound system is a surefire way of getting them psyched for the historical battle site (which, although it's just across the street, can't be reached without wending your way past lots and lots of Rivercenter shops). The theater also shows nature movies produced especially for the large screen, and occasionally commercial films, such as *The Perfect Storm.* Early 2001 saw the debut of a second, 50-foot-high screen with 3-D capability and a state-of-the-art sound system, making this the first commercial IMAX theater in the country to double its big-screen pleasures. Your ticket also buys you entry into The Texas Adventure (see below).

**Plaza Wax Museum & Ripley's Believe It or Not.** 301 Alamo Plaza. ☎ **210/224-9299.** Either attraction $10.95 adults, $4.95 children 4–12; both attractions $14.95 adults, $7.95 children 4–12. Memorial Day to Labor Day, daily 9am–10pm; remainder of the year, Sun–Thurs 9am–7pm, Fri–Sat 9am–10pm (ticket office closes an hour before listed closing times). Streetcar: All lines.

Adults may get the bigger charge out of the waxy stars—Denzel Washington and Brad Pitt are among the latest to be added to an impressive array—and some of the oddities collected by the globe-trotting Mr. Ripley, but there's plenty for kids to enjoy at this two-fer attraction. The walk-through wax Theater of Horrors, although tame compared to the *Friday the Thirteenth* adventures, usually elicits some shudders. At Believe It Or Not, youngsters generally get a kick out of learning about people around the world whose habits—such as sticking nails through their noses—are even weirder than their own.

✪ **San Antonio Children's Museum.** 305 E. Houston St. ☎ **210/21-CHILD.** Admission $4; children under 2 free. Mon 9am–noon; Tues–Fri 9am–3:30pm; Sat 9am–6pm; Sun noon–4pm. Bus: 7 or 40. Streetcar: Red line.

Opened in 1995, San Antonio's children's museum offers a wonderful introduction to the city for the pint-sized and grown-up alike. San Antonio history, population, and geography are all explored through such features as a miniature River Walk, a multicultural grocery store, a bank where kids can use their own ATM (hmmm . . . do we want them to know how easy it is?)—even a teddy bear hospital. Activities range from crawl spaces and corn-grinding rocks to a weather station and radar room. Don't miss this place if you're traveling with children up to age 10.

**Splashtown.** 3600 N. Pan Am Expressway (exit 160, Splashtown Dr., off I-35). ☎ **210/ 227-1100.** www.splashtownsa.com. Admission $20 adults, $15 children under 48 in.; seniors over 65 and children under 2 free; after 5pm, $12 for any age. Daily June–Aug; weekends May and Sept (call ahead or check Web site for exact times).

Cool off at this 8-acre water park, which includes a huge wave pool, hydro tubes nearly 300 feet long, a Texas-size water bobsled ride, more than a dozen water slides, and a two-story playhouse for the smaller children. A variety of concerts, contests, and special events are held here.

**The Texas Adventure.** 307 Alamo Plaza. ☎ **210/227-8224.** Admission $8.50 adults, $7.50 seniors and military, $5.50 children 3–11 (includes Alamo IMAX theater admission). Daily 10am–8pm in winter; 10am–10pm in summer. Streetcar: Red, Brown, and Blue lines.

San Antonio's latest foray into the high-tech history field, the world's first Encountarium F!X Theatre retells the battle for the Alamo with special effects that include life-size holographic images of the Alamo heroes and cannon fire roaring through a sophisticated sound system. The depiction of events is more accurate than in most such displays, but noise and smoke aside, this isn't terribly exciting, since the ghostly holograms do little more than hold forth about who they are. Still, it's included in the price of the Alamo IMAX theater (see above) and takes only 30 minutes.

## 4  Special-Interest Sightseeing

### FOR MILITARY HISTORY BUFFS

San Antonio's military installations are crucial to the city's economy, and testaments to their past abound. Those who aren't satisfied with touring Fort Sam Houston (see "More Attractions," above) can also visit the **Hangar 9/Edward H. White Museum** at Brooks Air Force Base, Southeast Military Drive at the junction of I-37 (☎ **210/ 536-2203**). The history of flight medicine, among other things, is detailed via exhibits in the oldest aircraft hangar in the Air Force. Admission is free, and it's open Monday to Friday 7:30am to 4pm, except the last 2 weeks of December. Lackland Air Force Base (12 miles southwest of downtown off U.S. 90 at Southwest Military Drive exit) is home to the **Air Force History and Traditions Museum,** 2051 George Ave., Bldg. 5206 (☎ **210/671-3055**), which hosts a collection of rare aircraft and components dating back to World War II. Admission is free; it's open Monday to Friday 8am to 4:30pm. Although Randolph Air Force Base (17 miles northeast of downtown off I-35) doesn't have any museums per se, much of the base is historically interesting and the **Taj Mahal** wing commander's (Bldg. no. 100) is on the National Register of Historic Places. Call ☎ **210/652-4407** for information on tours, restricted to active military or groups of 10 or more; 3 weeks' advance notice is needed. In all cases, phone ahead before you go; the bases are sometimes restricted.

### FOR JOCKS

**Alamodome.** 100 Montana St. ☎ **210/207-3652** (recorded information) or 210/207-3641. Tour $4 adults, $2 seniors over 55 and children 4–12. Tours Tues–Sat 11am and 1pm (travelers with disabilities can call to arrange private tours by appointment). Parking is free in the south lot (Durango Blvd.) on days that no events are scheduled. Streetcar: Yellow, Purple, and Brown lines.

You don't have to be a sports nut to tour San Antonio's $186 million athletic arena, even when there's no team playing here, but it helps. It also helps to be in good shape, because the 45-minute tour involves lots of walking and some stair climbing (consider that each of the two locker rooms alone measures nearly 5,000 square feet). The Alamodome has the world's largest retractable seating system, and its roof encompasses 9 acres. Call ahead; tours are sometimes canceled because of special events and holidays.

## FOR THOSE INTERESTED IN HISPANIC HERITAGE

A Hispanic heritage tour is almost redundant in San Antonio, which is a living testament to the role Hispanics have played in shaping the city. **Casa Navarro State Historical Park, La Villita, Market Square, San Antonio Missions National Historical Park,** and the **Spanish Governor's Palace,** all detailed above, give visitors a feel for the city's Spanish colonial past, while the new Nelson A. Rockefeller wing of the **San Antonio Museum of Art,** also discussed earlier, hosts this country's largest collection of Latin American art. The sixth floor of the main branch of the **San Antonio Public Library** (see above) hosts an excellent noncirculating Latino collection, featuring books about the Mexican-American experience in Texas and the rest of the Southwest. It's also the place to come to do genealogical research into your family's Hispanic roots.

The city's exploration of its own Hispanic roots is ongoing. At 310 W. Houston St., you can see the spectacular 86-foot-high neon sign of the **Alameda Theater,** opened in 1949 as one of the last of the grand movie palaces and the largest ever dedicated to Spanish-language entertainment. Among its many impressive features were private nursemaids for the patrons' children and gorgeous "deco tropical" tilework hand-created in San Antonio. Described as being "to U.S. Latinos what Harlem's Apollo Theater is to African-Americans," the Alameda is scheduled to reopen after a $16 million restoration in fall 2001 as a multi-venue performance hall and teaching facility for Latino arts and culture. It's part of the planned **Centro Alameda cultural zone** on downtown's west side, a project that will include the first Smithsonian Institution affiliate in the nation, slated to debut in 2002.

Cultural events and blow-out festivals, many of them held at Market Square, abound. **The Guadalupe Cultural Arts Center,** which organizes many of them, is detailed in chapter 8. In HemisFair Park, the **Mexican Cultural Institute,** 600 HemisFair Plaza Way (☎ 210/227-0123), sponsored by the Mexican Ministry of Foreign Affairs, hosts Latin American film series, concerts, conferences, performances, contests, and workshops—including ones on language, literature, and folklore as well as art. The institute also hosts shifting displays of art and artifacts relating to Mexican history and culture, from pre-Columbian to contemporary.

For information on the various festivals and events, contact the **San Antonio Hispanic Chamber of Commerce** (☎ 210/225-0462). Another good resource for Latin *cultura* is the **"Guide to Puro San Antonio,"** available from the San Antonio Convention and Visitors Bureau (☎ 800/447-3372).

## 5 Walking Tour: Downtown

One of downtown San Antonio's great gifts to visitors on foot is its wonderfully meandering early pathways—not laid out by drunken cattle drivers as has been wryly suggested, but formed by the course of the San Antonio River and the various settlements that grew up around it. Turn any corner in this area and you'll come across some fascinating testament to the city's historically rich past.

*Note:* Stops 1, 5, 6, 7, 9, 11, 13, and 14 are described earlier in this chapter. Entrance hours and admission fees (if applicable) are listed there. See chapter 4 for additional information on stop no. 2 and chapter 7 for additional information on stop no. 3.

**Start:** The Alamo.

**Finish:** Market Square.

**Time:** Approximately 1½ hours, not including stops at shops, restaurants, or attractions.

**Best Times:** Early morning during the week, when the streets and attractions are less crowded. If you're willing to tour the Alamo museums and shrine another time, consider starting out before they open (9am).

**Worst Times:** Weekend afternoons, especially in summer, when the crowds and the heat render this long stroll rather uncomfortable. (If you do get tired, you can always pick up a streetcar within a block or two of most parts of this route.)

Built to be within easy reach of each other, San Antonio's earliest military, religious, and civil settlements are concentrated in the downtown area. The city spread out quite a bit in the next 2½ centuries, but downtown still functions as the seat of the municipal and county government, as well as the hub of tourist activities.

Start your tour at Alamo Plaza (bounded by E. Houston St. on the north); at the plaza's northeast corner, you'll come to the entrance for:

**1. The Alamo** (see also "The Top Attractions," above), originally established in 1718 as the Mission San Antonio de Valero. The first of the city's five missions, it was moved twice before settling into this site. The heavy limestone walls of the church and its adjacent compound later proved to make an excellent fortress; in 1836, the fighters for Texas's independence from Mexico took a heroic, if ultimately unsuccessful, stand against Mexican general Santa Anna here.

When you leave the walled complex, walk south along the plaza to:

**2. The Menger Hotel** (see also chapter 4), built by German immigrant William Menger in 1859 on the site of Texas's first brewery, which he had opened with partner Charles Deegan in 1855. Legend has it that Menger wanted a place to lodge hard-drinking friends who used to spend the night sleeping on his long bar. Far more prestigious guests—presidents, Civil War generals, writers, stage actors, you name it—stayed here over the years, and the hotel turns up in several short stories by frequent guest William Sidney Porter (O. Henry). The Menger has been much expanded since it first opened, but retains its gorgeous, three-tiered Victorian lobby.

On the south side of the hotel, Alamo Plaza turns back into North Alamo Street. Take it south 1 block until you reach Commerce Street, where you'll spot:

**3. Joske's** (now Dillard's, see chapter 7), San Antonio's oldest department store. The more modest retail emporium opened by the Joske Brothers in 1889 was swallowed up in 1939 by the huge modernist building you see now, distinctive for its intricate Spanish Renaissance–style details; look for the miniaturized versions of Mission San José's sacristy window on the building's ground-floor shadowboxes.

Walk a short way along the Commerce Street side of the building to:

**4. St. Joseph's Catholic Church,** built for San Antonio's German community in 1876. This Gothic revival–style house of worship is as notable for the intransigence of its congregation as it is for its beautiful stained-glass windows. The worshipers' refusal to move from the site when Joske's department store was rising up all around it earned the church the affectionate moniker "St. Joske's."

Head back to Alamo Street and continue south 2 blocks past the San Antonio Convention Center to reach:

**5. La Villita** (see "The Top Attractions," above), once the site of a Coahuiltecan Indian village. It was settled over the centuries by Spanish, Germans, and, in the '30s and '40s, a community of artists. A number of the buildings have been continuously occupied for more than 200 years. The "Little Village" on the river was restored by a joint effort of the city and the San Antonio Conservation Society, and now hosts a number of crafts shops and two upscale restaurants in addition to the historic General Cós House and the Arneson River Theatre.

Just south of La Villita, you'll see HemisFair Way and the large iron gates of:

6. **HemisFair Park** (see "More Attractions," above), built for the 1968 exposition held to celebrate the 250th anniversary of San Antonio's founding. The expansive former fairgrounds are home to two museums, a German heritage park, and an observation tower—the tallest structure in the city and a great reference point if you get lost downtown. The plaza is too large to explore even superficially on this tour, so come back another time.

Retrace your steps to Paseo de la Villita and walk 1 block west to Presa Street. Take it north for about half a block until you see the Presa Street Bridge and descend from it to:

7. **The River Walk** (see "The Top Attractions," above). You'll find yourself on a quiet section of the 2.6-mile paved walkway that lines the banks of the San Antonio River through a large part of downtown and the King William Historic District. The bustling cafe, restaurant, and hotel action is just behind you, on the stretch of the river that winds north of La Villita.

Stroll down this tree-shaded thoroughfare until you reach the St. Mary's Street Bridge (you'll pass only one other bridge, the Navarro Street Bridge, along the way) and ascend here. Then walk north half a block until you come to Market Street. Take it west 1 long block, where you'll find:

8. **Main Plaza** (Plaza de Las Islas), the heart of the town established in 1731 by 15 Canary Island families sent by King Philip V of Spain to settle his remote New World outpost. Much of the history of San Antonio—and of Texas—unfolded on this modest square. A peace treaty with the Apaches was signed (and later broken) on the plaza in 1749; in 1835, freedom fighters battled Santa Anna's troops here before barricading themselves in the Alamo across the river. Much calmer these days, the plaza still sees some action as home to the Romanesque-style Bexar County Courthouse, built out of native Texas granite and sandstone in 1892.

Walk along the south side of Main Plaza to the corner of Main Avenue. Across the street and just to the north you'll encounter:

9. **San Fernando Cathedral** (see "More Attractions," above), the oldest parish church building in Texas and site of the earliest marked graves in San Antonio. Three walls of the original church started by the Canary Island settlers in 1738 can still be seen in the rear of the 1868 Gothic revival cathedral. Among those buried within the sanctuary walls are Eugenio Navarro, brother of José Antonio Navarro (see stop no. 13, below), and Don Manuel Muñoz, first governor of Texas when it was a province of a newly independent Mexico.

On the north side of the cathedral is Trevino Street; take it west to the next corner and cross the street to reach:

10. **Military Plaza** (Plaza de Armas), once the drill ground for the Presidio San Antonio de Béxar. The garrison, established in 1718 to protect the Mission San Antonio de Valero, was moved to this nearby site 4 years later. Military Plaza was one of the liveliest spots in Texas for the 50 years after Texas won its independence. In the 1860s, it was the site of vigilante lynchings, and after the Civil War it hosted a bustling outdoor market. At night, the townsfolk would come to its open-air booths to buy chili con carne from their favorite chili queen. The plaza remained completely open until 1889, when the ornate City Hall was built at its center.

The one-story white building you'll see directly across the street from the west side of the plaza is:

# Walking Tour: Downtown San Antonio

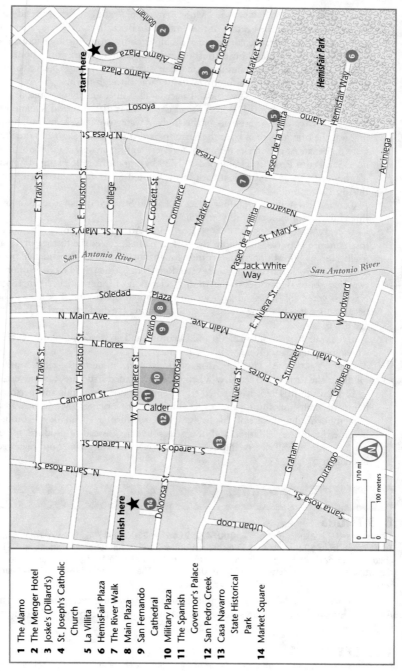

1  The Alamo
2  The Menger Hotel
3  Joske's (Dillard's)
4  St. Joseph's Catholic
    Church
5  La Villita
6  HemisFair Plaza
7  The River Walk
8  Main Plaza
9  San Fernando
    Cathedral
10 Military Plaza
11 The Spanish
    Governor's Palace
12 San Pedro Creek
13 Casa Navarro
    State Historical
    Park
14 Market Square

11. **Spanish Governor's Palace** (see "More Attractions," above), former residence and headquarters of the captain of the Presidio de Béxar (but not of any Spanish governors); from here, the commander could watch his troops drilling across the street. The source of the house's misnomer is not entirely clear; as the home of the highest local authority and thus the nicest digs in the area, the "palace" probably hosted important Spanish officials who came through town.

   From the front of the Governor's Palace, walk south until you come to the crosswalk; just west across Dolorosa Street is a drainage ditch, the sad remains of:

12. **San Pedro Creek.** The west bank of this body of water, once lovely and full flowing, was the original site of both the Mission San Antonio de Valero and the Presidio de Béxar. At the creek's former headwaters, approximately 2 miles north of here, San Pedro Park was established in 1729 by a grant from the king of Spain; it's the second-oldest municipal park in the United States (the oldest being the Boston Common).

   Continue west along Dolorosa Street to Laredo Street and take it south about three quarters of a block until you come to:

13. **Casa Navarro State Historical Park** (see "More Attractions," above). The life of José Antonio Navarro, for whom the park is named, traces the history of Texas itself: He was born in Spanish territory, fought for Mexico's independence from Spain, then worked to achieve Texas's freedom from Mexico. (He was one of only two Texas-born signatories to the 1836 Declaration of Independence.) In 1845, Navarro voted for Texas's annexation to the United States, and a year later, he became a senator in the new Texas State Legislature. He died here in 1871, at the age of 76.

   Trace your steps back to Laredo and Dolorosa, and go west on Dolorosa Street; when you reach Santa Rosa, you'll be facing:

14. **Market Square** (see "The Top Attractions," above), home to the city's Market House at the turn of the century. When the low, arcaded structure was converted to El Mercado in 1973, it switched from selling household goods and personal items to crafts, clothing, and other more tourist-oriented Mexican wares. Directly behind and west of this lively square, the former Haymarket Plaza has become the Farmer's Market, and now sells souvenirs instead of produce. Here, you can enjoy a well-deserved lunch at Mi Tierra or La Margarita, both reviewed in chapter 5.

## 6 Organized Tours

### BUS TOURS

**Gray Line.** 217 Alamo Plaza. ☎ **800/472-9546** or 210/226-1706. www.grayline.com. Tours range from $22 adults and $11 children under 12 (3½ hours) to $38 adults and $19 children (full day); children under 5 free. Lunch not included in tour prices. Earliest tours depart at 8:30am, latest return at 6:30pm; daily except Thanksgiving, Christmas, New Year's Day, Easter, and Battle of Flowers Parade.

Gray Line serves up a large menu of guided bus tours, covering everything from San Antonio's missions and museums to forays south of the border or to the Hill Country. Call for details.

### TROLLEY TOURS

**Lone Star Trolley.** 301 Alamo Plaza (in front of Plaza Wax Museum & Ripley's Believe It or Not). ☎ **210/224-9299.** Tickets $9.50 adults, $4 children 3–12 ($2 more for a 2-day pass). Daily 10am–4:45pm.

Lots of people confuse the red-and-green Lone Star Trolleys with the plain green (and unguided) city-run streetcars. Boarding these will cost you a bit more—but you'll also be learning a lot about what you're looking at. Hour-long tours touch on all the downtown highlights, taking you to the King William Historic District, Market Square, and more. If you want to get off at any of these sights, you can pick up another trolley (they run every 45 min.) after you're finished.

## RIVER CRUISES

**Yanaguana Cruises.** Ticket offices: Rivercenter Mall; River Walk, across the street from the Hilton Palacio del Rio Hotel; Holiday Inn Riverwalk on St. Mary's (weekends only). ☎ **210/ 244-5700.** www.sarivercruise.com. Tickets $5.25 adults, $3.25 seniors and active military, $1 children under 6. Boats depart daily every 15–20 minutes from 10am–9pm (longer hours in summer).

Maybe you've sat in a River Walk cafe looking out at people riding back and forth in open, flat-bottom barges. Go ahead—give in and join 'em. An amusing, informative tour, lasting from 35 to 40 minutes, will take you more than 2 miles down the most built-up sections of the Paseo del Rio, with interesting sights pointed out along the way. You'll learn a lot about the river—and find out what all those folks you watched were laughing about. The company also runs a non-narrated shuttle (see "By River Taxi" in the "Getting Around" section of chapter 3 for details).

## 7 Staying Active

Most San Antonians head for the hills—that is, nearby Hill Country—for outdoor recreation. Some suggestions of sports in or around town follow; see chapter 16 for more.

**BIKING**    There aren't many scenic cycling trails within San Antonio itself—locals tend to ride in **Brackenridge Park;** in **McAllister Park** on the city's north side, 13102 Jones-Maltsberger (☎ 210/207-PARK or 210/207-3120); and around the area near **SeaWorld of Texas**—but there are a number of appealing places to bike in the vicinity. If you didn't bring your own two-wheeler, **Britton's Bicycles,** 4230 Thousand Oaks (☎ **210/656-1655;** www.brittonbikes.com), can deliver one to your hotel. The store is a good resource, too, for cycling events around town. You might also log on to the San Antonio Wheelmen's Web site, **www.sa.wheelman.com**, for details on organized rides in the area.

**FISHING**    Closest to town for good angling are **Braunig Lake,** a 1,350-acre, city-owned reservoir, a few miles southeast of San Antonio off I-37, and **Calaveras Lake,** one of Texas's great bass lakes, a few miles southeast of San Antonio off U.S. 181 South and Loop 1604. A bit farther afield (astream?) but still easy to reach from San Antonio are **Canyon Lake,** about 20 miles north of New Braunfels, and **Medina Lake,** just south of Bandera. Fishing licenses—sold at most sporting goods and tackle stores and sporting goods departments of large discount stores such as Wal-Mart or K-Mart, as well as county courthouses and Parks and Wildlife Department offices—are required for all nonresidents; for current information, call ☎ **800/792-1112** (in Texas only) or 512/ 389-4800. **Hill Country Outfitters,** 18030 Hwy. 281 N., Suite 108 (☎ **210/ 491-4416;** www.hillcountryoutfitters.com), runs guided fly-fishing trips in the area ($275 for one person, $300 for two) and leases private creeks and streams for a day (from $75).

**GOLF**    Golf has become a big deal in San Antonio, with more and more visitors coming to town expressly to tee off. Of the city's six municipal golf courses, two of the most notable are **Brackenridge,** 2315 Ave. B (☎ **210/226-5612;** www.ci.sat.tx.us/sapa), the oldest (1916) public course in Texas, featuring oak- and pecan-shaded fairways; and northwest San Antonio's $4.3 million **Cedar Creek,** 8250 Vista Colina (☎ **210/695-5050**), repeatedly ranked as South Texas's best municipal course in golfing surveys. Other options for unaffiliated golfers include the 200-acre **Pecan Valley,** 4700 Pecan Valley Dr. (☎ **210/333-9018;** www.thetexasgolftrail.com), which crosses the Salado Creek seven times and has an 800-year-old oak near its 13th hole; the high-end **Quarry,** 444 E. Basse Rd. (☎ **210/824-4500;** www.quarrygolf.com), on the sight of a former (you guessed it) quarry and one of San Antonio's newest public courses; and **Canyon Springs,** 24400 Canyon Golf Rd. (☎ **888/800-1511** or 210/497-1770; www.canyonspringscc.com), at the north edge of town in the Texas Hill Country, lush with live oaks and dotted with historic rock formations. There aren't too many resort courses in San Antonio because there aren't too many resorts, but the two at **La Cantera,** 16401 La Cantera Pkwy. (☎ **800/446-5387** or 210/558-4653)—the original one designed by Jay Morish and Tom Weiskopf, and the Arnold Palmer creation that debuted in early 2001—have knockout designs and dramatic hill-and-rock outcroppings to recommend them. To get a copy of the free San Antonio Golfing Guide, call ☎ **800/447-3372.**

**HIKING**  **Friedrich Wilderness Park,** 21480 Milsa (☎ **210/698-1057**), operated by the city of San Antonio as a nature preserve, is crisscrossed by 5½ miles of trails that attract bird watchers as well as hikers; a 2-mile stretch is accessible to people with disabilities. The park offers free guided hikes, lasting about 2 hours, the first Saturday of every month at 9am. **Enchanted Rock State Park,** near Fredericksburg, is the most popular spot for trekking out of town (see chapter 16).

**RIVER SPORTS**  For tubing, rafting, or canoeing along a cypress-lined river, San Antonio river rats head 35 miles northwest of downtown to the 2,000-acre **Guadalupe River State Park,** 3350 Park Rd. 31 (☎ **830/438-2656;** www.tpwd. state.tx.us). On Hwy. 46, just outside the park, you can rent tubes, rafts, and canoes at the **Bergheim Campground,** FM 3351 in Bergheim (☎ **830/336-2235**). Standard tubes run $6 per person (but the ones with a bottom for your cooler, at $7, are better), rafts are $15 per person (children 12 and under half-price), and canoes go for $25. The section of the Guadalupe River near Gruene is also extremely popular; see the "New Braunfels" section of chapter 16 for details.

**SWIMMING/WATER PARKS**  Most hotels have swimming pools, but if yours doesn't, the **Parks and Recreation Department** (☎ **210/207-3113;** www.ci.sat.tx. us/sapar) can direct you to the nearest municipal pool. Both **SeaWorld** and **Six Flags Fiesta Texas,** detailed in the "The Top Attractions" section, above, are prime places to get wet (the latter has a pool in the shape of Texas and a waterfall that descends from a cowboy hat). **Splashtown** water recreation park is described in the "Especially for Kids" section, above. Many San Antonians head out to New Braunfels to get wet at the **Schlitterbahn,** the largest water park in Texas; see the "New Braunfels" section of chapter 16 for additional information.

**TENNIS**  You can play at the lighted courts at the **Fairchild Tennis Center,** 1214 E. Crockett (☎ **210/226-6912**), and **McFarlin Tennis Center,** 1503 San Pedro Ave. (☎ **210/732-1223**), both municipal facilities. The former is free; the very reasonable fees for the latter are $1.50 per hour per person ($1 for students and seniors), $2.50 after 5pm.

# 8  Spectator Sports

**AUTO RACING**    The best local drag-race action March through October is at the **San Antonio Speedway,** 14901 S. Hwy. 16, 4 miles south of Loop 410 (☎ **210/ 628-1499;** www.saspeedway.com). Another good option is the **Alamo Dragway,** 15030 Watson Rd. (☎ **210/628-1371**).

**BASEBALL**    From early April through early September, the minor league **San Antonio Missions** play at the Nelson Wolff Stadium, 5757 Hwy. 90 West. All home games for this Seattle Mariners farm club start at 7:05pm, except Sunday games, which start at 6:05pm. Tickets range from $4.50 for adult general admission to $8.50 for seats in the lower box. Call ☎ **210/675-7275** for schedules and tickets, or check the Web site at www.samissions.com.

**BASKETBALL**    Spur madness hits San Antonio every year from mid-October through May, when the city's only major-league franchise, the **San Antonio Spurs,** shoot hoops at the huge Alamodome (see "Special-Interest Sightseeing," above). For most games, tickets are sold only for the dome's lower level, where prices range from $17.50 for seats behind the basket to $55.50 for seats on the corners of the court. Nosebleed-level seats, running from $5 to $8, open up for the most popular contests. Tickets are available at the Spurs Ticket Office (south end of the Alamodome) or via Ticketmaster San Antonio (☎ **210/224-9600;** www.ticketmaster.com). Get schedules, players' stats, promotional news—everything you might want to know or buy relating to the team—on line at www.nba.com/spurs. It's also the place to track the progress of the Spurs' new stadium, the SBC Center, for which ground was broken in spring 2000.

**GOLF**    The **SBC Championship,** an Official Senior PGA Tour Event, is held each October at the Dominion Country Club, 1 Dominion Dr. (☎ **210/698-3582**). One of the oldest professional golf tournaments, now known as the **Westin Texas Open at La Cantera,** showcases the sport in September at 16401 La Cantera Pkwy. (☎ **201/ 558-4653**). Call the San Antonio Golf Association (☎ **800/TEX-OPEN** or 210/ 341-0823) for additional information.

**HORSE RACING**    Opened in 1995, the $79 million **Retama Park,** some 15 minutes north of San Antonio in Selma (☎ **210/651-7000;** www.rctamapark.com), is now the hottest place to play the ponies; take exit 174-A from I-35, or the Lookout Road exit from Loop 1604. The five-level Spanish-style grandstand is impressive, and the variety of food courts, restaurants, and lounges is almost as diverting as the horses. Live racing is generally from mid-April through October on Wednesday or Thursday through Sunday. Call for thoroughbred and quarter horse schedules. Simulcasts from top tracks around the country are shown year-round. General admission is $2.50 adults, $1.50 seniors; clubhouse, $3.50 adults, $2.50 seniors; simulcast, $1. Kids 15 and under and members of the military, active or retired, can enter gratis. Call ahead for the dates of "Fifty-Cent Fridays," when parking, admission, programs, beer, soft drinks, and hot dogs cost . . . you guessed it.

**ICE HOCKEY**    The first hockey team in city history, the Central Hockey League's **San Antonio Iguanas** dropped their first puck at the Freeman Coliseum (3201 E. Houston St.) in 1994. CHL tickets cost $6.50 to $15.50. Try ☎ **210/227-4449** or www.sa-iguanas.com for information.

**RODEO**    If you're in town in early February, don't miss the chance to see 2 weeks of Wild West events like calf roping, steer wrestling, and bull riding at the annual **San**

**Antonio Stock Show and Rodeo.** You can also hear major live country-and-western talent—Martina McBride, Alabama, Willie Nelson, John Michael Montgomery, George Jones, and Loretta Lynn were on the 2000 roster—and you're likely to find something to add to your luggage at an exposition hall, packed with Texas handcrafts. Contact the San Antonio Livestock Exposition Inc., P.O. Box 200230, San Antonio, TX 78220 (☎ **210/225-5851;** www.sarodeo.com), for additional advance information. Smaller rodeos are held throughout the year in nearby **Bandera County,** the self-proclaimed "Cowboy Capital of the World." Contact the Bandera County Convention and Visitors Bureau (☎ **800/364-3833** or 830/796-3045; www. banderacowboycapital.com) for more information.

# San Antonio Shopping

## 7

San Antonio offers the retail-bound a nice balance of large malls and little enclaves of specialized shops. You'll find everything here from the utilitarian to the unusual: huge Sears and Kmart department stores, a Saks Fifth Avenue fronted by a 40-foot pair of cowboy boots, a mall with a river running through it, and some lively Mexican markets.

You can count on most shops around town being open from 9 or 10am until 5:30 or 6pm Monday through Saturday, with shorter hours on Sunday. Malls are generally open Monday through Saturday 10am to 9pm and on Sunday noon to 6pm. Sales tax in San Antonio is 7.875%.

## 1 The Shopping Scene

Most out-of-town shoppers will find all they need **downtown,** between the large Rivercenter Mall, the boutiques and crafts shops of La Villita, the colorful Mexican wares of Market Square, the Southwest School of Art and Craft, and assorted retailers and galleries on and around Alamo Plaza. More avant-garde boutiques and galleries, including Blue Star, can be found in the adjacent area known as Southtown.

San Antonians tend to shop the **Loop 410 malls**—especially North Star, Central Park, and the Alamo Quarry Market near the airport— and cruise the upscale strip centers along Broadway in **Alamo Heights** (the posh Collection and Lincoln Heights are particularly noteworthy). Weekends might see locals poking around a number of terrific **flea markets.** For bargains on brand labels, they head out to New Braunfels and San Marcos, home to three large **factory outlet malls** (see chapter 16 for details).

## 2 Shopping A to Z

### ANTIQUES

In addition to the places that follow, a number of antiques shops line Hildebrand between Blanco and San Pedro, and McCullough between Hildebrand and Basse.

**Center for Antiques.** 8505 Broadway. ☎ **210/804-6300.** www. centerforantiques.com.

More than 100 different vendors ply their goods at this huge (more than 35,000 sq. ft.) warehouse near the airport, making the Center for Antiques an eclectic and interesting place to shop; if you have time for only one antiques forage in San Antonio, this is the place. There are booths specializing in knickknacks, others in old records, jewelry, or clothes, and still others in good-quality furniture for serious collectors. Some contemporary Southwestern crafts are sold here, too.

**The Land of Was.** 3119 Broadway. ☎ **210/822-5265.**

Every inch of space on the two floors of this shop is crammed with stuff—some of it strange and funky, more of it rare and pricey. The store is especially strong on Spanish colonial and Mexican antiques; if you're seeking an altarpiece or a treasure chest, try here first.

## ART GALLERIES

In the Southtown section near King William, the **Blue Star Arts Complex,** 1400 S. Alamo (☎ **210/227-6960**), is the up-and-coming place to buy art; see "More Attractions," in chapter 6, for details. Downtown is also beginning to hold its own in the art world, as more and more galleries enter the area. For a copy of the **San Antonio Gallery Guide,** prepared by the San Antonio Art Gallery Association, stop by the San Antonio Convention and Visitors Bureau, 317 Alamo Plaza (☎ **800/447-3372** or 210/207-6700). You can also check out the art scene online at the Office of Cultural Affairs' Web site, **www.ci.sat.tx.us/daca/Galleries.htm**, with links to several local galleries.

**Finesilver Gallery.** 816 Camaron St., Suites 1 and 2. ☎ **210/354-3333.** www.finesilver.com.

Just north of downtown near Flores Street, a converted uniform manufacturing plant is home to this large contemporary art gallery (as well as to offices for creative types like architects and Web designers). Expect minimalist and conceptual or whatever's on the cutting edge.

**Galería Ortíz.** 102 Concho (in Market Sq.). ☎ **210/225-0731.** www.galeriaortiz.com.

If a big-name artist is represented or temporarily shown in town, it'll be at Galería Ortíz, San Antonio's premier Southwestern gallery. The emphasis is on local San Antonio artists and Native American and New Mexican painters.

**Nanette Richardson Fine Art.** 513 E. Houston St. ☎ **210/224-1550.** www.nanetterichardson.com.

This downtown gallery, and the newer one near the Quarry (see "Malls/Shopping Complexes," below), at 555 E. Basse Rd., Suite 105 (☎ **210/930-1343**), carries a wide array of oils, watercolors, bronzes, ceramics, and handcrafted wood furnishings. Most of the art is traditional and representational, and the quality is uniformly high.

## CRAFTS

See also Alamo Fiesta, Red Iguana, San Angel Folk Art, and Tienda Guadalupe in "Gifts/Souvenirs," below.

**Southwest School of Art and Craft.** 300 Augusta. ☎ **210/224-1848.**

The gift shop at the restored Ursuline Academy for girls (see "More Attractions," in chapter 6, for details) sells handcrafted pottery, jewelry, clothing, and carryalls, most made by local artisans, and none of it run-of-the-mill.

## DEPARTMENT STORES

**Dillard's.** 102 Alamo Plaza (Rivercenter Mall). ☎ **210/227-4343.** www.dillards.com.

You'll find branches of this Arkansas-based chain in many Southwestern cities and in a number of San Antonio malls; all offer nice mid- to upper-range clothing and housewares, but the Dillard's in the Rivercenter Mall has a section specializing in Western fashions. Enter or exit on Alamo Plaza so you can get a look at the historic building's ornate facade (see "Walking Tour: Downtown," in chapter 6, for details).

**Saks Fifth Avenue.** 650 North Star Mall. ☎ **210/341-4111.**

Forget low-key and unobtrusive; this is Texas. Sure, this department store has the high-quality, upscale wares and attentive service one would expect from a Saks Fifth Avenue, but it also has a 40-foot-high pair of cowboy boots standing out front.

## FASHIONS

The following stores offer clothing in a variety of styles; if you're keen on the cow-puncher look, see "Western Wear," below.

### CHILDREN'S FASHION

**Bambinos.** 5934 Broadway. ☎ **210/822-9595.**

Whether your child goes in for the English Country look or veers more towards punk-rocker, you'll find something to suit his or her (okay—your) tastes at this delightful store, which also carries a great selection of kiddie room furnishings and toys. The focus is on the younger set—infants up to age 7.

### MEN'S FASHION

**Satel's.** 5100 Broadway. ☎ **210/822-3376.**

This family-run Alamo Heights store has been the place to shop for menswear in San Antonio since 1950; classic, high-quality clothing and personal service make it a standout. The neighborhood's most famous former resident, Tommy Lee Jones, has been spotted here.

**Todd's Inc.** 7400 San Pedro, Suite 722 (North Star Mall). ☎ **210/349-6464.**

Mexico's elite come to Todd's to buy their suits, casual wear, and accessories. Fine style doesn't come cheap, however; shop here only if you're prepared to part with some big bucks.

### WOMEN'S FASHION

**Adelante Boutique.** 6414 N. New Braunfels Ave. (in Sunset Ridge). ☎ **210/826-6770.**

The focus here is on the ethnic and the handmade, with lots of colorful, natural fabrics and free-flowing lines. The store also offers a nice selection of leather belts and whimsical jewelry and gifts.

**✪ Kathleen Sommers.** 2417 N. Main. ☎ **210/732-8437.**

This small shop on the corner of Main and Woodlawn has been setting trends for San Antonio women for years. Kathleen Sommers, who works mainly in linen and other natural fabrics, designs all the clothes, which bear her label. The store also carries great jewelry, bath items, books, fun housewares, and a selection of unusual gifts, including the San Antonio–originated Soular Therapy candles.

**Mirabella.** 5910 Broadway. ☎ **210/829-4435.**

Super-stylish but friendly Mirabella owner Misti Riedel buys clothes according to the credo, "Girls just wanna have fun." If it's sexy, colorful, creative, and wearable, you'll find it here. Good looks never come cheap, but many of the designers represented on the racks of this cozy shop are not well known, which means costs are by no means prohibitive either. And if you're lucky, there'll be a sale on.

# FOOD

✪ **Central Market.** 4821 Broadway. ☎ **210/368-8600.**

Free valet parking at a supermarket? On Saturday and Sunday, so many locals converge to take advantage of the huge array of delectable samples, that it's easy to understand why the store is willing to help alleviate parking stress. You'll feel as though you've died and gone to food heaven as you walk amid gorgeous mounds of produce (I've never seen so many types of chiles), cheeses and other dairy products (ditto), sauces, pastas, etc., etc. If you don't want to just graze, there are freshly prepared hot and cold gourmet foods, including a soup and salad bar, and a seating area in which to enjoy them. Wine tastings and cooking classes draw crowds in the evenings.

# GIFTS/SOUVENIRS

✪ **Alamo Fiesta.** 2025 N. Main at Ashby. ☎ **210/738-1188.**

Head just north of downtown to this two-level store near Monte Vista for a huge selection of Mexican folk art and handicrafts—everything from tinwork to colorful masks and piñatas—at extremely reasonable prices. Less touristy than most such shops, Alamo Fiesta is geared to local Hispanic families looking to celebrate special occasions.

**The Red Iguana.** 918 South Alamo St. ☎ **210/281-9667.**

A high-quality array of Mexican arts and crafts—polished and painted gourds, shoemakers' forms covered with *milagros,* intricately wrought silver jewelry (vintage and new), Spanish colonial–style paintings, and colorfully embroidered clothing, to name a few—have been gathered and/or created by Eduardo Tijerina, whose two-level gallery is one of Southtown's most interesting shops. You can find everything here from $15 T-shirts to paintings that run into four figures.

**San Angel Folk Art.** 1404 S. Alamo, Suite 410 in the Blue Star Arts Complex. ☎ **210/226-6688.**

Combing the crafts markets of Mexico might be more fun, but exploring this large store in the Blue Star Arts Complex is a pretty good substitute. Painted animals from Oaxaca, elaborate masks from the state of Guerrero—this place is chock-a-block with the colorful, whimsical, and well made. Of course, prices are better south of the border, but hey, you're saving on the airfare.

**Sloan/Hall.** 5922 Broadway. ☎ **210/828-7738.**

A cross between The Body Shop, Sharper Image, and Borders, only more concentrated and more upscale, this addictive boutique carries an assortment of toiletries, gadgets, books, and those uncategorizable items that you probably don't need but find you desperately want.

**Tienda Guadalupe Folk Art & Gifts.** 1001 S. Alamo. ☎ **210/226-5873.**

This incense-scented shop in the Southtown/King William area is brimming with things Hispanic: painting and handicrafts from Latin America, Mexican antiques and religious items, and more. Come here to pick up a Day of the Dead T-shirt or anything else relating to the early November holiday celebrated with great fanfare in San Antonio.

# JEWELRY

See also "Crafts" and "Gifts/Souvenirs."

✪ **Chamade Jewelers.** 504 Villita St. (La Villita). ☎ **210/224-7753.** www.lavillita.com/chamade.

Expect the unexpected and the beautiful at this dazzling jewelry store, representing more than 30 U.S. and international artists. You'll find everything from classically

# Love Potion No. 9

Ask a proprietor of a **botanica,** "What kind of store is this?" and you'll hear anything from "a drugstore" to "a religious bookstore." But along with Christian artifacts (including glow-in-the-dark rosaries and dashboard icons), botanicas carry magic floor washes, candles designed to keep the law off your back, wolf skulls, amulets, herbal remedies, and, of course, love potions. The common theme is happiness enhancement, whether by self-improvement, prayer, or luck.

Many of San Antonio's countless small botanicas specialize in articles used by *curanderas:* traditional folk doctors or medicine men and women. Books directing laypersons in the use of medicinal herbs sit next to volumes that retell the lives of the saints. It's easy enough to figure out the use of the *santos* (saints), candles in tall glass jars to which are affixed such labels as "Peaceful Home," "Find Work," and "Bingo." *Milagros* (miracles) are small charms that represent parts of the body—or mind—that a person wishes to have healed. Don't worry that many of the labels are in Spanish; the person behind the counter will be happy to translate.

**Papa Jim's,** 5630 S. Flores (☎ **210/922-6665**), is the best known of all the botanicas; for a small extra charge, Papa Jim will bless almost anything you buy. And his mail-order business will help take care of any problem you might experience down the road.

designed gold rings with precious gemstones to funny sterling silver earrings encasing beans for one ear and rice for the other. Some of the creations are crafted by local and Southwest artisans, including Native Americans; others come from as far afield as France, Italy, China, and Indonesia.

**Gavin Metalsmith.** 4024 McCullough St. ☎ **210/821-5254.**

For contemporary metal craft at its most creative, come to this small women's crafts gallery, where the exquisite original pieces range from wedding rings to salt-and-pepper shakers. The artists whose work is sold here incorporate lots of unusual stones into (mostly) silver and white gold settings. They also frequently do custom work, for fair prices.

## MALLS/SHOPPING COMPLEXES

✪ **Alamo Quarry Market.** 255 E. Basse Rd. ☎ **210/225-1000.**

Alamo Quarry Market may be its official name, but no one ever calls San Antonio's hottest newcomer to the mall scene anything but "The Quarry" (from the early 1900s until 1985, the property was in fact a cement quarry). The four smokestacks, lit up dramatically at night, now signal play, not work. There are no anchoring department stores, but a series of large emporiums (Old Navy; Bed, Bath & Beyond; Office Max; and Borders) and smaller upscale boutiques (Laura Ashley, Aveda, and Lucchese Gallery—see "Western Wear," below) will keep you happily spending. A multiplex cinema and an array of refueling stations—Chili's and Starbucks, as well as the more upscale Koi Kowa (see chapter 5) and Piatti's, an Italian eatery well liked by locals—complete this temple to self-indulgence.

**Central Park Mall.** Loop 410 and Blanco. ☎ **210/344-2236.**

Lots of shoppers ogle the goods at North Star Mall and then head next door to Central Park, where they can actually afford to buy something. Anchored by Bealls and

Sears department stores, this mall has lots of popular chains among its 90-plus stores, and many reasonably priced places to eat in its food court.

**Crossroads of San Antonio Mall.** 4522 Fredericksburg Rd. (off Loop 410 and I-10). ☎ **210/735-9137.**

Located near the South Texas Medical Center, this is San Antonio's bargain mall, featuring Burlington Coat Factory, Montgomery Ward, and SteinMart department stores alongside smaller discount shops. The recent addition of glitzier shops and Tuesday morning line dancing is part of an effort to draw San Antonians to this low-profile shopping destination.

**Heubner Oaks Shopping Center.** 11745 I-10. ☎ **210/697-8444.**

This upscale open-air mall houses a variety of yuppie favorites, including Old Navy, The GAP, Banana Republic, Victoria's Secret, and Eddie Bauer. When your energy flags, retreat to one of several casual dining spots like La Madeleine, serving good fast French food, or head straight to Starbucks for a caffeinated shopping boost.

✪ **Los Patios.** 2015 NE Loop 410, at the Starcrest exit. ☎ **210/655-6171.**

The self-proclaimed "other River Walk" features about a dozen upscale specialty shops in a lovely 18-acre wooded setting. You'll find shops carrying imported clothing, crafts, jewelry, and antique furniture among other offerings here. Although the food at Los Patios's two restaurants isn't especially notable, the setting is hard to beat: The Brazier looks out over Salado Creek (the restaurant was flooded in 2000, but should be reopened by the time you read this), and the Gazebo has a patio shaded by oaks.

**North Star Mall.** Loop 410, between McCullough and San Pedro. ☎ **210/340-6627.**

Starring Saks Fifth Avenue and upscale boutiques like Abercrombie & Fitch, Pappagallo, Aveda, Laura Ashley, and Williams-Sonoma, this is the crème de la crème of the San Antonio malls. But there are many sensible shops here, too, including a Mervyn's department store. Food choices also climb up and down the scale, ranging from a Godiva Chocolatier to a Luby's Cafeteria.

**Rivercenter Mall.** 849 E. Commerce, between S. Alamo and Bowie. ☎ **210/225-0000.** www.shoprivercenter.com.

There's a festive atmosphere at this bustling, light-filled mall, fostered, among other things, by its location on an extension of the San Antonio River. You can pick up a ferry from a downstairs dock or listen to bands play on a stage surrounded by water. Other entertainment options include the IMAX theater, the multiple-screen AMC, the Cyber Zone video arcade, and the Rivercenter Comedy Club. The shops—more than 130 of them, anchored by Dillard's and Foleys—run the price gamut, but tend toward upscale casual. If you get hungry, there's everything from Dairy Queen and A&W Hot Dogs to Morton's of Chicago, along with the restaurants at the huge Rivercenter Marriott.

# MARKETS

**Market Square.** 514 W. Commerce St. (near Dolorosa). ☎ **210/207-8600.**

Two large indoor markets, El Mercado and the Farmer's Market—often just called, collectively, the Mexican market—occupy adjacent blocks on Market Square. Competing for your attention are more than 100 shops and pushcarts, eight restaurants, and an abundance of food stalls. The majority of the shopping booths are of the border town sort, filled with onyx chess sets, cheap sombreros, and the like, but you can also find a few higher quality boutiques, including Galería Ortíz (see above). Come here for a bit of local color, good people-watching, and food—in addition to the sit-down Mi Tierra and La Margarita, detailed in chapter 5, there are loads of primo places for street snacking. You'll often find yourself shopping to the beat of a mariachi band.

## FLEA MARKETS

**Bussey's Flea Market.** 18738 I-35 North. ☎ **210/651-6830.**

Unless you're heading to New Braunfels or Austin, Bussey's is a bit out of the way. But these 20 acres of vendors selling goods from as far afield as Asia and Africa are definitely worth the drive (about a half-hour north of downtown). Crafts, jewelry, antiques, incense—besides perishables, it's hard to imagine anything you couldn't find at this market.

**Eisenhauer Road Flea Market.** 3903 Eisenhauer Rd. ☎ **210/653-7592.**

The all-indoors, all–air-conditioned Eisenhauer, complete with snack bar, is a good flea market to hit at the height of summer. You'll see lots of new stuff here—purses, jewelry, furniture, toys, shoes—and everything from houseplants to kinky leatherwear. Closed Monday and Tuesday.

**Flea Mart.** 12280 Hwy. 16 S. (about 1 mile south of Loop 410). ☎ **210/624-2666.**

On weekends, Mexican-American families make a day of this huge market, bringing the entire family to exchange gossip, listen to live bands, and eat freshly made tacos. There are always fruits and vegetables, electronics, crafts, and new and used clothing—and you never know what else.

## TOYS

The following stores (along with Bambinos—see "Fashions," above) carry unusual but often pricey toys. If your child is especially hard on playthings or your cash supply is running low, consider buying used toys at **Kids Junction Resale Shop,** 2267 NW Military Hwy. (☎ **210/340-5532**), or **Too Good to Be Threw,** 7115 Blanco (☎ **210/340-2422**).

**Monarch Collectibles.** 2012 NW Military Hwy. ☎ **800/648-3655** or 210/341-3655.

Welcome to doll heaven. Many of the models that fill Monarch's four rooms—about 3,000 dolls in all—are collectible and made from delicate materials like porcelain and baked clay, but others are cute and cuddly. Some come with real hair and eyelashes, and some are one of a kind. Doll furniture is also sold here—with a 6,000-square-foot dollhouse to showcase it—along with plates and a few stuffed animals. An entire room is devoted to Barbies. (Maybe the other dolls don't want to play with them.)

**Playworks.** 1812 Nacogdoches (at N. New Braunfels). ☎ **210/828-3400.**

It's a tossup who's going to spend more time oohing and aahing their way through this store, children or their parents. Along with the detailed Playmobil universe, imported from Germany, Playworks carries all kinds of life-science projects: Ant farms, Grow-A-Frog, butterfly gardens . . . you'd be amazed at the creatures that are sent through the mail. For something more huggable, there are also Steif teddy bears, as well as the largest selection of Madame Alexander dolls in town. Adults will have trouble staying away from the nostalgia toys: pogo sticks, stilts, and puppet theaters. A second Playworks store is located at 1931 NW Military Hwy. (☎ **210/340-2328**).

## WESTERN WEAR

**Boot Hill.** Rivercenter Mall, 849 E. Commerce, Ste. 213. ☎ **210/223-6634.** www.boothillwesternstore.com.

This one-stop shopping center for all duds Western, from Tony Lama boots to Stetson hats and everything in between, is one of the few left in town that's locally owned. Arnold Schwarzenegger and Ashley Judd are among the big names that have been outfitted here. This is a great store with terrific goods, but as an Arizonan, I feel compelled to mention that the *real* Boot Hill is in my home state (hey, y'all have got the Alamo). Boot Hill has another branch in the northwest, at 8023 Callaghan Rd. near I-10 West (☎ **210/341-4685**), as well as a major presence on the Internet.

○ **Lucchese Gallery.** 255 E. Basse, Suite 800. ☎ **210/828-9419.** www.lucchese.com.

The name says it all: Footwear is raised to the level of art at Lucchese. If it ever crawled, ran, hopped, or swam, these folks can probably put it on your feet. The store carries boots made of alligator, elephant, ostrich, kangaroo, stingray, and lizard. Come here for everything from executive to special-occasion boots, all handmade and expensive and all serious Texas status symbols. Lucchese also carries jackets, belts, and sterling silver belt buckles.

✪ **Paris Hatters.** 119 Broadway. ☎ **210/223-3453.**

What do Pope John Paul II, Prince Charles, Jimmy Smits, and Dwight Yoakam have in common? They've all had headgear made for them by Paris Hatters, in business since 1917 and still owned by the same family. About half of the sales are special orders, but the shelves are stocked with high-quality ready-to-wear hats, including Kangol caps from Britain, Panama hats from Ecuador, and, of course, Stetson, Resistol, Dobbs, and other Western brands. A lot of them can be adjusted to your liking while you wait. Check out the pictures and newspaper articles in the back of the store to see which other famous heads have been covered here.

## WINES

See also Central Market under "Food."

**Gabriel's.** 837 Hildebrand. ☎ **210/735-8329.**

A large, warehouse-style store, Gabriel's combines good selection with good prices. You never know what oenological bargains you'll find on any given day. The Hildebrand store is slightly north of downtown; there's also another location near the airport at 7233 Blanco (☎ **210/349-7472**).

**SeaZar's Fine Wine & Spirits.** 6422 N. New Braunfels, in the Sunset Ridge Shopping Center. ☎ **210/822-6094.**

A temperature-controlled wine cellar, a large selection of beer and spirits, a cigar humidor, and a knowledgeable staff all make this a good choice for aficionados of the various legal vices. Thirsty in the northwest? There's a branch at 16625 Huebner Rd. (☎ **210/479-0315**).

# San Antonio After Dark    **8**

San Antonio has its symphony and its Broadway shows, and you can see both at one of the most beautiful old movie palaces in the country. But much of what the city has to offer is less mainstream. Latin influences lend spice to some of the best local night life: San Antonio is America's capital for Tejano music, a unique blend of German polka and northern Mexico ranchero sounds, with a dose of pop for good measure. You can sit on one side of the San Antonio River and watch colorful dance troupes like Ballet Folklórico perform on the other. A Latino Laugh Festival, first held in the summer of 1996, has become an annual event. And Southtown, with its many Hispanic-oriented shops and galleries, celebrates its art scene with the monthly First Friday, a kind of extended block party.

Keep in mind, too, that the Fiesta City throws big public parties year-round: Fiestas Navideñas and Las Posadas around Christmastime; Fiesta San Antonio and Cinco de Mayo events in spring; the Texas Folklife Festival in summer; and the Day of the Dead celebration in fall (see also "San Antonio Calendar of Events," in chapter 2).

For the most complete listings of what's on while you're visiting, pick up a free copy of the weekly alternative newspaper, the **Current,** or the Friday "Weekender" section of the **San Antonio Express-News.** You can also check out the **San Antonio Arts & Cultural Affairs Hotline** at ☎ **800/894-3819** or 210/207-2166 (www.ci.sat.tx.us/daca). There's no central office in town for tickets, discounted or otherwise. You'll need to reserve seats directly through the theaters or clubs, or, for large events, through **Ticketmaster** (☎ **210/224-9600;** www.ticketmaster. com). Generally, box office hours are Monday to Friday 10am to 5pm, and 1 to 2 hours before performance time. The Majestic and Empire also have hours on Saturday 10am to 3pm.

## 1 The Performing Arts

The San Antonio Symphony is the city's only resident performing arts company of national stature, but smaller, less professional groups keep the local arts scene lively, and cultural organizations draw world-renowned artists. The city provides them with some unique venues—everything from standout historic structures like the Majestic, Empire, Arneson, and Sunken Garden theaters to the 1990s high-tech Alamodome. Because, in some cases, the theater is the show and, in others, a single venue offers an eclectic array of performances, I've included a category called "Major Arts Venues," below.

## CLASSICAL MUSIC

**San Antonio Symphony.** 222 E. Houston St. ☎ **210/554-1000** or 210/554-1010 (box office). www.sasymphony.org. Tickets $15–$52.

San Antonio's symphony is one of the finest in the United States. Founded in 1939, the orchestra celebrated its 50th anniversary by moving into the stunning Majestic Theatre, the reopening of which was planned to coincide with the event (check the Web site for a spectacular picture of the stage). The symphony offers two major annual series, classical and pops. The former showcases the talents of music director Christopher Wilkens and a variety of guest performers (Pinchas Zukerman in the 2001 season, for example); for the latter, the orchestra plays second fiddle to the likes of James Taylor and Johnny Mathis.

## THEATER

**Actors Theater of San Antonio at the Woodlawn.** 1920 Fredericksburg Rd. ☎ **210/738-2872.** Tickets $8–$13.

Established in the early 1980s, the Actors Theater uses local talent for its productions, which tend to be in the off-Broadway tradition. Recent award-winning dramatic performances have included *When You Comin' Back, Red Rider?, The Last Night of Ballyhoo,* and *Lucifer's Child; You're A Good Man, Charlie Brown* and *Chicago* numbered among the musicals. The company is housed in a former movie theater; it was built in 1945 by the same architect who created the Majestic Theatre (see "Major Arts Venues," below), but the Actors Theater is as sleek in its art deco lines as the Majestic is ornate. The film *The Alamo* premiered here, and its star John Wayne turned up for the opening.

**Josephine Street Theater.** 339 W. Josephine St. ☎ **210/734-4646.** Tickets $18 adults, $16 seniors and military, $12 students, $8 children 12 and under.

This community-based company puts on an average of five productions a year at the art deco–style Josephine Street Theater, built in 1945. The award-winning group does mostly musicals—*Oliver, The Sound of Music, Bye, Bye Birdie,* and *42nd Street* featured in the 2000 season—but has also performed dramatic classics. The theater is only 5 minutes from downtown and around the corner from several restaurants and nightclubs.

**Jump-Start Performance Company.** 108 Blue Star Arts Complex (1400 S. Alamo). ☎ **210/227-JUMP.** Tickets $8–$10.

Whether it's an original piece by a member of the company or a work by a guest artist, anything you see at Jump-Start is likely to push the social and political envelope. This is the place to find the big-name performance artists like Karen Finley or Holly Hughes who tour San Antonio, and also to discover who's cutting it on the local cutting edge.

**Magik Theatre.** Beethoven Hall, 420 S. Alamo (HemisFair Park). ☎ **210/227-2751.** Tickets $8 adults, $7 seniors, $6 children. Performances Tues–Fri 9:30 and 11:30am; Sat–Sun 2pm; Fri–Sat 7pm. Reservations required.

As San Antonio's only professional family theater, established in 1993, the Magik has been getting more popular as word spreads of its delightful entertainment. A daytime series provides light fare for ages 3 and up, including *Charlie and the Chocolate Factory, The Best Christmas Pageant Ever,* and *Charlotte's Web.* Evening performances, recommended for those 6 and older, may include weightier plays such as *To Kill a Mockingbird* and *The Dreams of Anne Frank,* but may be no heavier than *Peter Pan: A Rock Opera* or *Anne of Green Gables.* About half the plays are adaptations of published scripts, while the other half are originals, created especially for the theater. Games played with the kids before performances release enough steam to turn them into (generally) polite spectators, and the children can interact with the genial professional actors after they leave the stage.

**San Pedro Playhouse.** 800 W. Ashby (at San Pedro Ave.). ☎ **210/733-7258.** www. members.tripod.com\San_Pedro_Playhouse. Tickets $20 adults, $18 seniors and active military, $11 students, $8 children 10 and under.

This local troupe presents a wide range of plays in a neoclassical-style performance hall built in 1930. The first public theater to open in San Antonio, it's being renovated in 2001, but will remain open. A recent season included the musicals *Sweeney Todd, Hello Dolly,* and *Scrooge,* as well as Tennessee Williams's *The Glass Menagerie.*

## MAJOR ARTS VENUES

See also the "For Those Interested in Hispanic Heritage" section of chapter 6 for information on the Alameda Theater.

✪ **Arneson River Theatre.** La Villita. ☎ **210/207-8610.** www.lavillita.com.

If you're visiting San Antonio in the summer, be sure to see something at the Arneson. Built by the Works Project Administration in 1939 as part of architect Robert Hugman's design for the River Walk, this unique theater stages shows on one side of the river while the audience watches from an amphitheater on the other. Most of the year, performance schedules are erratic and include everything from opera to Tejano, but May through August run on a strict calendar: the Fandango folkloric troupe every Wednesday, and the Fiesta Noche del Rio on Thursday to Saturday. Both offer lively music and dance with a south-of-the-border flair.

**Beethoven Home and Garden.** 422 Pereida. ☎ **210/222-1521.**

San Antonio's German heritage is celebrated at this venue, a converted 1894 Victorian mansion in the King William area. The season starts in April, with music and dance performances for the citywide Fiesta. This is followed by monthly concerts with the Mannerchor (men's choir), which dates back to 1867, as well as brass bands, dancers, singers, and other choirs, through September. Traditional German food, drink, and revelry make Oktoberfest an autumn high point. The hall closes down after the first Saturday in December, when a Kristkrindle Markt welcomes the holiday season with an old country–style arts-and-crafts fair.

**Carver Community Cultural Center.** 226 N. Hackberry. ☎ **210/207-7211** or 210/ 207-2234 (box office). www.thecarver.org. Tickets $10–$46.

Located near the Alamodome on the east edge of downtown, the Carver's theater was built for the city's African-American community in 1929, and hosted the likes of Ella Fitzgerald, Charlie "Bird" Parker, and Dizzy Gillespie over the years. It continues to serve the community while providing a widely popular venue for an international array of performers in a variety of genres, including drama, music, and dance. The 2000 to 2001 season saw performances as diverse as Koko Taylor & Her Blues Machine, Aeros (dance by Romanian gymnasts), the London Opera's *Carmen,* and Isaac Hayes. The cultural center is undergoing a major renovation as part of a $12 million Carver Complex project, so some performances may be held at different San Antonio venues.

**The Empire Theatre.** 208 E. Houston St. ☎ **210/226-5700.**

Among the celebrities who trod the boards of the Empire Theatre before its motion picture prime were Roy Rogers and Trigger; Mae West put in an appearance, too. Fallen into disrepair and shuttered for 2 decades, this 1914 opera house made its grand re-debut in 1998 after a massive renovation by the Las Casas Foundation. Layers of thick, white paint were chipped off to reveal beautiful plasterwork, which was restored to its original rich colors; pounds of 23-karat gold leaf were painstakingly reapplied by hand. Smaller than its former rival the Majestic (see below and chapter 6), just down the block, the Empire hosts a similarly eclectic array of acts, from David Crosby and the Preservation Hall Jazz Band to children's theater and shows like *Always Patsy Cline.*

**Guadalupe Cultural Arts Center.** 1300 Guadalupe. ☎ **210/271-3151.** www. guadalupeculturalarts.org.

There's always something happening at the Guadalupe Center, the heart of Latino cultural activity in San Antonio. Visiting and local directors put on six or seven plays a year; the resident Guadalupe Dance Company might collaborate with the city's symphony or invite modern masters up from Mexico City. The Xicano Music Program celebrates the popular local conjunto and Tejano sounds; an annual book fair brings in Spanish-language literature from around the world; and the CineFestival, running since 1977, is one of the town's major film events. And then there are always the parties thrown to celebrate new installations at the theater's art gallery and its annex.

**Laurie Auditorium.** Trinity University, 715 Stadium Dr. ☎ **210/999-8117** (taped box office information line) or 210/999-8119.

Some pretty high-powered people turn up at the Laurie Auditorium, on the Trinity University campus in the north-central part of town. Everyone from Margaret Thatcher to Colin Powell has taken part in the university's Distinguished Lecture Series, subsidized by grants and open to the public for free. The 2,700-seat hall also hosts major players in the popular and performing arts: Bill Cosby was among those who took the stage in the 2000 to 2001 season. Dance recitals, jazz concerts, and plays, many with internationally renowned artists, are held here, too.

✪ **Majestic Theatre.** 230 E. Houston. ☎ **210/226-3333.**

This theater introduced air-conditioning to San Antonio—the hall was billed beforehand as "an acre of cool, comfortable seats"—and society women wore fur coats to its opening, held on a warm June night in 1929. The Majestic hosts some of the best entertainment in town—the symphony, major Broadway productions, big-name solo performers—and, thanks to a wonderful restoration of this fabulous showplace, completed in 1989, coming here is still pretty cool. See chapter 6 for details.

**Sunken Garden Theater.** Brackenridge Park, N. St. Mary's St. (Mulberry Ave. entrance). ☎ **210/207-3076.**

Built by the WPA in 1936 in a natural acoustic bowl in Brackenridge Park, the Sunken Garden Theater boasts an open-air stage set against a wooded hillside; cut-limestone buildings in Greek revival style hold the wings and the dressing rooms. This appealing outdoor arena offers a little bit of everything—rock, country, hip-hop, rap, jazz, Tejano, Cajun, and sometimes even the San Antonio Symphony. Bob Dylan, Kenny G., and Merle Haggard have all performed here, and the bard has been coming around almost every summer since 1990 for a week and a half of Shakespeare in the Park.

# A DINNER THEATER

**Alamo Street Restaurant & Theatre.** 1150 S. Alamo. ☎ **210/271-7791.** www. armadillo.nu. Show only $13; show and food $25. Usually dinner at 6pm, performance 8pm; Sun matinees, lunch at noon, performance at 2pm.

No matter which of its two venues you decide to attend, you're bound to have a good time at the King William district's Alamo Street Theatre. Interactive comedies and murder mysteries take place in the Green Room Dinner Theatre, where meals are buffet style. Entrees change depending on the accompanying comedy or thriller, but there are always soups, salads, veggies, and desserts to die for (as it were). Upstairs, on The Mainstage, there are lectures, concerts, musicals, comedies, and dramas, sans food. The church, now occupied by the Alamo Street Theater, was built in 1912 and is on the National Register of Historic Places. The interactive plays take place in what were once choir rooms; The Mainstage is in the old sanctuary.

# 2  The Club & Music Scene

The closest San Antonio comes to having a club district is the stretch of North St. Mary's between Josephine and Magnolia—just north of downtown and south of Brackenridge Park—known as the Strip. This area was hotter—or is that cooler?— about a decade ago, but it still draws young locals to its restaurants and lounges on the weekend. The River Walk clubs tend to be touristy, and many of them close early because of noise restrictions. As we went to press, the future was uncertain for downtown's **Sunset Station,** 1174 E. Commerce (☎ **210/222-9481**), a new multi-venue entertainment complex in the city's original train station. Presently, it is not subject to the residential regulations that prevent the River Walk venues from rocking into the wee hours, but stay tuned.

## COUNTRY & WESTERN

✪ **Floore Country Store.** 14664 Old Bandera Rd./Hwy. 16, Helotes (2 miles north of Loop 1604). ☎ **210/695-8827.** Cover $5–$25.

John P. Floore, the first manager of the Majestic Theatre and an unsuccessful candidate for mayor of San Antonio, opened up this country store in 1942. A couple of years later, he added a cafe and a dance floor—at half an acre, the largest in south Texas. And not much has changed since then. Boots, hats, and antique farm equipment hang from the ceiling of this typical Texas roadhouse, and the walls are lined with pictures of Willie Nelson, Hank Williams, Sr., Conway Twitty, Ernest Tubb, and other country greats who have played here. There's always live music on weekends; Dwight Yoakum, Robert Earl Keen, and Lyle Lovett have all turned up—along with Willie. The cafe still serves homemade bread, homemade tamales, and old-fashioned sausage.

**Leon Springs Dancehall.** 24135 I-10 (Boerne Stage Rd. exit). ☎ **210/698-7072.** Cover usually $5; kids under 12 free.

This lively 1880s-style dance hall can—and often does—pack some 1,200 people into its 18,000 square feet. Lots of people come with their kids when the place opens at 7pm; the crowd turns older (but not much) as the evening wears on. Some of the best local country-and-western talent is showcased here on Friday and Saturday nights, the only two nights the dancehall is open.

## ROCK

**Taco Land.** 103 W. Grayson St. ☎ **210/223-8406.** Cover $3 Fri–Sat; free during the week.

Loud and not much to look at—low ceilings, red vinyl booths, garage pin-up calendars stapled to the ceiling—tiny Taco Land is the hottest alternative music club in San Antonio, showcasing everything from mainstream rock to surf punk. Some of the bands that turn up may seem less than impressive, but, hey, you never know: Nirvana played here before they hit the big time. Name notwithstanding, Taco Land only began serving tacos fairly recently.

# Conjunto: An American Classic

Cruise a San Antonio radio dial or go to any major city festival, and you'll most likely hear the happy, boisterous sound of conjunto. Never heard of it? Don't worry, you're not alone. Although conjunto is one of our country's original contributions to world music, for a long time few Americans outside Texas knew much about it.

**Conjunto** evolved at the end of the 19th century, when South Texas was swept by a wave of German immigrants who brought with them popular polkas and waltzes. These sounds were easily incorporated into—and transformed by— Mexican folk music; the newcomer accordion, cheap and able to mimic several instruments, was happily adopted, too. With the addition at the turn of the century of the *bajo sexto,* a 12-string guitarlike instrument used for rhythmic bass accompaniment, conjunto was born.

**Tejano** (Spanish for "Texas") is the 20th-century offspring of conjunto. The two most prominent instruments in Tejano remain the accordion and the *bajo sexto,* but the music incorporates more modern forms, including pop, jazz, and country-and-western, into the traditional conjunto repertoire. At clubs not exclusively devoted to Latino sounds, what you're likely to hear is Tejano.

Long ignored by the mainstream, conjunto and Tejano were brought into America's consciousness by the murder of Hispanic superstar **Selena.** Before she was killed, Selena had already been slotted for crossover success—she had done the title song and put in a cameo appearance in the film *Don Juan de Marco* with Johnny Depp—and the movie based on her life boosted awareness of her music even further.

San Antonio is to conjunto music what Nashville is to country. The most famous *bajo sextos,* used nationally by everyone who is anyone in conjunto and Tejano music, were created in San Antonio by the Macías family—the late Martín and now his son, Alberto. The undisputed king of conjunto, **Flaco Jimenez**—a mild-mannered triple-Grammy winner who has recorded with the Rolling Stones, Bob Dylan, and Willie Nelson, among others—lives in the city. And San Antonio's **Tejano Conjunto Festival,** held every May (see "San Antonio Calendar of Events," in chapter 2), is the largest of its kind, drawing aficionados from around the world—there's even a conjunto band from Japan.

Most of the places to hear conjunto/Tejano are off the beaten tourist path, on the city's west side, and they come and go fairly quickly. Your hotel should be able to recommend one that's currently big. You can also phone **Salute!** (see below) to find out which night of the week they're featuring a Tejano or conjunto band. The best place to hear the lively music is at one of San Antonio's many festivals.

**White Rabbit.** 2410 N. St. Mary's St. ☎ **210/737-2221.** Cover varies.

One of the few alternative rock venues on the Strip—and one of the only ones large enough to have a raised stage—the Rabbit attracts a mostly young crowd to its black-lit recesses. Those 18 to 20 years old are allowed in for a higher cover.

## JAZZ & BLUES

✪ **The Landing.** Hyatt Regency Hotel, River Walk. ☎ **210/223-7266.** www.landing.com. Cover $6.50 Fri–Sat only.

You might have heard cornetist Jim Cullum on the airwaves: His American Public Radio program, *Riverwalk, Live from the Landing,* initiated in 1988, is now broadcast on more than 225 stations nationwide. The Landing is one of the best traditional jazz clubs in the country; if you like big bands and Dixieland, there's no better place to listen to music downtown. Jim Cullum and his band have backed some of the finest jazz artists of our time. The Landing Cafe features an eclectic menu with lots of New Orleans–style touches.

**Salute!** 2801 N. St. Mary's St. ☎ **210/732-5307.** Cover $3–$5 weekends; free during the week.

The live jazz at this tiny club tends to have a Latin base, but you never know what you're going to hear—anything from synthesized '70s sounds to conjunto.

**Tycoon Flats.** 2926 N. St. Mary's St. ☎ **210/737-1929.** No cover.

A friendly music garden, Tycoon Flats is a fun place to kick back and listen to blues, rock, acoustic, or jazz. The burgers are good, too. Bring the kids—an outdoor sandbox is larger than the dance floor. There's never any cover for the almost nightly live music.

## A DANCE CLUB

**Polly Esther's.** 212 College St. ☎ **210/220-1972.** Cover $3–$8, depending on night.

Coincidence that the last four digits in the telephone number of this lively, three-level River Walk club match the year that the disco craze started to take hold? I think not. Even if you've sworn off strobe forever, your arms and feet are likely to take on a life of their own once you hear that funky beat—especially if you indulge in one of the club's signature liqueur drinks. They sound innocuous (Peanut Butter 'n' Jelly, for example) and taste syrupy sweet, but pack a major wallop.

## A COMEDY CLUB

**Rivercenter Comedy Club.** 849 E. Commerce St. (Rivercenter Mall, third level). ☎ **210/229-1420.** www.hotcomedy.com. Cover $9 Mon–Thur, $12 Fri–Sun.

This club books big names in stand-up like Dennis Miller and Garry Shandling, but it also takes advantage of local talent. Every other Monday, two ComedySportz teams improvise on athletic themes suggested by the audience. Every Friday is open-mike night in the Ha!Lapeno Lounge, and you can watch the Local Comedians Invitational Comedy Showcase for free on Saturday afternoons at 3:30.

## THE GAY SCENE

In addition to the Bonham (see below), Main Street just north of downtown has three gay clubs in close proximity (it's been nicknamed the "gay bar mall"). **Pegasus,** 1402 N. Main (☎ **210/299-4222;** no cover), is your basic cruise bar; **The Silver Dollar,** 1418 N. Main (☎ **210/227-2623;** no cover), does the country-and-western thing; and **The Saint,** 1430 N. Main (☎ **210/225-7330;** www.saintsshowbar.com; $4 over 21, $5 ages 18–21), caters to dancing fools.

**Bonham Exchange.** 411 Bonham. ☎ **210/271-3811.** No cover for ages 21 and over before 10pm (9pm on Wed), then $5; $5 all the time ages 17–20.

Tina Turner, Deborah Harry, and LaToya Jackson—the real ones—have all played this high-tech dance club near the Alamo. While you may find an occasional cross-dressing show here, the mixed crowd of gays and straights, young and old, come mainly to move to the beat under wildly flashing lights. All the action—five bars, three dance floors, three levels—takes place in a restored German-style building dating back to the 1880s. Roll over, Beethoven.

## 3 The Bar Scene

Most bars close at 2am, although some alternative spots stay open until 3 or 4am.

**Blue Star Brewing Company Restaurant & Bar.** 1414 S. Alamo, no. 105 (Blue Star Arts Complex). ☎ **210/212-5506.**

Preppies and gallery types don't often mingle, but the popularity of this brewpub in the Blue Star Arts Complex with college kids demonstrates the transcendent power of good beer. (The pale ale is especially fine.) And if a few folks who wouldn't know a Picasso from a piccolo wander in to see some art after dinner, the owners will have performed a public service. The food's good, too.

**Cadillac Bar & Restaurant.** 212 S. Flores. ☎ **210/223-5533.**

During the week, lawyers and judges come to unwind at the Cadillac Bar, set in a historic stucco building near the Bexar County Courthouse and City Hall. On the weekends, singles take over the joint. A deejay spins on Wednesday and Saturday nights, but on Fridays, the sounds are live and local—anything from '70s disco to classic rock to pop. Full dinners are served on a patio out back.

**Cappycino's.** 5003 Broadway. ☎ **210/828-6860.**

Although it's by no means deficient in the caffeine department, don't mistake Cappycino's for a coffee bar: The name derives from neighboring Cappy's restaurant (see chapter 5), of which it's an offshoot. The forte here is yuppie hard stuff, including classic cocktails, tequilas, and single-malt scotches. A skinny but high-ceilinged lightwood dining room and a plant-filled patio create a relaxed setting for drinking and dining off the stylish Southwest bistro menu.

**Durty Nellie's Irish Pub.** 715 River Walk (Hilton Palacio del Rio Hotel). ☎ **210/222-1400.**

Chug a lager and lime, toss your peanut shells on the floor, and sing along with the piano player at this wonderfully corny version of an Irish pub. You've forgotten the words to "Danny Boy"? Not to worry—18 old-time favorites are printed on the back of the menu. After a couple of Guinnesses, you'll be bellowing "H-A, double R-I, G-A-N spells Harrigan," loud as the rest of 'em.

**Houston Street Alehouse.** 420 E. Houston. ☎ **210/354-4694.** www.houstonalehouse.com.

A hundred bottles of beer on the wall, and all of them different brands—not to mention the 25 brews on tap. Add a large selection of martinis, some expensive cigars, and lots of glass, wood, and brass, and you've got your basic collegiate bar, only a few blocks from the River Walk.

**Howl at the Moon Saloon.** 111 W. Crockett St. ☎ **210/212-4695.** www.howlatthemoon. com.

It's hard to avoid having a good time at this rowdy River Walk bar next to the Hard Rock Cafe; if you're shy, one of the dueling piano players will inevitably embarrass you into joining the crowd belting out off-key oldies from the '60s, '70s, and '80s. Not to worry. You're not likely to see most of these people ever again.

✪ **La Tuna.** 100 Probant. ☎ **210/224-8862.**

Gallery groupies tend to gather at this bar in Southtown's Blue Star Arts district—look for the brightly colored sign on a tiny concrete-and-corrugated aluminum building—but lots of less-creative types drop by for a beer, too. You can sit on the patio and watch the trains roll slowly by a block away; after downtown parades, the floats cruise past on their way back to the warehouses. There's music on Saturday night, weather permitting, year-round; in winter, a bonfire blazes from a pit built into the patio.

**The Laboratory.** 7310 Jones-Maltsberger. ☎ **210/824-1997.** www.labbrew.com.

One of the few microbreweries in San Antonio, and the only place in town that makes an "authentic" Bavarian *hefeweizen,* "The Lab" used to be the laboratory for the old Alamo Quarry cement factory. Stress tests were once conducted in the room where the beer is now brewed, but the only stress these days involves working up the nerve to walk up to that attractive stranger. For fortification, you can down dauntingly large sandwiches, nachos, and the like in the huge, two-level main room or on an outdoor patio, where trees do their best to hide the brightly lit Quarry shopping mall nearby. There's live music Monday and Thursday through Saturday.

✪ **Menger Bar.** Menger Hotel, 204 Alamo Plaza. ☎ **210/223-4361.**

More than 100 years ago, Teddy Roosevelt recruited men for his Rough Riders unit at this dark, wooded bar; they were outfitted for the Spanish-American War at nearby Fort Sam Houston. Constructed in 1859 on the site of William Menger's earlier successful brewery and saloon, the bar was moved from its original location in the Victorian hotel lobby in 1956, but 90% of its historic furnishings remain intact. You can still see an "X" on the bar (modeled after the bar in the House of Lords in London) put there by prohibitionist Carrie Nation, and Spanish Civil War uniforms hang on the walls. It's still one of the prime spots in town to toss back a few.

**Nile's Wine Bar.** 7319 Broadway. ☎ **210/826-8463.**

The quintessential yuppie hangout, this softly lit former farmhouse has its extensive wine list conveniently arranged by taste rather than vintage or price. Whites, for example, start out light and fruity and move to full-bodied and dry. The selections change approximately every 2 months, except for a few favorites. Nile's serves only appetizers, mainly assorted cheese plates, so you might want to fuel up at Beto's (see chapter 5) next door if you don't want to get too lightheaded. An eclectic array of live bands, including some singer/songwriters from Austin, turn up Thursday through Saturday.

**Polo's Lounge.** Fairmount Hotel, 401 S. Alamo St. ☎ **210/224-8800.**

For a piano, bass, and sax trio in a high-tone atmosphere, come to Polo's on a Friday or Saturday night. You can sink into a plush leather couch or perch on a stool at the marble bar and enjoy some jazz, swing, or Broadway sounds. This romantic spot tends to draw an older crowd, who can afford the drinks.

**Stone Werks Caffe and Bar.** 7300 Jones-Maltsberger. ☎ **210/828-3508.**

Right next door to The Laboratory (see above), Stone Werks attracts a slightly older (30-something) crowd than its neighbor, but it's equally lively, with local cover bands getting the crowd moving on the dance floor from Thursday through Saturday. It's also got an equally distinctive setting: It's housed in a 1920s building that used to be the Alamo Cement Company's office. An oak-shaded patio is surrounded by a fence handsculpted from cement by Mexican artist Dionicio Rodriguez.

**Swig.** 111 W. Crockett, no. 205. ☎ **210/476-0005.**

Craving a chocolate martini? Belly up to the freeform bar at the River Walk's latest nod to retro chic. Single-barrel bourbon, single-malt scotch, as well as a wide selection of beer and wines fill out the drinks menu, but James Bond's preferred poison is always the top seller. Nightly live jazz adds to the pizzazz. The catch (or draw) here is those big cigars.

✪ **Tex's.** San Antonio Airport Hilton and Conference Center, 611 NW Loop 410. ☎ **210/ 340-6060.**

If you want to hang with the Spurs, come to Tex's, regularly voted San Antonio's best sports bar in the *Current* readers' polls. Three satellite dishes, two large-screen TVs, and 17 smaller sets keep the bleachers happy, as do the killer margaritas and giant burgers. Among Tex's major collection of exclusively Texas sports memorabilia are a signed Nolan Ryan jersey, a football used by the Dallas Cowboys in their 1978 Super Bowl victory, and one of George Gervin's basketball shoes (the other is at the newer Tex's on the River, at the Hilton Palacio del Rio).

✪ **Tower of the Americas.** 222 HemisFair Park. ☎ **210/223-3101.** www. toweroftheamericas.com.

No matter what, or how much, you have to drink, you'll get higher here than anywhere else in San Antonio—more than 700 feet high, in fact. Just below the observation-deck level, the bar at the Tower of the Americas Restaurant affords dazzling views of the city at night. Sample a Top of the Tower—light rum, vodka, apricot brandy, and fruit juices—and you might never want to come down.

✪ **Zinc.** 209 N. Presa St. ☎ **210/224-2900.**

Brought to you by the folks who own Boudro's restaurant, this chic wine bar, open until 2am nightly, is perfect for a romantic after-hours glass of champagne. Hardwood floors, brick walls, and a cozy library make the space appealing; on temperate nights, head for the pretty back patio.

## 4 Movies

There's not that much of an alternative cinema scene in San Antonio. Art and foreign movies turn up primarily at the **Crossroads Mall Theater,** Crossroads Mall, no. 14 Loop 410 at Fredericksburg Road (☎ **210/737-0291**). The **Guadalupe Cultural Arts Center** (see "Major Arts Venues," above) and the **McNay and Witte Museums** (see chapter 6) often have interesting film series, and the **Esperanza Center,** 922 San Pedro (☎ **210/228-0201;** www.esperanzacenter.org), offers a gay and lesbian cinema festival annually. In addition to *Alamo, the Price of Freedom,* the **IMAX Theater,** Rivercenter Mall, 217 Alamo Plaza (☎ **210/225-4629;** www.imax-sa.com), shows high-action films like *Jurassic Park* or *The Perfect Storm* suited to the big, big screen. In late 2001, the Aztec Theater will add its large-scale Iwerks format to the River Walk megaview options.

*Note:* The free weekly alternative, the *Current,* can't always be relied on to list film times or even titles. If you want to check out the flicks, pick up the Friday *San Antonio Express-News* and flip to the "Weekender" section.

# Planning a Trip to Austin

## 9

Planning a trip is not only half the fun of getting there; it also helps ensure your enjoyment when you arrive. See chapter 2 for additional information about planning your trip (the "Money" section discusses ATM networks and traveler's check agencies, and "Insurance" talks about trip cancellation, medical, and lost luggage insurance).

## 1 Visitor Information

Call the **Austin Convention and Visitors Bureau,** 201 E. Second St., Austin, TX 78701 (☎ **800/926-2282**), to receive a general information packet in the mail; the same toll-free number will connect you to a menu with recorded data on everything from the city's current events to its outdoor recreation and tour possibilities, or to a representative who can answer any of your specific questions. Austin is one of the country's most plugged-in cities. You can get tourism information online from the CVB at **www.austin360.com/acvb**. The Austin municipal site, **www.ci.austin.tx.us**, is a good source for the scoop on city services, including parks and recreation; you can also get links to almost all other Austin sites from it by clicking on the "Web Connections in Austin" option of the "Quick Connections" menu. The *Austin Chronicle,* the city's alternative newspaper, is also online: **www.auschron.com**.

See this same section in chapter 2 for suggestions on getting information about other parts of Texas.

## 2 When to Go

Because Austin doesn't have an overabundance of hotel rooms, it's always important to book ahead of time. Summer season is typically busy, but legislative sessions (the first half of odd-numbered years) and University of Texas events (graduation, say, or home-team games) can also fill up the town's lodgings quickly.

### CLIMATE

May showers follow April flowers in the Austin/Texas Hill Country area; by the time the late spring rains set in, the bluebonnets and most of the other wildflowers have already peaked. Mother Nature thoughtfully arranges mild, generally dry weather in which to enjoy her glorious floral arrangements in early spring—an ideal and deservedly popular time to visit. Summers can be steamy—the past several summers have seen atypically long stretches of triple-digit temperatures—but Austin offers plenty of great places to cool off, among them the Highland Lakes and Barton Springs. Fall foliage in this leafy area is another treat, and it's hard to beat a Texas evening by a cozy fireplace—admittedly more for show than for warmth in Austin, which generally enjoys mild winters.

**Austin's Average Monthly Temperature & Rainfall**

|  | Jan | Feb | Mar | Apr | May | June | July | Aug | Sept | Oct | Nov | Dec |
|---|---|---|---|---|---|---|---|---|---|---|---|---|
| Avg. Temp. (°F) | 52.0 | 54.5 | 60.8 | 68.2 | 75.3 | 81.9 | 84.0 | 83.8 | 79.3 | 70.5 | 59.7 | 53.2 |
| Rainfall (in.) | 1.66 | 2.06 | 1.54 | 2.54 | 3.07 | 2.79 | 1.69 | 2.41 | 3.71 | 2.84 | 1.77 | 1.46 |

# Austin Calendar of Events

A party for a fictional donkey and a tribute to canned meat? Austin wouldn't be Austin if some of its festivals weren't offbeat. Other events are more traditional, many capitalizing on the great outdoors and the large community of local musicians. The major annual events are listed below; see also chapter 15 for information on the various free concerts and other cultural events held every summer.

## January

- **Red Eye Regatta,** Austin Yacht Club, Lake Travis. The bracing lake air at this keelboat race should help cure what ails you from the night before. For information, try ☎ **512/266-1336;** www.austinyachtclub.org. New Year's Day.

## February

- **Carnival Brasileiro,** City Coliseum. Conga lines, elaborate costumes, samba bands, and confetti are all part of this sizzling event, started by homesick Brazilian University of Texas students in 1975. Call ☎ **512/452-6832.** First or second Saturday of the month.

## March

- **Star of Texas Fair and Rodeo,** Travis County Exposition Center. This 15-day Wild West extravaganza features rodeos, cattle auctions, a youth fair, a parade down Congress Avenue, and lots of live country music. ☎ **512/467-9811;** www.startexas.org. First half of the month.
- **Kite Festival,** Zilker Park. Colorful handmade kites fill the sky during this popular annual contest. Call ☎ **512/478-0905.** Second Sunday of the month.
- ✪ **South by Southwest (S×SW) Music and Media Conference & Festival.** The Austin Music Awards kick off this huge conference, which organizes hundreds of concerts at more than two dozen city venues. Aspiring music industry professionals sign up months in advance; keynote speakers have included Johnny Cash. ☎ **512/467-7979;** www.sxsw.com (see also chapter 15). Around the third week of March (during U.T.'s spring break).
- **Jerry Jeff Walker's Birthday Weekend,** various locations. Each year, the legendary singer/songwriter performs at such places as the Broken Spoke and the Paramount Theatre, and takes part in a golf tournament with other musicians. The man knows how to throw a party. ☎ **512/477-0036;** www.jerryjeff.com. Last weekend of the month.
- **Spamarama,** Auditorium Shores. The awards for creative cooking with Spam are the highlight of this hilarious event, judged by Texas celebrities; there's also a live music Spam Jam. ☎ **512/447-1605;** www.spamarama.com. Late March/early April.

| What Things Cost in Austin | U.S. $ | U.K. £ |
| --- | --- | --- |
| Taxi from the airport to downtown | 23.00–25.00 | 15.90–17.30 |
| Bus ride between any two downtown points | Free | Free |
| Local telephone call | 0.35 | 0.25 |
| Double at the Four Seasons (very expensive) | 250.00–325.00 | 173.10–225.00 |
| Double at the La Quinta Inn–Capitol (moderate) | 99.00–119.00 | 68.50–82.40 |
| Double at the Austin Motel (inexpensive) | 60.00–88.00 | 41.55–61.00 |
| Lunch for one at the Shoreline Grill (expensive) | 13.00 | 9.00 |
| Lunch for one at Las Manitas (inexpensive) | 6.00 | 4.15 |
| Dinner for one, without drinks, at Jeffrey's (very expensive) | 50.00 | 34.60 |
| Dinner for one, without drinks, at Manuel's (moderate) | 17.00 | 11.75 |
| Dinner for one, without drinks, at The Iron Works (inexpensive) | 8.50 | 5.90 |
| Pint of beer at brewpub | 3.50 | 2.40 |
| Coca-Cola | 1.00 | 0.70 |
| Cup of espresso | 1.50 | 1.05 |
| Admission to Austin Museum of Art—Downtown | 3.00 | 2.10 |
| Roll of ASA 100 Kodacolor film, 36 exposures | 6.50 | 4.50 |
| Movie ticket | 1.50–7.00 | 1.05–4.85 |
| Austin Symphony ticket | 17.00–33.00 | 11.80–22.85 |

- **Zilker Garden Festival,** Zilker Botanical Gardens. There's plenty of flower power at this huge gathering—sales booths, gardening demonstrations, and a variety of entertainment. Call ☎ **512/477-8672.** Late March/early April.

**April**

- **Capitol 10,000.** Texas's largest 10K race winds its way from the state capitol through West Austin, ending up at Town Lake. Call ☎ **512/445-3598** for details. Early April.
- **Old Settlers Music Festival,** Dripping Springs. More than 30 bluegrass bands descend on nearby Dripping Springs to take part in this Americana roots music fest, which also includes songwriter workshops, arts-and-crafts booths, and children's entertainment. ☎ **512/346-1629;** www.bluegrassfestival.com. Early April.
- **Austin Fine Arts Festival,** Austin Museum of Art at Laguna Gloria. Set on the shores of Lake Austin, the museum's major fundraiser features a juried art show, an auction, and lots of kids' activities. ☎ **512/458-6073;** www.amoa.org. Early April.

- **Texas Hill Country Wine and Food Festival** (most events at the Four Seasons Hotel). Book a month in advance for the cooking demonstrations; beer, wine, and food tastings; and celebrity chef dinners. For the food fair, just turn up with an appetite. Call ☎ **512/329-0770.** First weekend after Easter.
- **Eeyore's Birthday Party,** Pease Park. Costume contests, face painting, and live music celebrate A. A. Milne's donkey at this huge rites-of-spring fest. Calling all aging (and nouveau) hippies. Call ☎ **512/448-5160.** Last Saturday of the month.

## May

- **O. Henry Pun-Off,** O. Henry Museum. One of the punniest events around, this annual battle of the wits is for a wordy cause—the upkeep of the O. Henry Museum. Call ☎ **512/472-1903.** First Sunday of the month.
- **Old Pecan Street Spring Arts and Crafts Festival,** Sixth Street. Eat and shop your way along Austin's restored Victorian main street while bands play in the background. ☎ **512/441-9015;** www.roadstarproductions.com. First weekend of the month.
- **Cinco de Mayo,** Fiesta Gardens. Mariachis, flamenco dancers, Tejano music, tacos, and tamales are all part of the traditional Mexican freedom celebration. Call ☎ **512/499-6720.** May 5.

## June

- ✪ **Juneteenth Freedom Festival,** Travis County Exposition Center and east Austin. This huge, 5-day celebration of African-American emancipation features parades, a jazz and blues festival, gospel singing, a rap competition, and a children's rodeo and carnival. Call ☎ **512/472-6838** for ticket and event details. Around June 15.
- **Hyde Park Historic Homes Tour.** The Victorian and early 20th-century homes of Austin's first residential suburb are open to the public one weekend a year. The contact number changes annually, so contact the Austin Convention and Visitors Bureau (☎ **800/926-2282**) for information. Father's Day weekend.

## July

- **Austin Symphony Orchestra,** Auditorium Shores. Cannons, fireworks, and of course a rousing rendition of the "1812 Overture" contribute to the fun at this noisy freedom celebration. Call ☎ **512/476-6064.** July 4.
- *Austin Chronicle* **Hot Sauce Festival,** Waterloo Park. The largest hot sauce contest in the world features more than 300 salsa entries, judged by celebrity chefs and food editors. The bands that play this super party are hot, too. ☎ **512/454-5766;** www.auschron.com. Last Sunday of the month.

## August

- **Fall Creek Vineyards Celebration & Grape Stomp,** Lake Buchanan. Grape squishing, footprint T-shirts, and wine tastings are all part of the fun. ☎ **512/476-4477;** www.fcv.com. Last two Saturdays in August.

## September

- ✪ **Diez y Siez,** Fiesta Gardens. Mariachis and folk dancers, conjunto and Tejano music, as well as fajitas, piñatas, and clowns help celebrate Mexico's independence from Spain. The highlight is the crowning of the Fiestas Patrias Queen. Call ☎ **512/476-7502.** Four days around September 16.
- **Fall Jazz Festival,** Zilker Hillside Theater. Zilker Park swings with 2 days of free concerts by top local jazz acts. Call ☎ **512/397-1468.** Second weekend of September.

**October**
- **Pumpkin Festival,** Travis County Farmer's Market. Children's Halloween festivities include a costume parade, apple bobbing, and pumpkin painting. Call ☎ **512/454-1002.** Near the end of the month.
- **Halloween,** Sixth Street. 100,000 costumed revelers take over 7 blocks of historic Sixth Street. Call ☎ **512/476-8876.** October 31.

**November**
- **Dia de los Muertos (Day of the Dead),** Congress Avenue. Death is embraced as part of the life cycle in this Hispanic festival, involving Latino music, a parade, and, of course, food. Call ☎ **512/480-9373** for date, but usually celebrated on November 2 (All Soul's Day).

**December**
- **Zilker Park Tree Lighting.** The lighting of a magnificent 165-foot tree is followed by the Trail of Lights, a mile-long display of life-size holiday scenes. Call ☎ **512/499-6700.** First Sunday of the month (tree lighting); second Sunday through December 24 (Trail of Lights).
- **Christmas Open House,** French Legation. Père Noël (the French Santa Claus) and costumed guides help host this lively gift bazaar, held in an 1840 historic house. Call ☎ **512/472-8180.** First Sunday of the month.
- **Armadillo Christmas Bazaar,** Austin Music Hall. Revel in Tex-Mex food, live music, and a full bar at this high-quality art, craft, and gift show. ☎ **512/447-1605;** www.armadillobazaar.com. Starting around 2 weeks before Christmas.

## 3  Tips for Travelers with Special Needs

### FOR TRAVELERS WITH DISABILITIES

See this section in chapter 2 for details on **Mobility International USA** and on the **Access-Able Travel Source** Web site. There's an active **Americans with Disabilities** (ADA) office in Austin, but it's best to call the **Austin Convention and Visitors Bureau** (☎ **800/926-2282, ext. 4594** or 512/404-4594) if you have questions about whether any of the hotels or other facilities you're interested in are in compliance with the act.

### FOR GAY & LESBIAN TRAVELERS

A university town and probably the most left-leaning enclave in Texas, Austin is generally gay-friendly. Oddly enough, though, it has fewer gay bars than the far more conservative San Antonio. **Book Woman,** 918 W. 12th St., at Lamar (☎ **512/472-2785;** http://bookwoman.citysearch.com.), and **Lobo,** 3204-A Guadalupe St. (☎ **512/454-5406**), are the best places to find gay and lesbian books and magazines, as well as the free *Austin Gay-Friendly Resource Directory,* published by Austin Media Visions every November, and *This Week in Texas,* a resource for the whole state. The Web site of the Lesbian and Gay Rights Lobby of Texas political group in Austin, **www.lbgsa.org/links/local.htm,** provides links to these and every other gay and lesbian resource in the city.

### FOR SENIORS

The **Old Bakery and Emporium,** 1006 Congress Ave. (☎ **512/477-5961**), not only sells crafts and baked goods made by senior citizens, but also serves as a volunteer center for people over 50. It's a good place to find out about any senior activities in town.

Another excellent resource is the monthly *Senior Advocate* newspaper, 3710 Cedar St., Box 17, Austin, TX 78705 (☎ **512/451-7433**), which you can pick up, gratis, at Albertson's supermarkets, bingo halls, libraries, and many other places. You can also call or write in advance for a subscription. The **"101 Things for Seniors"** pamphlet published by the Austin Convention and Visitors Bureau, 201 E. Second St., Austin, TX 78701 (☎ **800/926-2282**), covers everything from cultural events to garage sales.

See chapter 2 for information about the **American Association of Retired Persons (AARP)** and **Elderhostel.** Elderhostel classes in Austin often focus on the natural beauties of the region; there's usually a seminar at the Lady Bird Johnson Wildflower Center.

## FOR FAMILIES

Austin's free monthly publication **"Our Kids,"** which can be found at libraries, bookstores, children's clothing stores, The Children's Museum, the Austin Visitors Center, and Randall's, Whole Foods, and Sun Harvest grocery stores, gives a detailed day-by-day calendar of children-oriented events in town, as well as recommendations for local attractions that youngsters would enjoy. For a subscription ($15 per year), contact Our Kids, 500 San Marcos St., Suite 200-D, Austin, TX, 78702 (☎ **512/236-8417;** fax 512/236-8197). Not as up to date as "Our Kids," but still a good general resource, *Kidding Around Austin,* by Drew D. Johnson and Cynthia Brantley Johnson (John Muir Publications), is available at most local bookstores for $7.95. See also this section of chapter 2 for information about the *Family Travel Times* newsletter, "Travel with Your Children."

## FOR STUDENTS

There are endless resources for students in this university town. Just stop by the **University of Texas Student Union Building** (see map in chapter 13) to check out the scene. Austin's oldest institution of higher learning, **Huston Tillotson College,** 600 Chicon St. (☎ **512/505-3000**), in east Austin, is especially helpful for getting African-American students oriented. The AYH Hostel (see chapter 11) is another great repository of information for students.

One of the best sources for information and bookings of discounted airfares, rail fares, and lodgings is the **Council on International Educational Exchange (CIEE),** 205 E. 42nd St., New York, NY 10017 (☎ **800/2-COUNCIL** or 212/822-2600; www.counciltravel.com), with offices throughout the United States; in Austin, the Council Office is at 2000 Guadalupe St., Austin, TX 78705 (☎ **512/472-4931**). See this section of chapter 2 for details on **Hostelling International–American Youth Hostels (HI-AYH).**

## 4 Getting There

### BY PLANE

**THE MAJOR AIRLINES**    America West (☎ 800/235-9292; www.americawest. com), **American** (☎ 800/433-7300; www.americanair.com), **Continental** (☎ 800/ 525-0280; www.flycontinental.com), **Delta** (☎ 800/221-1212; www.delta.com), **Northwest** (☎ 800/225-2525; www.nwa.com), **Southwest** (☎ 800/435-9792; www.iflyswa.com), **TWA** (☎ 800/221-2000; www.twa.com), and **United** (☎ 800/ 241-6522; www.united.com) all fly into Austin. **Aerolitoral** (☎ 800/237-6639; www.aerolitoral.com), a subsidiary of Aeromexico, makes regular runs to Monterrey, Mexico. **Austin Express** (☎ 888/325-2879; www.austinexpress.com) is the city's commuter airline.

**FINDING THE BEST AIRFARE**   All the airlines run seasonal specials that can lower fares considerably. If your dates of travel don't coincide with these promotions, however, the least expensive way to travel is to purchase tickets 21 days in advance, stay over Saturday night, and travel during the week. (See chapter 2 for more advice on fighting, and winning, the airfare wars.)

Within these parameters, typical prices from New York to Austin were around $510 at press time, with very little difference between the carriers. From other cities, flight costs ranged substantially. The best fare from Chicago to Austin (on Southwest) hovered around $200; you could also get a flight from Los Angeles to Austin on American, United, and Southwest for that same price.

## BY CAR

**I-35** is the north–south approach to Austin; it intersects with **Hwy. 290,** a major east–west thoroughfare, and **Hwy. 183,** which also runs roughly north–south through town. If you're staying on the west side of Austin, hook up with **Loop 1,** almost always called Mo-Pac by locals.

Stay on I-35 north and you'll get to Dallas/Fort Worth in about 4 hours. Hwy. 290 leads east to Houston, approximately 2½ hours away, and west via a scenic Hill Country route to I-10, the main east–west thoroughfare. I-10 can also be picked up by heading south to San Antonio, some 80 miles away on I-35.

In case you're planning a state capital tour, it's 896 miles from Austin to Atlanta; 1,911 miles to Boston; 921 miles to Springfield, Illinois; 671 miles to Santa Fe; 963 miles to Phoenix; and 1,745 miles to Sacramento, California.

## BY TRAIN

To get to points east or west of Austin on the Sunset Limited by **Amtrak,** 250 N. Lamar Blvd. (☎ **800/872-7245** or 512/476-5684; www.amtrak.com), you'll have to pass through San Antonio (see the "By Train" section of chapter 2). Trains depart from Austin to San Antonio nightly. The Texas Eagle runs from Austin to Chicago daily.

## BY BUS

You'll also be going through San Antonio if you're traveling east or west to Austin via **Greyhound,** 916 E. Koenig Lane (☎ **800/231-2222** or 512/458-3823; www. greyhound.com); see chapter 2 for details. There are approximately 14 buses between the two cities each day, with one-way fares running around $15.

# 10

# Getting to Know Austin

Thousands of acres of parks, preserves, and lakes have been set aside for public enjoyment in Austin, making it an unusually people-friendly city. It's easy to miss all that, however, when you're busy negotiating the city's freeways. As soon as possible, get out of your car and smell the flowers: Just a few blocks south of downtown's office towers lie the green shores of Town Lake, where you'll begin to see what Austin is really all about.

Central Austin is, very roughly, bounded by Town Lake to the south, Hwy. 290 to the north, I-35 to the east, and Mo-Pac (Loop 1) to the west. South Austin, east of Mo-Pac, tends to be blue-collar residential, although the northern sections of South Austin have been gentrified; the number of high-tech companies in this area is growing now that the city's new international airport has moved into the neighborhood. High-tech development is also proceeding apace in north Austin, which is seeing a good deal of residential growth, too. The flat former farmland of older east Austin is home to largely Hispanic and African-American communities, while some of the city's most opulent mansions are perched on the lakeshores and hills of west Austin.

## 1 Orientation

### ARRIVING

**BY PLANE** Opened in May 1999, the $675 million **Austin-Bergstrom International Airport** (☎ **512/495-7550**), located on the site of the former Bergstrom Air Force Base, just off Hwy. 71/Ben White Boulevard, some 8 miles southwest of the capitol, is the town's transportation darling.

Not only does the airy glass-and-granite structure replace an outdated facility with an expanded new one, but it was also designed to capture the spirit of Austin from the second you step off the plane. The passenger terminal, named after the late Texas Congresswoman Barbara Jordan, boasts a stage area for performances by Austin musicians (see sidebar), hosts local businesses like BookPeople and Travelfest, and features Austin food concessions such as Amy's Ice Cream, Matt's El Rancho, and The Salt Lick—with prices comparable to those in town, so you won't feel ripped off. There's an ATM machine and an information booth on the lower level open 7am to 11pm. Naturally, it's also got a geek's dream of a Web site, **www.ci.austin.tx.us/newairport**, featuring a virtual reality tour of the terminal, flight schedules and links

# You Paid What?

47,000 hotels, 700 airlines, 50 rental car companies. And a few million ways to save money.

**Travelocity.com**
A Sabre Company

**Go Virtually Anywhere.**

**Will you have enough stories to tell your grandchildren?**

Yahoo! Travel

# Leaving on a Jet Plane? Tuneful Take-Offs

Who could have predicted that musicians would ever scramble for an airport gig? But with music lovers flying in from all over, the Austin airport's stage has turned out to be a great place for local bands to get national exposure—who knows what record company exec might be fortuitously stranded? The music mirrors the eclecticism of Austin's scene, including R&B, honky-tonk, jazz, conjunto, world, pop, Western retro—you name it. Don't expect to be entertained every time you fly in or depart, though. Performances generally take place on Wednesday and Thursday from 4 to 6pm, Friday from 5 to 7pm, and Sunday from 3 to 5pm. Check the airport's Web site to find out what bands might fit in with your flight plans.

to the airlines and car-rental companies, descriptions of all the concessions, the latest bulletins on noise-pollution control, and more.

Taxis from the major companies in town (usually) form a queue outside the terminal; they're not always in sight. To ensure off-hour pickup in advance, phone **American Yellow Checker Cab** (☎ 800/456-TAXI) before you leave home. The ride between the airport and downtown generally costs around $25. The flag-drop charge is $1.50, and it's $1.75 for every mile after that.

If you're not in a huge rush to get to your hotel, **SuperShuttle** (☎ 800/BLUE-VAN or 512/258-3826; www.supershuttle.com) is a less-expensive alternative to cabbing it, offering comfortable minivan service to hotels and residences. Prices range from $9 one-way ($16 round-trip) to a downtown hotel to $10 ($18) to a central hotel and $15 ($26) to a hotel in the northwest part of town. The drawback is that you often share your ride with several other people, who may get dropped off ahead of you. You don't have to book in advance for arrival, but you do need to phone 24 hours ahead of time to arrange for a pickup when you're ready to return.

For details about public transportation from the airport, phone **Capital Metro Transit** (☎ 512/474-1200; TDD ☎ 512/385-5872), or click on the "Parking-Transportation" section of the airport Web site. See also the "By Bus" section, below, and "By Public Transportation" in "Getting Around," later in this chapter, for additional information.

Most of the major car-rental companies—Advantage, Alamo, Avis, Budget, Dollar, Hertz, National Interrent, and Thrifty—have outlets at the airport, and you can now just walk across the road from the terminal building to pick up (and drop off) your car; see "Car Rentals" in the "Getting Around" section, below, for details. The trip from the airport to downtown by car or taxi could take anywhere from 25 minutes to an hour, depending on the time of day and the current state of highway repairs; during rush hour, there are often backups all along Hwy. 71. Be sure to slot in extra time when you need to catch a flight. *Tip:* If you're heading downtown from the airport, you're best off taking Riverside Drive—one of the earliest exits on Hwy. 71—and then Congress Avenue north rather than staying on Hwy. 71 and using I-35. If you want to get to the northwest, take Hwy. 183 all the way, again avoiding the often-congested I-35.

**BY TRAIN**   The **Amtrak** station (☎ 512/476-5684) is at Lamar and West First Street, in the southwest part of downtown. There are generally a few cabs around to meet the trains, but if you don't see one, a list of phone numbers of taxi companies is posted near the pay phones. Some of the downtown hotels offer courtesy pickup from the train station. A cab ride shouldn't run more than $4 or $5 (there's a $3 minimum charge). There's not much at the station beyond a couple of vending machines.

---

**Inside Info**
_____

Inside Line (☎ 512/416-5700) can clue you in on Austin information from the essential to the esoteric—everything from weather forecasts and restaurant reviews to financial news and bat facts. Punch extension 4636 for instructions on how to use the system.

---

**BY BUS**    The bus **terminal** is near Highland Mall, about 10 minutes north of downtown and just south of the I-35 motel zone. Some places to sleep are within walking distance, and many others are a short cab ride away; a few taxis usually wait outside the station. If you want to go downtown, you can catch either bus no. 7 (Duval) or no. 15 (Red River) from the stop across the street. A cab ride downtown—about 10 minutes away on the freeway—should cost from $8 to $10.

## VISITOR INFORMATION

The **Austin Convention and Visitors Bureau,** 201 E. Second St. (☎ 800/926-2282; www.austintexas.org), down the street from the Convention Center in the southeast section of downtown, is open Monday through Friday 8:30am to 5pm, Saturday 9am to 5pm, and Sunday noon to 5pm (closed Thanksgiving Day and Christmas). You can pick up tourist information pamphlets downtown at the **Old Bakery and Emporium,** 1006 Congress Ave. (☎ 512/477-5961), open Monday to Friday 9am to 4pm, and the first two Saturdays in December 10am to 3pm. In the **Capitol Complex Visitors Center,** 112 E. 11th St. (☎ 512/305-8400; www.tspb.state.tx.us, click on "visitors center"), open daily 9am to 5pm, there's a Texas Department of Transportation travel information center that dispenses information on the entire state. Those particularly interested in Austin's African-American community might contact the **Capital City African American Chamber of Commerce,** 5407 N. I-35, Suite 304 (☎ 512/459-1181).

The free alternative newspaper, the *Chronicle,* distributed to stores, hotels, and restaurants around town every Thursday, is the best source of information about Austin events. It's got a close rival in *XLent,* the free weekend entertainment guide put out by the *Austin-American Statesman,* which also turns up on Thursday at most of the same places that carry the *Chronicle.*

## CITY LAYOUT

In 1839, Austin was laid out in a grid on the northern shore of the Colorado River, bounded by Shoal Creek to the west and Waller Creek to the east. The section of the river abutting the original settlement is now known as Town Lake, and the city has spread far beyond its original borders in all directions. The land to the east is flat Texas plain; the rolling Hill Country begins on the west side of town.

**MAIN ARTERIES & STREETS**    I-35, forming the border between central and east Austin and—try not to think about it—straddling the Balcones Fault Line, is the main north–south thoroughfare; Loop 1, usually called Mo-Pac (it follows the course of the Missouri-Pacific railroad, although some people like to say it got its name because it's "mo' packed"), is its westside equivalent. Hwy. 290, running east and west on the north end of town, frequently changes its name (to 2222, Northland, and Koenig), as does 183, or Research Boulevard. Ben White Boulevard, a major east–west road to the south of town, is another incarnation of Hwy. 290, connecting with Hwy. 71 east of I-35. Important north–south city streets include Lamar, Guadalupe, and Burnet. If you want to get across town north of the river, use Cesar Chavez (once known as First

St.), 15th Street (which turns into Enfield west of Lamar), Martin Luther King Jr. Boulevard (the equivalent of 19th St., and often just called MLK), 38th Street, and 45th Street.

**FINDING AN ADDRESS** Congress Avenue was the earliest dividing line between east and west, while the Colorado River marked the north and south border of the city. Addresses were designed to move in increments of 100 per block, so that 1500 N. Guadalupe, say, would be 15 blocks north of the river. This system still works reasonably well in the older sections of town, but breaks down where the neat street grid does (look at a street map to see where the right angles end). All the east–west streets were originally named after trees native to the city (for example, Sixth St. was once Pecan St.); many that run north and south, such as San Jacinto, Lavaca, and Guadalupe, retain their original Texas river monikers.

**STREET MAPS** A number of the car-rental companies give out surprisingly detailed street maps of central Austin. If you're going farther afield, I'd recommend the **Gousha** city maps, available at most convenience stores, drugstores, newsstands, and bookstores.

## Neighborhoods in Brief

With a few exceptions, locals tend to speak in terms of landmarks (the University of Texas) or geographical sections (east Austin) rather than neighborhoods. In recent years, booming bedroom communities like Round Rock have grown up to the north of Austin; the west, in the direction of Hill Country, has seen such affluent residential developments as the separately incorporated Westlake Hills. Following are descriptions of some of the city's older and closer-knit areas.

**Downtown** The original city, laid out by Edwin Waller in 1839, runs roughly north–south from the river (Cesar Chavez) to the capitol (15th St.) and east–west between I-35 and Lamar. This prime sightseeing and hotel area has seen a resurgence in the past 2 decades, with more and more music clubs, restaurants, shops, and galleries moving onto and around Sixth Street. Businesses are also coming back to the beautiful old office buildings that line Sixth Street and Congress Avenue, as well as to the newer towers that lay partially abandoned after the savings-and-loan and oil crashes of the 1980s. The latest subsection of downtown to take off is the Warehouse District, centered on Third and Fourth streets just west of Congress; new restaurants and watering holes seem to pop up there every time you turn around.

**South Congress** The once-derelict stretch of Congress Avenue that lies to the south of Town Lake and ends (presently) at Oltorf Street is being gentrified—or at least trendified—by the young and the hip. It's rapidly becoming lined with abstract art galleries, antiques boutiques, and retro clothing shops; a former porno theater is now a high-tech firm. Naturally, this area has been nicknamed "SoCo."

**Fairview Park & Travis Heights** These adjoining neighborhoods between Congress and I-35 from Town Lake to Oltorf Street were Austin's first settlements south of the river. At the end of the 19th century, these bluffs became desirable as Austin residents realized they were not as likely to be flooded as the lower-ground areas north of the Colorado. Many mansions in what had become a working-class district have lately been reclaimed by the newly rich kids and boomers who are helping to develop South Congress Avenue.

**East Austin** The section east of I-35 between Cesar Chavez and Martin Luther King Jr. Boulevard is home to many of Austin's Latino and African-American residents.

Mexican restaurants and markets dot the area, which also hosts a number of African-American heritage sites, including Huston-Tillotson College, Metropolitan African Methodist Episcopal Church, George Washington Carver Museum, and Madison Cabin. Hispanic festivals are often held at Parque Zaragosa.

**French Place**   One of Austin's newest reclaimed neighborhoods, this area just east of I-35 between Manor and 38½ streets vies with South Congress for yuppie/artist ingress. It's a quiet, tree-lined section with some beautifully landscaped homes, some shabby rental properties, and everything in between. Art galleries are beginning to crop up in the warehouses near MLK.

**Old West Austin**   Of the neighborhoods that developed as downtown Austin expanded beyond Shoal Creek, Clarksville, just east of Mo-Pac, is among the most interesting: Founded by a former slave in 1871 as a utopian community for freed blacks, it's now an artists' enclave that's fast becoming populated by wealthy California techies. Directly to the north, from about West 15th to West 24th streets, Enfield boasts a number of beautiful homes and upscale restaurants. Larger mansions line the northern shores of Lake Austin, in the section known as Tarrytown; it's just south of Mount Bonnell and a beautiful stretch of land where, some historians say, Stephen F. Austin himself planned to retire.

**University of Texas**   The original 40 acres allotted for the building of an institution of higher education just north of the capitol have expanded to 357, and Guadalupe Street, along the west side of the campus, is now a popular shopping strip known as the Drag. Many of the large old houses in the area had been converted to apartments, but the trend has turned toward restoring them to family residences. West Campus is still the hangout for students, poststudents, and young artists who will move to South Austin when they get older and richer. There's a band in every garage.

**Hyde Park**   North of the university between 38th and 45th streets, Hyde Park got its start in 1891 as one of Austin's first planned suburbs; renovation of its Victorian and early Craftsman houses began in the 1970s. There's a real neighborhood feel to this pretty area, where children ride tricycles and people walk their dogs along quiet, tree-lined streets.

## 2 Getting Around

### BY PUBLIC TRANSPORTATION

Austin's public transportation system, **Capital Metropolitan Transportation Authority** (www.capmetro.austin.tx.us), is excellent, including more than 50 bus lines and a variety of ticket prices. The regular adult one-way fare on Metro routes is 50¢; express service from various Park & Ride lots costs $1; five 'Dillo routes—Red, Orange, Yellow, Blue, and Silver—are free. You'll need exact change or fare tickets (see below) to board the bus; free transfers are good for 3 hours on weekdays, 4 hours on weekends. Call ☎ **800/474-1201** or 512/474-1200 (512/385-5872 for TDD) from local pay phones for point-to-point routing information. You can also pick up a schedule booklet at any HEB, Fiesta, or Albertson grocery store or at the Capital Metro Information Center, 106 E. Eighth St., just off Congress, behind Hit or Miss.

**DISCOUNT FARES**   With the exception of Special Transit Service and Public Event shuttles, passengers 65 and older or those with mobility impairments may ride all fixed bus routes for free upon presenting a Capital Metro ID card to the driver. Cards are available for $3 from the Capital Metro Information Center (open Monday to Friday 7:30am to 5:30pm). University of Texas students also ride for free upon presentation of a UT ID card; all other students who get a Capital Metro ID card pay half-price. If you buy a Ticket Book, available at the same place as schedule booklets (see above), you can get 20 50¢ tickets for only $5—a 50% savings. Children 5 years or younger ride free when accompanied by adults.

## BY CAR

Between its long-standing traffic oddities and the more recent—but rampant—construction, driving in Austin is, to put it politely, a challenge. Don't fall into a driver's daze anywhere in town; you need to be as vigilant on the city streets as you are on highways. The former are rife with signs that suddenly insist LEFT LANE MUST TURN LEFT or RIGHT LANE MUST TURN RIGHT—generally positioned so they're noticeable only when it's too late to switch. A number of major downtown streets are one-way; many don't have street signs or have signs so covered with foliage they're impossible to read. Driving is particularly confusing in the university area, where streets like "32½" suddenly turn up. Multiply the difficulties at night, when you need x-ray vision to read the ill-lit street indicators.

The highways are no more pleasant. I-35—nicknamed "the NAFTA highway" because of the big rigs speeding up it from Mexico—is mined with tricky on-and-off ramps and, around downtown, a confusing complex of upper and lower levels; it's easy to miss your exit or find yourself exiting when you don't want to. The rapidly developing area to the northwest, where Hwy. 183 connects I-35 with Mo-Pac and the Capital of Texas Highway, requires particular vigilance, as the connections occur very rapidly. There are regular lane mergings and sudden, precipitous turnoffs.

Nervous? Good. Better a bit edgy than lost or injured. Consult maps in advance and, when driving around the university or downtown, try to gauge the number of blocks before turns so you won't have to be completely dependent on street signs. You can also check the Texas Department of Transportation's (TXDot) Web site, **www.dot. state.texas.us**, for the latest information on road conditions, including highway diversions, construction, and closures.

**CAR RENTALS**    If you're planning to travel at a popular time, it's a good idea to book as far in advance as you can, both to secure the quoted rates and to ensure that you get a car. Some of the companies I phoned in early October to inquire about the winter holiday season were already filled up for Christmas.

**Advantage** (☎ 800/777-5500; www.arac.com), **Alamo** (☎ 800/327-9633; www. goalamo.com), **Avis** (☎ 800/831-2847; www.avis.com), **Budget** (☎ 800/527-0700; www.budgetrentacar.com), **Dollar** (☎ 800/800-4000; www.dollarcar.com), **Hertz** (☎ 800/654-3131; www.hertz.com), **National** (☎ 800/227-7368; www.nationalcar. com), and **Thrifty** (☎ 800/367-2277; www.thrifty.com) all have representatives at the airport.

Lower prices are usually available for those who are flexible about dates of travel or who are members of frequent-flyer or frequent hotel stay programs or of organizations such as AAA or AARP. Car-rental companies are eager to get your business, so they're as likely as not to ask whether you belong to any group that will snag you a discount, but if the clerk doesn't inquire, it can't hurt to mention every travel-related program you're a member of; you'd be surprised at the bargains you might turn up. See chapter 3 for more tips about car rental.

**PARKING**    Unless you have congressional plates, you're likely to find the selection of parking spots downtown extremely limited during the week (construction isn't making the situation any better). Bring pockets full of quarters and prepare to feed the meter at intervals as short as every 15 minutes. There are a number of lots around the area, costing anywhere from $3 to $7, but the most convenient ones tend to fill up quickly.

Although there's virtually no street parking available near the capitol before 5pm during the week, there is a free visitor garage on 15th and San Jacinto (2-hr. time limit).

The university area is similarly congested during the week. Trying to find a spot near the shopping strip known as the Drag can be just that. Cruise the side streets; you're eventually bound to find a lot that's not filled. The two most convenient on-campus parking garages are near San Jacinto and East 26th streets and off 25th Street between San Antonio and Nueces; there is also a parking lot near the LBJ Library. Log on to **www.utexas.edu/business/parking/resources** for details on additional places to put your car on campus and for parking maps.

**DRIVING RULES**    Unless indicated, right turns are permitted on red after coming to a full stop. Seat belts and child-restraint seats are mandatory in Texas.

## BY TAXI

Among the major cab companies in Austin are **Austin Cab** (☎ 512/478-2222), **Roy's Taxi** (☎ 512/482-0000), and **American Yellow Checker Cab** (☎ 512/452-9999). Rates are regulated by the city: It's $1.50 for the flag-drop fee, $1.75 for each additional mile.

## BY BIKE

Although an increase in traffic has rendered Austin's streets less bicycle-friendly than they once were, it's still a relative Mecca for two-wheelers. Many city streets have separate bicycle lanes, and lots of scenic areas have been set aside for hiking and biking; see the "Staying Active" section of chapter 13 for details. *Note:* Austinites were so up in arms about a helmet law passed in 1996, they forced its repeal a year later. Go figure; you'd think all those techies would want to keep their heads intact.

## ON FOOT

Crossing wide avenues such as Congress is not as easy as it might be, because lights tend to be geared toward motorists rather than pedestrians, but downtown Austin and the other older sections of the city are generally very walkable. And Austin is dotted with lovely, tree-shaded spots for everything from strolling to in-line skating. The jaywalking laws are not generally enforced, except downtown.

## Fast Facts: Austin

**American Express**    The branch at 2943 W. Anderson Lane (☎ 512/452-8166; www.americanexpress.com) is open Monday to Friday 9am to 6pm.

**Area Code**    The telephone area code in Austin is **512**.

**Baby-sitters**    Grandparents Unlimited (☎ 512/280-5108) and Austin's Capital Grannies (☎ 512/371-3402) are licensed and bonded child-care providers that use seniors or older reliable people. If it's boundless energy you're after, the Student Employment Referral Service at the University of Texas (☎ 512/475-6243) can refer you to a college student.

**Business Hours**    Banks and offices are generally open Monday to Friday 8 or 9am to 5pm. Some banks offer drive-through service on Saturday 9am to noon or 1pm. Specialty shops and malls tend to open around 9 or 10am, Monday to Saturday; the former close at about 5 or 6pm, the latter at around 9 or 10pm. You can also shop at most malls and boutiques on Sunday from noon until 6pm. Bars and clubs tend to stay open until midnight during the week, 2am on weekends.

**Camera Repair**    A good, reliable choice is Precision Camera & Video, 3810 N. Lamar Blvd. (☎ **512/467-7676**).

**Car Rentals**    See "By Car," earlier in this section.

**Climate**    See "When to Go," in chapter 9.

**Dentist**    Call the Dental Referral Service at ☎ **800/917-6453.**

**Doctor**    The Medical Exchange (☎ **512/458-1121**) and Seton Hospital (☎ **512/324-4450**) both have physician referral services.

**Driving Rules**    See "By Car," earlier in this section.

**Drugstores**    See "Pharmacies," below.

**Embassies/Consulates**    See "Fast Facts: For the Foreign Traveler," in Appendix B.

**Emergencies**    Call ☎ **911** if you need the police, the fire department, or an ambulance.

**Eyeglass Repair**    TSO and Lenscrafters are two fast, dependable chains with many convenient locations around town.

**Hospitals**    Brackenridge, 601 E. 15th St. (☎ **512/324-7000**), and St. David's, 919 E. 32nd St. at I-35 (☎ **512/397-4240**), have good and convenient emergency-care facilities.

**Hot Lines**    Suicide Hotline (☎ **512/472-4357**); Poison Center (☎ **800/764-7661**); Domestic Violence Crisis Hotline (☎ **512/928-9070**); Sexual Assault Crisis Hotline (☎ **512/440-7273**).

**Information**    See "Visitor Information," earlier in this chapter.

**Laundry/Dry Cleaners**    Reliable dry cleaners in the downtown area are Ace Cleaners, 1117 S. Congress Ave. (☎ **512/444-2332**); Washburn's Town & Country, 1423 S. Congress Ave (☎ **512/442-1467**); and Sweet Cleaner's, 613 Congress (☎ **512/477-4083**). The only laundromat anywhere near downtown is Kwik Wash, 1000 W. Lynn (☎ **512/473-3725**), not within walking distance of any hotels, but a close drive.

**Libraries**    Downtown's Faulk Central Library, 800 Guadalupe St. (☎ **512/499-7599**), and adjoining Austin History Center, 810 Guadalupe St. (☎ **512/499-7480**), are excellent information resources. To find the closest local branch, check the Austin Public Libraries Web site: www.ci.austin.tx.us/library/.

**Liquor Laws**    See this section in chapter 3. Briefly, you have to be 21 to drink in Texas, it's illegal to have an open container in your car, and liquor cannot be served before noon on Sunday except at brunches (if it's billed as complimentary).

**Lost Property**    You can check with the police to find out whether something you've lost has been turned in by calling ☎ **512/974-5000.** If you leave something on a city bus, call ☎ **512/389-7454;** on a train heading for Austin or at the Amtrak station, ☎ **512/476-5684;** on a Greyhound bus or at the station, ☎ **512/458-4463;** at the airport, ☎ **512/530-COPS.**

**Luggage Storage/Lockers**    At the Greyhound station, there's only one size locker; the price is $2 per 6 hours. You can check your luggage at the Amtrak station for $1.50 per bag per 24 hours. As we went to press, lockers had not yet been installed at Austin's airport.

**Maps**    See "City Layout," earlier in this chapter.

**Newspapers/Magazines**    The daily *Austin American-Statesman* (www.austin360. com/statesman/editions/today) is the only large-circulation, mainstream newspaper in town. The *Austin Chronicle* (www.auschron.com), a free alternative weekly, focuses on the arts, entertainment, and politics. Monday through Thursday, the University of Texas publishes the surprisingly sophisticated *Daily Texan* (www. dailytexanonline.com) newspaper, covering everything from on-campus news to international events.

**Pharmacies**    You'll find many Walgreens and Eckerd drugstores around the city; most HEB grocery stores also have pharmacies. The Walgreens at Capitol Plaza, I-35 and Cameron Road (☎ 512/452-9452), is open 24 hours. Call ☎ 800/925-4733 to find the Walgreens branch nearest you.

**Police**    The non-emergency number for the Austin Police Department is ☎ 512/974-5000.

**Post Office**    The city's main post office is at 8225 Cross Park Dr. (☎ 512/ 342-1252); more convenient to tourist sights are the Capitol Station, 111 E. 17th St., in the LBJ Building, and the Downtown Station, 510 Guadalupe St. For information, phone ☎ 800/275-8777.

**Radio**    On the FM dial, turn to KMFA (89.5) for classical music, KUT (90.5) for National Public Radio talk programming (and—too much—eclectic music), KASE (100.7) for country, KUTZ (98.9) for contemporary rock, and KGSR (107.1) for folk, reggae, rock, blues, and jazz. AM stations include KVET (1300) for news and talk and KJCE (1300) for soul and Motown oldies.

**Restrooms**    The Capitol Complex, hotels, malls, and parks are your best bet. But good luck finding a restroom downtown on Sunday morning, when most of the stores and restaurants are closed.

**Safety**    Austin has been ranked one of the top five safest cities in the United States, but that doesn't mean you can throw common sense to the wind. It's never a good idea to walk down dark streets alone at night, and major tourist areas always attract pickpockets; keep your purse or wallet in a safe place.

**Taxes**    The tax on hotel rooms is 15%. Sales tax, added to restaurant bills as well as to other purchases, is 8.25%.

**Taxis**    See "By Taxi," earlier in this section.

**Television**    If you want to tune into your favorite network TV shows, you'll find CBS (KEYE) on Channel 5, ABC (KVUE) on Channel 3, NBC (KXAN) on Channel 4, Fox (KTBC) on Channel 2, and PBS (KLRU) on Channel 9. If you're interested in local issues—and sounds—you might want to try two cable channels: Channel 8, with nonstop local news (interspersed with updates of state and international news), and Channel 15, the city-run Austin Music Network, featuring a variety of sounds but emphasizing Austin and Texas artists.

**Time Zone**    Austin is on central time and observes daylight saving time.

**Transit Information**    Call Capital Metro Transit (☎ 800/474-1201 or 512/ 474-1200 from local pay phones; TDD 512/385-5872).

**Useful Telephone Numbers**    Find the time and temperature at ☎ 512/ 973-3555.

**Weather**    Check the weather at ☎ 512/451-2424 or www.kvue.com/weather/.

# Austin Accommodations

## 11

**E**ndless chain motels strung along I-35 notwithstanding, Austin has a room shortage. Resistance to development, strict residential zoning laws, and, for a long time, uncertainty about the opening date and the location of the new airport have all added to the pinch. The situation is changing—motels have begun to crop up like mushrooms near Bergstrom International Airport, and some excellent historic restorations have been completed in the downtown area—but finding a room can still be a difficult endeavor.

Even if there's no way of predicting when that major microchip convention is going to come to town, you can make some sense out of what might seem like random runs on hotel space by keeping two things in mind: the state legislature and the University of Texas (enrollment almost 50,000). Lawmakers and lobbyists converge on the capital for 140-day sessions at the start of odd-numbered years, so you can expect fewer free rooms in the first half of 2001 and 2003. And figure that the beginning of fall term, graduation week, and important home games of the Longhorns football team—U.T.'s Darrell K. Royal–Texas Memorial Stadium has nearly 80,000 seats—are going to draw parents and sports fans en masse. And during the third week in March, record label execs and aspiring artists attending the huge annual S×SW music conference take up all the town's rooms. It's always a good idea to book as far in advance as possible, but it's essential if your trip coincides with these events.

Low rates and quick freeway access to both downtown and the northwest help fill the motels that line I-35 north of the old airport. But you'll get a far better feel for what makes Austin special if you stay in the verdant Town Lake area, which includes both the historic downtown area near the capitol and the newly resurgent South Congress area; the hotels here are also on or near a 10-mile hike-and-bike trail. The leafy enclaves near the University of Texas, especially the Hyde Park neighborhood, are ideal for those willing to trade some modern perks for hominess and character. Convenient to various high-tech complexes and to the new airport are, respectively, the expanding accommodation clusters in the northwest and southern sections of town. Those with a penchant for playing on the water or putting around should consider staying out near the lakes and golf courses to the west.

Austin has some glitzy high-rises but only a few historic hotels and motels; if it's character you're after, you might opt for one of the town's many bed-and-breakfasts. The **Austin Area Bed and Breakfast Association** currently has seven members; for information, log on to **www.austinareabandb.com** or call the Woodburn House (☎ **512/458-4335**). For Austin inns that belong to Historic Accommodations of Texas, check the Web site at **www.hat.org** or contact the organization at P.O. Box 139, Fredericksburg, TX 78624 (☎ **800/HAT-0368**; e-mail: info@hat.org).

The prices listed below are only rough approximations based on rack rates, the officially established, undiscounted tariffs, which you should never have to pay. Most hotels catering to business travelers offer substantially lower prices on the weekends, while some bed-and-breakfasts have reduced rates Sunday through Thursday. If you don't mind changing rooms once, you can get the best of both discount worlds. Also be sure to inquire about reduced-price packages—which may include extras such as meals, parking, and admission to attractions—and reduced rates for senior citizens, families, and active-duty military personnel. Reservation agents don't always volunteer this information, so you should always take the initiative and ask about specials. In fact, it's a good idea to call both the 800 number and the hotel itself; sometimes the central reservation agent isn't aware of local deals.

In the following reviews, unless otherwise specified, you can assume that all the hotels in the Very Expensive and Expensive categories offer such standard amenities as room service, laundry and dry-cleaning services, and cable TV with free movie channels. See chapter 4 for a further breakdown of price categories and for an explanation of hotel pet policy notations. The rates noted in the listings do not take into account the city's 15% hotel sales tax.

Incidentally, wherever you bunk (except maybe the B&Bs) in Austin, you're likely to be in high-tech heaven; I've never been in a city where I've connected at higher speeds or more easily from hotel and motel rooms than Austin.

## 1 Downtown/South Congress

### VERY EXPENSIVE

**Doubletree Guest Suites.** 303 W. 15th St., Austin, TX 78701. ☎ **800/222-TREE** or 512/478-7000. Fax 512/478-3562. www.doubletreehotelaustin.com. 189 units. A/C TV TEL. $269 1-bedroom suite; $349 2-bedroom suite. Corporate (Mon–Thurs), extended-stay, Internet booking, and other discounts available. AE, DC, DISC, MC, V. Self- or valet parking $15. Pets accepted with $100 deposit at $20 per day.

Lobbyists sock in for winter legislative sessions at this tony all-suites high-rise, a stone's throw from the state capitol. It would be hard to find more comfortable temporary quarters: At 625 square feet, the standard one-bedroom suites are larger than the typical New York apartment.

All are decorated in attractive Western style with Texas details and offer cushy fold-out sofas and large mirrored closets; bathrooms are spacious, too. Many rooms have balconies with capitol views. Full-sized refrigerators, toasters, stoves, coffeemakers, and cookware allow guests to prepare meals in comfort and, unlike kitchens in many all-suite hotels, the ones here are separate, so you don't have to stare at dirty dishes after you eat. (The maid washes them every day, anyway.) For folks who don't like to cook on vacation, there's also 24-hour room service. You'll get a fresh supply of coffee every day and, if you request it, a newspaper delivered to your door during the week.

**Dining:** For hearty seafood, Tex-Mex, or steak, dine indoors or out at the white tableclothed 15th Street Cafe, serving three meals a day. You can sink your teeth (and your diet) into a chicken-fried steak sandwich with jalapeños at the more casual adjoining lounge.

# Downtown Austin Accommodations

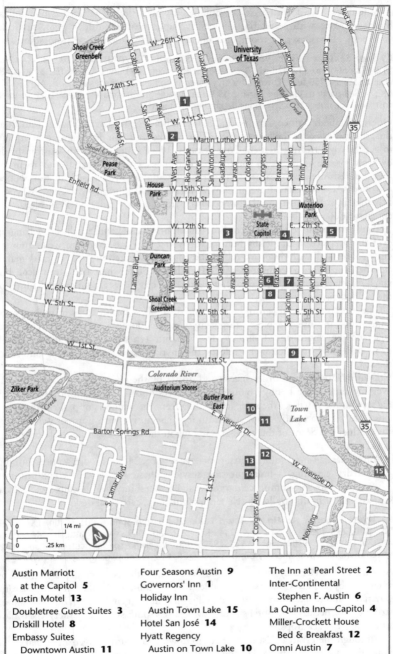

Austin Marriott
  at the Capitol **5**
Austin Motel **13**
Doubletree Guest Suites **3**
Driskill Hotel **8**
Embassy Suites
  Downtown Austin **11**

Four Seasons Austin **9**
Governors' Inn **1**
Holiday Inn
  Austin Town Lake **15**
Hotel San José **14**
Hyatt Regency
  Austin on Town Lake **10**

The Inn at Pearl Street **2**
Inter-Continental
  Stephen F. Austin **6**
La Quinta Inn—Capitol **4**
Miller-Crockett House
  Bed & Breakfast **12**
Omni Austin **7**

**Amenities:** Safe-deposit boxes, complimentary hotel shuttle within a 2-mile radius, business center with secretarial services available, heated outdoor pool, sundeck, whirlpool, saunas, exercise room, coin-operated laundry, guest library, shoeshine.

✪ **Four Seasons Austin.** 98 San Jacinto Blvd., Austin, TX 78701. ☎ **800/332-3442** or 512/478-4500. Fax 512/478-3117. www.fourseasons.com. 291 units. A/C TV TEL. $250–$325 double; $375–$950 suite. Lower rates on weekends, romance packages available. AE, CB, DC, MC, V. Self-parking $8; valet parking $13. Pets beagle size or smaller accepted at no extra cost; advance notice to reservations department required.

Queen Elizabeth, Prince Charles, and King Philip of Spain have all bedded down at this, the most luxe of the luxe hotels on Town Lake. But you don't have to be royalty to get the royal treatment at the Four Seasons. The Posture Luxe beds, custom-made by Sealy for the hotel, are so comfortable that many guests arrange to buy them for their homes. Allergic to feathers? Plush pillows without any animal affiliation will be provided. And if you're traveling on business, you'll appreciate the new Wayport Ethernet in-room high-speed connections, with network printing available at the concierge desk.

Polished sandstone floors, a cowhide sofa, horn lamps, and an elk head hanging over the fireplace in the lobby remind you you're in Texas, but airy, well-equipped guest rooms—all with minibars, robes, and hair dryers—are European country manse elegant. Not all are as enormous as the Presidential Suite where the queen slept, but you'll still have plenty of space to stretch out. The city views are fine, but the ones of the lake are prime.

The exercise oriented can indulge at one of the best health clubs in town, gratis. (And you can't use the old "I-forgot-my-workout-clothes" excuse here; the hotel will lend you shorts and T-shirts.) More sybaritic types can achieve that polished, pampered glow brought on by one of the myriad massages and wraps offered at the spa.

**Dining/Diversions:** Order snacks and drinks by the pool, or gaze out at the lake over cocktails in the Lobby Lounge, which serves hors d'oeuvres from midday until the wee hours. You'll get the same idyllic vista from the windows or patio of the excellent Café, serving creative New American regional cuisine with European and Pacific Rim influences. Some of the best bat watching in the city draws diners to vie for seating at dusk.

**Amenities:** 24-hour multilingual concierge service, 24-hour room service, 24-hour laundry/dry cleaning, 1-hour pressing service, physician on call, complimentary morning newspaper, complimentary overnight shoeshine, health club/spa, Jacuzzi, saunas, pool, running trails, bicycle rentals, gift shop, car-rental desk.

✪ **Hyatt Regency Austin on Town Lake.** 208 Barton Springs Rd., Austin, TX 78704. ☎ **800/233-1234** or 512/477-1234. Fax 512/480-2069. www.hyatt.com. 447 units. A/C TV TEL. $260–$300 double; $295–$495 suite. Weekend specials, corporate and state-government rates available. AE, CB, DC, DISC, JCB, MC, V. Self-parking $5; valet parking $9.

Austin's Hyatt Regency brings the outdoors in, with its signature atrium lobby anchored by a Hill Country–type tableau of a limestone-banked flowing stream, waterfalls, and oak trees. It's impressive all right, but the genuine item outside is more striking still: Because the hotel sits on Town Lake's south shore, its watery vistas have stunning city backdrops.

Although the Hyatt is just minutes from downtown, outdoor recreation makes the hotel tick. Bat tours and other Town Lake excursions depart from a private dock, which also rents paddleboats and canoes. In addition, guests can rent mountain bikes to ride on the hike-and-bike trail, right outside the door.

All the rooms, decorated in vibrant Southwest tones and rich woods, have nice desks, hair dryers, ironing boards, and irons. Special business-plan rooms offer fax machines and two-line phones, along with access to printers, copy machines, and office supplies. Gold Passport floors for frequent travelers provide coffee and tea areas and newspaper delivery to rooms. In all categories, the accommodations on the higher floors facing Town Lake are the most coveted.

**Dining/Diversions:** Townies as well as hotel guests come to the casual La Vista restaurant for its great fajitas and tasty selection of low-fat dishes. The atrium's Branchwater Lounge is hooked up to La Vista's kitchen, so you can order from its menu or, in the evening, just enjoy a drink and some country-and-western music.

**Amenities:** Currency exchange; staff fluency in French, German, and Spanish; business center; ATM; fitness room, outdoor pool, and whirlpool; newsstand; self-serve laundromat.

## EXPENSIVE

**Austin Marriott at the Capitol.** 701 E. 11th St., Austin, TX 78701. ☎ **800/228-9290** or 512/478-1111. Fax 512/478-3700. www.marriot.com. 369 units. A/C TV TEL. $199–$225 double; suites from $300. Weekend discounts, holiday rates. AE, CB, DC, DISC, JCB, MC, V. Self-parking $7; valet parking $10. Pets accepted with $50 deposit.

Austin's Marriott offers a convenient downtown location and lots of perks for business travelers, including guaranteed quick check-in and in-room hair dryers, coffeemakers, and irons. The walls of windows on the atrium levels of the blocky high-rise lend the public areas an open, airy look. Rooms, done in soft yellows and greens, also feel unconfined; the ones on the higher floors have terrific city views, and those on the west side all look out on the state capitol, 4 blocks away. Booking accommodations on the concierge floor will get you mineral water, plants, and an electric shoeshine machine in your room, along with newspaper delivery in the morning, snack delivery in the evening, and access to a lounge where complimentary continental breakfast and afternoon hors d'oeuvres are offered.

**Dining/Diversions:** The Marriott's sports lounge, with a casual menu, boasts two pool tables and TVs that broadcast games from around the world. In the evening, you can also imbibe in the more low-key lobby lounge. The skylit Allie's American Grille is the hotel's main restaurant, featuring somewhat Southwestern American and continental fare. A kiosk in the lobby serves designer coffees, muffins, and bagels in the morning.

**Amenities:** Indoor/outdoor pool, whirlpool, sauna, exercise room, gift shop, guest washer and dryer, video arcade.

○ **Driskill Hotel.** 604 Brazos St., Austin, TX 78701. ☎ **800/252-9367** or 512/474-5911. Fax 512/474-2214. www.driskillhotel.com. 205 units. A/C TV TEL. $205–$270 double; suites from $350. AE, CB, DC, DISC, MC, V. Valet parking $14. Pets 25 lbs. and under accepted for $50 fee.

Lyndon Johnson holed up here during the final days of his presidential campaign, anxiously awaiting the election results. Ann Richards held her inaugural ball at the Driskill when she became governor, and the hotel hosted Tommy Lee Jones's wedding reception. This is where the Daughters of the Republic of Texas gathered to decide the fate of the Alamo, and Texas lawmen met to set an ambush for Bonnie and Clyde. Since 1886, cattle baron Jesse Driskill has perched on a column atop his grand hotel, literally stone-faced, surveying it all.

The magnificent halls of this historic hotel had become a tad shabby, but a $35 million renovation, celebrated with the new millennium, restored their former sheen—and then some. This place is a born-again dazzler, especially the public areas, which are dripping with marble and crystal. The guest rooms—100 of them in a 1929 addition, the rest in the original structure—feature beautiful reproductions of the original 19th-century furnishings, plus such modern amenities as three dual-line phones and high-speed T1 connections (if you arrive with a next-generation laptop, you can check your e-mail on your TV screen). Some of the king rooms are quite small, though, and dominated by the large bed so there's little room to move about (at least the sink and mirror are outside the tiny bathroom). You might want to check the size before settling in.

**Dining/Diversions:** Adjoining the hotel's cushy piano bar (see chapter 15), the Driskill Grill is a swank Texas dining room serving excellent new Southwestern fare.

**Amenities:** 24-hour room service, 24-hour concierge service, complimentary shoeshine, foreign currency exchange, foreign newspapers available. A fully equipped health club with the latest exercise equipment and spa treatments opened in 2000.

**Embassy Suites Downtown Austin.** 300 S. Congress Ave., Austin, TX 78704. ☎ **800/ EMBASSY** or 512/469-9000. Fax 512/480-9164. www.embassy-suites.com. 262 units. A/C TV TEL. $189–$209 double. Rates include full breakfast. AE, CB, DC, DISC, MC, V. Free indoor parking garage; valet parking $8.

Embassy Suites are generally a good deal for those traveling on business or with families, and this link in the national chain has a great location to boot. It's convenient to the new airport, and it's a straight shot south of the state capitol and only a few blocks west of the row of restaurants on Barton Springs Road. And when you step outside the hotel's door, you're only a few minutes on foot from the Town Lake hike-and-bike trail.

All the attractive, modern suites have two TVs, two telephones (both with data ports and speakers), microwave, refrigerator, wet bar, coffeemaker and coffee supplies, full-size ironing board and iron, and hair dryer. Living rooms feature queen-size sleeper sofas and well-lighted work areas. About a third of the suites look out on downtown, the lake, and the hills. The open atrium arrangement of the rooms is its own security system, but the hotel also offers nighttime security escort service around the grounds. On top of all this, Embassy Suites has a hard-to-beat guarantee policy: You don't pay if you're not satisfied. Chances are they don't lose much money at this property.

**Dining:** The free full breakfast is one of the hotel's draws: cooked-to-order eggs, pancakes, and other griddle fare along with fresh fruit, cereal, and baked-goods in the morning. From 5:30 to 7:30pm, it's complimentary cocktails with salty snacks. If you don't want to drink your dinner, drop in at the Capital City Bistro, a moderately priced Italian grill.

**Amenities:** Room service, complimentary transportation to the airport and the downtown business district within a 2-mile radius, complimentary newspapers, pool, whirlpool, sauna, exercise room, guest laundry, gift shop, video-game room.

**Inter-Continental Stephen F. Austin.** 701 Congress Ave., Austin, TX 78701. ☎ **800/ 327-0200** or 512/457-8800. Fax 512/457-8896. www.interconti.com. 189 units. A/C TV TEL. $199–$250 double; $299 Club level; $350–$675 suite. Lower weekend rates. AE, DC, DISC, MC, V. Valet parking $16.

Built in 1924 to compete with the Driskill (see above) a block away, the Stephen F. Austin was another favorite power center for state legislators, along with celebrities like Babe Ruth and Frank Sinatra. Closed in 1987 and reopened in spring 2000 after being gutted and completely revamped, the hotel is once again fit for movers and shakers, although now they're most likely to be high-tech and music industry execs.

The public areas are elegant, but not quite as grand as those in the Driskill. The tradeoff is more spacious, less fussy rooms, done in soothing earth tones. Luxe amenities include terry robes, down duvets, alarm clock/CD players, magnifying mirrors, in-rooms safes large enough to fit a laptop—and every type of in-room business perk, including T1 lines and high-speed Internet access, that the bearer of said laptop could desire. Beware the sensitive, sensor-operated minibar, however, which may register a charge for jellybeans, say, if you just move, rather than consume, the contents of the jar. (*Note:* The staff is happy to adjust your bill if your refrigerator falsely accuses you of midnight snacking.)

**Dining:** Stephen F's, with terrace seating overlooking Congress Avenue and the capitol, instantly became downtown's new watering hole for those ranking high on (or looking to ascend) the org chart. The full-service Café Julienne, serving Mediterranean style cuisine, is fine, but the real buzz is about Star Canyon, the latest from Texas celebrity chef Stephen Pyle (not yet open when I visited).

**Amenities:** Fitness center and spa with indoor lap pool, sauna, and exercise room; business center; 24-hour room service; multilingual concierge; packing and unpacking service upon request; complimentary umbrellas for guest use; courtesy newspapers.

**Omni Austin.** 700 San Jacinto Blvd., Austin, TX 78701. ☎ **800/THE-OMNI** or 512/476-3700. Fax 512/320-5882. www.omnihotels.com. 375 units. A/C TV TEL. $215 double; $235 Omni Club; $349–$539 condo suite. AE, CB, DC, DISC, MC, V. Self-parking $8; valet parking $12.

Part of the posh Austin Center office and retail complex, the Omni's spectacular 200-foot rise of sun-struck glass and steel leaves you feeling simultaneously dwarfed and exhilarated. Rooms are far less overwhelming—they're not especially large and ceilings tend to be low. But they're attractive enough, in a bland contemporary way, and well equipped with irons and ironing boards, hair dryers, and makeup mirrors. Omni Club rooms on the 13th and 14th floors offer such upgraded amenities as terrycloth robes, pants press, bathroom scale, and bottled water. The complimentary continental breakfast and afternoon hors d'oeuvres and cocktails are all par for an executive-level course, but you're also treated here to the ultimate bedtime comfort snack: fresh-baked cookies and milk. If you need to hole up for a while and your company is footing the bill, your best bet is the condominium rooms—studio efficiencies with full kitchens, walk-in closets, and jetted tubs.

It'd be tough to beat the views from the Omni's rooftop pool, perched 20 stories high. You can also bask on the adjoining sundeck or soak in the Jacuzzi while gazing out over the city.

**Dining:** The hotel's dining and entertainment, all on the lobby level, include the Atrium Lounge; the full-service restaurant, Anchos, with breakfast and lunch buffets and continental cuisine at dinner; and Anchos Express, a coffee and snack kiosk for business noshers on the go.

**Amenities:** Free newspaper delivery, business center services, massage therapists, pool, sundeck, Jacuzzi, exercise room, sauna, shops, car-rental agency, travel agency, hair and nail salon.

## MODERATE

**Holiday Inn Austin Town Lake.** 20 N. I-35, Austin, TX 78701. ☎ **800/HOLIDAY** or 512/472-8211. Fax 512/472-4636. http://holidayinntown.citysearch.com. 322 units. A/C TV TEL. $129–$139 double. Weekend and holiday rates, corporate discounts available. Children under 18 stay free in parents' room. AE, CB, DC, DISC, MC, V. Free surface or garage parking. Pets accepted for $25 fee and $100 deposit.

The most upscale Holiday Inn in Austin, this high-rise is also the best situated: It's on the north shore of Town Lake, at the edge of downtown and just off I-35. Guest rooms are stylish, with simulated brick walls, light wood furniture, and Southwest patterns; the ones looking out on Town Lake are the most expensive. Fifty of the accommodations have additional sofa sleepers, which can translate into real family savings. All the rooms have hair dryers and coffeemakers. A rooftop pool large enough for laps affords fine lake views.

Dabber's sports bar and lounge holds its happy-hour specials from 5 to 7pm; you can watch the games here or shoot some pool. Monday through Friday, breakfast and lunch at the Pecan Tree Restaurant are all-you-can-eat bargains; dinner is served here, too.

Amenities include room service, valet dry cleaning during the week, complimentary airport transportation, exercise room, outdoor heated pool, sundeck, sauna, whirlpool, gift shop, and coin-operated guest laundry.

✪ **Hotel San José.** 1316 S. Congress Ave., Austin, TX 78704. ☎ **800/574-8897** or 512/444-7322. Fax 512/444-7362. www.sanjosehotel.com. 40 units. A/C TV TEL. $69–$125 double (lower end with shared bathroom); $145–$350 suite. Rates include continental breakfast. Corporate/entertainment discounts available. AE, DC, MC, V. Free parking. Dogs permitted with $100 deposit.

Hip young businesses have been infiltrating the once-seedy section south of Town Lake since the early 1990s, but the debut of this revamped 1930s motor court at the end of the decade announced that the area had officially arrived. There are nods to local design—red Spanish tile roofs, cowhide throw rugs, and Texas pine beds—but the dominant atmosphere is Zen, with Japanese-style outdoor landscaping and rooms so stripped down, they may seem stark to some. Of course, being of the moment in Austin requires the high-tech basics: high-speed Internet access, speaker phones with data ports, and VCRs and CD players (there's a well-stocked library for each of these media). Homemade granola, fresh breads and pastries, and great coffee are served up, gratis, in the morning; at night, the lobby and patio area overlooking the boutique pool turn into a bar as popular with locals as it is with hotel guests. And, from the start, the San José guaranteed its hipness by locating right across the street from the venerable Continental Club.

**La Quinta Inn–Capitol.** 300 E. 11th St., Austin, TX 78701. ☎ **800/NU-ROOMS** or 512/476-1166. Fax 512/476-6044. www.laquinta.com. 145 units. A/C TV TEL. $99–$119 double; $150 suite. Children under 18 stay free with parents. AE, DC, DISC, MC, V. Valet parking $10.

Practically on the grounds of the state capitol, this is a great bargain for both business and leisure travelers. Rooms are more attractive than your typical motel—TVs are large and the rich-toned furnishings look far from cheesy—and perks such as free local phone calls (on data port phones with voice mail), in-room coffeemakers, and free continental breakfast keep those annoying extras off your bill. Same-day laundry and dry cleaning are available during the week and a renovation, completed in 2001, has freshened up the rooms and added ironing boards and hair dryers to all of them. The sole drawback is that there's no restaurant on the premises, and there aren't many places to eat in the area on weekends if you don't feel like getting in your car.

✪ **The Miller-Crockett House Bed & Breakfast.** 112 Academy Dr., Austin, TX 78704. ☎ **888/441-1641** or 512/441-1600. Fax 512/474-5910. www.millercrockett.citysearch. com. E-mail: kat@millercrocket.com. 5 units. A/C TV TEL. Sun–Thurs $109 double, $129 suite; $119 private bungalow; Fri–Sat $139 double, $159 suite, $149 private bungalow. Rates include full breakfast. AE, MC, V. Free off-street parking.

Sure, it's got all the B&B accoutrements, including gracious veranda-wrapped quarters dating back to 1888, 1½-acre grounds spread with ancient live oaks, and the requisite generous gourmet breakfasts, and there are lovely antiques in several of the rooms. But don't expect ducks and gingham—or even your typical B&B guests. The cast and crew for the *Newton Boys,* including Matthew McConnaughey, stayed here, as have members of several bands, such as the Barenaked Ladies; depending on who's visiting, the music at breakfast could range from the Buena Vista Social Club to Jimi Hendrix. And if you want to escape the B&B experience entirely, you can hole up in one of the appealing Southwest-decor bungalows, with separate kitchens.

Wherever you bunk, you won't suffer from luxury deprivation. The guest quarters all have robes, cable TV with VCR, and phones with voice mail and Internet access. And you can't beat the location, near Town Lake (you can borrow a mountain bike to ride the trails) and the trendy South Congress area.

## INEXPENSIVE

✪ **Austin Motel.** 1220 S. Congress St., Austin, TX 78704. ☎ **512/441-1157.** Fax 512/444-2610. www.austinmotel.com. E-mail: coolpool@austinmotel.com. 41 units. A/C TV TEL. $60–$88 double; $115 suite. AE, CB, DC, DISC, MC, V. Free parking. Limited number of rooms for pets; $10 fee.

It's not only nostalgia that draws repeat guests to this Austin institution, established in 1938 and in the current owner's family since the 1950s. A convenient (but not quiet) location, in the trendy new area just south of downtown, and reasonable rates help, too. Other assets are a classic kidney-shaped pool, a great neon sign, a coin laundromat, free HBO, free coffee in the lobby (donuts, too, on Sun), and El Sol y La Luna, a good Latin restaurant that's popular with Town Lake athletes on weekend mornings. Ask to see the room—all are different and some are more recently renovated—before settling in.

**Hostelling International–Austin.** 2200 S. Lakeshore Blvd., Austin, TX 78741. ☎ **800/725-2331** or 512/444-2294. Fax 512/444-2309. www.hiaustin.org. E-mail: hiaustin@swbell.net. 39 beds in 4 dorms. $15.50 for AYH members, $3 additional for nonmembers. AE, MC, V. Free parking.

Youth- and nature-oriented Austin goes all out for its hostelers at this winning facility, located on the hike-and-bike trail, with views of Town Lake that many people pay through the nose for. In addition to being an excellent all-around resource for visitors, the hostel organizes various daytime and nighttime activities, including live music several nights a week. Facilities include a laundry room and kitchen; kayak and bike rentals are available. The building, which once served as a boathouse, is solar paneled.

## 2 University/Hyde Park

## MODERATE

**Brook House.** 609 W. 33rd St., Austin, TX 78705. ☎ **800/871-8908** or 512/459-0534. www.austinbedandbreakfast.com. E-mail: brookhouse@earthlink.net. 6 units. A/C TV TEL. $79–$119 double. Rates include breakfast. Lower weekday rates available. AE, CB, DC, DISC, MC, V. Free parking.

This 1922 colonial revival–style on a quiet block north of the University of Texas used to be a crash pad; chances are that Janis Joplin, who lived in the area in the 1960s, dropped in now and then. Although it's been a respectable bed-and-breakfast since 1985, the Brook House has still got good vibes.

You'd be hard-pressed to find better rates for such sunny, appealing quarters. The main house contains three lovely but unfussy rooms, two with their own screened porches, and all with antique furnishings. A romantic private cottage has its own kitchen and sitting deck, as does the lower of the two bedrooms in the separate carriage house. All the rooms offer cable TV, telephones with voice mail and data ports, coffeemakers, irons, and hair dryers. On nice days, a full breakfast—lots of fresh-baked goods, fruit, juices, and a hot dish—is served outside on the peaceful covered patio.

**The Inn at Pearl Street.** 809 W. MLK, Jr. Blvd., Austin, TX 78701. ☎ **800/494-2261** or 512/477-2233. Fax 512/795-0592. www.innpearl.com. E-mail: lodging@sprintmail.com. 9 units. Weekdays $109 doble, $125–$150 suite, $175 cottage; weekends $125 double, $150–$175 suite, $200 cottage. Rates include continental breakfast weekdays, full breakfast weekends. Packages available. 2-night minimum most weekends. AE, DC, DISC, MC, V. Free off-street parking.

Located on a rise above one of Austin's busier streets, this 1896 Greek revival–style house manages to preserve the peace. Although it's unassuming on the outside, the home is an interior decorator's dream. You'll be ogling all the public areas, with their silk wallpaper and Oriental rugs, and asking other guests for a peek in their rooms (or at least wanting to). The Gothic suite features a medieval-style draped canopy bed, as well as its own marble bathroom with a Jacuzzi tub. It adjoins a mint-green sun porch with a refrigerator and tape deck. The Far East room, resplendent in red, gold, and black, has a gorgeous inlaid chest and other Asian treasures. On nice days, you can enjoy breakfast on a 1,600-foot tree-shaded deck. Although this place appeals to vacationers, business travelers also like the direct phone line with voice mail in every room, as well as the weekday morning breakfast buffet (it's quick 'n' easy, but don't expect anything gourmet).

In early 2001, a carriage house on the grounds and three rooms in the trilevel Burton House next door were made available. Rooms in the latter, like those in the main house, have exotic themes (Italian, safari, and Oxford); two offer private balconies. A Texas motif dominates in the carriage house, which has its own kitchen.

**Woodburn House.** 4401 Ave. D, Austin, TX 78751. ☎ **888/690-9763** or 512/458-4335. Fax 512/458-4319. www.woodburnhouse.com. E-mail: woodburn@hotmail.com. 5 units. A/C TEL. $98–$100 double; $138 suite. Rates include breakfast. Corporate and monthly rates available. AE, MC, V. Free parking.

Herb and Sandra Dickson's late Victorian home couldn't look more firmly rooted. You'd never guess that, in danger of being bulldozed in 1980, it was jacked up, loaded on a flatbed trailer, and shifted from its original location 6 blocks away. Now settled in as the first bed-and-breakfast in Hyde Park, the Woodburn House is not only a delightful place to stay, but also a prime source of information about the historic neighborhood.

The inn's turn-of-the-century origins are apparent: Lustrous moldings made of Louisiana long-leaf pine, hardwood floors, and a built-in corner cabinet recall an age of meticulous attention to detail. Such original attributes are complemented throughout by American period antiques handed down over the years by the Dickson family. The bedrooms are similarly filled with delicate antiques. Breakfasts are designed to be heart healthy, but you can't tell the difference: Strawberry-filled crêpes topped with yogurt, apple-cinnamon pancakes, or a Mexican casserole might turn up on any given morning, along with delicious home-baked bread.

## INEXPENSIVE

✪ **The Adams House.** 4300 Ave. G, Austin, TX 85751. ☎ **512/453-7696.** Fax 512/453-2616. www.theadamshouse.com. E-mail: reservations@theadamshouse.com. 4 units. A/C TEL. $75–85 double; $125 suite. AE, MC, V. Free parking.

A welcome addition to the historic Hyde Park neighborhood, which has many lovely homes but few open to the public, this B&B was built as a single-story bungalow and expanded into a more grandiose colonial revival in 1931. A preservation architect restored its 12-foot ceilings and slate floors, among other details. Although the house is beautifully furnished, it has a friendly, open feel to it—in part because of its airiness, and in part because of the hospitable Lock family, who own and run it, with their adorable cocker spaniel, Dulce. All the rooms are lovely, but the nicest is the suite with a king-size four-poster bed and a sun porch with a fold-out couch. During the week, guests can enjoy fresh-baked breads along with fresh fruit and cereals; weekends offer dishes like omelets stuffed with spinach, yeast waffles, or Mexican *migas* (tortilla with meat and eggs and/or other items).

**Governors' Inn.** 611 W. 22nd St., Austin, TX 78705. ☎ **800/871-8908** or 512/477-0711. Fax 512/476-4769. www.governorsinnaustin.com. E-mail: governorsinn@earthlink.net. 10 units. A/C TEL. $69–$119 double. Rates include breakfast. AE, CB, DC, DISC, MC, V. Free parking.

Lisa Weidemann, who owns the Brook House (see above), also runs the Governors' Inn, which has a rather different feel. This 1897 neoclassical residence is more spacious and citified, in part because it's only 2 blocks from the busy UT campus. Guest rooms, named for long-dead and thus uncontroversial governors of Texas, are a bit more formal, too, decorated in floral prints and boasting good antique pieces. Rooms vary quite a bit in size and layout, but most are reasonably large. This bed-and-breakfast also harbors that rarity, a real single—it's small but not claustrophobic. Three rooms open directly onto a covered porch, and the others have access to it. Breakfast, which includes a hot dish along with cereals and fruit, is served buffet style during the week.

Weidemann spent almost 10 years with the Four Seasons Hotels, so she knows how to mix the convenience of a luxury hotel with the warmth of a B&B. All the rooms offer cable TV, private telephone lines with voice mail and data ports, coffeemakers, irons, and hair dryers.

## 3  Along I-35 North

### EXPENSIVE

**Doubletree Hotel Austin.** 6505 N. I-35, Austin, TX 78752. ☎ **800/222-TREE** or 512/454-3737. Fax 512/454-6915. 350 units. A/C TV TEL. $164–$194 double; $194–$224 suite. Corporate, weekend rates; romance package available. AE, CB, DC, DISC, MC, V. Self-parking $6.50; valet parking $8.65.

Leisure travelers should take advantage of the plummeting weekend rates at this tony business-oriented hotel. Once you step inside, you'll feel as though you're in a private luxury property rather than a chain lodging just off the freeway. The reception area has polished Mexican-tile floors and carved-wood ceiling beams, while an adjoining colonnade boasts a massive cherry hutch and other antiques from Mexico, along with 19th-century English wall tapestries.

In keeping with the hacienda theme, rooms are arranged around a lushly land-scaped courtyard, dotted with umbrella-shaded tables. Writing desks and separate sitting areas allow business to be conducted comfortably in the airy, spacious guest quarters, which are decorated traditionally in hues of gold and blue. An upgrade to the concierge floor will get you extra room amenities, as well as free continental breakfast and afternoon hors d'oeuvres. Executive level quarters offer two phone lines, ergonomic chairs, upgraded workstations with office caddies, and complimentary use of the business center. Wherever you stay, you needn't walk very far to reach your car; all the sleeping floors have direct access, via room key, to the parking garage.

**Dining/Diversions:** Resembling the library of a large estate, the Courtyard Lounge sports a fireplace, large-screen TV, and billiards table. Breakfast, lunch, and dinner are served at the Courtyard Cafe, overlooking multilevel waterscapes and profuse greenery; the evening menu is continental with a Texas flair.

# Greater Austin Accommodations & Dining

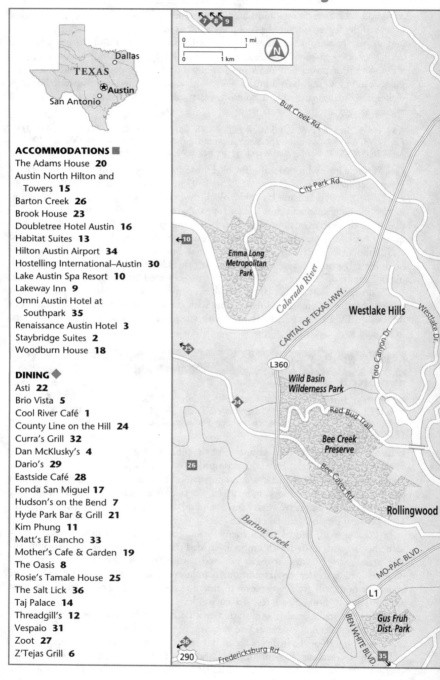

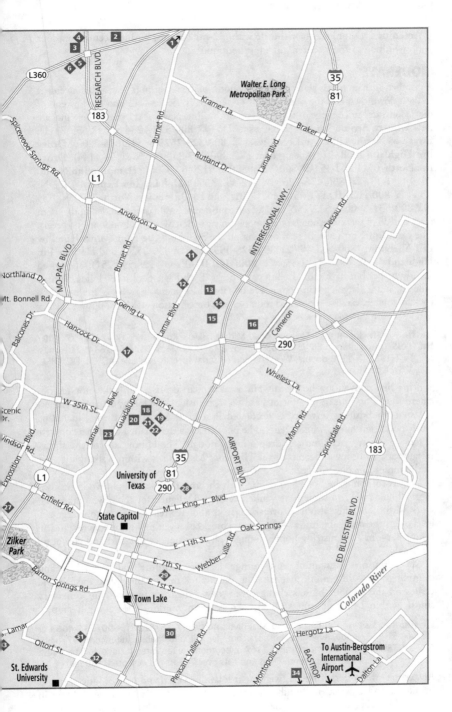

**Amenities:** Complimentary shuttle within 2-mile radius, business center, outdoor pool, whirlpool, fitness center, gift shop/boutique.

# MODERATE

A number of chain hotels along the freeway north of the old airport—an area convenient to both downtown and the northwest, if not especially scenic—fall into the low end of the "Moderate" price range or the high end of the "Inexpensive" category. These include **Best Western Atrium North,** 7928 Gessner Dr. (☎ **800/528-1234** or 512/339-7311); **Days Inn North,** 820 E. Anderson Ave. (☎ **800/325-2525** or 512/835-2200); **Drury Inn Highland Mall,** 919 Koenig Lane (☎ **800/325-8300** or 512/454-1144); **Drury Inn North,** 6511 N. I-35 (☎ **800/325-8300** or 512/467-9500).; **Hampton Inn North,** 7619 N. I-35 (☎ **800/426-7866** or 512/452-3300); **Holiday Inn Express,** 7622 N. I-35 (☎ **800/HOLIDAY** or 512/467-1701); and **La Quinta Inn North,** 7100 N. I-35 (☎ **800/531-5900** or 512/452-9401). Free continental breakfast is included in the room rates, and all of the above hotels offer a pool (only the Best Western's is indoors, however). The Days Inn North also has baby-sitting on the premises. **The Four Points Hotel by ITT Sheraton,** 7800 N. I-35 (☎ **800/325-3535** or 512/836-8520), and **Holiday Inn Highland Mall,** 6911 N. I-35 (☎ **800/HOLIDAY** or 512/459-4251), are priced slightly higher but have more facilities and perks. Each has a pool (the Holiday Inn's is indoors, and it's large), an on-premises restaurant where guests enjoy a free full breakfast, cocktail lounge, exercise room, and room service; the Sheraton also has a business center and a coin-op guest laundry.

**Austin North Hilton and Towers.** 6000 Middle Fiskville Rd., Austin, TX 78752. ☎ **800/ HILTONS** (reservations), 800/347-0330, or 512/451-5757. Fax 512/467-7644. 240 units. A/C TV TEL. $120–$170 double. Weekend and seasonal specials available. AE, CB, DC, DISC, MC, V. Free parking.

Austin's first convention hotel, this Hilton is a nice surprise: A blocky, nondescript exterior gives no hint of the gracious public areas inside. The lobby, a favorite gathering spot for business travelers, is decorated in a Lone Star Texas theme, including hardwood floors and cowhide chairs. The pool area is a tree-shaded oasis in a concrete desert—a desert where you can drop a lot of dough. The Hilton adjoins the shops, restaurants, and movie theaters of the Highland Mall and is within walking distance of the tonier Lincoln Village.

Rooms combine the Lone Star theme with cheerful florals and light wood furnishings; all are large, and some have vaulted ceilings. Designed for those who take their work with them, they also have oversized desks and two telephones. A concierge-key level offers the usual amenities—continental breakfast, evening hors d'oeuvres, and an honor bar—in an unusually homey lounge, plus business center, fax, and computer terminals.

Ma Ferguson's restaurant and lounge features comfort food—chicken and dumplings, say—in a room that takes up the lobby's theme. Blue-plate specials and dishes on the copious buffets change every day. Amenities include complimentary shuttle within 2 miles, business center, exercise room, outdoor pool, and gift shop.

✪ **Habitat Suites.** 500 E. Highland Mall Blvd., Austin, TX 78752. ☎ **800/535-4663** or ☎/fax 512/467-6000. www.habitatsuites.com. E-mail: info@habitatsuites.com. 97 units. A/C TV TEL. $127 1-bedroom suite; $167 2-bedroom suite. Rates include full breakfast. AE, DC, DISC, MC, V. Free parking. Dogs and cats over 2-years-old accepted, $50 fee.

An "ecotel" that offers Kukicha twig tea, at least one vegan and macrobiotic entree at breakfast, and a book of Buddha's teaching in the bedside-table drawer? Only in Austin. Don't be put off by the generic name and nondescript location on the outskirts of Highland Mall; lush gardens (tended without chemical fertilizers, natch) and little front porches or decks are among the many details that make this motor lodging far from generic. The rooms themselves don't have much character, but they're extremely large (the two-bedroom duplex suites have separate entrances) and satisfy business travelers' needs with full kitchens and dual-line data phones with voice mail; local calls are free. They also offer real fireplaces and windows that open. Suites are available for chemically sensitive people at no extra charge. The "quiet hours" in effect from 9pm to 9am, and the general marriage of eco-consciousness and friendliness with function, make this an unusually soothing and pleasant place to stay, whether for work or play. Amenities include a heated outdoor pool and whirlpool (with ionized water, of course), coin-op laundry, children's playscape, and hospitality hour with beer, wine, and light snacks during the week.

## INEXPENSIVE

The following familiar names along north I-35 consistently offer rooms for under $80: **Econo Lodge,** 6201 Hwy. 290 East (☎ **800/553-2666** or 512/458-4759; restaurant); **Motel 6 North,** 9420 N. I-35 (☎ **800/466-8356** or 512/339-6161; guest laundry); **Quality Inn North,** 909 E. Koenig Lane (☎ **800/228-5151** or 512/452-4200; cocktail lounge); **Ramada Inn North,** 9121 N. I-35 (☎ **800/843-9077** or 512/836-0079; restaurant, cocktail lounge); **Ramada Limited,** 5526 N. I-35 (☎ **800/880-0709** or 512/451-7001; whirlpool); **Super 8 Highland Mall,** 6000 Middle Fiskville Rd. (☎ **800/800-8000** or 512/467-8163; exercise room, room service, restaurant); and **Travelodge Suites North,** 8300 N. I-35 (☎ **800/255-3050** or 512/835-5050; kitchenettes, guest laundry). In addition to the facilities noted, all offer outdoor pools and include continental breakfast in their rates, except for the Ramada Inn North, which lays on a full morning meal.

## 4  Northwest Austin

### EXPENSIVE

**❖ Renaissance Austin Hotel.** 9721 Arboretum Blvd., Austin, TX 78759. ☎ **800/ HOTELS-1** or 512/343-2626. Fax 512/346-7945. 478 units. A/C TV TEL. $237 double; $233 club floor; $240–$1,500 suite. Weekend packages available. AE, CB, DC, DISC, MC, V. Free self-parking; valet parking $10.

Anchoring the upscale Arboretum mall on Austin's northwest side, the luxurious Renaissance caters to executives visiting the nearby computer firms. But on weekends, when rates are slashed, even underlings can afford to take advantage of the hotel's many amenities, including an excellent health club and direct access to the myriad allures of the mall (movie theaters among them). Guests buzz around the eateries, elevator banks, and lounges of a nine-story-high atrium lobby, but the space is sufficiently large to avoid any sense of crowding.

Silk wallpaper, lacquer chests, and Japanese-design draperies and bedspreads, in muted tones, add an Asian flavor to the oversized guest rooms, all with comfortable sitting areas as well as coffeemakers, irons and ironing boards, and hair dryers. In addition, many of the suites offer refrigerators, wet bars, and electric shoe buffers. Rooms on the Club Floor include bathrobes and extended services such as express checkout, concierge, and free continental breakfast and afternoon hors d'oeuvres.

**Dining/Diversions:** Who knows what wheels of high-tech intrigue have been oiled in the hotel's clubby Lobby Bar, where cocktails are expertly mixed to the tunes of a live piano? Discussions can be fueled all night long at the nearby Pavillion, with a 6am to midnight (2am on weekends) menu of deli sandwiches, snacks, and desserts. Another place to chow down in the lobby is the Garden Cafe, offering a full breakfast-and-lunch menu. Upstairs, the northern Italian Trattoria Grande doubles as a power-lunch spot and a romantic evening retreat. Business and leisure travelers alike are drawn to the happy hour and complimentary buffet at Tangerine's nightclub; many linger on to dance the night away.

**Amenities:** Complimentary shoeshine and newspaper delivery, 24-hour room service, indoor and outdoor pools, exercise room, whirlpool, sauna, access to jogging-and-walking trail, gift shop.

## MODERATE

Chain properties that fall into the "Moderate" range in this part of town include the **Homewood Suites Hotel Austin Northwest/Arboretum,** 10925 Stonelake Blvd., Austin, TX 78759 (☎ **800/225-5466** or 512/349-9966), where rooms have fully equipped kitchens (many also have wood-burning fireplaces), and amenities include an on-site fitness center, sports court, outdoor pool, whirlpool, and shop (rates include a full breakfast); and its lower-priced sister property, the **Hampton Inn NW,** 3908 W. Braker Lane, Austin, TX 78759 (☎ **800/225-5466** or 512/349-9898), which offers an outdoor pool, an exercise room, and free continental breakfast.

**✪ Staybridge Suites.** 10201 Stonelake Blvd., Austin TX 78759. ☎ **800/238-8000** or 512/349-0888. Fax 512/349-0809. www.staybridge.com. 121 units. A/C TV TEL. $119 studio suite; $139 1-bedroom. Extended stay, weekend discounts. AE, DC, DISC, MC, V. Free parking. Pets accepted with $75 fee.

Although it's designed with business travelers in mind—it's smack in the center of the high-tech corridor and offers such top-notch amenities as two-line phones, data port and high-speed Internet access, voice mail, and a 24-hour business center—this cheery Holiday Inn property is also ideal for families, who can take advantage of the kitchen in every suite, the multiple TVs (with VCR), the complimentary breakfast buffet, the pool in a leafy courtyard, and the free laundry facilities that adjoin the exercise room (the latter is small but has the latest in cardio machines). Both types of travelers appreciate the proximity to the Arboretum and other upscale shopping complexes, as well as the many restaurants in this burgeoning area.

## 5 West Austin

### VERY EXPENSIVE

**✪ Barton Creek Resort.** 8212 Barton Club Dr., Austin, TX 78735. ☎ **800/336-6158** or 512/329-4000. Fax 512/329-4597. www.bartoncreek.com. E-mail: BC.Conference.Sales@ ourclub.com. 302 units. A/C MINIBAR TV TEL. $230–$280 double; suites from $345. Spa and golf packages available. AE, DC, MC, V. Free self- or valet parking.

Sure it's a conference resort, but with four 18-hole championship golf courses, a plethora of pools and tennis courts, and a state-of-the-art European-style spa and fitness center, just how much work do you suppose actually gets done here, anyway? If you don't happen to be employed by a generous company, go ahead and book a room on your own; Barton Creek has put together a variety of golf-and-spa packages designed to draw leisure travelers.

This place is gorgeous. Spread out over 4,000 gently rolling and wooded acres in west Austin, the hotel complex includes two main buildings resembling European châteaux and a new nine-story tower connecting the spa and the conference center. All three structures host accommodations as large and as high-toned as one might expect, with 10-foot ceilings, custom-made Drexel Heritage pieces, and marble-topped sinks and vanities. Some have balconies, and rooms in the back offer superb views of the Texas Hill Country.

## (†) **Family-Friendly Hotels**

**Four Seasons Austin** (*p. 130*)   Tell the reservations clerk that you're traveling with kids, and you'll be automatically enrolled in the free amenities program: Age-appropriate snacks—cookies and milk for children under 10, popcorn and soda for those older—along with various toys and games will be waiting for you when you arrive.

**Hyatt Regency Austin on Town Lake** (*p. 130*)   This hotel no longer has a camp for kids, but there's a play area with toys in the hotel's La Vista restaurant as well as a playscape near the pool. Subject to availability, rooms for children 3 to 12, adjoining adult rooms, are half-price.

**Embassy Suites Downtown Austin** (*p. 132*)   Large quarters give children enough space to play, and the hotel's Town Lake location allows for lots of running around outside. There's also a video-game room on the first floor.

A $50 million expansion, completed in 2000, added a second Tom Fazio–designed golf course to an earlier Fazio one, plus those by golf greats Ben Crenshaw and Arnold Palmer. Don't worry if your drive is not up to par; a Golf Advantage School can help set it straight. A large pool complex, with cabanas, bar, and separate kids' swimming area, is another recent acquisition. And although aromatherapy is among the featured services, Barton Creek's spa is nothing to sneeze at. You can get buffed, pummeled, and wrapped to your heart's content.

**Dining/Diversions:** Barton Creek's renovation did away with the resort's very formal restaurant. The main, full-service spot is the Hill Country dining room, which overlooks the resort pool and one of the golf courses. There are lunch and breakfast buffets, and dinners there include continental and Southwest fare as well as Smart Cuisine selections. Other gathering grounds include the casual Austin Grill, open for early lunch or late dinner, and Jim Bob's, a bar with a pool table.

**Amenities:** Same-day dry cleaning and pressing, complimentary newspaper delivery, tennis clinic, indoor and outdoor pools, spa, hair salon, indoor track, steam room, Jacuzzi, weight room, aerobics, sauna, sporting clays, Ping-Pong, volleyball, jogging course.

**✪ Lake Austin Spa Resort.** 1705 S. Quinlan Park Rd., Austin, TX 78732. ☎ **800/ 847-5637** or 512/372-7300. Fax 512/266-1572. www.lakeaustin.com. E-mail: reserve@ lakeaustin.com. 40 units. A/C TV TEL. $350 per person for 1 night, double occupancy (standard); $375 per person (luxury). Rates include all meals, classes, and activities. 3-, 4-, and 7-night packages; seasonal specials available. AE, MC, DISC, V. Free parking.

If you had to create the quintessential Austin spa, it would be laid-back, located on a serene body of water, offer lots of outdoor activities, and feature super-healthy food that lives up to the locals' high culinary standards. You'll sign off on every item of that wish list here. The spa takes advantage of its proximity to the lovely Texas Hill Country by offering such activities as combination canoe/hiking trips or excursions to view the wildflowers. The aromatic ingredients for such soothing spa treatments as the honey-mango scrub are grown in the resort's garden, which is also the source for the herbs used at mealtimes. Newly redone rooms, many in cottages with private gardens, fireplaces, and hot tubs, are casual elegant, with all natural fabrics, locally crafted furniture, and Saltillo tile floors. Some spas create their own stress by inspiring style competitions among guests; here, single women are more likely than not to bond with each other.

**Dining:** A new chef is turning out excellent food that doesn't taste nearly as healthy as it is.

**Amenities:** Hiking, biking, water aerobics, kick-boxing, yoga, tai chi, kung fu, circuit training, toning, Pilates, canoeing, kayaking, fishing, trips to Central Market . . . you name it. Spa with wide range of body treatments and massages; classes including cooking, personal care, stress management; indoor and outdoor pools; sauna; steam room; Jacuzzi; weight and cardio room; jogging track.

## EXPENSIVE

**Lakeway Inn.** 101 Lakeway Dr., Austin, TX 78734. ☎ **800/LAKEWAY** or 512/261-6600. Fax 512/261-7322. www.dolce.com. 239 units. A/C TV TEL. $125–$240 double. Romance, golf, spa, and holiday packages available. AE, DC, DISC, MC, V. Free self-parking; valet parking $8.

Not as glitzy as Barton Creek nor as New Age-y as the Lake Austin Spa, this conference resort in a planned community on Lake Travis is great for those seeking traditional recreation at prices that won't break the bank.

There's something for everyone in the family. At the resort's marina, you can rent pontoons, ski boats, sculls, sailboats, water-skis, WaveRunners, fishing gear and guides—just about everything but fish that promise to bite. Lakeway's lovely 32-court tennis complex, designed for indoor or outdoor, day or night games, has a pro shop with trainers and even a racquet-shaped swimming pool. Duffers can tee off from 36 holes of golf on the property, get privileges at other courses nearby, or brush up on their game at the Jack Nicklaus–designed Academy of Golf. Just want to kick back and be pampered? In addition to Lakeway's small spa, guests can book treatments at the excellent Millennium day spa nearby.

The main lodge of this older property was razed and rebuilt at the end of the 1990s, but, oddly, the rooms were reincarnated with a rather dark and staid 1970s look. Still, they're spacious and comfortable, with all the requisite conference attendee business amenities and, best of all, lake views.

**Dining:** Both the full-service Travis Restaurant & Bar, featuring creative new Texas cuisine at dinner, and the nouveau rustic lobby bar in the main lounge serve up spectacular sun-setting-on-the-lake views.

**Amenities:** Room service, valet laundry and dry cleaning, playground, marina, two outdoor pools, volleyball court, tennis, well-equipped exercise room, spa, jogging-and-walking trails, two golf courses, pro shops, gift shop.

## 6 Near the Airport

## EXPENSIVE

**Hilton Austin Airport.** 9515 New Airport Dr., Austin TX 78719. ☎ **800/347-0330** or 512/385-6767. Fax 512/385-6763. www.hilton.com. 263 units. $199 double. Weekend discounts. AE, CB, DC, DISC, MC, V. Self-parking $6; valet parking $12.

Opened in early 2001, Austin's only full-service airport hotel occupies a striking landmark building: The former administrative center for Bergstrom Air Force base was built in the 1960s, and it's distinctly, distinctively, round. The underground tunnels and fallout shelters designed to protect the Commander in Chief, should he have required a secure hideout in Texas's capital, were capped off during the Hilton's construction, but the building remains rock-solid—and blissfully soundproof.

Of course, the emphasis now is on the mechanics of civilian business—always oiled by pleasure—and this hotel has the requisites: Large, comfortable rooms equipped with all the amenities (two-line phones, modem hookups, irons, hair dryers, etc.), a good fitness center, and an outdoor pool. Centered under a transparent dome, the lobby is light and airy, and the theme throughout is cheery Texas Hill Country (lots of limestone and wood). You're unlikely to recall the building's genesis until you read the posted histories of the military figures for whom all the conference rooms are named.

**Dining:** The Hilton's full-service restaurant, Creeks, picks up the Hill Country theme in its nighttime menu, which always includes a few game dishes. Buffets are laid on for both breakfast and lunch. The Lobby bar lets you lubricate those deals under the impressive lobby rotunda.

**Amenities:** Room service, valet/laundry service, outdoor pool, fitness center, business center, gift shop, complimentary airport transfers.

**Omni Austin Hotel at Southpark.** 4140 Governor's Row (at I-35 and Ben White Blvd.), Austin, TX 78744. ☎ **800/THE-OMNI** or 512/448-2222. Fax 512/448-4744. www. omnihotels.com. 313 units. A/C TV TEL. $159 double. Weekend discounts. AE, CB, DC, DISC, MC, V. Free valet and self-parking.

Conveniently located near the new airport, this Omni primarily attracts a corporate crowd, but you never know who might turn up; actor Dennis Hopper, rocker Ted Nugent, and baseball's Nolan Ryan have all stayed here at one time or another, and scenes from *Miss Congeniality* were filmed here. Whoever you are, you can expect friendly and efficient service from a staff who actually seem happy you're here.

Sleeping quarters are the picture of updated traditional taste, their mahogany furnishings complemented by gold, crimson, and green with black accents; all come with coffeemakers, hair dryers, irons and ironing boards, and high-speed Internet connections. King rooms offer working desks as well as easy chairs with ottomans. Open long hours, the Omni Austin's health club stands out in a town where many hotels have only minimal exercise facilities. It includes a lap-length pool that's half indoors, half outdoors, a whirlpool, a sauna, and an exercise room with a full array of all-new aerobic equipment and weight machines.

**Dining/Diversions:** Everyone looks upbeat sitting around the sunken bar in the lobby or tanking up on an espresso in the morning. The skylit Onion Creek Grille serves breakfast and lunch (with a pasta bar) in a casual setting that turns more formal when the candles and white tablecloths come out at night. Next door, Sweetwater's sports bar, with a peanut shell–strewn floor, serves burgers, sandwiches, and nachos from 11am until midnight or 1am.

**Amenities:** Complimentary airport and area transportation, indoor/outdoor pool, exercise room, whirlpool, sauna, basketball court, newsstand/gift shop, ATM.

## MODERATE

The two new chain properties in the moderate range that are the closest to the airport are the **Holiday Inn Express & Suites,** 2751 E. Hwy. 71 (☎ **800/HOLIDAY** or 512/385-1000), and **La Quinta Inn and Suite Austin Airport,** 7625 E. Ben White Blvd. (☎ **800/531-5900** or 512/386-6800); both offer a fitness center, a swimming pool, complimentary breakfast bars, and excellent in-room business amenities, such as irons, two-line phones, and hair dryers.

Motels that are slightly farther from the airport (on I-35 south in the vicinity of Ben White Blvd.) and not as new, but that fall into the lower end of the "Moderate" category, include **Fairfield Inn South,** 4525 S. I-35 (☎ **800/228-2800** or 512/797-8899; indoor pool, whirlpool, exercise room); and **Hampton Inn South,** 4141 Governor's Row, at I-35 and Ben White Boulevard (☎ **800/225-5466** or 512/ 442-4040; outdoor pool, exercise room). Both include continental breakfast in their room rates.

## INEXPENSIVE

The following offer cut-rate lodgings in the South I-35/Ben White Boulevard area convenient to the Austin-Bergstrom International Airport: **Best Western Seville Plaza Inn,** 4323 S. I-35 (☎ **800/528-1234** or 512/447-5511; restaurant, cocktail lounge, game room, guest laundry); **Exel Inn Austin South,** 2711 S. I-35 (☎ **800/ 356-8013** or 512/462-9201; in-room irons and ironing boards, hair dryers, guest laundry, exercise room); **La Quinta Inn–Ben White,** 4200 S. I-35 (☎ **800/ 531-5900** or 512/443-1774); and **Motel 6 South,** 2704 S. I-35 (☎ **800/466-8356** or 512/444-5882). In addition to the facilities noted, all have outdoor pools, and all except the Motel 6 South throw in continental breakfast (but that property offers free coffee—and has the lowest rates).

# Austin Dining

## 12

You would expect to eat well in a town where lawmakers schmooze power brokers, high-tech firms try to lure outside talent, and academics can be tough culinary graders. With more restaurants per capita than any other city in the United States, Austin doesn't disappoint. Chic industrial spaces vie for diners' dollars with gracious 100-year-old houses and plant-filled hippie shacks. Inside, the food ranges from the stylish but reasonably priced cuisine once dubbed "Nouveau Grub" by *Texas Monthly* magazine to tofu burgers, barbecue, and enchiladas.

Downtown's West End/Warehouse district, near Fourth and Colorado streets, is the hot new area to eat, with chic restaurants opening at a precipitous rate. The other rapidly expanding restaurant area is the northwest, near the Arboretum, where many popular downtown restaurants are installing branches. This modern industrial complex–filled area is not the most scenic, but those relocating and doing business around here are glad for the trend.

At many of the more established downtown restaurants, you can enjoy a meal with a view of Town Lake. Fast-food joints tend to be concentrated to the north, off I-35. If you're looking for authentic Mexican, the east side is the place. Barton Springs Road, near Zilker Park; the Enfield area around Mo-Pac; Lake Austin, near the Tom Miller Dam; and the tiny town of Bee Cave to the far west are also popular dining enclaves, but there's good food to be found in almost every part of town. Wherever you eat, think casual. There isn't a restaurant in Austin that requires men to put on a tie and jacket, and many upscale dining rooms are far better turned out than their wealthy techno-geek clientele.

It's a good idea to eat at off-hours, either early or late, if the restaurant you're interested in doesn't take reservations (an irritatingly large number of places don't). If you arrive at a popular place at prime time—around 8pm—you may find yourself waiting an hour or more for a table. Make reservations whenever you can, and make them as far in advance as possible—dining out can be a competitive sport in Austin.

In addition, at some of the hottest restaurants, the buzz is literal: Many Austin eateries, especially those in converted homes, have terrible acoustics, and the rooms are LOUD. At the height of the dinner rush, you're likely to find yourself shouting to your companion. Quiet, romantic tête-à-têtes are hard to come by—but you can argue in complete privacy, because no one's likely to hear a thing.

Note, too, that the downtown area still tends to be deserted on the weekend; many restaurants popular with businesspeople during the week are closed for lunch on Saturday and for both lunch and dinner on Sunday.

See chapter 5 for an explanation of culinary categories.

## 1  Restaurants by Cuisine

### AMERICAN
Dan McKlusky's (p. 162)
Eastside Café (p. 158)
Hyde Park Bar & Grill (p. 158)
The Oasis (p. 164)

### ASIAN
Mars (p. 154)
Mongolian Barbecue (p. 155)

### BARBECUE
County Line on the Hill (p. 163)
The Iron Works (p. 154)
The Salt Lick (p. 165)

### CARIBBEAN
Gilligan's (p. 150)

### CHINESE
Kim Phung (p. 159)

### CONTINENTAL
Green Pastures (p. 160)

### DELI
Katz's (p. 154)

### FRENCH
Aquarelle (p. 149)
Chez Nous (p. 150)
Sardine Rouge (p.149)

### FUSION
Saba Blue Water Café (p. 154)
Sardine Rouge (p. 149)

### INDIAN
Clay Pit (p. 153)
Taj Palace (p. 159)

### ITALIAN
Asti (p. 158)
Basil's (p. 149)
Mezzaluna (p. 152)
Pizza Nizza (p. 156)
Vespaio (p. 160)

### JAPANESE
Kyoto (p. 153)

### MEDITERRANEAN
Bitter End Bistro & Brewery (p. 152)
Louie's 106 (p. 150)
Mars (p. 154)

### MEXICAN (NORTHERN & TEX-MEX)
Chuy's (p. 156)
Dario's (p. 161)
Güero's (p. 161)
Las Manitas (p. 155)
Manuel's (p. 153)
Matt's El Rancho (p. 161)
The Oasis (p. 164)
Rosie's Tamale House (p. 165)

### NEW AMERICAN
Bitter End Bistro & Brewery (p. 152)
Brio Vista (p. 162)
Castle Hill Cafe (p. 156)
Granite Cafe (p. 158)
Hudson's on the Bend (p. 163)
Jeffrey's (p. 155)
Shoreline Grill (p. 152)
Zoot (p. 155)

### PIZZA
Pizza Nizza (p. 156)

### REGIONAL MEXICAN
Curra's Grill (p. 160)
Güero's (p. 161)
Fonda San Miguel (p. 157)
Manuel's (p. 153)

### SEAFOOD
Gilligan's (p. 150)
Shoreline Grill (p. 152)

### SOUTHWEST
Cool River Café (p. 162)
Z'Tejas Grill (p. 163)

## STEAKS

Cool River Café (p. 162)
Dan McKlusky's (p. 162)
Sullivan's (p. 152)

## TEXAN

Shady Grove (p. 157)
Threadgill's (p. 159)

## VEGETARIAN

Eastside Café (p. 158)
Mother's Cafe & Garden (p. 159)
West Lynn Cafe (p. 157)

## VIETNAMESE

Kim Phung (p. 159)

## 2  Downtown/Capitol

### VERY EXPENSIVE

**Aquarelle.** 606 Rio Grande. ☎ **512/479-8117.** Reservations recommended on weekends. Main courses $18–$30; prix-fixe $40 (market menu), $45 (vegetarian menu), $65 (menu gourmand). AE, DC, DISC, MC, V. Mon–Thurs 6–10pm; Fri–Sat 6–10:30pm. FRENCH.

Isn't it romantic? A converted neoclassical house with gilded mirrors, fresh flowers, tiny candle lamps flickering on the tables, strains of "La Vie en Rose" floating in the background—well, you get the picture—Aquarelle is a traditionally pretty addition to Austin's growing Francophile scene. The food also stays traditionally Gallic; Jacque Richard, the Loire-born chef, doesn't believe in messing with success. All the prix-fixe menus are a good bet (there are not many cities where you'd find a vegetarian version), but such dishes as the warm foie gras with raspberries, currants, and strawberries or the puff pastry with scallops in cream sauce are worth going à la carte. One caveat: You might want to make sure Richard is in the kitchen when you visit; a meal prepared by the staff wasn't quite as stellar.

**✪ Sardine Rouge.** 311 W. 6th St. ☎ **512/473-8642.** Reservations recommended on weekends. Main courses $19–$52. AE, MC, DC, V. Mon–Fri 11:30am–2pm; Mon 6–10pm; Tues–Thurs 6–10:30pm; Fri–Sat 6–11pm; Sun 6–9pm. FRENCH/FUSION.

It's back to the future at Sardine Rouge, where the latest in culinary trends (sweetbread spring rolls, say) vie with retro chic details—a tuxedoed piano player tickling the ivories on a white baby grand, showy tableside preparations, a palate cleanser before the entree—to create one of Austin's most exciting new eateries. The dining room is stunningly stylish, from the art moderne stained-glass windows to the dramatic deco chandeliers and the unusual lily-shaped sorbet dishes. The food presentation isn't too shabby, either. Although Asian-influenced dishes such as sesame-and-wasabi grilled tuna are interesting, it's the classics that shine: the incredibly rich, cognac-laced lobster bisque and amazing bananas Foster, among others. This place is pricey, no doubt about it, but the excellent service and memorable setting make any occasion you celebrate here worthy of the expense.

### EXPENSIVE

**Basil's.** 900 W. 10th St. ☎ **512/477-5576.** Reservations recommended, especially on weekends. Pastas $12–$15; main courses $13–$26. AE, CB, DC, DISC, MC, V. Daily 6–10:30pm. ITALIAN.

Pretty in pink, with lace curtains, oak trim, and lazily swirling ceiling fans, Basil's dining room is a romantic backdrop for fine northern Italian cuisine. You'll find the traditional dishes here, but turned out with innovative touches. For example, the spaghetti primavera is heaped with vegetables served al dente, and many of the preparations include colorful carrot or spinach noodles.

Consider starting with a half order of the primavera instead of a salad; it's a delicious way to get your greens in for the day. You might follow it with one of the restaurant's specialty fish dishes: the Pesce Angelica, sautéed with crab and artichokes in a mustard cream sauce, or the scampi in white-wine and garlic sauce. The wine list is extensive, and Amy's ice cream, a popular local brand, makes a sweet successor to the meal.

**○ Chez Nous.** 510 Neches St. ☎ **512/473-2413.** Reservations accepted for 5 or more. Main courses $15.50–$25.50; menu du jour $19.50. AE, DC, MC, V. Tues–Fri 11:45am–2pm; Tues–Sun 6–10:30pm. FRENCH.

Just around the corner from the Sixth Street action, this intimate little restaurant feels closer to Paris, France than to Paris, Texas. Lace curtains, fresh flowers in anisette bottles, and Folies-Bergère posters create a casual Left-Bank atmosphere. Since 1982, Chez Nous's friendly French owners have been offering fine bistro fare in Austin.

Items on the à la carte dinner menu are reasonably priced, but the real bargain is the menu du jour, which includes a choice of soup, salad, or pâté; one of three designated entrees; and crème caramel, chocolate mousse, or Brie for dessert. The main courses might include an excellent *poisson poivre vert* (fresh fish of the day with a green-peppercorn sauce) or a simple but delicious roast chicken. Everything from the pâtés to the profiteroles (puff pastry filled with ice cream and dripping with warm chocolate) is made on the premises.

**Gilligan's.** 407 Colorado St. ☎ **512/474-7474.** Reservations recommended on weekends. Main courses $12–$29. AE, DC, DISC, MC, V. Mon–Thurs 5–10pm; Fri–Sat 5–11pm. CARIBBEAN/SEAFOOD.

If you like your seafood with a kick, get yourself to Gilligan's, located in one of the converted buildings in the warehouse district (the building started out as a restaurant more than 100 years ago and spent time as—among other things—a garage, telephone supply house, and disco). You might start with the calamari with Cajun seasonings and move on from there to the tuna mignon with pineapple-mango salsa or the macadamia-crusted mahi-mahi. There's also a selection of Caribbean-style nonfish dishes, including wild boar potstickers and Jamaican jerk chicken. Portions are huge, and many entrees come with delicious coconut rice; accompaniments like jicama slaw and West Indian black beans are winners, too. Don't be misled by the name: This is no collegiate meat mart, but a skylit, sophisticated place, with colorful tropical murals and nightly music, including some terrific reggae bands.

**Louie's 106.** 106 E. Sixth St. ☎ **512/476-1997.** Reservations recommended for lunch, accepted only for 6 or more at dinner. Tapas $2–$7; main courses $13.75–$23.50. AE, CB, DC, DISC, MC, V. Mon–Fri 11:15am–4:30pm; Mon–Thurs 5–10:30pm; Fri–Sat 5–11pm; Sun 5–10pm. MEDITERRANEAN.

Looking for a place to cut a serious deal? Louie's has all the requisites: a location in the historic Littlefield office building, the tony atmosphere of a private club, an award-winning wine list, even a separate cigar room for puffing expensive stogies. But this is not to suggest it doesn't double as a pleasure palace, especially on the weekends when a classical guitarist entertains waiting diners in the glossy outside corridor.

You can enjoy Louie's updated versions of traditional Spanish tapas—portobello mushroom–potato blini, beef carpaccio with capers—at the bar of the large, high-ceiling dining room, or at one of the downstairs or mezzanine-level tables. Larger portions of similar appetizers are also available on the regular lunch and dinner menus. A classic paella Valencia (saffron rice with seafood and sausage) makes for a good, hearty entree, as does the pork chop with garlic mashed potatoes. Portions are substantial; pace yourself.

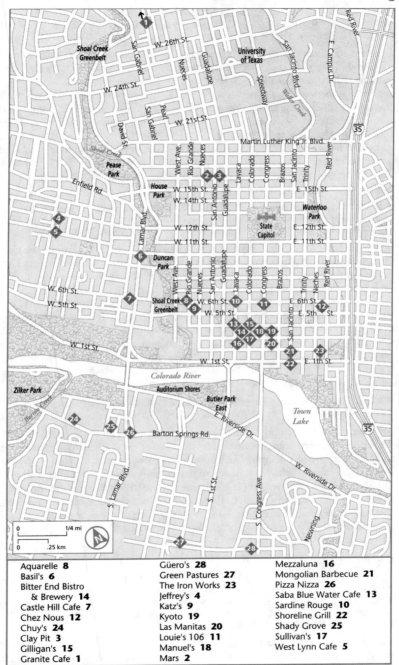

Aquarelle **8**
Basil's **6**
Bitter End Bistro
& Brewery **14**
Castle Hill Cafe **7**
Chez Nous **12**
Chuy's **24**
Clay Pit **3**
Gilligan's **15**
Granite Cafe **1**

Güero's **28**
Green Pastures **27**
The Iron Works **23**
Jeffrey's **4**
Katz's **9**
Kyoto **19**
Las Manitas **20**
Louie's 106 **11**
Manuel's **18**
Mars **2**

Mezzaluna **16**
Mongolian Barbecue **21**
Pizza Nizza **26**
Saba Blue Water Cafe **13**
Sardine Rouge **10**
Shoreline Grill **22**
Shady Grove **25**
Sullivan's **17**
West Lynn Cafe **5**

⭐ **Mezzaluna.** 310 Colorado St. ☎ **512/472-6770.** Reservations not accepted. Pizzas and pasta $7.50–$16.95; main courses $15.95–$24.95. AE, DC, DISC, MC, V. Mon–Thurs 11:30am–10:30pm; Fri 11:30am–11pm; Sat 5–11pm; Sun 6–11pm. ITALIAN.

One of the first restaurants to open in the now chic warehouse district, Mezzaluna is still ahead of the pack (and always packed). The menu has moved in a slightly more traditional direction over the years—toppings on the wood-fired pizzas are no longer as offbeat as they were in the past—but you can still find such unusual ingredients as cracked red chiles in the seafood risotto. All the main dishes are terrific, but the chef is especially successful with salmon. The restaurant offers exclusive Italian wines by the glass to introduce diners to interesting bottles—which gives you something to do while waiting, sometimes more than an hour on the weekend. The buzz is that the newer Mezzaluna Gateway in the northwest, 9901 Capital of Texas Hwy. North, Gateway Shopping Center (☎ **512/372-8030**), isn't quite as good, but that may just be die-hard downtowners defending their turf.

**Shoreline Grill.** 98 San Jacinto Blvd. ☎ **512/477-3300.** Reservations recommended (patio is first-come, first-served). Main courses $13–$28. AE, CB, DC, DISC, MC, V. Mon–Thurs 11am–10pm; Fri 11am–10:30pm; Sat 5–10:30pm; Sun 5–10pm. SEAFOOD/NEW AMERICAN.

Fish is the prime bait at this tony grill, which looks out over Town Lake and the Congress Avenue Bridge, but in late spring through early fall, bats run a close second. During this period, when thousands of Mexican free-tailed bats emerge in unison from under the bridge at dusk, patio tables for viewing the phenomenon are at a premium.

When they're not going batty, diners focus on such starters as semolina-crusted oysters or portobello mushrooms with basil and queso fresco. Menus change seasonally; in summer, entree-sized salads are offered. Drum, a moist, meaty fish from the Gulf, is worth trying, however it's prepared; the cinnamon-glazed salmon with red chile polenta is excellent, too. Non-aquatic dishes include Parmesan-crusted chicken with penne pasta and prime rib with horseradish cream. There's always at least one interesting vegetarian entree. Service is prompt and cheerful.

**Sullivan's.** 300 Colorado St., Suite 200. ☎ **512/495-6504.** Reservations suggested. Main courses $13–$27. AE, DC, DISC, MC, V. Mon–Sat 5:30–11pm (bar opens at 4:30pm). STEAKS.

An anomaly in super-casual Austin: Serious business suits rule at Sullivan's, but then, the setting and menu seem to demand it. This is classic men's club territory, with miles of dark cherry wood and cushy black booths and enough beef consumed at each sitting to keep cattle ranchers happy. Midwestern grain-fed cattle are the stars, whether in bone-in cowboy rib-eye cuts (24 oz.) or diminutive (8 oz.) filet mignon. Accompaniments such as creamed spinach or horseradish mashed potatoes come à la carte, but they're low priced and large enough to serve two. Some of the deals cut here may be as big as the meat, but the atmosphere is by no means hushed; the popular bar is especially raucous.

## MODERATE

**Bitter End Bistro & Brewery.** 311 Colorado St. ☎ **512/478-2337.** Reservations accepted for 6 or more. Pizzas $7.50–$8.50; main courses $12.50–$24; Sun and Mon prix-fixe dinner $14.50 and $16.50. AE, CB, DC, DISC, MC, V. Mon–Tues 11:30am–midnight; Wed–Fri 11:30am–1am; Sat 5pm–1am; Sun 5pm–midnight. Bar open until 1am Sun–Tues, 2am Wed–Sat. NEW AMERICAN/MEDITERRANEAN.

The food is as good as the beer at this brewpub—and the beer is very good indeed, especially the smooth, light E-Z Wheat and the toasty Uptown Brown. One of the earliest of the downtown warehouses to have been renovated, the Bitter End is all tall windows, brick walls, and galvanized metal light fixtures. But such touches as a rustic wood bar and large, comfy booths keep the atmosphere from becoming too austere.

Curry-steamed mussels, semolina-fried calamari, or a refreshing salade niçoise are all auspicious ways to begin. Nicely prepared entrees have included wood-roasted salmon with tortilla strips, grilled beef tenderloin in red wine, and vegetable risotto. Pizzas, topped with such ingredients as grilled beer sausage, provolone, and goat cheese, are deliciously imaginative, too. And this is one of the few restaurants in town where you can dine after 10:30pm.

**Clay Pit.** 1600 Guadalupe St. ☎ **512/322-5131.** Reservations recommended. Main courses $10.95–$21.95. AE, DC, DISC, MC, V. Mon–Fri 11am–2pm; Tues–Sun 5–11pm. INDIAN.

An elegant setting—a historic building with wood floors and exposed limestone walls, lit with soft lamps and votive candles—and sumptuous recipes, including creative curries and other sauces rich with nuts, raisins, and tongue-titillating spices, put this brainchild of a husband-and-wife team and a New Delhi–trained chef a cut above the usual tandoori-centered Indian restaurant. The starter of perfectly cooked coriander calamari is served with a piquant cilantro aïoli. For an entree, consider *khuroos-e-tursh,* baked chicken breast stuffed with nuts, mushrooms, and onions and smothered in a cashew-almond cream sauce, or one of the spicy, exciting vegetarian dishes. An assortment of *naan* bread, from savory to sweet, is available for sopping up these sauces. The excellent, knowledgeable staff is a wonderful complement to the food.

**Kyoto.** 315 Congress Ave. (upstairs). ☎ **512/482-9010.** Reservations accepted for 7 or more. Sushi $1.50–$10.50; main courses $7–$26. AE, DC, DISC, MC, V. Tues–Fri 11am–2pm; Mon–Thurs 6–10:30pm; Fri–Sat 6–11pm. JAPANESE.

Dine at the sushi bar or in one of the long, narrow dining rooms of this attractive Japanese restaurant, and you can keep your shoes on; opt for a cushioned and bamboo-matted tatami room, and you'll have to remove them. Shod or unshod, you'll enjoy Kyoto's well-prepared specialties, especially the sushi, which is flown in fresh. There's a nice variety, mostly fairly standard, but the Texas rolls with jalapeños are a tasty nod to local cuisine.

There are plenty of choices for those who prefer their food cooked—the soft, pork-filled *gyoza* dumplings, for starters. The Seafood Delight platter lays on crab claws, teriyaki salmon, and shrimp and scallop shish kebabs, among other delights; the beef teriyaki and deep-fried chicken *karaage* are very satisfying, too. Sweet ginger or green-tea ice cream make clean, light finishes to the meal. There's another location in the northwest at 4815 W. Braker Lane, Suite 580 ( ☎ **512/346-5800**).

**Manuel's.** 310 Congress Ave. ☎ **512/472-7555.** Reservations accepted for 5 or more. Main courses $6.75–$17. AE, DC, DISC, MC, V. Mon–Thurs 11am–10pm; Fri–Sat 11am–11pm. MEXICAN/REGIONAL MEXICAN.

One of the few moderate holdouts in a downtown dining scene that's rapidly heading uptown price-wise, Manuel's is sleek, chic, and lively. Downtown executives are among the many who come to unwind at Manuel's lively happy hour (daily 4 to 7pm), with half-price hors d'oeuvres and salsa music (see the "Only in Austin" section, later in this chapter, for the musical Sunday brunch).

The food, which includes dishes from the interior of Mexico, is a creative cut above many Tex-Mex places. You can get well-prepared versions of the standards, but Manuel's also offers hard-to-find specialties such as the *chile relleno en nogada,* stuffed with pork and topped with walnut–cream brandy sauce. The excellent *enchiladas banderas* are arrayed in the colors of the Mexican flag: a green *tomatillo verde* sauce; a white sour-creamy *suiza;* and a red *adobada,* made with ancho chiles. A northwest branch, in Great Hills, 10201 Jollyville Rd. ( ☎ **512/345-1042**), lays on live music Thursday and Saturday nights.

**Mars.** 1610 San Antonio St. ☎ **512/472-3901.** Reservations recommended on weekends. Main courses $11–$21. AE, DISC, MC, V. Sun–Thurs 5:30–10:30pm; Fri–Sat 5:30–11pm. MEDITERRANEAN/ASIAN.

In Austin's growing constellation of interesting restaurants, Mars still shines bright. Chef James Fischer picked up some interesting culinary influences when he lived in Cairo, which explains the hummus and baba ganoush that turn up alongside the pot-stickers, ribs, and spring rolls. The tandoori pork tenderloin marinated in soy, sake, honey, star anise, and cloves comes out tender and succulent, while the shrimp in green Thai curry is deliciously spicy. (Don't worry; three-alarm dishes are marked on the menu with little chiles.) The Greek noodle bowl—a Greek salad, only with linguini rather than lettuce—is tasty, filling, and inexpensive. The dining room is a bit dark for some tastes, with deep reddish-rust walls that allude to the red planet and a ceiling resembling the night sky, but the food more than compensates for any trouble you might have seeing the menu.

**Saba Blue Water Café.** 208D W. Fourth St. ☎ **512/478-7222.** Reservations accepted for parties of 6 or more. Tapas $3–$9; main courses $12–$19. AE, DC, DISC, MC, V. Mon 4pm–midnight; Tues–Fri 4pm–2am; Sat 5pm–2am. Food served until midnight. FUSION.

An aquatic-oriented color scheme, ocean-inspired artwork, and a menu heavy on seafood make for a hip, tropical dining experience far from any beach. Right on the main strip of downtown's popular warehouse district, this bar and restaurant boasts distinctive Asian/Caribbean/Mexican fusion fare, with an emphasis on light "bites." You can graze your way through the likes of seaweed-wrapped tuna pieces flash-fried and served with a delightful honey-wasabi sauce, lobster and brie empanadas, or masa-fried oyster tostadas. Not satisfied with smaller dishes? Saba also serves up enticing entrees like plantain-crusted chicken with ginger mashed potatoes or calypso pork tenderloin with roasted sweet potatoes. End your meal by getting lost in the Bermuda Triangle, a chocolate shell layered with chocolate mousse and chocolate cake and topped with chocolate shavings.

## INEXPENSIVE

**The Iron Works.** Red River and E. First sts. ☎ **800/669-3602** or 512/478-4855. Reservations accepted for large parties only. Sandwiches $3–$4; plates $5.80–$15.60; by the pound $4–$10.50. AE, DC, MC, V. Mon–Sat 11am–9pm. BARBECUE.

Some of the best barbecue in Austin is served in one of the most unusual settings. Until 1977, this building housed the ironworks of the Weigl family, who came over from Germany in 1913. You can see their ornamental craft all around town, including the State Capitol. Cattle brands created for Jack Benny ("Lasting 39"), Lucille Ball, and Bob Hope are displayed in front of the restaurant. The fall-off-the-bones-tender beef ribs are the most popular order, with the brisket running a close second. Lean turkey breast and juicy chicken are also smoked to perfection.

**Katz's.** 618 W. Sixth St. ☎ **512/472-2037.** Reservations not accepted. Sandwiches $5.25–$9.25; main courses $6.75–$16. AE, DISC, MC, V. Daily 24 hours. DELI.

Even if it doesn't quite achieve New York deli status—for one thing, the staff is not nearly rude enough, and for another, you can get jalapeños in your cream cheese—Katz's is as close as you'll come in Austin. The matzo balls are as light and the cheesecake as dense as they're supposed to be, and the corned beef sandwiches come in the requisite gargantuan portions. The venerable upstairs Top of the Marc jazz club may have closed, but Katz's is still a great place to come after hitting the other Sixth Street clubs, whether you're craving challah French toast or *kasha varnishkas* at 4am.

**Las Manitas.** 211 Congress Ave. ☎ **512/472-9357.** Reservations not accepted. Breakfast $3.85–$5.25; lunch $3–$8. AE, DISC, MC, V. Mon–Fri 7:30am–4pm; Sat–Sun 7am–2:30pm. MEXICAN.

This funky family-owned Mexican diner, decked out with local artwork and colorful booths and tables, is an Austin classic; don't leave town without checking it out. A rack of alternative newspapers at the door sets the political tone, but businesspeople and slackers alike pile into this small place for breakfasts of *migas con queso* (eggs scrambled with corn tortillas, cheddar cheese, and ranchero sauce) or *chilaquiles verdes* (tortilla strips topped with green tomatillo sauce, Jack cheese, and onions). The delicious refried beans are prepared with bacon but, this being Austin, most of the rest of the food is cooked in canola or olive oil; vegetarian items are highlighted and smoothies as well as Mexican beer turn up on the menu.

**Mongolian Barbecue.** 117 San Jacinto Blvd. ☎ **512/476-3938.** Reservations accepted for parties of 10 or more. Lunch $5.50; dinner $7.50. AE, DISC, MC, V. Mon–Thurs 11am–3pm and 5–9pm; Fri–Sat 11am–3pm and 5–10pm. ASIAN.

Across the street from the Convention Center, this all-you-can-eat Asian stir-fry buffet is a great place to grab a quick (if you come before 11:30am and beat the lines during the week) delicious lunch or a casual dinner. Equipped with a bowl, you'll work your way through a long bar containing a wealth of uncooked vegetables and meats—bell peppers, zucchini, mushrooms, beef, pork, and chicken—to a section displaying such sauces and ingredients as soy, ginger, garlic, and sesame oil. Recipes are posted to guide those seeking traditional tastes like sweet-and-sour or hot garlic Szechuan. Once you've made your final selections, hand them to the nimble chef, who presides over a huge grill. Although he may cook up to 10 dishes at once, he somehow manages to get all of them right.

## 3  Near West Side

### VERY EXPENSIVE

⊙ **Jeffrey's.** 1204 W. Lynn. ☎ **512/477-5584.** Reservations recommended. Main courses $21.75–$31.75. AE, DC, DISC, MC, V. Mon–Thurs 6–10pm; Fri–Sat 5:30–10:30pm; Sun 6–9:30pm. NEW AMERICAN.

David Garrido, Jeffrey's boyish executive chef, exudes culinary passion. You might catch him excitedly explaining to an admiring patron how he went out at dawn to buy just the right mushrooms for one of his daily specials. While his innovative Texas fare is dazzling, the setting for his performance is low-key. People walk into this three-room former storefront, in the artsy Clarksville neighborhood, wearing anything from a T-shirt to a tux.

You can't tell what will turn up on the ever-changing menu, but you can depend on flavors and textures that dance wildly together without tripping. Appetizers might include the likes of a foie gras and leek tart with cherries or crispy oysters topped with five-alarm honey-garlic butter. Duck and shrimp with butternut squash ravioli was among the entree successes on a recent menu. Desserts such as Chocolate Intemperance live up to their diet-destroying promise, and the wine list is outstanding.

### EXPENSIVE

⊙ **Zoot.** 509 Hearn. ☎ **512/477-6535.** Reservations recommended, especially on weekends. Main courses $18–$28. AE, CB, DC, DISC, MC, V. Daily 5:30–10pm. NEW AMERICAN.

Texas chauvinism and eco-consciousness come together at Zoot to produce a cuisine that's creative, fresh, and delicious. This cozy Enfield restaurant, set in a 1920s cottage, uses only organic vegetables, and designs its dishes around ingredients grown in the area. Appetizers such as the orange-sesame marinated beef satay show an Asian influence, but the backbone of the menu, which changes seasonally, is its new takes on American standards. You'll be sure to encounter some version of chicken with smoked corn custard or grilled beef tenderloin—regulars complained too loudly when those items were rotated off the menu. Vegetarians will be thrilled to find something to eat besides pasta—perhaps vegetable samosas on basmati rice in a mint-and-cumin yogurt sauce. The presentations are always gorgeous.

## MODERATE

**Castle Hill Cafe.** 1101 W. Fifth St. ☎ **512/476-0728.** Reservations accepted for parties of 6 or more. Main courses $11–$20. AE, DISC, MC, V. Mon–Fri 11am–2:30pm; Mon–Sat 6–10pm (5:30pm Oct–May). NEW AMERICAN.

Surrounded on three sides by trees, Castle Hill feels tucked away somewhere remote, but it's just a block beyond downtown's western border, near two major thoroughfares. With its dark-wood tables, rich Southwestern tones, and abundant Oaxacan folk art, this favored yuppie haunt balances comfort and creativity.

Exciting arrays of flavor emerge from the kitchen, different ones for each season. The empanadas filled with curried lamb and raisins and topped with a cilantro-yogurt sauce make a superb appetizer, as do the crab-crayfish cakes with apple-rosemary vinaigrette. Imaginatively conceived and beautifully arranged dinners might include beef tenderloin marinated in port wine and served with wild mushroom whipped potatoes or shrimp enchiladas with toasted piñon sauce.

## INEXPENSIVE

**Chuy's.** 1728 Barton Springs Rd. ☎ **512/474-4452.** Reservations accepted for parties over 12 for weekday lunch only. Main courses $6–$9. AE, CB, DC, DISC, MC, V. Sun–Thurs 11am–10:30pm; Fri–Sat 11am–11:30pm. MEXICAN.

One of the row of low-priced, friendly restaurants that line Barton Springs Road just east of Zilker Park, Chuy's stands out for its determinedly wacky decor—hubcaps lining the ceiling, Elvis memorabilia galore—and its sauce-smothered Tex-Mex fare. You're not likely to leave hungry after specials like Southwest enchiladas, piled high with smoked chicken and cheese and topped with a fried egg; or a huge sopapilla stuffed with grilled sirloin. The margaritas are good and the T-shirts, designed by local artists, even better.

There are two other Chuy's in town, one in the north on 10520 N. Lamar Blvd. (☎ **512/836-3218**), the other to the northwest on 11680 N. Research Blvd. (☎ 512/342-0011).

**Pizza Nizza.** 1608 Barton Springs Rd. ☎ **512/474-7070.** Reservations accepted. Main courses $6.50–$8.50; pizza $14–$18. AE, DC, DISC, MC, V. Daily 11am–10pm. ITALIAN/PIZZA.

This pizzeria does a thriving delivery business, but unless the place where you're staying has a large pecan tree growing in its center, it's a lot more interesting to place your order at the counter and then eat at one of the colorful glass-topped tables painted in Roman mosaic style. Pastas such as cannelloni stuffed with chicken, Italian sausage, ricotta, mozzarella, and provolone, and doused in tomato cream sauce are not only delicious, but also bargain priced. The pizzas are billed as offering "the most toppings in Austin," and with selections like hamburger, basil pesto, and smoked bacon, who would doubt it? The lunch specials—a dinner salad plus a large slice with three toppings—are a real deal at $4.95.

**ⓘ   Family-Friendly Restaurants**

**Chuy's** (*p. 156*)   Teens and aspiring teens will enjoy this colorful, inexpensive restaurant, with its cool T-shirts, Elvis kitsch, and green iguanas crawling up the walls.

**Threadgill's** (*p. 159*)   This bustling, cheerful diner has an impressive music history—surely your kids have heard of Janis Joplin?—and an inexpensive "miniature" menu for ages 12 and under.

**Katz's** (*p. 154*)   The Kid's Club Menu here not only has small fry–friendly items such as chicken fingers and peanut butter–and–sliced banana sandwiches, but it also includes connect-the-dot, maze, and word games to keep youngsters occupied.

✪ **Shady Grove.** 1624 Barton Springs Rd. ☎ **512/474-9991.** Reservations accepted weekends only. Main courses $7–$10. AE, CB, DC, DISC, MC, V. Sun–Thurs 11am–10:30pm; Fri–Sat 11am–11pm. TEXAN.

If your idea of comfort food involves chiles, don't pass up Shady Grove. The inside dining area, with its Texas kitsch roadhouse decor and cushy booths, is plenty comfortable, but most people head for the large, tree-shaded patio when the weather permits. After a day of fresh air at nearby Barton Springs, Freddie's Airstream chili, cooked with 10 different spicy peppers, might be just the thing. All the burgers are made with high-grade ground sirloin, and if you've never had a Frito pie (chili in a corn-chip bowl), this is the place to try one. Large salads—among them, noodles with Asian vegetables—or the hippie sandwich (grilled eggplant, veggies, and cheese with pesto mayonnaise) will satisfy less hearty appetites.

✪ **West Lynn Cafe.** 1110 W. Lynn. ☎ **512/482-0950.** Reservations accepted for 6 or more. Main courses $7–$10. AE, DC, DISC, MC, V. Mon–Thurs 11:30am–10pm; Fri 11:30am–10:30pm; Sat 11am–10:30pm; Sun 11am–9:30pm (brunch Sat–Sun 11am–3pm). VEGETARIAN.

Although this sunny, soaring-ceiling restaurant, part homey, part techno-chic, is totally vegetarian, it doesn't attract just a Birkenstocks-with-socks crowd. Health-conscious sophisticates and artsy neighborhood locals also come to enjoy well-prepared dishes that range over the world's cuisine, accompanied by nice, reasonably priced wine. You can enjoy everything from Thai red pepper curry and Szechuan stir-fry to pesto primavera, mushroom Stroganoff, spanakopita, and artichoke enchiladas. Some dishes are rich, but many nondairy, low-cholesterol selections are highlighted, too. Soft background jazz helps create a soothing atmosphere, although if you come at prime dining time, you may have trouble hearing it.

## 4  University/North Central

### EXPENSIVE

✪ **Fonda San Miguel.** 2330 W. North Loop. ☎ **512/459-4121.** Reservations recommended. Main courses $14.95–$21.95. AE, CB, DC, DISC, MC, V. Mon–Thurs 5:30–9:30pm; Fri–Sat 5:30–10:30pm; Sun brunch 11:30am–2pm (bar opens 30 min. earlier). REGIONAL MEXICAN.

Like American Southwest chefs who look to Native American staples such as blue corn for inspiration, Mexico City chefs have had their own back-to-the-roots movement. Such trends as using ancient Aztec ingredients are carefully tracked and artfully translated by Roberto Santibañez at Fonda San Miguel, the top fine-dining spot for Mexican regional cuisine. You'll discover here that food from the northern Mexico state of Sonora, on which most Tex-Mex fare is based, represents Mexico in the same limited way that hearty Midwestern cooking represents the United States.

The huge dining room, with its carved wooden doors, colorful paintings, and live ficus tree, is a gorgeous backdrop to such appetizers as Veracruz-style ceviche or quesadillas with *huitlacoche,* a corn fungus as rare as French truffles. *Conchinita pibil,* pork baked in banana leaves, is one of the Yucatán offerings. Hearty appetites will also enjoy the grilled beef tenderloin from the Tampico region. Familiar northern Mexican fare, extremely well prepared, is also on the menu.

⚫ **Granite Cafe.** 2905 San Gabriel St. ☎ **512/472-6483.** Reservations suggested. Main courses $12–$32. AE, CB, DC, DISC, MC, V. Mon–Thurs 11:30am–10pm; Fri 11:30am–11pm; Sat 5:30–11pm; Sun 11:30am–3pm (brunch) and 5:30–9pm. NEW AMERICAN.

The west UT campus's favorite foodie haunt had been failing for a bit, but under a new chef, the Granite Cafe has reemerged as one of Austin's premier restaurants for contemporary Texas cuisine. A sophisticated, modern main dining room with bold artwork is complemented by a leafy outdoor deck on the second level. Creative starters include meaty *pepita*-crusted crabcakes with *guajillo* corn salsa and a warm spinach salad with apples and walnuts dressed in sherry-bacon vinaigrette. The daily specials are always tempting, but you can't go wrong with the perfectly cooked duck on sweet-potato flan or the seared tuna on fried green tomatoes. Leave room for such desserts as the triple-threat bananas "tres leches," a light cake layered with banana cream, caramelized bananas, and a caramel-cream sauce.

## MODERATE

**Asti.** 408C E. 43rd St. ☎ **512/451-1218.** Reservations recommended on weekends. Pizzas, pastas $8–$15.75; main courses $13.50–$16. AE, DC, DISC, MC, V. Mon–Fri 11am–11pm; Sat 5–11pm. ITALIAN.

This is the Italian place everyone wants in their neighborhood: casual, consistently good, and reasonably priced. An open kitchen and retro Formica-topped tables create a hip, upbeat atmosphere. The designer pizzas make a nice light meal, and northern Italian specialties such as the Calabrese-style trout and the pan-seared salmon with white beans are winners. Skip the unexciting risottos, though, and save room for such desserts as the creamy espresso sorbet or the amazing chocolate mousse cannoli.

**Eastside Café.** 2113 Manor Rd. ☎ **512/476-5858.** Reservations recommended. Main courses $7.50–$14.95. AE, DC, DISC, MC, V. Mon–Thurs 11am–10pm; Sat 10am–11pm; Sun 10am–10pm (brunch Sat–Sun 10am–3pm). AMERICAN/VEGETARIAN.

Located in a nondescript neighborhood—just east of the university and northeast of the capitol—that's turning trendy, the Eastside Café is hugely popular with herbivores and carnivores alike. Diners enjoy eating on a tree-shaded patio or in one of a series of cheery, intimate rooms in a classic turn-of-the-century bungalow.

This restaurant gears its menu to all appetites; you can get half orders of all the pasta dishes, including an excellent artichoke manicotti, and of some salads, such as the mixed field greens topped with warm goat cheese. The main courses emphasize light meats and fish—sesame-breaded catfish, say, or Szechuan chicken. Each morning, the gardener informs the head chef which of the vegetables in the restaurant's large organic garden are ready for active duty. An adjoining store carries gardening tools and restaurant cookware.

**Hyde Park Bar & Grill.** 4206 Duval St. ☎ **512/458-3168.** Reservations not accepted. Main courses $6.25–$14.95. AE, CB, DISC, MC, V. Daily 11am–midnight (weekend brunch 11am–3pm). AMERICAN.

This comfy, converted old house, with its dark wood bar and frosted glass partitions, draws a local crowd every night of the week. And why not? It's got something for everyone, from vegetarian lasagna, turkey burgers, and frequent salad specials for the righteous to Reuben sandwiches and chicken-fried steak for the diet-be-damned. The latter swear that the breaded(!) French fries are the best in town, and even the calorie conscious fall sooner or later for the rich, delicious chocolate mousse cake.

**Taj Palace.** 6700 Middle Fiskville Rd. ☎ **512/452-9959.** Reservations accepted for 6 or more only. Main courses $7.95–$13.95; all-you-can-eat lunch buffet Mon–Fri $6.50, Sat–Sun $7.95; Mon night dinner buffet $10.95; Tues night vegetarian buffet $9.95. AE, DC, DISC, MC, V. Mon–Fri 11am–2pm; Sat–Sun 11:30am–2:30pm; Sun–Thurs 5:30–10pm; Fri–Sat 5:30–10:30pm. INDIAN.

In a strip center off I-35, just north of Highland Mall, statues of Ganesh, Krishna, and other Hindu deities preside over dining rooms decorated with colorful masks and Japoori-style wall hangings. Order a breadbasket to sample such treats as *naan* or *aloo paratha,* baked in a tandoor oven. The oven also produces low-fat specialties like fish *tikka,* served on skewers. Dishes like *malai kofta,* cheese and vegetable dumplings in a cream and almond sauce, or lamb *bhuna gosht,* sautéed with fried onions, bell peppers, and curry, are richly delicious.

## INEXPENSIVE

✪ **Kim Phung.** 7601 N. Lamar Blvd., no. 1. ☎ **512/451-2464.** Reservations accepted for 6 or more. Lunch specials $3.50–$3.75; main courses $5.50–$8.50. DISC, MC, V. Daily 10:30am–9pm. VIETNAMESE/CHINESE.

The rest of Austin has caught on to what the Asian community to the north has known for some time: Kim Phung is one of the best, most efficient, and least expensive restaurants in town. The low-key strip-mall setting doesn't detract from the main draw: huge portions of terrific Vietnamese and Chinese food. Wonderfully crisp spring rolls come topped with a thick peanut sauce. Entrees such as kung pao shrimp are fine, but the vermicelli noodle dishes (especially the ones heaped with chicken, garlic, and hot peppers), the grilled tofu, and the charbroiled shrimp are outstanding. The house specialty *pho* noodle soup allows you to choose the main ingredients and then add cilantro, basil, jalapeño, lime, or sprouts to taste. Thai-style coffee, served thick and dark over ice with a dollop of condensed milk, is a delicious caffeine finish.

**Mother's Cafe & Garden.** 4215 Duval St. ☎ **512/451-3994.** Reservations for parties of 6 or more only. Soups and salads $2.50–$6.50; main courses $4.95–$8.50. DC, DISC, MC, V. Mon–Fri 11:15am–10pm; Sat–Sun 10am–10pm (Sat–Sun brunch 10am–3pm). VEGETARIAN.

If you want to treat your body right and keep your taste buds happy at the same time, head over to Mother's. The Save the Earth crowd that frequents this Hyde Park cafe enjoys an international array of veggie dishes, with heavy south-of-the-border representation. You'll find classic chiles rellenos, burritos, and nachos, along with more unusual tofu enchiladas. A three-cheese spinach lasagna is especially popular. The tropical shack–style back garden is appealing, and the young staff is friendly, but not nauseatingly so. There's a good, inexpensive selection of local beers and wines.

**Threadgill's.** 6416 N. Lamar Blvd. ☎ **512/451-5440.** Reservations not accepted. Sandwiches and specials $5–$6.95; main courses $5.95–$15.95. MC, V. Daily Mon–Sat 11am–10pm; Sun 11am–9pm. TEXAN.

Kenneth Threadgill obtained Travis County's first legal liquor license after the repeal of Prohibition in 1933, turning his Gulf gas station into a club. His Wednesday night hootenannies became legendary in the 1960s, with performers like Janis Joplin turning up regularly. The Southern-style diner added on in 1980 continues in the down-home casual tradition of the adjoining club. Threadgill's is renowned for its huge chicken-fried steaks, as well as its vegetables. You can get Creole cabbage, broccoli-rice casserole, garlic-cheese grits, and Cajun-Italian eggplant in combination plates or as sides, and seconds are free.

Eddie Wilson, the current owner of Threadgill's, was the founder of the now defunct Armadillo World Headquarters, Austin's most famous music venue—which is why, when he opened a downtown branch at 301 W. Riverside (☎ **512/472-9304**) in 1996, he called it Threadgill's World Headquarters. Across the street from the old Armadillo, it's filled with music memorabilia from the club. Although it has the same menu, this Threadgill's is larger than the original and has a state-of-the-art sound system. There's live music here every Thursday night, while the uptown original brings in bands on Wednesdays.

## 5 South Austin

### EXPENSIVE

✪ **Green Pastures.** 811 W. Live Oak Rd. ☎ **512/444-4747.** Reservations advised. Main courses $18–$29.50. AE, DISC, MC, V. Daily 11am–2pm and 6–10pm. CONTINENTAL.

Peacocks strut their stuff among the 225 live oaks surrounding this 1894 mansion, which has remained in the hands of the same renowned Austin family since 1916, and which the current owner's mother converted into a restaurant in 1945. In this gracious setting, you'll find Southern comfort, impeccable service, and a continental menu that nods only gently toward current culinary trends. The lunch crowd may be a bit blue-haired, but nighttime draws Austinites of all stripes.

Although the menu changes seasonally, you'll always find two popular dishes on it: duck Texana, wrapped in bacon and served with blackcurrant sauce, and beef tenderloin with béarnaise. The Texas pecan ball (vanilla ice cream rolled in nuts and dripping fudge) is enough to weaken the strongest resolve, but you might prefer to go for baroque—flaming bananas Foster for two.

**Vespaio.** 1610 S. Congress Ave. ☎ **512/441-6100.** Reservations accepted only for Tues, Wed, and Sun 5:30–6:30pm. Pizzas and pastas $8–$19; main courses $14–$26.50. AE, CB, DC, DISC, MC, V. Tue–Sun 5:30–10:30pm (bar open 5pm–midnight). ITALIAN.

Austin's trendiest new Italian restaurant, Vespaio draws long lines of hipsters who, if they're lucky, nab a perch at the see-and-be-seen bar and do lots of head swiveling. It's a great setting—a swanked-up old storefront with lots of exposed brick and glass—and the food is worth waiting for, but you can drop quite a bit of dough on expensive wines while you're doing so. Best bet: Get an order (they're huge) of the crispy calamari while you're waiting for a table. The cannelloni stuffed with veal, prosciutto, and béchamel sauce is super, and the house duck and figs is so popular that the restaurant sometimes runs out; come early to avoid fowl disappointment.

### MODERATE

✪ **Curra's Grill.** 614 E. Oltorf. ☎ **512/444-0012.** Reservations accepted for 12 or more only. Main courses $5.95–$15.95. AE, CB, DISC, MC, V. Daily 7am–10pm. REGIONAL MEXICAN.

You're likely to find this funky, colorful restaurant packed at any time of day, but it's worth the wait for the best interior Mexican food in South Austin. A couple of breakfast tacos and a cup of special Oaxacan dark roast coffee are a great way to jump-start your day. For lunch, consider the octopus ceviche and the *crema de calabaza* (cream of zucchini) soup, or perhaps the tacos *al pastor,* stuffed with chile-grilled pork and served with cilantro, onions, pineapple, and avocado sauce. The chiles rellenos topped with cream pecan sauce make a super dinner entree, but if you're sharing, the tamale platter

# Sweet Tooth

Austin's home-grown brand of ice cream, **Amy's**, is not only wonderfully rich and creamy, but watching the colorfully clad servers juggling the scoops is always a kick. Amy's has six Austin locations, including one on the west side of down-town, 1012 W. Sixth St. at Lamar Boulevard (☎ **512/480-0673**), and one at the Arboretum, 10000 Research Blvd. (☎ **512/345-1006**). And if you don't have a chance to try it in town, you can catch this tasty treat at the airport.

lets you sample from the five kinds available, including veggie and pecan-pineapple. All main courses come with rice and your choice of black, refried, or charro beans. The mango margaritas are tops in the potent potables department.

✪ **Güero's.** 1412 S. Congress. ☎ **512/447-7688.** Reservations not accepted. Main courses $7–$12.60. AE, DC, DISC, MC, V. Mon–Fri 11am–11pm; Sat–Sun 8am–11pm. MEXICAN/ REGIONAL MEXICAN.

This sprawling converted feed store has become the center of the newly hip South Austin scene, but it's fine for families, too; there's even a plate for children under 12. Although menu listings are stylishly tongue-in-cheek—the entry for one pork dish describes it as being the same as the beef version "except piggish"—the food is seri-ously good. You can enjoy health-conscious versions of Tex-Mex standards as well as dishes from the interior of Mexico: snapper *á la veracruzana* (with tomatoes, green olives, and jalapeños), say, or Michoacán-style tamales. Lots of plates come topped with cheese, guacamole, and sour cream, but you can also get delicious, low-fat entrees like the chicken *al carbón* (breast meat grilled in *achiote*, a Yucatán spice), served with whole-wheat tortillas and beans. There's live music on Sunday afternoon.

**Matt's El Rancho.** 2613 S. Lamar Blvd. ☎ **512/462-9333.** Reservations not accepted after 5pm on weekends, except for large groups. Main courses $6–$18.25. AE, CB, DC, DISC, MC, V. Sun–Mon and Wed–Thurs 11am–10pm; Fri–Sat 11am–11pm. MEXICAN.

Lyndon Johnson hadn't been serving in the U.S. Senate very long when Matt's El Ran-cho first opened its doors. Although owner Matt Martinez outlived LBJ and other early customers, plenty of his original patrons followed when he moved his restaurant south of downtown in 1986. They came not out of habit, but because Matt (and now his son, Matt, Jr.) has been dishing up consistently tasty food since 1952.

Some of the items show the regulars' influence. For instance, you can thank former land commissioner Bob Armstrong for the tasty cheese, guacamole, and spiced-meat dip that bears his name. Chiles rellenos and grilled shrimp seasoned with garlic and soy are perennial favorites. Although the place can seat almost 500, you might still have to wait for an hour on weekend nights. Just lounge out on the terrace, sip a fresh lime margarita, and chill. The new branch at the Austin airport is not quite as atmos-pheric, nor is the menu as extensive, but you'll get a taste of what draws the crowds to this relatively nontouristy (for the time being, anyway) part of town.

## 6 East Austin

### INEXPENSIVE

**Dario's.** 1800 E. Sixth St. ☎ **512/479-8105.** Reservations for large parties only. Main courses $4.20–$7. DC, DISC, MC, V. Mon–Thurs 7am–3pm (Wed til 4pm); Fri–Sun 7am–10pm. MEXICAN.

One of the most enduring of the many family-run Mexican restaurants in Hispanic East Austin, Dario's is nothing to look at: Tables are Formica, walls are pseudo-wood paneled, and there are few decorations to liven things up. But most of the people who gather here concentrate on what's on their plates—combinations such as the Dario's no. 1: one taco, one cheese enchilada, one tamale with chili con carne, guacamole, Spanish rice, refried beans, and two tortillas ($5.75). On Sunday, Dario's is packed with post-Mass parishioners and post-Saturday night revelers, who come for the reputed hangover cure: a large bowl of *menudo* (just don't ask about the ingredients . . .).

## 7 Northwest

### VERY EXPENSIVE

✪ **Brio Vista.** 9400-B Arboretum Blvd. ☎ **512/342-2642.** Reservations accepted. Main courses $15–$30. AE, CB, DC, DISC, MC, V. Mon–Fri 11am–2pm; Mon–Thurs 6–10pm; Fri–Sat 6–10:30pm; Sun 6–9:30pm (bar open nightly from 5pm). NEW AMERICAN.

Its clean, light lines and soaring archways—not to mention the hilly vistas spread out beyond the elegant patio and the floor-to-ceiling interior windows—lend this dining room a Mediterranean air, but the menu is all creative American. You might start with one of the best Caesar salads in town or a melt-in-your-mouth chicken liver pâté, followed by seared salmon with crab-and-orzo salad or beef tenderloin with sweet corn grits. All the dishes are usefully paired with a recommended wine (or, in the case of the fried calamari, beer), which is typical of the attention to detail you'll find here. All in all, dining at Brio Vista is a soothing experience—once you find parking in the busy lot it shares with Z'Tejas (see below). It's best to turn your car over to the valet at dinner (no charge); at lunch, when the service isn't available, arrive before 11:45am or after 1pm to avoid a long asphalt patrol.

### EXPENSIVE

**Cool River Café.** 4001 Parmer Lane. ☎ **512/835-0010** or 512/835-8629 (reservations). Reservations recommended Thurs–Sat. Main courses $10.95–$29.95. AE, CB, DISC, MC, V. Mon–Sat 11am–11pm (bar Mon–Wed til 1am, Thurs–Sat til 2am; light food served until 12:30am). STEAKS/SOUTHWEST.

Austin's new, new thing, Cool River has something for everyone, from families to prowling singles. The food at this gigantic, self-styled "multi-functional entertainment facility" is good, although not quite as adventurous as the descriptions of some of the Southwestern dishes would lead one to expect. Stick with the certified Angus beef or simple chicken and fish preparations, and you won't go wrong.

But eating is almost beside the point. You come for the scene, which moves from the high-ceilinged, Alpine-style dining rooms through a cushy cigar lounge and past a bar to pool tables, a live music stage, an outdoor patio . . . this place seems endless. There's been an attempt to make this a dress-up destination, so cutoffs and shorts are discouraged, but during my last visit, the crowd was the typical "anything goes" Austin mix.

**Dan McKlusky's.** 10000 Research Blvd. (Arboretum). ☎ **512/346-0780.** Reservations recommended. Main courses $11.75–$33.50; sunset dinners 5–6:30pm, $11.75–$15.95. AE, CB, DC, DISC, MC, V. Mon–Fri 11:15am–2pm; daily 5–10pm. Jazz bar Fri–Sat 7pm–11pm. STEAKS/AMERICAN.

A bastion of traditionalism in a town turning California trendy, Dan McKlusky's offers sanctuary to folks tempted to say "gesundheit" when they hear the word *achiote*. Good, old-fashioned surf and turf—especially turf—draws people into the dimly lit dining rooms with exposed-brick walls.

An on-premises butcher cuts fresh, corn-fed beef to your specifications, so you can adjust the size and price of your steak to your appetite. You can also order as many chops or chicken breasts as you like, or customize an entire dinner, combining six fried shrimp, say, with an 8-ounce rib-eye. There's a lively jazz bar on Friday and Saturday nights.

The original Dan McKlusky's is downtown, at 301 E. Sixth St. (☎ **512/473-8924**).

## MODERATE

⭘ **Z'Tejas Grill.** 9400-A Arboretum Blvd. ☎ **512/346-3506.** Reservations recommended. Main courses $8.95–$17.95. AE, DISC, MC, V. Mon–Thurs 11am–10pm; Fri 11am–11pm; Sat 10am–11pm; Sun 10am–10pm. SOUTHWEST.

An offshoot of a popular downtown eatery (which has also branched off into other states), this northwest location improves a bit on the original. Not that the food is different here—both share a terrifically zippy Southwest menu—but the room is a lot more open, with floor-to-ceiling windows, a soaring ceiling, sophisticated Santa Fe–style decor, and, in cool weather, a roaring fireplace. Gorgonzola ravioli in a sun-dried tomato pesto makes a great starter, and if you see it on a specials menu, go for the smoked chiles rellenos, made with apricots and goat cheese. Entrees include the delicious pan-fried snapper topped with fresh crabmeat, and a tender rib eye livened up by smoked jalapeño cream sauce. Even if you think you can't eat another bite, order a peanut butter pie with chocolate graham cracker crust for the table. It will miraculously disappear.

If you can't make it to the northwest, try the original Z'Tejas at 1110 W. Sixth St. (☎ **512/478-5355**).

## 8  Far West Side

### VERY EXPENSIVE

⭘ **Hudson's on the Bend.** 3509 Hwy. 620 N. ☎ **512/266-1369.** Reservations recommended, essential on weekends. Main courses $29–$35. AE, DC, MC, V. Sun–Mon 6–9pm; Tues–Thurs 6–10pm; Fri–Sat 5:30–10pm (closing times may be earlier in winter; call ahead). NEW AMERICAN.

If you're game for game, served in a very civilized setting, come to Hudson's. Soft candlelight, fresh flowers, fine china, and attentive service combine with outstanding and out-of-the-ordinary cuisine to make this worth a special-occasion splurge. Sparkling lights draped over a cluster of oak trees draw you into a series of romantic dining rooms, set in an old house some 1½ miles southwest of the Mansfield Dam, near Lake Travis.

The chipotle cream sauce was sufficiently spicy so that it was hard to tell whether Omar's rattlesnake cakes tasted like chicken. But they were very good, as were the black-bean ravioli and duck and liver pâté appetizers. Pecan-smoked prime rib and a mixed grill of venison, rabbit, quail, and pheasant sausage are among the excellent entrees I've sampled; the last time I visited, I opted to go lighter with a superb trout served with tangy mango-habañero butter. Although portions are more than generous, finishing a slice of Key lime pie with graham-cracker crust posed no problem.

One caveat: The charming but acoustically poor setting can make Hudson's indoor dining rooms noisy on the weekends. Opt for the terrace when the weather is nice enough.

## MODERATE

**County Line on the Hill.** 6500 W. Bee Cave Rd. ☎ **512/327-1742.** Reservations not accepted. Plates $8.95–$16.95. AE, CB, DC, DISC, MC, V. Summer, Sun–Thurs 5–9:30pm; Fri–Sat 5–10pm; closes a half-hour earlier in winter. BARBECUE.

Some critics deride the County Line chain for its "suburban" barbecue, but Austinites have voted with their feet (or, rather, their cars). If you don't get here before 6pm, you

# Reel Barbecue

Forget cheap labor and right-to-work laws: One of the less-publicized induce-ments for filmmakers to come to Austin is the barbecue—slow-cooked over a wood-fueled fire, and so tasty it doesn't need sauce. The Austin Barbecue Loop, an unofficial feeding arena, describes a rough 30-mile radius from the state capi-tol. Sometimes the meat in these rib joints comes on butcher paper rather than plates, and there's usually little ceremony in the service—if there's any service at all. But who cares about amenities when you're dealing with this kind of flavor and aroma?

Gary Bond, film liaison for the Austin Convention and Visitors Bureau, has the skinny on the celluloid-barbecue connection. According to Bond, the eastern portion of the loop—where rolling prairies, farmland, and small towns conve-niently pass for Everywhere, USA—has received rave reviews from location scouts, stars, and producers alike. **Rudy Mikeska's** (☎ **512/352-5561**), in downtown Taylor, was featured in *The Hot Spot* as The Yellow Rose, the racy hangout of the Don Johnson character, while less than a block away, **Louie Mueller Barbecue** (☎ **512/352-6206**) served as a location for *Flesh and Bone*, starring Dennis Quaid and James Caan. To the south, in Elgin, crews from movie segments, music videos, and commercials have happily hit **Southside Market & BBQ** (☎ **512/281-4650**) on breaks. Still farther south, three hot meat purvey-ors in Lockhart have Hollywood dealmakers bickering about which is best: **Kreutz Market** (in either of its two incarnations, one of which is called Smitty's; ☎ **512/398-2361**), **Black's Barbecue** (☎ **512/398-2712**), or **Chisholm Trail** (☎ **512/398-6027**).

As for the west loop, the guys scouting for *Lolita* loved **Cooper's** (☎ **915/247-5713**) open pit in Llano, while **The Salt Lick,** near Driftwood (see review above), has hosted lots of wrap parties. In Austin itself, Nora Ephron couldn't tear herself away from **The Green Mesquite** (☎ **512/335-9885;** various locations).

can expect to wait as long as an hour and a half to eat. Should this happen, sit out on the deck and soak in the views of the Hill Country, or look at the old advertising signs hung on the knotty-pine planks of this 1920s roadhouse, formerly a speakeasy and a brothel. In addition to the barbecue—oh-so-slowly-smoked ribs, brisket, chicken, or sausage—skewered meat or vegetable plates are available. County Line on the Lake, near Lake Austin, 5204 FM 2222 (☎ **512/346-3664**), offering the same menu, is open for lunch as well as dinner.

✪ **The Oasis.** 6550 Comanche Trail, near Lake Travis. ☎ **512/266-2441.** Reservations not accepted. Main courses $10–$25. AE, DISC, MC, V. Mon–Thurs 11:30am–10pm; Fri–Sat 11:30am–11pm; Sun 11am–10pm. AMERICAN/MEXICAN.

This is where Austinites like to take out-of-town guests at sunset: From the 28 multi-level decks nestled into the hillside hundreds of feet above Lake Travis, visitors and locals alike cheer—both with toasts and applause—as the fiery orb descends behind the hills on the opposite bank. No one ever leaves unimpressed. The Oasis was never known for its food, but it's definitely improved in recent years. The chicken fajitas are great, as are the humongous crab-stuffed mushrooms. Add a margarita, and kick back. It doesn't get much mellower than this.

✪ **The Salt Lick.** 18300 FM 1826, Driftwood. ☎ **512/858-4959** or 888/SALT-LICK (mail order). Reservations for large parties only. Main courses $7–$16. No credit cards. Daily 11am–10pm. BARBECUE.

It's 11½ miles from the junction of 290 West and FM 1826 (turn right) to The Salt Lick, but you'll start smelling the smoke during the last 5 miles of your trip. Moist chicken, beef, and pork, as well as terrific homemade pickles, more than justify the drive. You're faced with a tough decision here: If you indulge in the all-you-can-eat family-style platter of beef, sausage, and pork ribs, you might have to pass on the fresh-baked peach or blackberry cobbler, which would be a pity. In warm weather, seating is outside at picnic tables under oak trees; in winter, fireplaces blaze in a series of large, rustic rooms. Unlike many Texas barbecue places, The Salt Lick prides itself on its sauce, which has a sweet and sour tang. If you like your BBQ with a brew, tote your own in a cooler; Hays County is dry.

Good news: Now you don't have to drive all the way out to the country for a smoked meat fix. It's not quite as atmospheric as the original, but The Salt Lick concession at the new airport is convenient and quick. If you get hooked on the barbecue at either place, you can have your brisket or smoked turkey shipped.

## INEXPENSIVE

**Rosie's Tamale House.** 13436 Hwy. 71, Bee Cave. ☎ **512/263-5245.** Reservations not accepted. Main courses $4.95–$9.15. No credit cards. Sun–Mon and Wed–Thurs 11am–10pm; Tues 5–10pm; Fri–Sat 11am–10:30pm. MEXICAN.

When Willie Nelson first started coming to Rosie's in 1973, he always asked for a taco, a beef enchilada, chile con queso, and guacamole. Rosie has moved to a larger place, down the road from her original converted gas station, and Nelson's standing order is now enshrined on the menu as Willie's Plate. But the singer still drops by, and Rosie is still here to greet him—and everyone else who comes in. The food isn't fancy, but it's filling and good. Before you leave, take out a dozen fresh tamales ($5.75) for a midnight snack and check out the back wall, lined with photos of famous and not-so-famous regular customers. This branch, in dry Hays county, is BYOB, but the two other Austin Rosie's—102 E. Oltorf (☎ **512/440-7727**) and 13776 Hwy. 183 (☎ **512/219-7793**)—run by family members, have full bars, and, unlike the original, accept credit cards.

## 9  Only in Austin

For information on Austin's funky, totally original cafe scene, see "Late-Night Bites," in chapter 15.

### A BAT'S-EYE VIEW

From late March through mid-November, the most coveted seats in town are the ones with a view of the thousands of bats that fly out from under the Congress Avenue Bridge in search of a hearty bug dinner at dusk. The **Shoreline Grill** (see above) and the **Cafe at the Four Seasons,** 98 San Jacinto Blvd. (☎ **512/478-4500**), are the two toniest spots for observing this astounding phenomenon, while **TGIF's** at the Radisson Hotel on Town Lake, 11 E. First St. (☎ **512/478-9611**), offers a casual, collegial roost.

### MUSICAL BRUNCHES

For a religious experience on Sunday morning that doesn't require entering a church or temple, check out the gospel brunch at **Stubb's Bar-B-Q,** 801 Red River St.

(☎ 512/480-8341). The singing is heavenly, and the pork ribs are divine. If you worship at the altar of the likes of Miles Davis, the Sunday jazz brunches at both locations of **Manuel's** (see "Downtown," earlier in this chapter) let you enjoy eggs with venison chorizo or corn gorditas with garlic and cilantro while listening to hot live jazz or Latin sounds. Check out www.manuels.com to find out who's gonna be sizzling while you're visiting.

## COFFEEHOUSES

Austin has often been compared to Seattle for its music scene and its green, college-town atmosphere. Although the city isn't quite up to, er, speed when it comes to coffeehouses, there are enough home-grown versions these days to constitute a respectable presence around downtown and the university.

**Little City,** 916 Congress Ave. (☎ 512/476-2489), with its ultra-chic design, is close to the downtown tourist sights, and the only local place to get a java fix near the capitol on Sunday. Another location, at 3403 Guadalupe, near the UT campus (☎ 512/467-2326), roasts its own beans. A couple of blocks farther south, **Texpresso,** 718 Congress Ave. (☎ 512/477-3275), is renowned for the incredibly creamy coffee drink that gives the place its name; it was invented by Austinite David Hall while he was working as a barista at a Beverly Hills boutique. In the warehouse district, **Ruta Maya,** 218 W. Fourth St. (☎ 512/472-9637), offers a funky atmosphere, Tuesday night poetry readings, eclectic live music—and perfectly brewed coffee. A similar mix prevails at **Flipnotics,** 1601 Barton Springs Road (☎ 512/322-9750), a two-story, indoor/outdoor "coffeespace" where you can sip great caffeine drinks or beer while listening to fine acoustic singer/songwriters (most nights). You don't have to get wired at **Spider House,** 2908 Fruth St. (☎ 512/480-9562), just north of the UT campus, where the likes of tempeh chili, Frito pie, great smoothies, and beer complement the coffee portion of the menu. The large, tree-shaded patio should get you mellow, too. Still, in the chill-out department, it's impossible to beat ✪ **Mozart's,** 3825 Lake Austin Blvd. (☎ 512/477-2900), with killer views of Lake Austin and great white-chocolate-almond croissants.

# Exploring Austin 13

Stroll up Congress Avenue and you'll see much the same sight as visitors to Austin did more than 100 years ago: a broad thoroughfare gently rising to the grandest of all state capitols. Obsessed from early on with its place in history, the city is not neglecting it now, either. The capitol recently underwent a complete overhaul; a grand new state history museum opened its doors near the capitol in 2001; and downtown's historic Sixth Street is turning back the clock with ongoing restorations. The town is on a cultural tear, too, as dual multimillion-dollar complexes are being built to house the city's two top art collections, and new galleries are opening all around town.

But it is Austin's myriad natural attractions that put the city on all the "most livable" lists. From bats and birds to Barton Springs, from the Highland Lakes to the hike-and-bike trails, Austin lays out the green carpet for its visitors. You'd be hard-pressed to find a city that has more to offer fresh-air enthusiasts.

It's also easy to sightsee here, even if you don't have a car. Bicycling is not the only free ride in town. There's no charge for transportation on the city's five 'Dillo lines, which cover most of the downtown tourist sites and the University of Texas. Other freebies include the Convention and Visitors Bureau's excellent guided walks and the state-sponsored tours of the governor's mansion and the state capitol.

## Suggested Itineraries

### If You Have 1 Day

You'll see much of what makes Austin unique if you spend a day downtown. You might start out with a cup of coffee and a pastry at the **Little City café,** then head over to the **Old Land Office Building,** interesting in itself and, as an information center, the ideal place to begin your tour of the capitol complex. The **capitol** and newer extension are next; you'll be impressed by the results of the costly restoration. You can either go from here to the **governor's mansion** (keep in mind that the last tour is at 11:40am Mon to Fri only) and the nearby historic **Bremond block** district for a taste of how the other half lived in the 19th century. Or visit the new **Bob Bullock Texas State History Museum,** where you'll get the big picture (via IMAX and otherwise). Have lunch at the history museum or, if you've gone to the governor's mansion, on historic **Sixth Street,** which is well worth a stroll in either case. A bit farther south is the north shore of **Town Lake,** where you can rest under the shade of an oak tree or join the athletic hordes in perpetual motion on the hike-and-bike trail. If you're in town from late March through October, book a table at the Shoreline Grill and **watch the bats** take off at dusk from under the Congress Avenue Bridge. Devote any energy you have left to the **live music** scene back on Sixth Street, which takes on an entirely new character at night.

### If You Have 2 Days

**Day 1**    Follow the itinerary outlined in "If You Have 1 Day," above.

**Day 2**    In the morning, head out to the **Lady Bird Johnson Wildflower Center,** where Texas's bountiful natural blooms are the stars. In the afternoon, visit the **LBJ Library, Texas Memorial Museum,** and **Jack S. Blanton Museum of Art** on the University of Texas campus; weekends, you can also tour the **UT Tower.** (If you're traveling with youngsters, **substitute** the excellent Children's Museum or the Jourdan Bachman Pioneer Farm.) At night, get your music fix away from the Sixth Street hordes—try **Antone's** for blues or the **Broken Spoke** for country.

### If You Have 3 Days

**Days 1–2**    Same as Days 1 and 2 in "If You Have 2 Days."

**Day 3**    Scope out the cityscape from **Mount Bonnell,** the highest point in Austin; then visit the historic **Hyde Park neighborhood,** including the **Elisabet Ney museum.** If the weather is nice, have lunch at one of the restaurants along Barton Springs Road, then spend the afternoon in **Zilker Park:** Go for a stroll at the lovely Botanical Gardens and afterward dip into the Barton Springs pool. Or if you're interested in history, substitute the sights on Austin's east side—the **George Washington Carver Museum,** the **State Cemetery,** and the **French Legation.** There are a number of good, inexpensive Mexican restaurants in the area. Alternatively, after Mt. Bonnell, you can head for **Lake Travis** and some serious waterplay. Just be sure to be at the **Oasis** in time to applaud the sunset.

### If You Have 4 Days

**Days 1–3**    Same as Days 1–3 in "If You Have 3 Days."

**Day 4**    Take a day trip to Fredericksburg or New Braunfels in the **Hill Country.** Fredericksburg lays on the Germanic charm a bit more, but New Braunfels competes with a discount mall and lots of river-rafting options.

### If You Have 5 Days or More

**Days 1–3**    Follow the strategy in "If You Have 3 Days," above.

**Days 4–5**    Stay overnight at a bed-and-breakfast in **Fredericksburg** and visit the **LBJ Ranch, Enchanted Rock State Park,** and some nearby **Hill Country** towns (see chapter 16).

## 1  The Top Attractions

✪  **Barton Springs Pool.** Zilker Park, 2201 Barton Springs Rd. ☎ **512/867-3080.** Admission $2.50 Mon–Fri, $2.75 Sat–Sun adults; $1 ages 12–17; 50¢ children 11 and under. Daily 5am–10pm except during pool maintenance (Thurs 8am–7pm). Lifeguard on duty Apr–Sept 8am–10pm; Oct to early Nov 8am–8pm; mid-Nov to Mar 9am–6pm. Gift shop and Splash!, Tues–Fri noon–6pm; Sat–Sun 10am–6pm. Bus: 30 (Barton Creek Sq.).

If the University of Texas is the seat of Austin's intellect, and the state capitol is its political pulse, Barton Springs is the city's soul. The Native Americans who settled

# Downtown Austin Attractions & Shopping

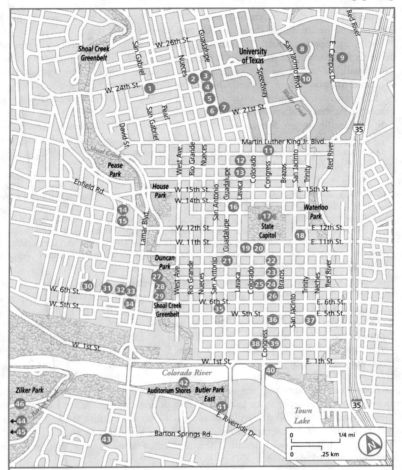

near here believed these waters had spiritual powers, and today's residents still place their faith in the abilities of the spring-fed pool to soothe and cool.

Each day, approximately 32 million gallons of water from the underground Edwards Aquifer bubble to the surface here; at one time, this force powered several Austin mills. Although the original limestone bottom remains, concrete was added to the banks to form uniform sides to what is now a swimming pool of about 1,000 feet by 125 feet. Maintaining a constant 68° temperature, the amazingly clear water is bracing in summer and warming in winter, when many hearty souls brave the cold for a dip. Lifeguards are on duty for most of the day, and a large bathhouse operated by the Parks and Recreation Department offers changing facilities and a gift shop. For details about the new Splash! environmental information center (☎ **512/481-1466**), see "Especially for Kids," below.

**The Bob Bullock Texas State History Museum.** 1800 N. Congress Ave. ☎ **512/ 936-4699.** www.TheStoryofTexas.com. Exhibit areas: $5 adults, $4.25 seniors 65 and over; free for ages 18 and under). IMAX theater: $6.50 adults, $5.50 seniors, $4.50 youth. Texas Spirit Theater: $5 adult, $4 senior, $3.50 youth. Combination tickets: Exhibits and IMAX, $9/$7.50/$4.50; exhibits and Spirit Theater $8/$6.50/$3.50; exhibits and both theaters $12.50/$10/$6. Mon–Sat 9am–6pm; Sun 1–6pm. Phone or check Web site for additional IMAX evening hours. Closed New Year's Day, Easter Sun, Thanksgiving, Christmas Eve, and Christmas Day. Bus: Orange and Blue 'Dillo.

Not yet open when we went to press (Apr 2001 is its slated debut), this new museum complex promises to be Austin's answer to the Alamo when it comes to glitzing up and enlarging Texas history.

The complex consists of three parts. Three floors of exhibits, arrayed around a huge, capitol-like rotunda centered by a 50-foot polished granite map of Texas, feature themed permanent displays—everything from Stephen F. Austin's diary to Neil Armstrong's space suit—and rotating special shows. (The premier exhibit is titled "It Ain't Braggin If It's True.") In the multimedia, special-effects Spirit Theater, the only one of its kind in Texas, you can experience the high-speed winds of the great Galveston hurricane and feel your seats shake as an East Texas oil well hits a gusher. Austin's only IMAX theater, with 3-D capabilities, will feature both a historical film tailored to the Texas history theme and independent movies designed to highlight the theater's capacity. There's also an indoor/outdoor cafe, a Texas Fair–themed store, and—that rarity—an underground parking garage.

✪ **Lady Bird Johnson Wildflower Center.** 4801 La Crosse Ave. ☎ **512/292-4100.** www.wildflower.org. Admission $4 adults, $2.50 students and seniors 60 and older; 4 and younger free. Tues–Sat 9am–4pm; Sun 1–4pm (grounds open Tues–Sun 9am–5:30pm). Take Loop 1 (Mo-Pac) south to Slaughter Lane; drive 0.8 mile to La Crosse Ave.

Talk about fieldwork: The researchers at this lovely, colorful complex have 178 acres of wildflowers for their personal laboratory. Founded by Lady Bird Johnson in 1982, the center is dedicated to the study and preservation of native plants—and where better to survey them than in the Texas Hill Country, famous for its glorious spring blossoms?

The main attractions are naturally the display gardens—among them, one designed to attract butterflies—and the wildflower-filled meadow, but the native stone architecture of the visitors center and observation tower is attention grabbing, too. Included among the interesting indoor displays is one of Lady Bird's wide-brimmed gardening hats and a talking lawnmower with a British accent. There are usually free lectures and guided walks on the weekends; phone or check the Web site for current programs. The facility's research library is the largest in the United States for the study of native plants. The excellent gift shop sells packets of information about the species that are indigenous to your home state, as well as plant books and many creative botanical-related items. The admission and gift shop proceeds help fund the nonprofit organization.

⭘ **LBJ Library and Museum.** University of Texas, 2313 Red River. ☎ **512/916-5136.** www.lbjlib.utexas.edu. Free admission. Daily 9am–5pm. Closed Christmas. Bus: Blue and Orange 'Dillos, UT Shuttle.

Set on a hilltop commanding an impressive campus view, the LBJ Library contains some 45 million documents relating to the colorful 36th president, along with gifts, memorabilia, and other historical objects. Johnson himself kept an office here from 1971, when the building was dedicated, until his death in 1973. Photos trace his long political career, starting with his early successes as a state representative and continuing through to the Kennedy assassination and the Civil Rights Movement. LBJ's success in enacting social programs is depicted in an Alfred Leslie painting of the Great Society. Johnson loved political cartoons, even when he was their target; examples from his large collection are among the museum's most interesting rotating exhibits. Adults and kids alike are riveted by the animatronic version of LBJ. Dressed in his clothes and speaking with a tape recording of his voice, the life-size, gesticulating figure seems eerily alive from afar.

⭘ **State Capitol.** 11th and Congress sts. ☎ **512/463-0063.** Free admission. Mon–Fri 7am–10pm; Sat–Sun 9am–8pm; 24 hours a day during legislative sessions (held in odd years, starting in Jan, for 140 straight days; 30-day special sessions are also sometimes called). Free 45-min. guided tours every 15 min. Mon–Fri 8:30am–4:30pm; Sat–Sun 9:30am–4:30pm. Bus: Yellow, Orange, Red, and Blue 'Dillo lines.

Begun in 1990 and completed in time for the 1995 legislative session, a massive renovation and expansion—to the tune of $187.6 million—restored Texas's capitol building to its former glory and added a striking new underground annex. A refurbishing of the capitol grounds was finished in 1997. Among other things, the old wrought-iron perimeter fence, topped with gold Lone Stars, was reconstructed (part of it was in storage) and reinstalled—but this time, the gates don't have to be shut to keep the cattle out.

The current 1888 capitol replaced an 1852 limestone statehouse that burned down in 1881; a land-rich but otherwise impecunious Texas government traded 3 million acres of public lands to contractors to finance its construction. Gleaming pink granite was donated to the cause, but a railroad had to be built to transport the material some 75 miles from Granite Mountain, near Marble Falls, to Austin. Texas convicts labored on the project alongside 62 stonecutters brought in from Scotland.

The result was the largest state capitol in the country, second only in size to the U.S. Capitol—but measuring 7 feet taller. The building covers 3 acres of ground; the cornerstone alone weighs 16,000 pounds, and the total length of the wooden wainscoting runs approximately 7 miles. A splendid rotunda and dome lie at the intersection of the main corridors; the House and Senate chambers are located at opposite ends of the second level. The legislative sessions are open to the public; go up to the third-floor visitors' balcony if you want see how politics are conducted Texas-style.

Almost 700,000 tons of rock were chiseled from the ground to make way for the new extension, connected to the capitol and four other state buildings by tunnels. Skylights provide natural illumination and afford spectacular views of the capitol dome. To complement the 1888 building, the annex was constructed with similar materials and incorporates many of the capitol's symbols and styles. The design of what has been called the "inside-out, upside-down capitol" is extremely clever; the large brass star on the outdoor rotunda, for example, also functions as a water drain.

## 2 More Attractions

### ARCHITECTURAL HIGHLIGHTS

**Moore/Andersson Compound.** 2102 Quarry Rd. ☎ **512/477-4557.** Tours $10 adults, $4 students. By appointment only.

Architecture buffs won't want to miss the hacienda-like compound where Charles Moore spent the last decade of his life—when he wasn't traveling, that is. The peripatetic American architect, who kept a low profile but had a great influence on postmodernism, built five homes; this one, which he designed with Arthur Andersson, perfectly demonstrates his combination of controlled freedom, whimsical imagination, and connection to the environment. The wildly colorful rooms are filled with folk art from around the world; odd angles, bunks, and dividers render every inch of space fascinating. In the evening, the compound is now used as a conference and lecture center. Tours are led by enthusiastic graduate students in historic preservation at the University of Texas, where Moore had held his last chair in architecture.

**Moonlight Towers.**

In May 1895, the first dam-generated electric current illuminated 4 square blocks around each of Austin's 31 new electric lights, or "moonlight towers." Some residents of the still-rural town worried that these 165-foot-high spires would confuse the roosters, who wouldn't be able to figure out when the sun was coming up. Seventeen of these cast- and wrought-iron towers, most of them downtown, remain part of Austin's street-lighting system. You can also see one in Hyde Park, at 41st Street and Speedway.

### A CEMETERY

**Texas State Cemetery.** 909 Navasota St. ☎ **512/463-0605.** www.cemetery.state.tx.us. Free admission. Grounds, daily 8am–5pm; visitors center, Mon–Fri 8am–5pm. Bus: 4–18 stop nearby.

The city's namesake, Stephen F. Austin, is the best-known resident of this east side cemetery, established by the state in 1851. Judge Edwin Waller, who laid out the grid plan for Austin's streets and later served as the city's mayor, also rests here, as do eight former Texas governors, various fighters in Texas's battles for independence, a woman who lived to tell the tale of the Alamo, and Barbara Jordan, the first black woman from the South elected to the U.S. Congress (in 1996, she became the first African American to gain admittance to these grounds). Perhaps the most striking monument, sculpted by Elisabet Ney (see "Museums & Galleries," below), commemorates Confederate General Albert Sidney Johnston, who died at the Battle of Shiloh.

A multimillion-dollar revamp begun in 1994 added much-needed pedestrian walkways and, in 1997, a visitors center, designed to suggest the long barracks at the Alamo. Two self-guided tour pamphlets are available. The one published by the cemetery details the new features and sketches the histories of some of the most important residents, while the one created by the Austin Convention and Visitors Bureau offers a wider historical context and gives some headstone highlights. This historic boneyard marked its 150th anniversary in 2001. Check the Web site for information on the various ceremonies and exhibitions that will be held throughout the year to mark the occasion.

### HISTORIC SITES

✪ **Capitol Complex Visitors Center.** 112 E. 11th St. (southeast corner of capitol grounds). ☎ **512/305-8400.** www.tspb.state.tx.us (click on "visitors center"). Free admission. Daily 9am–5pm. Free tours of the building upon request. Bus: Yellow, Orange, Red, and Blue 'Dillo lines.

The capitol wasn't the only important member of the state complex to undergo a face-lift: Texas also spent $4 million to gussy up its oldest surviving office building, the 1857 General Land Office. If the imposing German Romanesque structure looks a bit grand for the headquarters of an administrative agency, keep in mind that land has long been the state's most important resource. Among the employees of this important—and very political—office, charged with maintaining records and surveying holdings, was the writer O. Henry, who worked as a draftsman from 1887 to 1891; he based two short stories on his experiences here.

The building was rededicated as a visitors center for the Capitol Complex in 1994; the Texas Department of Transportation also distributes state travel information here. A Walter Cronkite–narrated video tells the history of the complex, and changing exhibits on the first floor highlight the Capitol Preservation Project; upstairs, displays focus on the Land Office and other aspects of Texas's past. You can buy replicas of the door hinges, to be used as bookends, and other capitol gifts at the gift shop, which also has a good collection of books on Texas history.

**Driskill Hotel.** 604 Brazos St. ☎ **512/474-5911.** Bus: Blue and Red 'Dillos.

Colonel Jesse Driskill was not a modest man. When he opened a hotel in 1886, he named it after himself, put busts of himself and his two sons over the entrances, and installed bas-relief sculptures of longhorn steers—to remind folks how he had made his fortune. Nor did he build a modest property: The ornate four-story structure, which originally boasted a skylit rotunda, has the largest arched doorway in Texas over its east entrance. So posh that the state legislature met here while the 1888 capitol was being built, the hotel has had its ups and downs over the years, but it was restored to its former glory in the late 1990s. You can pick up a history of the hotel at the front desk; if the concierge has time, he'll be happy to help orient you.

**French Legation.** 802 San Marcos. ☎ **512/472-8180.** Admission $3 adults, $2 seniors, $1 students (under 18); 5 and under free. Tours Tues–Sun 1–5pm. Go east on Seventh St., then turn left on San Marcos St.; the parking lot is behind the museum on Embassy and Ninth sts. Bus: 4 stops nearby (at San Marcos and 7th sts.).

The oldest residence still standing in Austin was built in 1841 for Count Alphonse Dubois de Saligny, France's representative to the fledgling Republic of Texas. Although his home was very extravagant for the then primitive capital, the flamboyant de Saligny didn't stay around to enjoy it for very long; he left town in a huff after his servant was beaten in retaliation for making bacon out of some pigs that had dined on the diplomat's linens. In the back of the house, considered the best example of French colonial–style architecture outside Louisiana, is a re-creation of the only known authentic Creole kitchen in the United States. A gift shop focuses on Texas history from the time of the republic to the present.

**Governor's Mansion.** 1010 Colorado St. ☎ **512/463-5516** (recording). Free admission. Tours offered every 20 min. Mon–Fri 10–11:40am; closed weekends, some holidays, and at the discretion of the governor. Bus: Red and Yellow 'Dillo lines.

Unless you slept through the entire 2000 election, you probably saw more shots of the Texas governor's mansion than you'd care to remember. Although it's one of the oldest buildings in the city (1856), this opulent house is far from a mere symbol or museum piece: State law requires that the governor live here whenever he or she is in Austin. If the governor happens to be hosting a luncheon, you might notice warm smells wafting from the kitchen if you're on the last mansion tour of the day.

Living in the mansion isn't exactly a hardship, although it was originally built by Abner Cook without any indoor toilets (there are now seven). The house was beauti-fully restored in 1979, but you can still see the scars of nails that were hammered into

# Greater Austin Attractions & Shopping

**ATTRACTIONS**

Austin Museum of Art-
  Laguna Gloria **15**
Austin Nature & Science
  Center **28**
Austin Zoo **43**
Celis Brewery **10**
Elisabet Ney Museum **26**
French Legation **30**
George Washington Carver
  Museum **29**
Hyde Park **25**
Lady Bird Johnson
  Wildflower Center **42**
Jourdan Bachman
  Pioneer Farm **9**
Moore/Andersson
  Compound **27**
Mt. Bonnell **14**
Texas State Cemetery **31**

**SHOPPING**

Antique Marketplace **16**
The Arboretum **2**
Artisans Gallery **2**
Austin Antique Mall **4**
Austin Country Flea Market **11**
Barton Creek Square **40**
Breed & Co. Hardware **23**
Central Market **20**
Clarksville Pottery **2** & **20**
Dillard's **1**
Eco-Wise **34**
Electric Ladyland **36**
El Taller Gallery **6**
Fire Island Hot Glass
  Studio, Inc. **32**
Gallery Shoal Creek **18**
The Gateway Comples **3**
Grape Vine Market **5**
Highland Mall **12**
Hog Wild **17**
Keepers **22**
Lakeline Mall **1**
Neiman Marcus Last Call **41**
Northcross Mall **7**
Russell Korman **19**
Saks **3**
Sheplers **13**
Terra Toys **38**
Therapy **33**
Toy Joy **24**
Travis County Farmers' Market **8**
Under the Sun **35**
26 Doors **21**
Whip in Convenience Store **39**
Yard Dog **37**

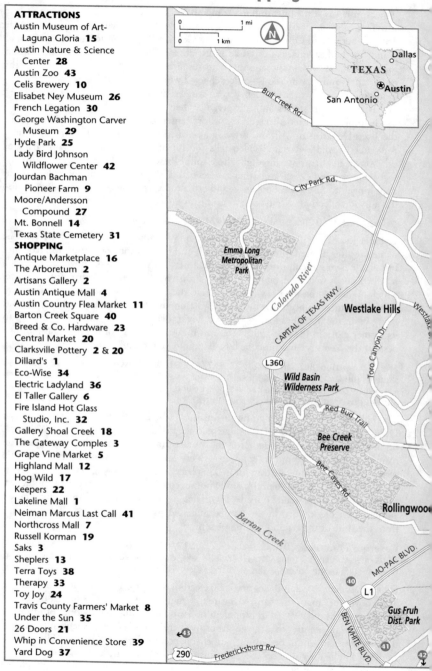

the banister of the spiral staircase to break Governor Hogg's young son Tom of the habit of sliding down it. The nation's first female governor, Miriam "Ma" Ferguson, entertained her friend Will Rogers in the mansion, and Governor John Connally recuperated here from gunshot wounds received when he accompanied John F. Kennedy on his fatal motorcade through Dallas. Among the many historical artifacts on display are a desk belonging to Stephen F. Austin and portraits of Davy Crockett and Sam Houston.

Come as close to opening time as you can; only a limited number of people are allowed to tour the mansion during the few hours it's open to the public. If you arrive later, you might either have a long wait or not get in at all.

**Neill-Cochran Museum House.** 2310 San Gabriel St. ☎ **512/478-2335.** Admission $2 adults; children under 10 free. Wed–Sun 2–5pm; free 20-min. tours given. Bus: Yellow 'Dillo, UT shuttle.

Abner Cook, the architect-contractor responsible for the governor's mansion and many of Austin's other gracious Greek revival mansions, built this home in 1855. It bears his trademark portico with six Doric columns and a balustrade designed with crossed sheaves of wheat. Almost all its doors, windows, shutters, and hinges are original—which is rather astonishing when you consider that the house was used as the city's first Blind Institute in 1856 and then as a hospital for Union prisoners near the end of the Civil War. The beautifully maintained 18th- and 19th-century furnishings are interesting, but many people come just to see the painting of bluebonnets that helped convince legislators to designate these native blooms the state flower.

**Old Bakery and Emporium.** 1006 Congress Ave. ☎ **512/477-5961.** Free admission. Mon–Fri 9am–4pm; first 3 Sat in Dec 10am–2pm. Bus: Red 'Dillo.

On the National Register of Historic Landmarks, the Old Bakery was built in 1876 by Charles Lundberg, a Swedish master baker, and continuously operated until 1936. You can still see the giant oven and wooden baker's spade inside. Rescued from demolition by the Austin Heritage Society, and now owned and operated by Austin's Parks and Recreation Department, the brick-and-limestone building is one of the few unaltered structures on Congress Avenue. It houses a gift shop, selling crafts handmade by seniors, a reasonably priced lunchroom, and a hospitality desk with visitors' brochures.

**Paramount Theatre.** 713 Congress Ave. ☎ **512/472-5470** (box office) or 512/472-5411. Bus: Red and Orange 'Dillo lines.

The Marx Brothers, Sarah Bernhardt, Helen Hayes, and Katharine Hepburn all entertained at this former vaudeville house, which opened as the Majestic Theatre in 1915 and functioned as a movie palace for 50 years. Restored to its original opulence, the Paramount now hosts Broadway shows, visiting celebrity performers, local theatrical productions, including an impressive Kids Classic series, and, in the summer, old-time films. There are no formal tours.

**Treaty Oak.** 503 Baylor St., between W. Fifth and Sixth sts. ☎ **512/440-5194.** www.ci.austin.tx.us/treatyoak. Bus: Silver 'Dillo.

Legend has it that Stephen F. Austin signed the first boundary treaty with the Comanches under the spreading branches of this 500-year-old live oak, which once served as the symbolic border between Anglo and Indian territory. Whatever the case, this is the sole remaining tree in what was once a grove of Council Oaks—which made the well-publicized attempt on its life in 1989 especially shocking. But almost as dramatic as the story of the tree's deliberate poisoning by an attention-seeking Austinite is the tale of its rescue by an international team of foresters. The dried wood from major limbs that they removed has been allocated to local artists, who are creating public artworks celebrating the tree. You can also buy items such as pen sets, gavels,

---

**❷  Did You Know?**

- Austin is home to the most highly educated citizens per capita, and has the highest bookstore sales per capita of the U.S.'s 50 largest cities.
- Sixty-five percent of Austinites use computers, making Austin the most computer-literate city in the United States.
- Austin is the only city in the world to preserve its first public electric lights—17 of the original 31 "moonlight towers" are still operating around the city. (A special moonlight tower was erected for scenes in the movie *Dazed and Confused* when it was filmed in Austin.)
- The University of Texas's Buford H. Jester Center, which hosts many of the college dormitories, has the largest kitchen in Texas, capable of serving more than 13,000 students a day.
- The world's first photograph, created by Joseph Nicèphore Nièpce in 1826, is at UT's Harry Ransom Humanities Research Center.
- Austin has more restaurants per capita than any other city in the United States.

---

clocks, and wooden boxes made out of the tree's severed limbs, as well as less expensive mementos. The proceeds go to the forestry unit of the City of Austin Parks and Recreation Department.

## LIBRARIES/RESEARCH CENTERS

**Austin History Center/Austin Public Library.** 810 Guadalupe St. ☎ **512/499-7599.** Free admission. Mon–Thurs 9am–9pm; Fri–Sat 9am–6pm; Sun noon–6pm. Closed most holidays. Bus: Yellow 'Dillo.

Built in 1933, the Renaissance revival–style public library not only embodies some of the finest architecture, ironwork, and stone carving of its era, but also serves as the best resource for information about Austin from before the city's founding in 1839 to the present. The center often hosts exhibitions drawn from its vast archives of historical photographs and sketches.

**Harry Ransom Humanities Research Center.** University of Texas. Harry Ransom Center, 21st and Guadalupe sts; Flawn Academic Center, west of the main tower. ☎ **512/471-8944.** Free admission. Exhibitions Mon–Fri 9am–4pm. Closed university holidays. Bus: Blue 'Dillo, UT Shuttle.

The special collections of the Harry Ransom Center (HRC) contain approximately 1 million rare books, 36 million manuscripts, 5 million photographs, and more than 100,000 works of art. Most of this wealth is the domain of scholars (although anyone can request a look at it), but permanent and rotating exhibits of HRC holdings are held in two buildings: the Harry Ransom Center and the Leeds Gallery of the Flawn Academic Center. A Gutenberg Bible—one of only five complete copies in the United States—is on permanent display on the first floor of the HRC, and you never know what else you might see: costumes from *Gone With the Wind,* the original manuscript of *Death of a Salesman,* or letters written by novelist Isaac Bashevis Singer.

## MUSEUMS & GALLERIES

**Austin Museum of Art—Downtown.** 823 Congress Ave. (at 9th St.) ☎ **512/495-9224.** www.amoa.org. Admission $3 adults, $2 seniors and students, $1 for everyone on Thurs; children under 12 free. (Shows frequently receive corporate sponsorship, so general admission is often free.) Tues–Wed and Fri–Sat 10am–6pm; Thurs 10am–8pm; Sun noon–5pm. Bus: Red and Orange 'Dillo lines.

Plans for a major downtown museum of art have been in the works for nearly 2 decades. This high-ceiling one-story space isn't it (architect Richard Gluckman is designing the $60 million facility that's slated to open a few blocks away in 2003), but it will do nicely for the time being. Major name shows—for example, a photography exhibit focusing on Tina Modotti and Edward Weston—are complemented by exhibits of lesser known local artists, of consistently high quality. The museum shop is a great place to pick up some artsy mugs or earrings.

**Austin Museum of Art—Laguna Gloria.** 3809 W. 35th St. ☎ **512/458-8191.** www.amoa.org. 1 mile past west end of 35th St. at the foot of Mt. Bonnell. Closed for renovations until 2004.

This intimate art museum sits on 28 palm- and pecan-shaded acres overlooking Lake Austin, believed by some to be part of a claim staked out for his retirement by Stephen F. Austin, who didn't live to enjoy the view. The lovely Mediterranean-style villa that houses the exhibits was built in 1916 by Austin newspaper publisher Hal Sevier and his wife, Clara Driscoll, best known for her successful crusade to save the Alamo from commercial development. The buildings and exhibition spaces have been shuttered as part of a $15 million renovation project, but the grounds and sculpture gardens remain open. Check the Web site for the current state of the renovations.

**Elisabet Ney Museum.** 304 E. 44th St. ☎ **512/458-2255.** Free admission. Wed–Sat 10am–5pm; Sun noon–5pm. Bus: 1 or 5.

Strong-willed and eccentric, German-born sculptor Elisabet Ney nevertheless charmed Austin society in the late 19th century. When she died, her admirers turned her Hyde Park studio into a museum. In the former loft and working area—part Greek temple, part medieval battlement—visitors can view plaster replicas of many of her pieces. Drawn toward the larger-than-life figures of her age, Ney had created busts of Schopenhauer, Garibaldi, and Bismarck by the time she was commissioned to make models of Texas heroes Stephen F. Austin and Sam Houston for an 1893 Chicago exposition. William Jennings Bryan, Enrico Caruso, Jan Paderewski, and four Texas governors were among the many visitors to her Austin studio.

**George Washington Carver Branch Library and Museum.** 1165 Angelina St. ☎ **512/472-4809.** Free admission. Tues–Thurs 10am–6pm; Fri–Sat noon–5pm. Bus: 2 and 120.

The many contributions of Austin's African-American community are highlighted at this museum, the first one in Texas to be devoted to black history. Rotating exhibits of contemporary artwork share the space with photographs, videos, oral histories, and other artifacts from the community's past. Cultural events are often held here, too. The museum's collection is housed in the city's first public library building, opened in 1926 and moved to this site in 1933. The newer George Washington Carver branch of the public library is next door.

**✪ Jack S. Blanton Museum of Art.** University of Texas, Art Building, 23rd St. and San Jacinto Blvd. ☎ **512/471-7324.** www.blantonmuseum.org. Free admission. Mon–Fri 9am–5pm (Thurs until 9pm); Sat–Sun 1–5pm. Closed university holidays. Bus: Blue and Yellow 'Dillo lines, UT Shuttle.

The good news: The Blanton is ranked among the top 10 university art museums in the United States, featuring some of the most important art in the country. Most notable is the Suida-Manning Collection, a superb gathering of Renaissance works by such masters as Veronese, Rubens, and Tiepolo that was sought after by the Metropolitan museum, among others. Other permanent holdings include the Mari and

James Michener collection of 20th-century American masters, the largest gathering of Latin American art in the United States, and a rare display of 19th-century plaster casts of monumental Greek and Roman sculpture.

The bad news: The structure being planned to highlight these impressive works won't be completed for a while yet. Scheduled to open in 2004 on MLK and Speedway (across from the Bob Bullock History Center), this art space will help connect the university with the capitol complex. In the meantime, you'll still be able to view portions of the impressive Blanton collection, although in a less than optimum setting.

**Jones Center for Contemporary Art.** 700 Congress Ave. ☎ **512/453-5312.** Admission $2 adults, $1 artists; children under 12 and seniors free. Tues–Wed and Fri 11am–7pm; Thurs 11am–9pm (free admission after 5pm); Sat 11am–5pm; Sun 1–5pm. Bus: Red 'Dillo.

The newest addition to downtown's art scene, the Jones Center is home to, and the exhibition venue for, the Texas Fine Arts Association (TFAA), which has promoted visual art in Texas since 1911. But the only blue hair here is of the spiked variety. Although the TFAA focuses on Texas art, it's likely to be as cutting-edge as anything you'd see in SoHo (in fact, a recent exhibition called "New New York" was a young Texas curator's take on the current Big Apple art scene). Genres range from representational to performance, and artists of all ethnicities are represented. This ain't your purty pictures of bluebonnets, hon'.

**MEXIC-ARTE Museum.** 419 Congress Ave. ☎ **512/480-9373.** Admission $3 adults, $1 children under 12 and seniors. Mon–Fri 10am–6pm; Sat 10am–5pm. Bus: Red 'Dillo.

The first organization in Austin to promote multicultural contemporary art when it was formed in 1983, MEXIC-ARTE has a small permanent collection of 20th-century Mexican art, including photographs from the Mexican revolution and a fascinating array of masks from the state of Guerrero. It's supplemented by visiting shows, including some from Mexico, such as a major retrospective of muralist Diego Rivera. The museum also programs an average of two music, theater, and performing arts events each month and runs mural tours to Mexico.

**O. Henry Museum.** 409 E. Fifth St. ☎ **512/472-1903.** Free admission. Wed–Sun noon–5pm. Closed Thanksgiving, Christmas, and New Year's Day. Bus: Blue 'Dillo.

When William Sidney Porter, better known as O. Henry, lived in Austin (1884–98), he published a popular satirical newspaper called *Rolling Stone.* He also held down an odd string of jobs, including a stint as a teller at the First National Bank of Austin, where he was later accused of embezzling funds. It was while he was serving time for this crime that he wrote the 13 short stories that established his literary reputation. The modest Victorian cottage in which O. Henry lived with his wife and daughter from 1893 to 1895 showcases the family's bedroom furniture, silverware, and china, as well as the desk at which the author wrote copy for the *Rolling Stone.*

**Texas Memorial Museum.** University of Texas, 2400 Trinity St. ☎ **512/471-1604.** www.utexas.edu/depts/tmm. Free admission (donations appreciated). Mon–Fri 9am–5pm; Sat 10am–5pm; Sun 1–5pm. Bus: 27.

During a whistle-stop visit to Austin in 1936, Franklin Roosevelt broke the ground for this museum, built to commemorate the centennial of Texas independence. Whatever your age, you'll probably remember going on a class trip to a place like this, with dioramas, stuffed animals, and other displays detailing the geology, anthropology, and natural history of your home state.

In addition to the requisite kid-pleasing dinosaur displays (including footprints outside the building), three things make this museum well worth a visit: an intriguing exhibit on the history of firearms; the original zinc goddess of liberty that once sat on top of the capitol; and a good gift shop, with lots of ethnic crafts and educational toys.

**Umlauf Sculpture Garden & Museum.** 605 Robert E. Lee Rd. ☎ **512/445-5582.** www.io.com/~tam/umlauf. Admission $3 adults, $2 seniors, $1 students; children 6 and under free. Wed–Fri 10am–4:30pm; Sat–Sun 1–4:30pm (Sat 10am–4:30pm June–Aug). Bus: 29 or 30.

This is a very user-friendly museum, one for people who don't enjoy being cooped up in a stuffy, hushed space. An art instructor at the University of Texas for 40 years, Charles Umlauf donated his home, studio, and more than 250 pieces of artwork to the city of Austin, which maintains the lovely native garden where much of the sculpture is displayed. Umlauf, whose pieces reside in such places as the Smithsonian Institution and New York's Metropolitan Museum, worked in many media and styles. He also used a variety of models; you'll probably recognize the portrait of Umlauf's most famous UT student, Farrah Fawcett. With advance notice, the museum can arrange American Sign Language tours for the deaf and "touch tours" for the blind.

**Women & Their Work Gallery.** 1710 Lavaca St. ☎ **512/477-1064.** www. womenandtheirwork.org. Free admission. Mon–Fri 9am–5pm; Sat noon–4pm. Bus: Red 'Dillo.

Founded in 1978, this gallery is devoted to more than visual art—it also promotes and showcases women in dance, music, theater, film, and literature. Regularly changing exhibits have little in common except innovation. In 2000, this art space got the nod for "Best Gallery" from both the editors and readers of the *Austin Chronicle*. The gift shop has a great selection of unusual crafts and jewelry created by female artists.

# AUSTIN OUTDOORS
## LAKES
**Highland Lakes.**

The six dams built by the Lower Colorado River Authority in the late 1930s through the early 1950s not only controlled the flooding that had plagued the areas surrounding Texas's Colorado River (not to be confused with the more famous river of the same name to the north), but also transformed the waterway into a sparkling chain of lakes, stretching some 150 miles northwest of Austin. The narrowest of them, Town Lake, is also the closest to downtown. The heart of urban recreation in Austin, it boasts a shoreline park and adjacent hike-and-bike trail. Lake Austin, the next in line, is more residential, but offers Emma Long Park as a public shore. Serious aquatic enthusiasts go all the way to Lake Travis, the longest lake in the chain, which offers the most possibilities for playing in the water. Together with the other Highland Lakes— Marble Falls, LBJ, Inks, and Buchanan—these compose the largest concentration of freshwater lakes in Texas. See also "Staying Active," below, for activity and equipment rental suggestions.

## NEIGHBORHOODS & HISTORIC BLOCKS
**Bremond Block.** Between Seventh and Eighth, San Antonio and Guadalupe sts. Bus: Yellow 'Dillo.

"The family that builds together, bonds together" might have been the slogan of Eugene Bremond, an early Austin banker who established a mini real-estate monopoly for his own kin in the downtown area. In the mid-1860s, he started investing in land on what was once Block 80 of the original city plan. In 1874, he moved into a Greek revival home made by master builder Abner Cook. By the time he was through, he had created a family compound, purchasing and enlarging homes for himself, two sisters, a daughter, a son, and a brother-in-law. Some were destroyed, but those that remain on what is now known as the Bremond Block are exquisite examples of elaborate late 19th-century homes.

**Hyde Park.** Between E. 38th and E. 45th, Duval and Guadalupe sts. Bus: 1.

Unlike Eugene Bremond (see above), developer Monroe Martin Shipe built homes for the middle, not upper, classes. In the 1890s, he created—and tirelessly promoted—a complex-cum-resort at the southwest edge of Austin. He even built an electric streetcar system to connect it with the rest of the city. By the middle of this century, Austin's first planned suburb had become somewhat shabby, but recent decades of gentrification have turned the tide. Now visitors can amble along pecan-shaded streets and look at beautifully restored residences, many in pleasing combinations of late Queen Anne and early Craftsman styles. Shipe's own architecturally eclectic home, at 3816 Ave. G, is a bit grander than some of the others, but not much.

**Sixth Street.** Between Lavaca Ave. and I-35. Bus: Silver 'Dillo.

Formerly known as Pecan Street—all the east–west thoroughfares in Austin were originally named for trees—Sixth Street was once the main connecting road to the older settlements east of Austin. During the Reconstruction boom of the 1870s, the wooden wagon yards and saloons of the 1850s and 1860s began to be replaced by the more solid masonry structures you see today.

After the grand new state capitol was built in 1888, the center of commercial activity began shifting toward Congress Avenue, and by the middle of the next century, Sixth Street had become a skid row. Restoration of the 9 blocks designated a National Register District began in the late 1960s. In the 1970s, the street blossomed into a live-music center. Austin's former main street is now lined with more than 70 restaurants, galleries, theaters, nightspots, and shops. The section east of Congress is still somewhat deserted during the day, when the roots of its sleazy past show in the occasional tattoo parlor and S&M leather shop. But that's changing, as wrecking balls seem to be swinging on every square inch of downtown. The streets west of Congress are seeing more and more upscale business activity every day, and on weekend nights a mostly young crowd throngs the sidewalks of the entire stretch for serious club crawling.

## A PANORAMA

✪ **Mount Bonnell.** 3800 Mt. Bonnell Rd. Free admission. Daily 5am–10pm. Take Mt. Bonnell Road 1 mile past the west end of W. 35th St.

For the best views of the city and Hill Country, ascend to this mountaintop park, at 785 feet the highest point in Austin and the oldest tourist attraction in town. It has long been a favorite spot for romantic trysts; rumor had it that any couple who climbed the 106 stone steps to the top together would fall in love (an emotion often confused with exhaustion). The peak was named for George W. Bonnell, Sam Houston's commissioner of Indian affairs in 1836.

## PARKS & GARDENS

**Emma Long Metropolitan Park.** 1706 City Park Rd. ☎ **512/346-1831** or 512/346-3807. Admission $5 per vehicle Mon–Thurs, $8 Fri–Sun and holidays. Daily 7am–10pm. Exit I-35 at 290 West, then go west (street names will change to Koenig, Allendale, Northland, and FM 2222) to City Park Rd. (near Loop 360). Turn south and drive 7.2 miles to park entrance. *Note:* Park closes to visitors when maximum capacity has been reached.

More than 1,100 acres of woodland and a mile of shore along Lake Austin make Emma Long Park—named after the first woman to sit on Austin's city council—a most appealing metropolitan space. Water activities revolve around two boat ramps, a fishing dock, and a protected swimming area, guarded by lifeguards on summer weekends. This is the only city park to offer camping, with permits ($6 for open camping, $15 hookups) available on a first-come, first-served basis. If you hike through the stands of oak, ash, and juniper to an elevation of 1,000 feet, you'll get a view of the city spread out before you.

**Zilker Botanical Garden.** 2220 Barton Springs Rd. ☎ **512/477-8672.** Free admission. Grounds open dawn–dusk. Garden center open Mon–Fri 8:30am–4pm; Sat 10am–5pm (Jan–Feb, 1–5pm); Sun 1–5pm (sometimes open earlier on weekends for special garden shows; phone ahead). Bus: 30.

There's bound to be something blooming at the Zilker Botanical Garden from March to October, but no matter what time of year you visit, you'll find this a soothing spot. The Oriental Garden created by Isamu Taniguchi is particularly peaceful; ask someone at the garden center to point out how Taniguchi landscaped the word *Austin* into his design. A butterfly garden attracts gorgeous winged visitors during April and October migrations, and you can poke and prod the plants in the herb garden to get them to yield their fragrances. One hundred million–year-old dinosaur tracks were discovered on the grounds in the early 1990s; they're not open to the public currently, but a garden designed to display them is currently under construction.

✪ **Zilker Park.** 2201 Barton Springs Rd. ☎ **512/476-9044.** Free admission. Daily 5am–10pm. Bus: 30.

Comprising 347 acres, the first 40 of which were donated to the city by the wealthy German immigrant for whom the park is named, this is Austin's favorite public playground. Its centerpiece is Barton Springs Pool (see "The Top Attractions," above), but visitors and locals also flock to the Zilker Botanical Garden, the Austin Nature Preserves, and the Umlauf Sculpture Garden and Museum, all described in this chapter. See also the "Especially for Kids" and "Staying Active" sections for details about the Austin Nature and Science Center, the Zilker Zephyr Miniature Train, and Town Lake canoe rentals. In addition to its athletic fields (eight for soccer, two for softball, and one for rugby), the park also hosts a nine-hole disk (Frisbee) golf course.

## NATURE PRESERVES

For information on **Wild Basin Wilderness Preserve,** see "Special-Interest Sightseeing," below.

**City of Austin Nature Preserves.** 200 S. Lamar Blvd. ☎ **512/402-0781.** www.ci.austin.tx.us/preserves. Free admission. Daily dawn–dusk. To locate the city's preserves, phone the above number or click on the names on the Web site.

The following are some highlights of the remarkably diverse group of natural habitats Austin boasts in its city-run nature preserves. At **Blunn Creek** (1100 block of St. Edward's Dr.), 40 acres of upland woods and meadows are traversed by a spring-fed creek; one of the two lookout areas is made of compacted volcanic ash. Spelunkers will like **Goat Cave** (3900 Deer Lane), which is honeycombed with limestone caves and sinkholes; you can arrange for cave tours by phoning the **Austin Nature Center** (☎ 512/327-8181). Lovely **Mayfield Park** (3505 W. 35th St.) directly abuts the Barrow Brook Cove of Lake Austin. Peacocks and hens roam freely around lily ponds, and trails cross over bridges in oak and juniper woods. Visitors to the rock-walled ramada (a shaded shelter) at the **Zilker Preserve** (Barton Springs Rd. and Loop 1), with its meadows, streams, and cliff, can look out over downtown Austin. All the preserves are maintained in a primitive state with natural surface trails and no rest rooms.

**Westcave Preserve.** Star Rte. 1, Dripping Springs. ☎ **830/825-3442.** www.westcave.org. Free admission Sat–Sun for tours at 10am, noon, 2, and 4pm (weather permitting). Take Hwy. 71 to Ranch Rd. 3238. Follow the signs 15 miles to Hamilton Pool, across the Pedernales River Bridge from the preserve.

If you don't like the weather in one part of Westcave Preserve, you might like it better in another: Up to a 25°F difference in temperature has been recorded between the highest area of this beautiful natural habitat, an arid Hill Country scrub, and the lowest, a lush woodland spread across a canyon floor. Because the ecosystem here is so delicate, the 30 acres on the Pedernales River may be entered only by guided tour. No reservations are taken; the first 30 people to show up at the allotted times are allowed in.

## OUTDOOR ART

**Philosophers' Rock.** Zilker Park, 2201 Barton Springs Rd., just outside the entrance to Barton Springs Pool. Free admission. Daily 5am–10pm. Bus: 30.

Glenna Goodacre's wonderfully witty bronze sculpture of three of Austin's most recognized personalities from mid-century—naturalist Roy Bedichek, humorist J. Frank Dobie, and historian Walter Prescott Webb—captures the essence of the three friends who used to schmooze together at Barton Springs Pool. No heroic posing here: Two of the three are wearing bathing trunks, which reveal potbellies, wrinkles, and sagging muscles, and all three are sitting down in mid-discussion. But the intelligence of their expressions and the casual friendliness of their pose have made this 1994 piece an Austin favorite.

✪ **Stevie Ray Vaughan Statue.** South side of town lake, adjacent to Auditorium Shores.

In contrast to the Philosophers' Rock (see above), Ralph Roehming's bronze tribute to Austin singer/songwriter Stevie Ray Vaughan is artificial and awkward. Although he's wearing his habitual flat-brimmed hat and poncho, the stiffly posed Stevie Ray looks more like a frontiersman with a gun than a rock star with a guitar. But his devoted fans don't care; flowers and messages can almost always be found at the foot of the statue.

## THE UNIVERSITY

**University of Texas at Austin.** Guadalupe and I-35, Martin Luther King Jr. Blvd. and 26th St. ☎ **512/471-3434.** www.utexas.edu.

In 1883, the 221 students and 8 teachers who made up the newly established University of Texas in Austin had to meet in makeshift classrooms in the town's temporary capitol. At the time, the two million acres of dry west Texas land that the higher educational system had been granted barely brought in 40¢ an acre for grazing. Now, nearly 50,000 students occupy 120 buildings on UT's main campus alone, and that arid west Texas land, which blew a gusher in 1923, has raked in more than $4 billion in oil money—two-thirds of it directed to the UT school system.

Currently, the status of the visitors center is in flux, but at the general information booth on the ground floor of the Main building (near 24th and Whitis), you can get campus maps and other UT Austin–related materials. Free campus tours for prospective students (but anyone can tag along) leave from its information desk weekdays at 11am and 2pm (only at 2pm in Dec and May) and Saturday at 2pm. Call ☎ **512/ 475-7399,** option 5, for recorded details.

See also "The Top Attractions," above, for more on the LBJ Library and Museum; listings earlier in this section for the Harry Ransom Humanities Research Center, Jack S. Blanton Museum of Art, and Texas Memorial Museum; the Walking Tour of university sights section, below; and information on visiting the UT Tower in the "Organized Tours" section.

## WINERIES & BREWERIES

**Celis Brewery.** 2431 Forbes Dr. ☎ **512/835-0884.** Free admission. Tours, followed by samplings, Tues–Sat 2 and 4pm, Fri also at 5:30pm. Shop Mon–Fri 8:30am–5pm. Take U.S. 290 East, just past the intersection with U.S. 183. Turn left at Cross Park Dr. and take it north to Forbes Dr.

Those with a taste for highly prized Belgian beers will want to tour the Celis Brewery on the northeast side of Austin. Pierre Celis found the spring-fed water and limestone terrain of the Austin area conducive to reproducing the "white" (wheat) beer that had been brewed for 500 years in his native Belgian town of Hoegaarden. The brewery was built around two huge, hand-hammered copper drums that Celis imported to give his beer the desired flavor. Clint Eastwood liked the suds here so much that he helped develop the brewery's Pale Rider Ale.

**Fall Creek Vineyards.** 2.2 miles northeast of Tow. ☎ **915/379-5361.** Free admission. Mon–Fri 11am–4pm for tasting and sales; Sat noon–5pm tours, tasting, and sales; Sun noon–4pm tasting and sales. Closed Sun Dec–Feb. For the most scenic route, take Hwy. 71 (Ben White Blvd.) west to Marble Falls, and pick up Hwy. 1431 West, which will dead-end into 261 North (called Lakeshore Dr. at Lake Buchanan). When you get to 2241, take it north past Tow, where it will trail off at the vineyards.

The wines sold at this 65-acre vineyard, praised by critics around the country, amply reward the long drive up to the northwest shore of Lake Buchanan. You may have already tried a glass or two at fine restaurants in Austin; here, you can sample the full range of award winners, including carnelians, Rieslings, and zinfandels. Special tours can be arranged through the Austin office (☎ **512/476-4477**).

**Hill Country Cellars.** 1700 Hwy. 183 North, Cedar Park. ☎ **512/259-2000.** Free admission. Tasting room open Fri–Sun noon–5pm; winery tours Sat–Sun 1, 2, and 3pm. Take U.S. Hwy. 183 North about ½ mile past FM 1431.

Stroll under a trellised wood arbor and enjoy the fermented product of the grapes grown on the premises of this vineyard/winery, about 20 minutes northwest of Austin. A 200-year-old native grapevine is the centerpiece of the picnic area, where various seasonal festivals are held.

**Slaughter Leftwich Winery.** 4209 Eck Lane. ☎ **512/266-3331.** www.slaughterleftwich. com. Free admission. Tastings Sat 1–5pm (call to check wine availability and hours). Eck Lane is off R.R. 620, 1 mile south of Mansfield Dam on the right (see map on Web site).

The Slaughter Leftwich vineyards produced the first chardonnays in the high-plains region of Texas. But you don't have to travel out to the Lubbock area to try these award-winning bottles; just take a scenic drive to a shady lane near Austin's Lake Travis. The winery and tasting room are in a native stone structure, built to resemble ones popular in the last century. If you like whites, the chardonnay is your best bet, but all the wines are reasonably priced, so it's hard to go very wrong.

## 3　Especially for Kids

The **Bob Bullock Texas State History Museum** and the **Texas Memorial Museum,** both described in earlier sections, are child-friendly, but outdoor attractions are still Austin's biggest kiddie draw. There's lots of room for children to splash around at **Barton Springs,** and even youngsters who thought **bats** were creepy are likely to be converted on further acquaintance with the critters. In addition, the following attractions are especially geared toward children.

**Austin Children's Museum.** Dell Discovery Center, 201 Colorado St. ☎ **512/472-2499.** www.austinkids.org. Admission $4.50; children under 2 free. Tues and Thurs–Sat 10am–5pm, Wed 10am–8pm, Sun noon–5pm; inquire about the Open Door Policy (free admission to all who ask). Closed Mon (except for "Baby Bloomers" tots) and some holidays. Bus: Red and Yellow 'Dillo lines.

Located in a large, new state-of-the-art facility, this excellent children's museum has something for all ages. Tots—who get exclusive run of the place almost every Monday morning 9:30am to 1pm ($4.50 per family)—enjoy low-key but creative playscapes. In-betweens take on a variety of "creation stations" and grown-up environments like a studio sound stage, and the Loft section challenges teens from 12 to 18 with workshops in different arts and media. Parents will get a kick out of the replica Austin cityscapes, including a model of the Congress Avenue Bridge and its bats. Visiting exhibits, such as "Chagall for Children" (you never know what budding artists you have in your midst), keep the museum continuously interesting.

**Austin Nature and Science Center.** Zilker Park, 301 Nature Center Dr. ☎ **512/327-8181.** Donations requested; occasional special exhibits charge separately. Mon–Sat 9am–5pm; Sun noon–5pm. Closed Thanksgiving and Christmas. Bus: 63.

Bats, bees, and crystal caverns are among the subjects of the Discovery Boxes at this museum in the 80-acre Nature Center, which features lots of interactive exhibits. The tortoises, lizards, porcupine, and vultures in the Wildlife Exhibit—among more than 50 orphaned or injured creatures brought here from the wild—also hold kids' attention. An Eco-Detective trail highlights pond-life awareness. Keep an eye out for the upcoming Dino Pit, sure to lure budding paleontologists.

**Austin Zoo.** 10807 Rawhide Trail. ☎ **512/288-1490.** www.austinzoo.org. Admission $6 adults, $5 seniors, $4 children 2–12; children under 2 free. Daily 10am–6pm. Closed Thanksgiving and Christmas. Take Hwy. 290 West to Circle Dr., turn right, go 1.5 miles to Rawhide Trail, and turn right.

This small zoo, some 14 miles southwest of downtown, may not feature the state-of-the-jungle habitats of larger facilities, but it's easier to get up close and personal with the critters here. Most of the animal residents, who range from turkeys and pot-bellied pigs to marmosets and tigers, were mistreated, abandoned, or illegally imported before they found a home here. It costs $2 to board the 1.5-mile miniature train for a scenic Hill Country ride, which lets you peer at some of the shyer animals. There are no food concessions, but plenty of picnic tables.

**Jourdan Bachman Pioneer Farm.** 11418 Sprinkle Cut Off Rd. ☎ **512/837-1215.** Admission $4 adults, $3 children over 3. Mon–Wed 9:30am–1pm (Thurs 9:30am–1pm June–Aug); Sun 1–5pm. Take exit 243 east off I-35 to Dessau Rd., turn left, go ½ mile and take a right on Sprinkle Cut Off Rd.

A glimpse of what life was like in the rural 1880s might help kids appreciate the simplicity (or lack) of their own chores—at least for a while. When Harriet Bachman and Frederic Jourdan set up housekeeping in northeast Austin in 1852, cattle herders drove past their property on the Chisholm Trail. Today's visitors to their farm can enter into the worlds of three typical late 19th-century Texas families: wealthy cotton farmers, homesteaders from Appalachia, and freed slaves turned tenant farmers. The costumed interpreters clearly relish playing their historic roles, and their enthusiasm is contagious. On Sunday afternoon, there's always something interactive for kids to do, from making sausage to milking cows.

**Splash! Into the Edwards Aquifer Exhibit and Gift Store.** Zilker Park, 2201 Barton Springs Rd. ☎ **512/481-1466.** Free admission. Tues–Sat 10am–5pm; Sun noon–5pm. Bus: 30 (Barton Creek Sq.).

The Edwards Aquifer, Austin's main source of water, is fed by a variety of underground creeks filtered through a large layer of limestone. You'll feel as though you're entering one of this vast ecosystem's sinkholes when you walk into the dimly lit enclosure— formerly the bathhouse at Barton Springs pool—where a variety of interactive displays grab kids' attention. Young visitors can make it rain on the city, identify water bugs, or peer through a periscope at swimmers. Although the focus is on the evils of pollution, the agenda is by no means heavy-handed. The exhibit is also great for adults who have always wondered about all the signs around town that announce ENTERING THE [FILL-IN-THE-CREEK] RECHARGE ZONE. (Does this mean slow down or speed up?)

**Zilker Zephyr Miniature Train.** Zilker Park, 2100 Barton Springs Rd. (just across from the Barton Springs Pool). ☎ **512/478-8286.** Admission $2.75 ages 12 and over, $1.75 seniors and ages under 12; free for infants (under age 1) on guardian's lap. Daily 10am–dusk. Bus: 30.

Take a scenic 25-minute ride through Zilker Park on a narrow-gauge, light-rail miniature train, which takes you at a leisurely pace along Barton Creek and Town Lake. The more than 2 miles of recently laid track makes the ride smoother than ever. The train departs approximately every hour on the hour during the week and every half hour on the half hour on the weekend, weather permitting.

## 4 Special-Interest Sightseeing

### AFRICAN-AMERICAN HERITAGE

The **George Washington Carver Museum** (see "More Attractions," above) is the best place to learn about Austin's African-American past, but a number of other sites in east Austin are worth visiting, too. Less than 2 blocks from the Carver Museum, on the corner of Hackberry and San Bernard streets, stands the **Wesley United Methodist Church.** Established at the end of the Civil War, it was one of the leading black churches in Texas. Diagonally across the street, the **Zeta Phi Beta Sorority,** Austin's first black Greek letter house, occupies the Thompson House, built in 1877; it's also the archival center for the Texas chapter of the sorority. Nearby, at the **State Cemetery** (see "More Attractions," above), you can visit the gravesite of congresswoman and civil rights leader Barbara Jordan, the first African American to be buried here.

About half a mile away, the sparsely furnished **Henry G. Madison Cabin** was built around 1863 by a black homesteader. When it was donated to the city in 1873, it was relocated to the grounds of the **Rosewood Park and Recreation Center,** 2300 Rosewood Ave. (☎ 512/472-6838). The cabin is no longer open regular hours, but if you phone in advance, you can arrange for someone to give a tour. You'll have to go across town, to the near west side, to explore the neighborhood known as **Clarksville,** founded by a former slave in 1871 as a utopian community for freed blacks; it's an almost entirely white artists' enclave now, however.

For a more up-to-date look at the Austin scene, visit **Mitchie's Fine Black Art & Gift Gallery,** 5706 Manor Rd., Suite B1 (☎ 512/323-6901), and **Bydie Arts & Gifts,** 412 E. Sixth St. (☎ 512/474-4343), both offering a good selection of African-American painting and sculpture.

### SKY GAZING

**Wild Basin Wilderness Preserve.** 805 N. Capital of Texas Hwy. ☎ **512/327-7622** or Inside Line ☎ 512/416-5700, category 3560 (updated recorded information). www.wildbasin.org. E-mail: hike@wildbasin.org. Free admission. Tours $3 adults, $1 ages 5–12; children under 5 free. Preserve open daily dawn–dusk; office Mon–Thurs 9am–4:30pm, Fri 9am–noon, Sat–Sun 9am–5pm. Tours twice monthly, weather permitting, generally 8 or 8:30pm to 9:30 or 10pm.

Sitting on a 227-acre peninsula high above Loop 360, the Wild Basin Wilderness Preserve is a perfect place to watch the moon rise over Austin. The clarity of the night sky from here is, well, stellar. In addition to its weekend daytime nature walks (phone or check Web site for times and prices), Wild Basin sponsors moonlighting and stargazing tours twice a month. Call ahead for exact dates: The moonlighting tour coincides with the full moon, and stargazing is scheduled for 3 or 4 days after the new moon. This popular heavenly peek is limited to 60, so make reservations as far in advance as possible by phone or e-mail.

# 5 Walking Tour: University of Texas

**Start:** The Arno Nowotny Building.
**Finish:** The Littlefield Fountain.
**Time:** 1 hour, not including food breaks or museum visits.
**Best Times:** On the weekends, when the campus is less crowded, more parking is available, and the Tower is open.
**Worst Times:** Morning and midday during the week when classes are in session and parking is impossible to find. (*Beware:* Those tow-away zone signs mean business.)

No ivory tower (although it has several of them), the University of Texas is as integral to Austin's identity as it is to its economy. To explore the vast main campus is to glimpse the city's future as well as its past: Here, state-of-the-art structures—including information kiosks that can play the school's team songs—sit cheek by jowl with elegant examples of 19th-century architecture. The following tour points out many of the most interesting spots on campus. Unless you regularly trek the Himalayas, however, you'll probably want to drive or take a bus between some of the first seven sights. (Parking limitations were taken into account in this initial portion of the circuit.) For a walking tour alone, begin at stop no. 8.

*Note:* Stops 2, 5, 6, 12, and 20 are also discussed earlier in this chapter, where their entrance hours are listed; stop no. 9 is detailed in the "Organized Tours" section, later in the chapter.

In 1839, the Congress of the Republic of Texas ordered a site set aside for the establishment of a "university of the first class" in Austin. Some 40 years later, when the flagship of the new University of Texas system opened, its first two buildings went up on that original 40-acre plot, dubbed College Hill. Although there were attempts to establish master-design plans for the university from the turn of the century onward, they were only carried out in bits and pieces until 1930, when money from an earlier oil strike on UT land allowed the school to begin building in earnest. Between 1930 and 1945, consulting architect Paul Cret put his mark on 19 university buildings, most of which show the influence of his education at Paris's Ecole des Beaux-Arts. If the entire 357-acre campus will never achieve stylistic unity or anything close to it, its earliest section has a grace and cohesion that make it a delight to stroll.

Although we start out at the oldest building owned by the university, this tour begins far from the original campus. At the frontage road of I-35 and the corner of Martin Luther King Jr. Boulevard, you can pull into the parking lot of:

1. **The Arno Nowotny Building.** In the 1850s, several state-run asylums for the mentally ill and the physically handicapped arose on the outskirts of Austin. One of these was the State Asylum for the Blind, built by Abner Cook around 1856. The ornate Italianate-style structure soon became better known as the headquarters and barracks of General Custer, who had been sent to Austin in 1865 to reestablish order after the Civil War. Incorporated into the university and restored for its centennial celebration, the building once served as a visitors center, but is now used for administration.

Take Martin Luther King Jr. Boulevard to Red River, then drive north to the:

2. **LBJ Library and Museum** (see also "The Top Attractions," earlier in this chapter), which offers another rare on-campus parking lot. (You'll want to leave your car here while you look at sights 3 through 6.) The first presidential library to be built on a university campus, the huge travertine marble structure oversees a beautifully landscaped 14-acre complex. Among the museum's exhibits is a seven-eighths scale replica of the Oval Office as it looked when the Johnsons

occupied the White House. In the adjoining Sid Richardson Hall are the Lyndon B. Johnson School of Public Affairs; the Barker Texas History Center, housing the world's most extensive collection of Texana; and the UT's visitors bureau.

Stroll down the library steps across East Campus Drive to 23rd Street, where, next to the large Burleson bells on your right, you'll see the university's $41 million:

**3. Performing Arts Center,** which includes the 3,000-seat Bass Concert Hall, the 700-seat Bates Recital Hall, and other College of the Fine Arts auditoriums. The state-of-the-art acoustics at the Bass Concert Hall enhance the sounds of the largest tracker organ in the United States. Linking contemporary computer technology with a design that goes back some 2,000 years, it has 5,315 pipes—some of them 16 feet tall—and weighs 48,000 pounds.

From the same vantage point to the left looms the huge:

**4. Darrell K. Royal/Texas Memorial Stadium,** where the first of the traditional UT–Texas A&M Thanksgiving Day games was played in 1924. The upper deck directly facing you was added in 1972. In a drive to finance the original stadium, female students sold their hair, male students sold their blood, and UT alum Lutcher Stark matched every $10,000 they raised with $1,000 of his own funds. The stadium's 1995 name change (from Texas Memorial Stadium) to honor legendary Longhorns football coach Darrell K. Royal angered some who wanted the stadium to remain solely a memorial to Texas veterans, and confused others who wonder if the very active Royal is still alive.

Continue west on 23rd; at the corner of San Jacinto, a long staircase marks the entrance to the:

**5. Art Building,** temporary home to the Jack S. Blanton Museum of Art (see "More Attractions," earlier in this chapter), until its larger facility is completed on MLK and Speedway.

Walk a short distance north on San Jacinto. A stampeding group of bronze mustangs will herald your arrival at the:

**6. Texas Memorial Museum** (see also "More Attractions," above), a monumental art moderne building designed by Paul Cret. Inside, on the first floor, the 16-foot-tall Goddess of Liberty defines the term *statuesque*. Liberty, who reigned atop the state capitol dome until 1986, was designed to be viewed from more than 300 feet away; up close and personal, she's a bit crude. The museum also houses a fascinating collection of antique firearms, some carved into exotic animal shapes.

When you exit the building, take Trinity, which, curving into 25th Street, will bring you back to the parking lot of the LBJ Library and to your car. Retrace your original route along Red River until you reach Martin Luther King Jr. Boulevard. Drive west; at the corner of San Jacinto, you'll see:

**7. Santa Rita No. 1,** an oil rig transported here from west Texas, where liquid wealth first spewed forth from it on land belonging to the university in 1923. The money was distributed between the University of Texas system, which got the heftier two thirds, and the Texas A&M system. Although not its main source of income, this windfall has helped make UT the second richest university in the country, after Harvard.

There's no parking in the area, so it's best to pay passing obeisance to the oil god, continue on to University Avenue, and then hang a left. There are public parking places around 21st Street and University, where you'll begin your walking tour at the:

**8. Littlefield Memorial Fountain,** built in 1933. Pompeo Coppini, sculptor of the magnificent bronze centerpiece, believed that the rallying together of the nation

# Walking Tour: The University of Texas

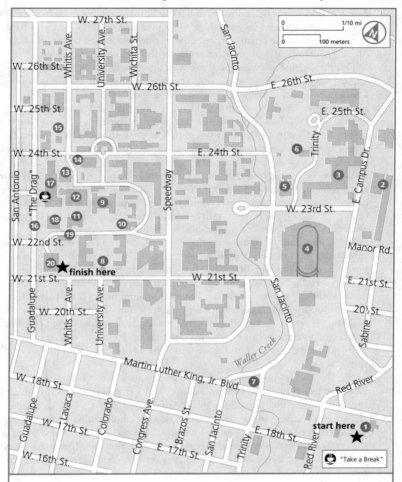

**1** Arno Nowotny Building

**2** LBJ Library and Museum

**3** Performing Arts Center

**4** Darrell K. Royal/Memorial Stadium

**5** Art Building

**6** Texas Memorial Museum

**7** Santa Rita No. 1

**8** Littlefield Memorial Fountain

**9** Main Building and Tower

**10** Garrison Hall

**11** Battle Hall

**12** Flawn Academic Center

**13** Hogg Auditorium

**14** Battle Oaks

**15** Littlefield Home

**16** The Drag

**17** Texas Union Building

**18** Goldsmith Hall

**19** Sutton Hall

**20** Harry Ransom Center

during World War I marked the final healing of the wounds caused by the Civil War. He depicted the winged goddess Columbia riding on the bow of a battleship sailing across the ocean—represented by three rearing sea horses—to aid the Allies. The two figures on the deck represent the Army and the Navy.

This three-tiered fountain graces the most dramatic entrance to the university's original 40 acres. Behind you stands the state capitol. Directly ahead of you, across an oak-shaded mall lined with heroic statues, is the:

9. **Main Building and Tower,** site of the university's first academic building, built in 1884. The 307-foot-high structure that now rises above the university was created by Paul Cret in 1937. It's a fine example of the Beaux Arts style, particularly stunning when lit to celebrate a Longhorn victory. Sadly, the clock tower's many notable features—the small classical temple on top, say, or the 17-bell carillon—will always be dogged by the shadow of the carnage committed by Charles Whitman, who, in August 1966, killed 16 people and wounded 31 before he was gunned down by a sharpshooter. Closed off to the public in 1975 after a series of suicide leaps from its observation deck, the tower reopened for supervised ascensions in 1999 (see "Organized Tours," below).

If you go climb the staircase on the east (right) side of the tower to the stone balustrade, you can see the dramatic sweep of the entire eastern section of campus, including the LBJ Library. The first building in your direct line of vision is:

10. **Garrison Hall,** named for one of the earliest members of the UT faculty, and home to the department of history. Important names from Texas's past—Austin, Travis, Houston, and Lamar—are set here in stone. The walls just under the building's eaves are decorated with cattle brands; look for the carved cow skulls and cactuses on the balcony window on the north side.

If you retrace your steps to the western (left) side of the Main Building, you'll see:

11. **Battle Hall,** regarded by many as the campus's most beautiful building. Designed in 1911 by Cass Gilbert, architect of the U.S. Supreme Court building, this hall was the first to be done in the Spanish Renaissance style that came to characterize so many of the structures on this section of campus; note the terracotta–tiled roof and broadly arched windows. On the second floor, you can see the grand reading room of what is now the Architecture and Planning Library.

When you exit Battle Hall, go left to the northern door, which faces the much newer:

12. **Flawn Academic Center.** A 200,000-volume undergraduate library shares space here with exhibits from the archives of the Humanities Research Center (see stop no. 20, below). Among the permanent displays in the Academic Center's Leeds Gallery is a cabin furnished with the effects of Erle Stanley Gardner, Perry Mason's creator. In front of the building, Charles Umlauf's *The Torch Bearers* symbolizes the passing of knowledge from one generation to the next.

If you continue walking along the eastern side of the Academic Center, you'll pass:

13. **The Hogg Auditorium,** another Paul Cret building, designed in the same monumental art moderne mode as his earlier Texas Memorial Museum, and recently renovated.

Go a few steps farther and you'll come to a group of trees that have been dubbed the:

14. **Battle Oaks.** The three oldest members of this small grove are said to predate the city of Austin itself. They survived the destruction of most of the grove to build a

Civil War fortress and a later attempt to displace them with a new Biology Building. It was this last, near-fatal skirmish that earned them their name. Legend has it that Dr. W. J. Battle, a professor of classics and an early university president, holed up in the largest oak with a rifle to protect the three ancient trees.

Just across the street at the corner of 24th and Whitis is the impressive:

**15.** Littlefield Home, built in high Victorian style in 1894. Major George W. Littlefield, a wealthy developer, cattle rancher, and banker, bequeathed more than $1 million to the university on the condition that its campus not be moved to land that his rival, George W. Brackenridge, had donated. During the week, when the UT Development Office is open, you can enter through the east carriage driveway to see the house's gorgeous gold-and-white parlors, griffin-decorated fireplace, and other ornate details.

Walk west about a block to Guadalupe to reach:

**16.** The Drag, as its name suggests, the main off-campus action strip. Bookstores, fast-food restaurants, and shops line the thoroughfare, which is usually crammed with students trying to grab a bite or a book between classes. On weekends, the pedestrian mall set aside for the 23rd Street Renaissance Market overflows with crafts vendors.

☕ **TAKE A BREAK**   Texas French Bread, 2270 Guadalupe St., at 23rd Street (☎ **512/474-2785**), next door to the Co-op, is just the spot for a healthy salad or sandwich and a good cup of coffee.

To get back to the university, cross Guadalupe at the traffic light in front of the huge Co-op, between 24th and 22nd streets. You'll now be facing the west mall.

On your left is the:

**17.** Texas Union Building, another Paul Cret creation. A beautifully tiled staircase leads up to the second level where, through the massive carved wooden doors, you'll see the Cactus Cafe, a popular coffeehouse and music venue (see chapter 15). This bustling student center hosts everything from a bowling alley to a formal ballroom.

Immediately across the mall to the right is:

**18.** Goldsmith Hall, one of two adjacent buildings where architecture classes are held. Also designed by Paul Cret, this hall has beautifully worn slate floors and a palm tree–dotted central courtyard.

Walk through the courtyard and go down a few steps; to your right is the second component of the School of Architecture:

**19.** Sutton Hall, designed by Cass Gilbert in 1918. Like his Battle Hall, it is gracefully Mediterranean, with terra-cotta moldings, a red-tile roof, and large Palladian windows.

If you enter Sutton Hall through the double doors at the front and exit straight through the back, you'll be looking directly at the chunky, contemporary:

**20.** Harry Ransom Center, home to the Humanities Research Center (HRC). The satirical portrait of a rich American literary archive in A. S. Byatt's best-selling novel *Possession* is widely acknowledged to have been based on HRC. On the first floor of this building, you can view the center's rare Gutenberg Bible.

When you leave the building, you'll be back on 21st Street, facing the fountain where the walking tour began.

## 6 Organized Tours

See also chapter 15 for details on touring the *Austin City Limits* studio.

### BOAT TOURS

**Capital Cruises.** Hyatt Regency Town Lake boat dock. ☎ **512/480-9264.** www.capitalcruises.com. Bat and sightseeing cruises $8 adults, $6.50 seniors, $5 children 4–12; dinner cruises (including tax and tip) $29.50 adults, $19.50 children. Bat cruise daily at sunset (call ahead for exact time), weather permitting; sightseeing cruise Sat–Sun at 1pm; dinner cruise Fri–Sun at 6pm. Reservations required for dinner cruises; for bat and sightseeing cruises, show up at the dock a minimum of 30 min. in advance.

From March through October, Capital Cruises plies Town Lake with electric-powered boats heading out on a number of popular tours. The bat cruises are especially big in summer, when warm nights are perfect for the enjoyable and educational hour-long excursions; the high point is seeing thousands of bats stream out from under their Congress Avenue Bridge roost. Dinner cruises, featuring fajitas from the Hyatt Regency's La Vista restaurant, are also fun on a balmy evening, and the afternoon sightseeing tours are a nice way to while away an hour on the weekend.

**Lone Star River Boat.** South shore of Town Lake, between the Congress Ave. and S. First St. bridges, just next to the Hyatt. ☎ **512/327-1388.** Scenic tours $9 adults, $7 seniors, $6 children under 12; bat tours $8 adults, $6 seniors, $5 children under 12. Scenic tours Sat–Sun 3pm Mar–Oct only. Bat tours nightly Apr–Oct only; call for exact times.

You'll set out against a backdrop of Austin's skyline and the state capitol on this riverboat cruise and move upstream past Barton Creek and Zilker Park. Along the way, you'll glimpse 100-foot-high cliffs and million-dollar estates. These scenic tours, accompanied by knowledgeable narrators, last 1½ hours. Slightly shorter bat-watching tours leave approximately half an hour before sunset, so call ahead to check.

**Vanishing Texas River Cruise.** P.O. Box 901, Burnet, TX 78611. ☎ **800/4-RIVER-4** or 512/756-6986. www.vtrc.com. Cruise $15 adults; $13 seniors, students, active military; $10 children 6–12; children 5 and under free. Tour days vary according to season and are contingent on reservations, but usually depart 11am. At Burnet, drive 3 miles west on Hwy. 29 to R.R. 2341, turn right, and go 13½ miles.

It's about 1½ hours from Austin to the Lake Buchanan dock from which these fascinating 2½-hour naturalist tours depart. A guide narrates the history of the area and points out the seasonal flora and fauna, among them bald eagles (Nov to Mar), migratory birds (Mar to May), and wild deer and turkey (June to Oct). There's a full-service snack bar aboard the vessel. Additional trips, most of them lasting 4 hours, are offered seasonally: On Saturday nights from May through October, it's a sunset dinner cruise; October through November, you can take in the autumn foliage; March through May brings on wildflowers and vineyards; and June through August, you can enjoy a swim and picnic on one of Lake Buchanan's sandy islands. Prices range from $19.95 for adults and $12.95 children 2 to 12 (without food) to $26.95 adults and $21.95 children, including one meal. Call for details, or check the Web site, which lists the latest schedules.

### AMPHIBIOUS TOUR

**Austin Duck Adventures.** Boarding in front of the Austin Convention and Visitors Bureau, 201 E. 2nd St. ☎ **512/4-SPLASH.** www.austinducks.com. Tours $16.50 adults, $14.50 seniors and students, $11 children 12 and under. Tours Wed–Fri 11am and 2pm; Sat 11am, 2pm, and 4pm; Sun 11am and 2pm most weeks, but call to check schedule.

It's a hoot—or should I say a quack? Whether or not you opt to shell out for a duck call whistle to blow at the folks you pass in the street, you'll get a kick out of this combination land and sea tour. You'll be transported in a six-wheel-drive amphibious vehicle originally created for NATO troops through Austin's historic downtown and the scenic west side before splashing into Lake Travis. Comedy writers helped devise the script for this 1½-hour tour, so it's amusing as well as informative.

# TRAIN TOURS

**Hill Country Flyer Steam Train Excursion. ☎ 512/477-8468.** www.atcrr.com. Coach $25 adults, $22 seniors, $15 children 13 and under; first-class $40 adults, $36 seniors, $24 children. Tours Sat 10am (return 5:30pm) June–Nov; 2-week advance reservations strongly suggested in high season.

The Austin Steam Train Association restored the five historic coaches and the 1916 locomotive that you'll board for a leisurely 33-mile excursion from Cedar Park, northwest of Austin. After crossing the South San Gabriel River, the train whistles past scenic Hill Country vistas, especially pretty in spring and fall. At the end of the line—the town of Burnet, near Lake Buchanan—an Old West gunfight is staged for passengers. There's a 3-hour stopover in Burnet. The River City Flyer takes a shorter excursion from Cedar Park to downtown Austin on Sundays, departing at 10am June to October ($25 adults, $22 seniors, $15 children; or $40, $36, and $24 in first-class). From spring through late fall, the River City Local goes on a 90-minute jaunt from downtown Austin (E. Fifth and Comal) to the city's east side ($10 adults, $9 seniors, $6 for children; no first-class) at 1pm every Sunday; it's not particularly scenic, frankly, but it's fun for those who have never ridden this kind of train. Check also about a variety of twilight specials offered throughout the year. The Hill Country and River City flyers pick up passengers at the Capitol Metro Park & Ride Lot at Hwy. 183 and Farm Road 1431 in Cedar Park.

# A LOFTY TOUR

**University of Texas Tower Observation Deck Tour.** UT Campus. **☎ 512/475-6633** or 877/475-6633 (outside Austin). Tours $3. Usually Sat–Sun on the hour 10am–5pm (additional hours late May–late August Thurs–Fri at 6, 7, 8 and 9pm, Sat hourly 2–9pm); no tours on Sun.

Off-limits to the public for nearly a quarter of a century, the observation deck of the UT Tower (see "Walking Tour: University of Texas," above) was remodeled with a new webbed dome and reopened in September 1999. Billed as tours, these excursions to the top of the tower are really supervised visits, although a guide gives a short, informative spiel and stays on hand to answer questions. You're permitted to bring a camera, binoculars, or videocam to take advantage of the spectacular, 360-degree view of Austin, but must leave behind everything else, including purses, camera bags and tripods, strollers, etc. (lockers are available at the nearby Texas Union for $1).

Deck tours are available by reservation only. They may be made in person at the Texas Union Information Center in the Texas Union building, corner of 24th Street and Guadalupe, or by phoning the above-listed numbers on Monday to Friday 8am to 5pm. Arrive 20 minutes before your reserved tour time to claim your ticket; otherwise, you'll forfeit your reservation. If you haven't booked, come by an hour before a scheduled tour and put your name on a waiting list for the next ascent. Unclaimed tickets are sold to standby patrons 10 minutes before the starting time for each tour.

# WALKING TOURS

Whatever price you pay, you won't find better guided walks than the informative and entertaining ones offered free of charge by the **Austin Convention and Visitors Bureau** (ACVB), 201 E. Second St. (☎ **800/926-2282** or 512/454-1545), from March through November. Ninety-minute tours of the historic Bremond Block leave every Saturday and Sunday at 11am; Congress Avenue/East Sixth Street is explored for an hour and a half on Thursday, Friday, and Saturday starting at 9am, Sunday at 2pm. The hour-long Capitol Complex tour is conducted on Saturday at 2pm and Sunday at 9am. All tours depart promptly from the south entrance of the capitol, weather permitting; come even a few minutes late, and you'll miss out. The ACVB also publishes five excellent self-guided tour booklets, including one on Hyde Park and another on the state cemetery. They make for interesting reading even if you don't have time to follow the routes.

## 7 Staying Active

**BALLOONING**   For an uplifting experience, consider a hot-air balloon ride over Hill Country. **Austin Aeronauts Hot Air Balloons** (☎ 512/440-1492; www.austinaeronauts.com) and **Airwolf Adventures** (☎ 512/251-4024) are both reputable operators with FAA-licensed pilots. Their scenic excursions, including champagne breakfast, generally last about an hour.

**BIKING**   A city that has a "bicycle coordinator" on its payroll, Austin is a cyclist's dream. Contact **Austin Parks and Recreation,** 200 S. Lamar Blvd. (☎ 512/499-6700), for information on the city's more than 25 miles of scenic paths, the most popular of which are the Barton Creek Greenbelt (7.8 miles) and the Town Lake Greenbelt (10.1 miles). The **Veloway,** a 3.1-mile paved loop in Slaughter Creek Metropolitan Park, is devoted exclusively to bicyclists and in-line skaters. You can rent bikes and get maps and other information from **University Cyclery,** 2901 N. Lamar Blvd. (☎ 512/474-6696); a number of downtown hotels rent or provide free bicycles to their guests. For information on weekly road rides, contact the **Austin Cycling Association,** P.O. Box 5993, Austin, TX 78763 (☎ 512/282-7413; www.ccsi.com/~aca/; e-mail: bikin-fred@macconnect.com), which also publishes a monthly newsletter, *Southwest Cycling News;* only local calls or e-mails are returned. For rougher mountain-bike routes, try the **Austin Ridge Riders;** their Web site, **www.io.com/austinridgeriders**, will have the latest contact information.

**BIRD WATCHING**   Endangered golden-cheeked warblers and black-capped vireos are among the many species you might spot around Austin. The **Travis Audubon Society** (☎ 512/926-8751; www.travisaudubon.org) organizes regular birding trips and even has a rare-bird hotline. Texas Parks and Wildlife publishes "The Guide to Austin-Area Birding Sites," which points you to the best urban perches; you should be able to pick up a copy at the Austin Convention & Visitors Bureau or at the offices of any of Austin's parks and preserves (see "More Attractions," above). Avid birders should also enjoy *Adventures with a Texas Naturalist* by Roy Bedichek; the author is one of the three friends depicted on the Philosophers' Rock, also listed in the "More Attractions" section.

**CANOEING**   You can rent canoes at **Zilker Park,** 2000 Barton Springs Rd. (☎ 512/478-3852), for $7.75 an hour, $28.50 all day (Sat, Sun, and holidays only Oct to Mar). **Capital Cruises,** Hyatt Regency boat dock (☎ 512/480-9264; www.capitalcruises.com), also offers hourly rentals on Town Lake. If your paddling skills are a bit rusty, check out the instructional courses of UT's **Recreational Sports Outdoor Program** (☎ 512/471-3116).

**FISHING**   Go on the fly with downtown's **Austin Angler,** 312½ Congress Ave. (☎ 512/472-4553; www.austinangler.com), an excellent place to pick up a license, tackle, and information on where to find the big ones. **Git Bit** (☎ 512/280-2861; www.gitbitfishing.com) provides guide service for half- or full-day bass-fishing trips on Lake Travis.

**GOLF**   For information about Austin's **six municipal golf courses,** call ☎ 512/ 480-3020; all offer pro shops and equipment rental, and their greens fees are very reasonable. Among them are the 9-hole **Hancock,** which was built in 1899 and is the oldest course in Texas; and the 18-hole **Lions,** where Tom Kite and Ben Crenshaw played college golf for the University of Texas.

**HIKING**   Austin's parks and preserves abound in nature trails; see "More Attractions," above, for additional information. Contact the **Colorado River Walkers of Austin** (☎ 512/495-6294; www.onr.com/user/dbarber/crw/homepage.htm) or the **Sierra Club** (☎ 512/472-1767; www.sierraclub.org/chapters/tx/austin) if you're interested in organized hikes. **Wild Basin Wilderness Preserve** (see the "Special-Interest Sightseeing" section, above), is another source for guided treks, offering periodic "Haunted Trails" tours along with its more typical hikes.

**ROCK CLIMBING**   Those with the urge to hang out on cliffs can call **Mountain Madness** (☎ 512/292-6624; www.mtmadness.com), which holds weekend rock-climbing courses at Enchanted Rock, a stunning granite outcropping in the Hill Country. **Austin Rock Gym,** 4401 Freidrich Lane, Suite 300 (☎ 512/474-4376; www.austinrockgym.com), offers more than 10,000 square feet of indoor rock climbing in a climate-controlled environment.

**SAILING**   Lake Travis is the perfect place to let the wind drive your sails; among the operators offering boat rentals in the Austin area are **Commander's Point Yacht Basin** (☎ 512/266-2333; www.cpyb.com), **Texas Sailing Academy** (☎ 512/261-6193; www.texassailing.com), and **Dutchman's Landing** (☎ 512/267-4289; www. dutchmanslanding.com); the first two companies also offer instruction.

**SCUBA DIVING**   The clarity of the limestone-filtered waters of Lake Travis makes it ideal for peeking around underwater. Boat wrecks and metal sculptures have been planted on the lake bottom of the private (paying) portion of **Windy Point Park** (☎ 512/266-3337), and Mother Nature has provided the park's advanced divers with an unusual underwater grove of pecan trees. Equipment rentals and lessons are available nearby from **Pisces** (☎ 512/258-6646; www.flash.net/~piscestx).

**SPELUNKING**   The limestone country in the Austin area is rife with dark places in which to poke around. In the city, two wild caves you can crawl into with the proper training are **Airman's Cave** on the Barton Creek Greenbelt and **Goat Cave Preserve** in southwest Austin. Check out **www.texascavers.com/tsa/** for links to statewide speleological sites, and see chapter 16 for other caves in nearby Hill Country.

**SWIMMING**   The best known of Austin's natural swimming holes is **Barton Springs Pool** (see "The Top Attractions," above), but it's by no means the only one. Other scenic outdoor spots to take the plunge include **Deep Eddy Pool,** 401 Deep Eddy Ave. at Lake Austin Boulevard (☎ 512/472-8546), and **Hamilton Pool Preserve,** 27 miles west of Austin, off Texas 71 on FM 3238 (☎ 512/264-2740). For lakeshore swimming, consider **Hippie Hollow** on Lake Travis, 2½ miles off FM 620 (☎ 512/473-9437), where you can let it all hang out in a series of clothing-optional coves, or **Emma Long Metropolitan Park** on Lake Austin (see "More Attractions," above). You can also get into the swim at a number of **free neighborhood pools;** phone ☎ 512/476-4521 for information.

**TENNIS**   The very reasonably priced **Austin High School Tennis Center,** 2001 W. Cesar Chavez St. (☎ 512/477-7802), **Caswell Tennis Center,** 2312 Shoal Creek Blvd. (☎ 512/478-6268), and **Pharr Tennis Center,** 4201 Brookview Dr. (☎ 512/ 477-7773), all have enough courts to give you a good shot at getting one. To find out about additional public courts, call ☎ 512/420-3020.

## 8 Spectator Sports

There are no professional teams in Austin, but a new minor league baseball team has captured local attention. College sports are very big, particularly when the University of Texas Longhorns are playing. The most comprehensive source of information on the various teams is **www.utexas.edu/athletics**, but you can phone the **UT Athletics Ticket Office** (☎ **512/471-3333**) to find out about schedules and **UTTM Charge-A-Ticket** (☎ **512/477-6060**) to order tickets.

**BASEBALL**   The **Longhorns baseball** team goes to bat February through May at Disch-Falk Field (just east of I-35, at the corner of Martin Luther King, Jr. Blvd. and Comal). Many players from this former NCAA championship squad have gone on to the big time, including five-time Cy Young award winner Roger Clemens. Nolan Ryan's **Round Rock Express,** a Houston Astro's farm club, won the Texas League championship in 1999, their first year in existence. See them at the Dell Diamond, 3400 E. Palm Valley Road in Round Rock (☎ **512/255-BALL** [information] or 512/244-4209 [ticket office]; www.roundrockexpress.com), a 7,800-seat stadium where you can choose from box seats, stadium seating, or even a grassy berm in the outfield.

**BASKETBALL**   The **Longhorns** and **Lady Longhorns basketball** teams, both Southwest Conference champions, play in the Frank C. Erwin Jr. Special Events Center (just west of I-35 on Red River between Martin Luther King, Jr. Blvd. and 15th St.) November through March.

**FOOTBALL**   It's hard to tell which is more central to the success of an Austin Thanksgiving: the turkey or the UT–Texas A&M game. Part of the Big 12 Conference, the **Longhorns football** team often fills the huge Darrell K. Royal/Texas Memorial Stadium (just west of I-35 between 23rd and 21st sts., E. Campus Dr. and San Jacinto Blvd.) during home games, played August through November.

**GOLF**   Celebrities such as Joe Namath and Dennis Quaid tee off for a good cause at the **East Austin Youth Classic,** held at Barton Creek Resort (☎ **512/329-4000**) in June. (It's been dubbed the "Ben-Willie-Darryl" because its benefactors are Ben Crenshaw, Willie Nelson, and Darryl Royal.)

**HOCKEY**   The **Austin Ice Bats** hockey team (☎ **512/927-PUCK;** www.icebats. com) has been getting anything but an icy reception. This typically rowdy team plays at the Travis County Exposition Center, 7311 Decker Lane (about 15 min. east of UT). Tickets, which run from $10 to $18, are available at any UTTM outlet or from Star Tickets (☎ **888/597-STAR** or 512/469-SHOW; www.startickets.com). The team generally plays on weekends mid-October through late March; a phone call will get you the exact dates and times.

**HORSE RACING**   Pick your ponies at **Manor Downs,** 8 miles east of I-35 on U.S. 290 East (☎ **512/272-5581;** www.manordowns.com). The track is open for live racing on Saturday and Sunday in February and Friday to Sunday, March through mid-April. Gates open at 11:30am, with the first weekend post at 1:30pm, the Friday post at 3:30pm. The rest of the year, you can see simulcast racing Wednesday to Sunday and holiday Mondays; call for the current schedule.

# Austin Shopping 14

When it comes to items intellectual, musical, or ingestible, Austin is a match for cities twice its size. Shopping here may not quite have evolved into an art as it has in glitzier Texas towns like Houston or Dallas, but Austin has a more than satisfying shopping range, plus several unique retail niches.

## 1 The Shopping Scene

Austin is seeing a revitalization of its urban retail scene. Downtown, specialty shops and art galleries are filtering back to the renovated 19th-century buildings along **Sixth Street** and **Congress Avenue.** Below Town Lake, **South Congress Avenue,** from Riverside south to Annie Street, is especially trendy, with art galleries and boutiques joining its rows of secondhand clothing stores. Other rich shopping enclaves to mine include the **West End** on Sixth Street west of Lamar and, nearby, north of 12th Street and West Lynn. In the vicinity of **Central Market,** between West 35th and 40th streets and Lamar and Mo-Pac, such small shopping centers as 26 Doors and Jefferson Square are similarly charming. Many stores on **the Drag**—the stretch of Guadalupe Street between Martin Luther King Jr. Boulevard and 26th Street, across from the University of Texas campus—are student oriented, but a wide range of clothing, gifts, toys, and, of course, books can also be found here.

Still, much of Austin's shopping has moved out to the malls. The newest growth area is in the northwest, where three upscale shopping centers, **The Arboretum, The Arboretum Market,** and **The Gateway complex** (consisting of the Gateway Courtyard, the Gateway Market, and Gateway Square), have earned the area the nickname "South Dallas." Bargain hunters go farther afield to the huge collections of factory outlet stores in San Marcos and New Braunfels; see chapter 16 for details.

Specialty shops in Austin tend to open around 9 or 10am, Monday through Saturday, and close at about 5:30 or 6pm; many have Sunday hours from noon until 6pm. Malls tend to keep the same Sunday schedule, but Monday through Saturday they don't close their doors until 9pm. Sales tax in Austin is 8.25%.

## 2  Shopping A to Z

# ANTIQUES

In addition to the one-stop antiques markets listed below, a number of smaller shops line Burnet Road north of 45th Street. See also the **Travis County Farmers' Market** under "Food," below.

**Antique Marketplace.** 5350 Burnet Rd. ☎ **512/452-1000.**

For people who like antiques but don't enjoy speaking in hushed tones, the Antique Marketplace offers bargains and treasures in a friendly, relaxed atmosphere. You'll find a little bit of everything under the roof of this large warehouse-type building in central Austin—Czech glass, funky collectibles, and expensive furnishings.

**Austin Antique Mall.** 8822 McCann Dr. ☎ **512/459-5900.**

You can spend anything from five bucks to thousands of dollars in this megacollection of antiques stores. More than 100 dealers in a 30,000-square-foot indoor space sell Roseville pottery, Fiesta dishes, Victorian furniture, costume jewelry, and much, much more. Think this is big? About 20 minutes north of Austin, the Antique Mall of Texas, 1601 S. I-35 (☎ **512/218-4290**), in Round Rock, run by the same people, has double the number of stalls.

**Whit Hanks Antiques.** 1009 W. Sixth St. ☎ **512/478-2101.** www.whithanks.com.

More than 50 high-quality dealers gather at tony Whit Hanks, just across the street from Treaty Oak. This is Austin's premier outlet for antiques. Even if you can't afford to buy anything, it's fun to ogle items from fine crystal and vases to Chinese cabinets and neoclassical columns. Two blocks west, West End Consignment, 1214 W. Sixth St., Suite 120 (☎ **512/478-2398**), offers 15,000 more square feet of fine antiques; it's an offshoot of the original that was sold to the staff.

# ART GALLERIES

**Country Store Gallery.** 1304 Lavaca St. ☎ **512/474-6222.** www.countrystore. citysearch.com.

Occupied by the architect and the superintendent of the state capitol during its construction in the late 19th century, this former boardinghouse now hosts the oldest art gallery in Austin and maybe all of Texas. The deer heads and branding irons on the walls complement bronzes and action paintings by well-known western artists such as Olaf Wieghorst. All told, more than 2,500 pieces, representing a variety of styles, are available in this 7,000-square-foot space.

**El Taller Gallery.** 8015 Shoal Creek Blvd., Suite 109. ☎ **800/234-7362** or 512/302-0100.

Located off Mo-Pac near Northcross Mall, this appealing showcase for Southwestern art sells Santa Fe pieces at Austin prices. Amado Peña, Jr., who once owned the gallery, is represented here, and you'll also find work by R. C. Gorman and other Native American artists. Handmade Pueblo pottery, Zapotec Indian weavings, and "critter" jewelry by Richard Lindsay are among the gallery's other interesting offerings.

**Gallery Shoal Creek.** 1500 W. 34th St. ☎ **512/454-6671.** www.gshoalcreek.com.

Since it opened in 1965, Shoal Creek has moved away from an exclusive emphasis on Western art to encompass work from a wide range of American regions. The focus is on contemporary painting in representational or impressionist styles—for example, Jerry Ruthven's Southwest landscapes or Nancy McGowan's naturalist watercolors. Like El Taller, this is an Austin outlet for many artists who also have galleries in Santa Fe.

**Wild About Music.** 721 Congress Ave. ☎ **877/708-1700** or 512/708-1700. www.wildaboutmusic.com.

Austin's commitment to music makes it a perfect location for this gallery and shop, strictly devoted to arts and crafts with a musical theme. Some of the pieces are expensive, but nearly all of them are fun. Come see the multimedia prints by Texas musician Joe Ely, the instrument-shaped furniture (a Moroccan prince picked up a guitar-shaped Jimi Hendrix chair), and the unique Texas music T-shirt collection. Gift items run the gamut from books and bola ties to watches and wind chimes.

**Yard Dog Folk Art.** 1510 South Congress Ave. ☎ **512/912-1613.** www.yarddog.com.

"Outsider" art, created in the deep, rural South, usually by the poor and sometimes by the incarcerated, is not for everyone, but for those interested in contemporary American folk art, this gallery is not to be missed. Not surprisingly, it's located in the hip South Congress area, where no one would be so uncool as to admit they find some of this stuff incredibly ugly.

## CRAFTS

**Eclectic.** 700 N. Lamar. ☎ **512/477-1816.**

A dazzling panoply of furniture, crafts, pottery, and paintings—new and old—from around the world is beautifully presented here. An outstanding jewelry section includes Native American pieces as well as bracelets, pins, and necklaces from Portugal, Thailand, and many other exotic places. Different countries are featured on a rotating basis.

**Tesoros Trading Co.** 209 Congress Ave. ☎ **512/479-8377.**

If you like exotic tchotchkes, be prepared to lose all sense of time when you enter this store. Colorful handwoven cloth from Guatemala, intricate weavings from Peru, glassware and tinwork from Mexico . . . all these and more are available at Tesoros, which, in addition to its high-quality folk art, also offers a limited amount of furniture, dishes, and housewares from Latin America. Plenty of reasonably priced items mingle with expensive treasures.

## DEPARTMENT STORES

**Dillard's.** Highland Mall. ☎ **512/452-9393.** www.dillards.com.

This Little Rock–based chain, spread throughout the Southwest, carries a nice variety of mid- to high-range merchandise. In Highland Mall, there are two separate outlets (with one central number)—one focusing on home furnishings and women's clothing, the other devoted to men's and children's wear. All the stores have country shops with good selections of stylish Western fashions. Two other locations are at the Barton Creek Mall (☎ **512/327-6100**) and the Lakeline Mall (☎ **512/257-8740**).

**Saks.** 9722 Great Hills Trail. ☎ **512/231-3700.** www.saksfifthavenue.com.

Austin came of age in the late 1990s with the opening of a link in this golden chain. Although smaller than many of the other Saks stores, it offers the high-tone fashions and accoutrements you'd expect, as well as personal shopper service.

## DISCOUNT SHOPPING

**Neiman Marcus' Last Call.** Brodie Oaks Shopping Center, 4115 S. Capital of Texas Hwy., at S. Lamar. ☎ **512/447-0701.** www.neimanmarcus.com.

Fans of Texas-grown Neiman Marcus will want to take advantage of Last Call, which consolidates fashions from 27 of the high-toned department stores and sells them for

50% to 75% off. Different merchandise shipments arrive every week. Not only can you find great bargains, but you needn't sacrifice the attention for which Neiman Marcus is famous. The staff here is as helpful as at all the other branches, and personal shopper service is available.

## ECO-WARES

**Eco-wise.** 110 W. Elizabeth. ☎ **512/326-4474.**

It's hard to typecast a shop that sells everything from greeting cards, natural insect repellent, and handwoven purses to building materials and home decorating supplies. The common denominator? Everything you'll find here is created with an eye toward the environment—that is, recycled or made from natural fabrics, and chemical free. The staff is incredibly knowledgeable and helpful, and customers are passionately loyal. The store offers baby and wedding shower registries for earth-friendly brides and grooms or moms and dads.

## ESSENTIAL OILS

**Sabia Botanicals.** 500 N. Lamar, Suite 150. ☎ **512/469-0447.**

All those soothing oils and lotions in their pretty bottles on the shelves seem to whisper, "Buy me, I'll make you feel better." This is aromatherapy central, but along with New Age products, the store also carries old-time herbal lines, such as Kiehl's.

## FASHIONS
### MEN

**By George Men.** 2346 Guadalupe St. ☎ **512/472-5536.**

This men's specialty shop strives to be unique—not only by offering distinctive items from the collections of well-established designers like Calvin Klein, Helmut Lang, and BCBG, but also by carrying lines of independents such as Thiory and T. Walko. You don't have to spend a fortune here, though. Austin businessmen seeking stylish suits mingle with UT students striving for a casual chic look.

**Keepers.** 1004 W. 38th St. ☎ **512/302-3664.** http://keepers.austin.citysearch.com.

Austinites seeking to make the transition from geek to fashion chic turn to this locally owned men's specialty store for friendly but expert advice and the latest in well-made men's clothing. You'll find an "image consultant" and expert tailors on the premises.

### OUTDOOR

**Run-Tex.** 422 W. Riverside Dr. ☎ **512/472-3254.** www.runtex.com.

If you've ever felt like saying "Feets, don't fail me now," you've come to the right place. Owned by the footwear editor for *Runner's World* magazine—and serving as the official wear-test center for that publication—this store not only has a huge inventory of shoes and other running gear, but also does everything it can to promote healthful jogging practices, even offering free running classes and a free injury-evaluation clinic (you'll have to pay for the sports massage at the Body Therapy Center, upstairs, however). The staff will make sure any footwear you buy is a perfect fit for your feet and running style. There's also a larger Run-Tex in Gateway Market, 9901 Capital of Texas Hwy. (☎ **512/343-1164**), a new location at 2201 Lake Austin Blvd., (☎ **512/477-9464**), and the related WalkTex, 4001 N. Lamar (☎ **512/454-WALK**), but the downtown store is right near the Austin runner's Mecca, Town Lake.

### WOMEN

See also **The Cadeau,** listed under "Gifts/Souvenirs," below.

**By George**. 524 N. Lamar Blvd. ☎ **512/472-5951.**

In its various locations, By George has long been a prime pick for Austin fashion victims, and this latest incarnation is the biggest and best yet. Pricey suits and dressy clothes, as well as lots of pamper-yourself potpourri and bath oils, make this store a favorite of the 30- and 40-something set; the college crowd sticks with the more casual outlet on the Drag, 2324 Guadalupe St. (☎ **512/472-2731**). But both shops offer hip, contemporary fashions in natural fabrics, and great purses and shoes to match.

**Therapy.** 1113 S. Congress Ave. ☎ **877/326-2331** or 512/326-2331. www.therapyclothing. com.

Many of Austin's top singer/songwriters come to this hip SoCo boutique to seek out clothing as clever as the store's name (any shopper worth her credit card knows the value of retail therapy). You'll find a small but constantly changing inventory of wonderfully inventive styles by local designers—everything from purses and casual halters to flowing skirts and evening gown—sold at prices that fall well below what you'd find at the large national stores. Aaah—feeling better already, aren't you?

## VINTAGE

**Electric Ladyland/Lucy in Disguise with Diamonds.** 1506 S. Congress Ave. ☎ **512/444-2002.**

Feather boas, tutus, flapper dresses, angel wings, and the occasional gorilla suit overflow the narrow aisles of Austin's best-known costume and vintage clothing outlet. The owner, who really *does* dress like that all the time, is a walking advertisement for her fascinating store. You can buy everyday clothes here like floral-print dresses and striped shirts—although even they require some degree of flamboyance—but you're likely to get sidetracked by rack after rack of outrageousness. If you're here at Halloween, this is the place to rent your costume.

**Under the Sun.** 1323A S. Congress Ave. ☎ **512/442-1308.**

One of South Congress's burgeoning retro boutiques, this is the place to come if you're looking for Western wear that's decades old but never saw the sweat of a cowpoke (don't expect it to come cheap, though). There's a large variety of clothing styles from the 1940s and 1950s, in all prices, as well as records and other nonwearable memorabilia.

## FOOD

**Central Market.** 4001 N. Lamar. ☎ **512/206-1000.** www.centralmarket.com.

You'll think you've died and gone to foodie heaven. Not only can you buy every imaginable edible item here—fresh or frozen, local or imported—but these gourmet megamarkets also have a restaurant section, with a top-notch chef serving up cowboy, bistro, Italian, vegetarian . . . you name it . . . all at very reasonable prices. A monthly newsletter announces what's fresh in the produce department, which jazz musicians are entertaining on the weekend, and which gourmet chef is holding forth at the market's cooking school (it has more classes for nonprofessional chefs than any other in the country). The Westgate Shopping Center branch, 4477 S. Lamar (☎ **512/899-4300**), opened in 1999 in South Austin, is as impressive as its history-making sibling north of UT.

**Travis County Farmers' Market.** 6701 Burnet Rd. ☎ **512/454-1002.**

Not only does this market offer great fresh fruit and vegetables from all around the Austin area, it also hosts monthly festivals honoring particular crops and/or growing seasons. April, for example, honors the 1015 "Y" onion, lauded as sweet, mild, and tear-free, while June celebrates peaches with contests for the best peach cobbler, peach ice cream, and peach preserves. Want something less produce-oriented? The market also has a barbecue restaurant, a cowboy restaurant, a Mexican restaurant, and a bakery. Those not interested in food can browse a store selling country-primitive antiques.

**Whole Foods Market.** 601 N. Lamar Blvd. ☎ **512/476-1206.** www.wholefoodsmarket. com.

From chemical-free cosmetics to frozen tofu burgers, Whole Foods covers the entire (organic) enchilada. It's the place to find anything that comes in a low-fat or otherwise pure version. If you need to fortify yourself before shopping this huge food emporium or want to try well-prepared versions of some of the store's products, head upstairs to the reasonably priced **Fresh Planet Cafe** (☎ 512/476-0902), open Monday to Saturday 11am to 9pm, Sunday 11am to 5pm. The northwest store in Gateway Market, 9607 Research Blvd. (☎ **512/345-5003**), is slightly smaller, but it's less frenetic and also has a cafe.

## GIFTS/SOUVENIRS

See also **Wild About Music,** listed under "Art Galleries," above.

**Artisans Gallery.** 10000 Research Blvd. (The Arboretum), Suite 258. ☎ **512/345-3001.**

Chock-a-block with colorful and creative clocks, boxes, picture frames, decanters, scarves, paperweights, and hair clips—all unique and handcrafted by artisans from all over the United States—this shop is an ever-metamorphosing delight. Several display cases of jewelry, ranging from glass bauble earrings to pricey silver chokers, round out the gift (and treat-yourself) cornucopia.

**The Cadeau.** 2316 Guadalupe St. (the Drag). ☎ **512/477-7276.**

*Cadeau* means "gift" in French, and this is the perfect place to find one, whether it be beautiful contemporary kitchenware, pottery, jewelry, clothing, bibelots, tchotchkes, or knickknacks. Be forewarned: Just when you think you've narrowed down your choice, you may suddenly realize you've missed two whole rooms full of goodies to choose from. To add to the dilemma, there's a newer location, at 4001 N. Lamar Blvd. (☎ **512/453-6988**), near Central Market.

## GLASS & POTTERY

**Clarksville Pottery & Galleries.** 4001 N. Lamar, Suite 200. ☎ **512/454-9079.** www.clarksvillepottery.com.

This pottery emporium, filled with lovely pieces created by local artisans, has moved from its namesake location in the artsy section of downtown to a prime spot near Central Market (see "Food," above). You'll find everything ceramic, from candleholders to bird feeders, as well as hand-blown glass, wood carvings, and contemporary jewelry in a variety of media; there's a unique selection of Judaica, too. A second outlet in the Arboretum Market, 9722 Great Hills Trail, Suite 380 (☎ **512/794-8580**), carries equally impressive stock.

**Fire Island Hot Glass Studio, Inc.** 3401 E. Fourth St. ☎ **512/389-1100.** http://fireisland. citysearch.com.

This glassblowing studio, about 2 miles east of I-35, is a bit off the beaten track, but it's a treat to watch the owners/artists, Matthew LaBarbera and his wife, Teresa Ueltschey, at their delicate craft. Demonstrations are given every Saturday morning (Sept to Jan and Mar to May) from 9am to noon; other times are available by appointment. You'll find the couple's elegant perfume bottles, oil lamps, bowls, and paperweights in fine galleries around Austin, but this showroom naturally has the largest selection. If you have a certain design in mind, you can special-order a set of goblets.

# HARDWARE & MORE

**Breed & Co. Hardware.** 718 W. 29th St. ☎ **512/474-6679.** www.breedandco.com.

You don't have to be a power-drill freak to visit Breed & Co. How many hardware stores, after all, have bridal registries where you can sign up for Waterford crystal? This darling of Austin do-it-your-selfers has everything from nails to tropical plants, organic fertilizer, gardening and cookbooks, pâté molds, and cherry pitters. You're sure to find something here you never knew you needed. A newer branch in the chic West-lake Hills area, 3663 Bee Cave Rd. (☎ **512/328-3960**), is the only store in Austin that carries Tiffany china.

# JEWELRY

See also **Artisans Gallery,** under "Gifts/Souvenirs," above.

**Russell Korman.** 3806 N. Lamar Blvd. ☎ **512/451-9292.**

You'd never know it from his current elegant digs, but Russell Korman got his start in Austin's jewelry trade by selling beads on the Drag. Although he's moved on to fine 14-karat gold, platinum, and diamond pieces, along with fine pens and watches—there's an experienced watchmaker on the premises—his store still has a considerable collection of more casual sterling silver from Mexico. Prices are very competitive, even for the most formal baubles.

# MALLS/SHOPPING CENTERS

**26 Doors.** 1206 W. 38th St. ☎ **512/338-9222.**

Not all the shops in 26 Doors boast the exquisite wooden antique entryways that give this Spanish-style shopping center its name, but all are intimate and charming. The specialty stores arrayed around a tiled, tree-shaded courtyard range from chic hair salons to toymakers.

**The Arboretum.** 10000 Research Blvd. (Hwy. 183 and Loop 360). ☎ **512/338-4437.**

It's worth a trip to the far northwest part of town to a shopping center so chic that it calls itself a market, not a mall. This two-level collection of outdoor boutiques surrounding the tony Renaissance Hotel doesn't include any department stores, but it does have a Barnes & Noble Superstore and a huge Pottery Barn. Your basic selection of yuppie shops—everything from upscale clothing stores to a cigar humidor—are present and accounted for. The Treetop Galleries section on the second floor features art galleries, a custom jeweler, and crafts shops. Dining options, including a sub shop and a T.G.I. Friday's, tend to be on the casual side. There's an outlet for Amy's, Austin's favorite locally made ice cream, as well as a Dan McKlusky's steakhouse (see chapter 12).

**Barton Creek Square.** 2901 S. Capital of Texas Hwy. ☎ **512/327-7040.**

Set on a bluff with a view of downtown, Barton Creek tends to be frequented by upscale west siders; the wide-ranging collection of more than 180 shops is anchored by Dillard's, Foley's, Sears, JCPenney, and Montgomery Ward. One of the newest malls in Austin, it's refined and low-key, but the presence of Frederick's of Hollywood and Victoria's Secret lingerie boutiques makes one wonder if the daytime soaps might not be onto something about the bored rich.

**The Gateway Complex.** Hwy. 183 and Capital of Texas Hwy. ☎ **512/418-1600.**

Comprising three not-so-distinct shopping areas, the Gateway Courtyard, the Gateway Market, and Gateway Square, this large, open complex includes everything from a handmade paper store and an audiobook store to national chains such as Blockbuster Music, REI, Old Navy, and CompUSA. There are also branches of Austin-based stores, including Run-Tex, TravelFest, and Whole Foods Market, discussed individually in this chapter, as well as a branch of Mezzaluna, detailed in chapter 12.

**Highland Mall.** 6001 Airport Blvd. ☎ **512/454-9656.**

Austin's first mall, built in the 1970s, is still one of the city's most popular places to shop. It's located at the south end of the hotel zone near the old airport, just minutes north of downtown on I-35. Reasonably priced casual-clothing stores like the GAP and Express vie with high-end shops such as Anne Taylor. Dillard's (two of 'em!), Foley's, and JCPenney department stores coexist with specialty stores like Papyrus and the Warner Bros. Studio Store. The tonier Lincoln Plaza shops are just to the south, on I-35. The food court is impressive.

**Lakeline Mall.** 11200 Lakeline Mall Dr., Cedar Park. ☎ **512/257-SHOP.**

Austin's newest shopping Mecca, in an upscale far northwest location, is notable for its attention-grabbing design, featuring lots of colorful reliefs and murals of the city. The shops, including Foley's, Dillard's, Mervyn's, Sears, and JCPenney, are not nearly so unusual, but there are some interesting smaller shops, from Dollar Tree, where everything costs a buck, to The Stockpot, with state-of-the art cookware.

**Northcross Mall.** 2525 W. Anderson Lane. ☎ **512/451-7466.**

Smaller than Highland and Barton Creek malls, Northcross is Austin's recreational shopping center, with the city's only ice-skating rink, a six-screen movie theater, and a large food court. It's also home to Oshman's Super Sport, a huge sporting-goods store where customers can try out equipment at a batting cage, basketball court, and in-line skating surface.

# MARKETS

**Austin Country Flea Market.** 9500 Hwy. 290 east (4 miles east of I-35). ☎ **512/928-2795** or 512/928-4711.

Every Saturday and Sunday year-round, more than 550 covered spaces are filled with merchants selling all the usual flea market goods and then some—new and used clothing, fresh herbs and produce, electronics, antiques. This is the largest flea market in central Texas, covering more than 130 paved acres. There's live music every weekend—generally a spirited Latino band to step up the shopping pace.

**Renaissance Market.** West 23rd and Guadalupe sts. (the Drag). ☎ **512/397-1468.**

Flash back or be introduced to tie-dye days at this hippie-ish crafts market, where vendors are licensed by the city of Austin (read: no commercial schlock). Billed as the only continuously operated, open-air crafts market in the United States, it's theoretically open daily 8am to 10pm, but most of the merchants turn up only on the weekends. You'll find everything from silver jewelry and hand-carved flutes to batik T-shirts. Many of the artisans come in from small towns in the nearby Hill Country.

# MUSIC

**Sound Exchange.** 2100A Guadalupe St. (the Drag). ☎ **512/476-8742.** www. soundexchange.com/austin.

Come to the Sound Exchange for hard-to-find older music, imports, and releases by local bands, especially in the rock-and-roll and punk-rock genres. You can get some pretty good bargains in vinyls, tapes, and CDs here, and browse obscure music magazines to your heart's content. The walls are plastered with posters announcing upcoming Austin shows.

**Waterloo Records and Video.** 600A N. Lamar Blvd. ☎ **512/474-2500.** www. waterloorecords.com.

Carrying a huge selection of sounds, Waterloo is always the first in town to get the new releases. If they don't have something on hand, they'll order it for you promptly. The store offers preview listening, compilation tapes of Austin groups, and tickets to all major-label shows around town. It also hosts frequent in-store promotional performances by both local and mid-sized national bands. There's a video annex just west of the record store (☎ **512/474-2525**) and, for purists, a vinyl section.

## OUTDOOR GEAR

See also **Run-Tex,** listed under "Fashions," above.

**The Whole Earth Provisions Co.** 2410 San Antonio St. ☎ **512/478-1577.** www. wholeearth.citysearch.com.

Austin's large population of outdoor enthusiasts flocks to this store to be outfitted in the latest gear and earth-friendly fashions. If you wouldn't think of hiking without a two-way radio or a Magellan positioning navigator, you can find them here. The Austin-based chain also carries gifts, housewares, educational toys, and travel books. There are additional locations at 1014 N. Lamar Blvd. (☎ **512/476-1414**) and Westgate Shopping Center, 4477 S. Lamar (☎ **512/899-0992**).

## TOYS

**Hog Wild.** 100A E. North Loop Blvd. ☎ **512/467-9453.**

Always regretted throwing out that Howdy Doody lunch box? You can get it back— for a few more bucks, of course—at this nostalgia-inducing little toy shop on the edge of Hyde Park. Photos of celebrity customers such as Quentin Tarantino and Mira Sorvino hang on the wall.

**Terra Toys.** 1708 S. Congress Ave. ☎ **800/247-TOYS** or 512/445-4489.

Steiff teddy bears, the wooden Playmobil world, and other high-quality imported toys are among the kiddie delights at Terra, just south of the river. The store also carries a variety of miniatures, train sets, books, and kites. For unique children's apparel, try the owners' other place, **Dragonsnaps,** 1700 S. Congress (☎ **512/445-4497**), just down the block.

**Toy Joy.** 2900 Guadalupe St. ☎ **512/320-0090.**

The name says it all; the only question is whether kids or grown-ups will have more Toy Joy here. Ambi and Sailor Moon are among the appealing children's lines sold in the large back room. Out front, things like lava lamps, yo-yos, and cartoon character watches keep both GenXers and baby boomers fascinated. Open until midnight on Friday and Saturday.

## TRAVEL

**Travelfest by Pace.** 1214 W. Sixth St. ☎ **800/590-3378** or 512/469-7906. www. pacetvl.com.

A concept whose time has clearly come, the country's first all-inclusive travel shop offers guidebooks, luggage, cameras, binoculars, over-the-counter medicines, travel-sized containers, and a full-service travel agency under one roof. Those planning a trip of any sort can come in and browse various useful directories or attend the free and frequent travel-related seminars. (Check the Web site for schedules.) The first store, 9503 Research Blvd. (☎ **800/343-3378** or 512/418-1515), was so successful that the owner opened this second, larger one in downtown's West End, and now there's a mini-branch at the Austin airport.

## WESTERN STORES

**Capitol Saddlery.** 1614 Lavaca St. (between 16th and 17th sts.). ☎ **512/478-9309.**

The custom-made boots of this classic three-level Western store near the capitol were immortalized in a song by Jerry Jeff Walker. Run by the same family for 7 decades, this place is a bit chaotic, but it's worth poking around to see the hand-tooled saddles, belts, tack, and altogether functional cowboy gear.

**Sheplers.** 6001 Middle Fiskville Rd. ☎ **512/454-3000** or 800/835-4004 (mail order). www.sheplers.com.

Adjacent to Highland Mall, the huge Austin branch of this growing chain of Western-wear department stores has everything the well-dressed urban cowboy or cowgirl might require. If you're already back home and get a sudden urge for a concho belt or bola tie, the mail-order and online business can see you through any cow-fashion crisis.

## WINE & BEER

See also **Central Market** in "Food," above.

**Grape Vine Market.** 7938 Great Northern Blvd. ☎ **512/323-5900.** www.grapevinemarket. com.

The recent arrival on the retail scene of this warehouse-size wine store, with its expert staff and huge selection of bottles at good prices, is yet another sign that, sophistication wise, Austin is coming of age (or is that vintage?). If you're seeking a unique wine gift, this is definitely the place to come. There's a good selection of brews and spirits, too.

**Whip In Convenience Store.** 1950 S. I-35. ☎ **512/442-5337.**

Like the name says, it's a convenience store, and like the address says, it's just off the freeway, so don't expect atmosphere. Do expect to find any obscure beer you're looking for, though, be it lager or stout, from Hill Country or New Delhi. At a conservative estimate, the cooler is filled with almost 400 different types of brews at any given time, with even more come Oktoberfest or other special beer-producing seasons. Wines also make a strong showing here (the staff is happy to track obscure bottles for you) and there are two humidors for imported cigars.

**Wiggy's.** 1130 W. Sixth St. ☎ **512/474-WINE.**

If liquor and tobacco are among your vices, Wiggy's can help you indulge in high style. In addition to its extensive selection of wines (more than 1,500) and single-malt scotches, this friendly west end store also carries a huge array of imported smokes, including humidified cigars. Prices are reasonable and the staff is very knowledgeable.

## 15

# Austin After Dark

It's hard to imagine an itch for entertainment, high or low, that Austin couldn't scratch. Live-music freaks enjoy a scene that rivals those of Seattle and Nashville, while culture vultures have local access to everything from classic lyric opera to high-tech modern dance. Ironically, the source of much of the city's high culture is literally crude: When an oil well on land belonging to the University of Texas system blew in a gusher in 1923, money for the arts was assured.

The best sources for what's on around town are the *Austin Chronicle* and *XLent,* the entertainment supplement of the *Austin-American Statesman;* both are free and available in hundreds of outlets every Thursday.

For a quick take on the local club action, call the **KLBJ** hotline at ☎ **512/832-4094.**

The **Austin Circle of Theaters Hotline** (☎ **512/320-7168**) can tell you what's on the boards each week. If you want to know who's kicking around, phone **Danceline** (☎ **512/474-1766**).

The **Ticketmaster** (www.ticketmaster.com) telephone number for the University of Texas, the locus for many of the city's performing-arts events, is ☎ **512/477-6060;** for other major venues, phone ☎ **512/494-1800.** Concerts at La Zona Rosa, the Backyard, and Austin Music Hall, and shows at the Paramount Theatre can be booked through **Star Tickets** (☎ **512/469-SHOW** or 888/597-STAR; www.startickets.com/Austin), with outlets in most Albertson's grocery stores.

The **Austix Box Office,** 4402 Burnet Rd. (☎ **512/454-8497;** www.austix.com), handles phone charges for many of the smaller theaters in Austin as well as half-price ticket sales (☎ **512/454-4253**). Call for a recorded listing of what's currently being discounted, then pick up tickets at the Austix Box Office (Wed to Sat 11:30am to 6:30pm), or at the **Austin Visitors Center,** 201 E. Second St. (Wed to Sat 11:30am to 5pm, Sun noon to 6pm).

## FREE ENTERTAINMENT

Starting in late April or early May, the city sponsors 10 weeks of free **Wednesday night concerts** at Auditorium Shores and **Sunday afternoon concerts** at the Beverly F. Sheffield Zilker Hillside Theater. Barring classical, they run the gamut of musical styles, from rock and reggae to country-and-western and Latin. Call ☎ **512/442-2263** for current schedules of these two series and of the free **Zilker Park Jazz Festival** in September. Every other Wednesday night, from June

# But There Are No Limits on the Entertainment

PBS's longest-running show (it first aired in 1975), **Austin City Limits** has showcased such major talent as Lyle Lovett, Garth Brooks, Mary Chapin Carpenter, the Dixie Chicks, and Phish. Originally pure country, it has evolved to include blues, zydeco, Cajun, Tejano—you name it. The show is taped live from August through February at the KLRU-TV studio, 2504B Whitis St. (near Dean Keeton, 1 block in from Guadalupe), but the schedule is very fluid, so you have to be vigilant to nab the free tickets, which are distributed on a first-come, first-served basis on the day of the taping. Log on to **www.pbs.org/klru/austin** and click on FAQ for details of how to get tickets, or phone the show's hot line at ☎ **512/475-9077.**

You don't have to plan in advance to get a free tour of the recording studio, where you can watch an interesting video clip of the show's highlights, stroll through the control room, and get up on the actual stage and play air guitar; they're held at the KLRU studio at 10:30am every Friday except holidays (call ☎ **512/478-0098** or 800/926-2282 to verify the schedule around holidays).

through August, the upscale Arboretum shopping center (10000 Research Blvd.) hosts a **Blues on the Green** concert series in their open-air courtyard; call ☎ **512/338-4437** for details. Some 70,000 people turn out to cheer the 1812 Overture and the fireworks at the Austin Symphony's **Fourth of July Concert** at Auditorium Shores (☎ **512/476-6064**).

From mid-July through late August, the **Beverly F. Sheffield Zilker Hillside Theater,** across from Barton Springs Pool, hosts a summer musical (☎ **512/397-1463**); "Will Rogers Follies" is featured in 2001. The series started in the late 1950s, and is the longest-running one in the United States. The summer **Austin Shakespeare Festival** is often held at the theater, too; call ☎ **512/454-BARD** for up-to-date information about locations and dates. More than 5,000 people can perch on the theater's grassy knoll to watch performances. Seating is first-come, first-served; bring your own blanket or lawn chairs.

## 1 The Club & Music Scene

The appearance of country-and-western "outlaw" Willie Nelson at the Armadillo World Headquarters in 1972 united hippies and rednecks in a common musical cause, and is often credited with the birth of the live-music scene on Austin's Sixth Street. The city has since become an incubator for a wonderfully vital, cross-bred alternative sound that mixes rock, country, folk, and blues. Although the Armadillo is defunct and Sixth Street is past its creative prime—with some notable exceptions, it caters pretty much to a rowdy college crowd—live music in Austin is very much alive, just more geographically diffuse. There's always something happening downtown in the warehouse district and on the stretch of Red River between 6th and 10th streets, voted the "Best Entertainment District" by the readers of the *Austin Chronicle* in 2000. Some venues, like the Continental Club, have long been off the beaten path; others, like the Backyard, more recently expanded the boundaries of Austin's musical terrain. Poke around; you can never tell which dive might turn up the latest talent (Janis Joplin, Stevie Ray Vaughan, and Jimmie Dale Gilmore all played local gigs). If you're here during S×SW (see box, below), you'll see the town turn into one huge, music-mad party.

*Note:* Categories of clubs in a city known for crossover are often very rough approximations; those that completely defy typecasting are dubbed "eclectic." Cover charges range from $5 to $12 for well-liked local bands. Note, too, that in addition to the clubs detailed below, several of the restaurants discussed in chapter 12, including **Threadgill's** and **Manuel's,** offer live music regularly.

## FOLK & COUNTRY

**Broken Spoke.** 3201 S. Lamar Blvd. ☎ **512/442-6189.**

This is the genuine item, a Western honky-tonk dating from 1964, with a wood-plank floor and a cowboy-hatted, two-steppin' crowd. Still, it's in Austin, so don't be surprised if the band wears Hawaiian shirts, or if tongues are firmly in cheek for some of the songs. Photos of Hank Williams, Tex Ritter, and other country greats line the walls of the club's "museum." You can eat in a large, open room out front (the chicken-fried steak can't be beat), or bring your long-necks back to a table overlooking the dance floor.

✪ **Continental Club.** 1315 S. Congress Ave. ☎ **512/441-2444.**

Although it also showcases rock, rockabilly, and new-wave sounds, the Continental Club holds on to its traditional country roots by celebrating events such as Hank Williams's birthday. A small, smoky club with high stools and a pool table in the back room, this is a not-to-be-missed Austin classic. It's considered by many to have the best happy hour music in town, and the folksy Tuesday blues with Toni Price is a real crowd pleaser.

**Jovita's.** 1617 S. First St. ☎ **512/447-7825.**

It's a winning recipe: Jovita's is part Mexican restaurant, part nightclub, part Mexican-American cultural center—and all South Austin landmark. How can you beat a place that's got terrific flautas and enchiladas, tasty margaritas, and some of the best sounds in town, ranging from salsa to country?

## JAZZ & BLUES

✪ **Antone's.** 213 W. Fifth St. ☎ **512/474-5314.**

Although Willie Nelson and crossover C&W bands like the Austin Lounge Lizards have been known to turn up at Clifford Antone's place, the club owner's name has always been synonymous with the blues. Stevie Ray Vaughan used to be a regular, and when major blues artists like Buddy Guy, Etta James, or Edgar Winter venture down this way, you can be sure they'll either be playing Antone's or stopping by for a surprise set. Clifford Antone's incarceration (for selling marijuana) and the club's relocation to the warehouse district hasn't changed anything—this is still where you come to hear the bad, sad songs.

**Elephant Room.** 315 Congress Ave. ☎ **512/473-2279.**

Stars on location in Austin mingle with T-shirted students and well-dressed older aficionados at this intimate downtown venue, as dark and smoky as a jazz bar should be. The focus is on contemporary and traditional jazz, although the bill branches out to rock on occasion.

## ROCK

**Emo's.** 603 Red River St. ☎ **512/477-EMOS.**

Austin's last word in alternative music, Emo's draws acts of all sizes and flavors, from Johnny Cash to Green Day. It primarily attracts college kids, but you won't really feel out of place at any age. (And when there's a cover, you'll get in cheaper than the under-21 crowd.) The front room holds the bar, pool tables, and pinball machines. You'll have to cross the outside patio to reach the back room where the bands play.

## Label It Successful—Austin's SxSW

When SxSW started out in 1987, as an offshoot of New York City's now defunct New Music seminar, it was primarily a way to showcase unsigned Texas bands. In less than a decade and a half, it has become the most anticipated convention on the industry calendar. Speakers and panelists over the years have included everyone from Tony Bennett to Neil Young, while Billy Bragg, Arlo Guthrie, Iggy Pop, Michelle Shocked, Soul Asylum, Toad the Wet Sprocket, and Lucinda Williams have been among the featured artists.

Fledgling musicians from around the world come here now to schmooze with A&R reps, publicists, journalists, radio personalities, managers, and other industry suits—with good reason. In the past, now-popular bands and singers like the Presidents of the United States of America, Lisa Loeb, and Letters to Cleo were signed by major labels after impressing the right people.

Some who have attended the conference from the start complain that it has changed, that it's no longer a showcase for new bands but a forum for groups that recording companies have already signed and want to publicize. So many hot names turn out now, too, that the unknowns have a hard time getting audience attention. The festival has also gotten more diffuse: Film and interactive (high-tech and Internet) components were added in the mid-1990s, and now they're almost as big as the original music segment. Attending actors have included everyone from Sandra Bullock to Billy Bob Thornton, directors such as Adam Egoyan and Quentin Tarantino have turned up, and Web site design contests have drawn a tremendous response.

In short, love it or hate it for being a sell-out; this event is huge, with some 15,000 industry professionals and 25,000 fans signing on for programs that might include 60 panels and workshops and 900 musical appearances at more than 40 venues around town. So even if you're not looking to make it big in the music, film, or Internet industries, this is still the hottest conference ticket around. Prices in 2001 ranged from $135 if you registered early for the film or interactive aspect alone, to $795 for the walkup Platinum rate, which affords access to all conference and music events. Special hotel and transportation packages are also offered.

**South by Southwest (SxSW) Music and Media Conference & Festival** is held during UT's spring break, usually the third week of March. For current schedules and speakers/performers, check the Web site at **www.sxsw.com** or contact SxSW Headquarters at P.O. Box 4999, Austin, TX 78765 (☎ **512/467-7979**; fax 512/451-0754; e-mail: sxsw@sxsw.com).

**Maggie Mae's.** 512 Trinity St. ☎ **512/478-8541.**

Good rock cover bands, a great selection of beers, and plenty of space set Maggie Mae's apart from the collegiate-crowded clubs lining Sixth Street. Five separate bars make ordering easy, and the live music plays upstairs and down. The outside courtyard is generally reserved for blues.

## SINGER/SONGWRITER

**Cactus Cafe.** Texas Union, University of Texas campus (24th and Guadalupe). ☎ **512/475-6515.**

A small, dark cavern with great acoustics and a fully stocked bar, UT's Cactus Cafe is singer/songwriter heaven, a place where dramatic stage antics take a back seat to engaged showmanship. The crowd's attentive listening attracts talented solo artists like Jimmy LaFave and nationally recognized Austin native Shawn Colvin, along with well-known acoustic combos. The adjacent **Texas Union Ballroom** (☎ **512/475-6645**) draws larger crowds with big names like Billy Bragg.          •

**Ego's.** 510 S. Congress Ave. ☎ **512/474-7091.**

Located in the parking garage of an apartment building, this '60s clubhouse is dark, smoky, seedy, and loads of fun. Locals throng here for the strong drinks and live nightly music, from piano to honky-tonk country. A couple of run-down pool tables and video games add to the funky charm. On Sundays, you can try your hand at finger painting—the supplies are provided, and who knows? Your masterpiece might be chosen to hang on the wall for a while.

**Saxon Pub.** 1320 S. Lamar Blvd. ☎ **512/448-2552.**

You'll recognize the Saxon Pub by the giant knight in shining armor in the parking lot, an old friend among lots of new faces along South Lamar Boulevard. This is a long-standing home to South Austin's large community of singer-songwriters. Don't be put off by the medieval kitsch outside; inside, the atmosphere is comfortable and no-nonsense.

**Speakeasy.** 412 Congress Ave. ☎ **512/476-8017.**

The walk down a dark alley in the warehouse district to reach this multilevel club is all part of the 1920s Prohibition theme, which, mercifully, is not taken to an obnoxious extreme. Rather, a swanky atmosphere is created by lots of dark wood and red velvet drapes on the side of the stage; walk up two flights of narrow stairs to enjoy a drink on the romantic Evergreen terrace, which affords a nice view of downtown. The booze is not bootleg and, with live music (mostly of the singer/songwriter type) nightly except Sunday when the place is closed, there's no prohibition on good times.

# ECLECTIC

✪ **The Backyard.** Hwy. 71 West at R.R. 620, Bee Cave. ☎ **512/263-4146** or 512/469-SHOW for tickets. Tickets $6–$8 local acts, $20–$45 national acts.

A terrific sound system and a casual country atmosphere have helped make this one of Austin's hottest venues, although it rarely hosts local bands any more. Since it opened in the early 1990s, the Allman Brothers, Joan Baez, The Band, Jimmy Cliff, Chick Corea, k.d. lang, Lyle Lovett, Bonnie Raitt, and Warren Zevon have all played the terraced outdoor amphitheater, which is shaded by ancient live oaks. Come early for dinner; the Waterloo Ice House serves a Texas menu, including barbecue from The Iron Works (see chapter 12). The food's all good and reasonably priced.

**Carousel Lounge.** 1110 E. 52nd St. ☎ **512/452-6790.**

In spite of (or maybe because of) its out-of-the-way location and bizarre circus theme—complete with elephant and lion-tamer murals and an actual carousel behind the bar—the Carousel Lounge is a highly popular local watering hole. You never know what will turn up on stage; this place has hosted everything from smaller musical acts to belly dancers.

**Cedar Street Courtyard.** 208 W. Fourth St. ☎ **512/495-9669.**

Join the martini-and-cigar crowd—which has included the likes of actor Denzel Washington and music legend Bob Dylan—in this sophisticated courtyard, where the nightly live sounds range from jazz to tango. Single gals take note: This place got the *Austin Chronicle*'s nod as the "Best Place to Watch Too Many Men Compete for Too Few Women."

**Hole in the Wall.** 2538 Guadalupe St. ☎ **512/472-5599.**

This intimate club, on the Drag just off the UT campus, has a long-standing tradition of trying anything once. It's a great coup for local performers to be booked here, and the audience often gets to say, "We saw them when" about popular Texas bands that later hit it big. There's a good bar food menu, plus pool tables in back.

**La Zona Rosa.** 612 W. Fourth St. ☎ **512/472-2293.** www.lazonarosa.com.

Another Austin classic, LZR has departed from its funky roots a bit to go upmarket, featuring bigger names and bigger covers than in the past. But the venue has remained the same—a renovated garage brightly painted with monsters and filled with kitschy memorabilia—and this is still a fun place to listen to good bands, from Greg Allman and Friends to Los Lobos.

**Stubb's Bar-B-Q.** 801 Red River St. ☎ **512/480-8341.**

Within the rough limestone walls of a renovated historic building you'll find great barbecue and country Texas fare and three friendly bars—plus terrific music, ranging from singer/songwriter solos to hip-hop open mics to all-out country jams. Out back, the Waller Amphitheater hosts some of the bigger acts. See also chapter 12 for Stubb's Sunday gospel brunches.

## COMEDY CLUBS

**Capitol City Comedy.** 8120 Research Blvd., Suite 100. ☎ **512/467-2333.** Tickets $8 Sun–Thurs, $12 Fri–Sat. Performances Tues–Thurs and Sun 8pm; Fri–Sat 8 and 10pm.

Top ranked on the stand-up circuit, Cap City books nationally recognized comedians like Bobcat Goldthwait and Victoria Jackson. The cream of the crop turn up on Friday and Saturday, of course, but you'll find plenty to laugh at (including lower prices) the rest of the week. Look for a move to downtown soon.

**Esther's Follies.** 525 E. Sixth St. ☎ **512/320-0553.** Tickets $16 Thurs, $18 Fri–Sat; $2 off for students. Performances Thurs 8pm; Fri–Sat 8 and 10pm.

You might miss a couple of the punch lines if you're not in on the latest twists and turns of local politics, but the no-holds-barred Esther's Follies doesn't spare Washington, either. It's very satirical, very irreverent, very Austin.

**Velveeta Room.** 525 E. Sixth St. ☎ **512/469-9116** or 512/478-MONK. Monk's Night Out $7; performances $8 Fri, $10 Sat. Monk's Night Out and open mic Thurs; Monk's Night Out and performances Fri–Sat. Times vary from 8pm to midnight.

For one-stop comedy consumption, go straight from Esther's to the Velveeta Room next door, a deliberately cheesy club serving more generic stand-up, local and national. Regular shows and Thursday's open mic alternate with Monk's Night Out, improv with lots of audience participation.

## DANCE CLUBS & DISCOS

Dancing fools head for Sixth Street, where they can hop from one club to another within a 5-block radius. Off that drag, the **Voodoo Room,** 318 E. Fifth St. (☎ **512/477-1641**), features techno and hip-hop DJs on the weekends, and **Polly Esther's,** 404 Colorado St. (☎ **512/418-1975**), is a retro-decor disco for those either too young to be allergic to 1970s and '80s sounds or old enough to have grown nostalgic for it.

## 2 The Performing Arts

Austin has its own symphony, theater, ballet, lyric opera, and modern dance companies, but it also draws major international talent to town. Much of the action, local and imported, goes on at the University of Texas's Performing Arts Center, but some terrific outdoor venues take advantage of the city's abundant greenery and mild weather.

## OPERA & CLASSICAL MUSIC

**Austin Chamber Music Center.** 4930 Burnet Rd., Suite 203. ☎ **512/454-7562** or 512/454-0026. www.austinchambermusic.org. Tickets $21–$35. Box office Mon–Fri 9am–5pm.

This teaching and performing group features an Intimate Concert series, open to the public but held at elegant private homes. They also host visiting national and international artists, such as the Maia Quartet from Juilliard, and hold an annual summer festival.

**Austin Lyric Opera.** 901 Barton Springs Rd. ☎ **800/31-OPERA** or 512/472-5992 (box office). www.austinlyricopera.org. Tickets $11–$100. Box office Mon–Fri 9:30am–4:30pm; Sat before a performance 10am–2pm.

Austin's first professional opera company, founded in 1985, currently presents four productions a year at the Bass Concert Hall. Major national and international artists hit the high notes in such operas as *Carmen* and *Madame Butterfly* for the 2000 to 2001 season.

**Austin Symphony.** 1101 Red River St. ☎ **888/4-MAESTRO** or 512/476-6064. www.austinsymphony.org. Tickets $17–$33 classical, $15 and $25 pops. Box office Mon–Fri 9am–5pm; concert days noon–5pm.

A resident in Austin since 1911, the symphony performs most of its classical works at Bass Concert Hall, although a new hall, which will also host Ballet Austin and the Austin Lyric Opera, is under construction. The informal Pops shows play to a picnic table–seated crowd at the Palmer Auditorium; Blood, Sweat, and Tears was featured in 2001. Casual Classics and Family series round out a very full, very creative musical program. In addition, in June and July at Symphony Square, every Wednesday from 9:30 until about 11:30am, kids can try out various orchestral instruments in the symphony's version of a petting zoo. Symphony Square is a complex comprising an outdoor amphitheater and four historic structures dating from 1871 to 1877. Narrow Waller Creek runs between the seats and the stage of the amphitheater.

## THEATER

**Frontera @ Hyde Park Theatre.** 511 W. 43rd St. ☎ **512/479-PLAY.** Tickets $8–$15. Box office Mon–Sat 1–6pm.

An intimate neighborhood theater in Austin's historic Hyde Park district presents the innovative, contemporary work of the Frontera theater company. Genres range from music and dance to performance art, subjects from baseball to racism to lesbianism, but you can count on whatever you see to be intellectually engaging. The annual 5-week-long FronteraFest, the largest fringe theater/performance art festival in the Southwest, showcases local and national talent of all kinds.

**Mary Moody Northen Theatre of St. Edward's University.** 3001 S. Congress Ave. ☎ **512/448-8484** (box office) or 512/448-8483. Tickets $10.

UT's College of Fine Arts is not the only act in town: St. Edward's University also has a thriving theater department, which gets support for its performances from a variety of professional directors and guest actors. The 2000 to 2001 season ranged from the classic *Death of A Salesman* to the more contemporary *Six Women Near Brain Death or Inquiring Minds Want to Know.*

**State Theater Company.** State Theater, 719 Congress Ave. ☎ **512/472-5143** (box office) or 512/472-7134. Tickets $20–$35. Box office Mon–Fri; performance Sat noon–5:30pm.

The former Live Oak Theatre company has taken on the name of its newly renovated venue, the beautiful old State Theater. Austin's most professional group of performers puts on a wide variety of works, from classics like Shakespeare's *Taming of the Shrew* to contemporary works like Edward Albee's *Three Tall Women*. Readings from nationwide participants in the Harvest Festival of New American Plays are held in the fall; the play that wins the contest is produced during the season. A second theater being renovated next door will hold newer works.

**Vortex Repertory Company.** The Vortex, 2307 Manor Rd. ☎ **512/454-TIXS** (box office) or 512/478-LAVA. www.vortexrep.org. Tickets $8–$20.

A converted warehouse with an outdoor courtyard and cafe, Vortex's theater space (just east of UT and I-35) complements the company's avant-garde program. Names of such original productions as *Dark Goddess, Despair's Book of Dreams,* and the *Sometimes Radio* may be familiar only to the initiated, but there are updated performances of more traditional fare, and Austin premieres of such established contemporary works as *Unidentified Human Remains*.

**Zachary Scott Theatre Center.** 1510 Toomey Rd. (John E. Whisenhunt Arena Stage) or 1421 W. Riverside Dr. (Kleberg Stage). ☎ **512/476-0541** (box office) or 512/476-0594. www.zachscott.com. Tickets $16–$31. Box office Mon–Sat noon–7pm.

Austin's oldest theater, incorporated in 1933, featured first-class stagings of such Broadway and off-Broadway fare as *The Master Class, Jelly's Last Jam,* and *Art* during the 2000 to 2001 season. Works are performed at two adjacent theaters—one on a three-sided thrust stage, the other in the round—at the edge of Zilker Park. It's a sneaker's throw from the parking lot to the hike-and-bike trail.

# DANCE

**Ballet Austin.** 3004 Guadalupe St. ☎ **512/476-2163** (box office) or 512/476-9051. www.balletaustin.org. Tickets $12–$51. Box office Mon–Fri 10am–6pm; Sat 10am–3pm.

This company's two-dozen professional dancers leap and bound in such classics as *The Nutcracker* and *Hamlet,* or more modern pieces like *Triple Exposure,* a suite of three ballets. Artistic director Stephen Mills has choreographed a wide array of works for prestigious companies in the United States and abroad. When in town, the troupe performs at Bass Concert Hall or, for children's shows, the Paramount Theatre.

**Sharir + Bustamante Dance Works.** 3724 Jefferson St., Suite 201. ☎ **512/458-8158** or 512/477-6060 (box office). Tickets $15 adults, $10 seniors and students. Box office Mon–Fri 10am–6pm; Sat 10am–3pm.

An aptly high-tech ensemble for plugged-in Austin, Sharir first stretched the boundaries of dance toward virtual reality in 1994 when the company included video projections and computer-generated images in its choreography. This exciting postmodern troupe, in residence at the University of Texas's College of Fine Arts, has been continuing its exploration of new technologies ever since. Most of the Austin performances are held at UT's Performing Arts Center, but there are also site-specific environmental pieces.

## ECLECTIC

**One World Theater.** 7701 Bee Caves Rd. ☎ **512/330-9500.** www.oneworldtheatre.org. Tickets $19–$90. Box office Mon–Fri 9am–6pm, plus noon to curtain time on show days.

It's tough to typecast a venue whose 2000 to 2001 season included Arlo Guthrie, Chuck Mangione, Herbie Hancock, Ballet Stars of Moscow, Ailey II, Melissa Manchester, Richie Havens—and Tibetan Monks. But you couldn't find a better venue than this intimate (300-seat) West Austin performance space to showcase these impressive talents. The Tuscan castle–style theater is charming, the acoustics are excellent, and the Hill Country views from the balcony are superb.

## 3 The Bar Scene

### BREWPUBS

**Bitter End B-Side Lounge & Tap Room.** 311 Colorado St. ☎ **512/478-5890.**

Adjoining the Bitter End Bistro & Brewery (see chapter 12), this intimate gathering spot serves up (canned) swing, jazz, and blues along with its excellent home brews. Additional draws are a cask-conditioned beer tap and a separate cigar room. Ahhh, yuppie heaven.

**Copper Tank Brewing Company.** 504 Trinity St. ☎ **512/478-8444.**

Within the confines of these thick limestone walls, sports fans catch games on one of the two large screens, couples dine from an eclectic menu, and singles hopefully scan the crowd, while beer aficionados of all stripes savor the light Whitetail Ale or the Big Dog Stout. Wednesday nights all drafts are a dollar. A small courtyard provides a haven from the madding crowd.

**Waterloo Brewing Company.** 401 Guadalupe St. ☎ **512/477-1836.**

The first brewpub in Texas—do-it-yourself suds weren't legal in the state until late 1993—Waterloo has a decent dining room on the first floor, a noisy game room upstairs, and six good microbrews on tap. The pale ale is excellent, and the full-bodied O. Henry's Porter is practically a meal in itself.

### A BRITISH PUB

**Dog & Duck Pub.** 406 W. 17th St. ☎ **512/479-0598.**

We have it on the authority of our British friends that this is the real McCoy, a comfy locale with a relaxing atmosphere. You'll be touring all the British Isles with the mix of darts, Irish jams, bagpipes, and hearty brews. The bangers and mash taste authentic, too—not that that's necessarily a good thing.

### GAY BARS

**Oilcan Harry's.** 211 W. Fourth St. ☎ **512/320-8823.**

Its name notwithstanding, this slick warehouse district bar attracts a clean-cut, upscale, mostly male crowd. This is the place to go if you're looking for a buttoned-down, Brooks Brothers kind of guy. There's dancing, but not with the same frenzy as at many of the other clubs.

**Rainbow Cattle Co.** 305 W. Fifth St. ☎ **512/472-5288.**

This is Austin's prime gay country-western dance hall. It's about 75% male but attracts a fair share of lesbian two-steppers as well.

# Late-Night Bites

If it's 3am and you have a hankering for a huge stack of pancakes to soak up that last Shiner you probably shouldn't have downed, Austin has you covered. Part Texas roadhouse, part all-night diner, Austin's cafes offer extra-late hours, funky atmosphere, and large quantities of hippie food. To call them cafes is a bit misleading—there's nothing remotely resembling Gallic chic here—but it's as good a term as any for these Austin originals.

One of the earliest on the scene and still hugely popular is **Kerbey Lane,** 3704 Kerbey Lane (☎ **512/451-1436**). Sunday mornings, locals spill out on the porch of the comfortable old house, waiting for a table so they can order the signature "pancakes as big as your head." Musicians finishing up late-night gigs at the Continental Club usually head over to the **Magnolia Cafe South,** 1920 S. Congress Ave. (☎ **512/445-0000**); on nice nights, enjoy the Love Veggies sautéed in garlic butter or the Deep Eddy burrito on an outdoor deck. Both cafes are open 24 hours daily. Kerbey Lane has two other locations, and Magnolia Cafe has one clone, but the originals are far more interesting.

## AN HISTORIC BAR

✪ **Scholz Garten.** 1607 San Jacinto Blvd. ☎ **512/474-1958.**

Since 1866, when councilman August Scholz first opened his tavern near the state capitol, every Texas governor has visited it at least once (and many quite a few more times). In recent years, Texas's oldest operating biergarten was sold to the owners of the popular Green Mesquite BBQ, giving it new life. The extensive menu now combines barbecue favorites with traditional bratwurst and sauerkraut; a state-of-the-art sound system cranks out the polka tunes; and patio tables as well as a few strategically placed TV sets help Longhorn fans cheer on their team—a Scholz's tradition in and of itself. All in all, this is a great place to drink in some Austin history.

## AN IRISH BAR

**Fadó Irish Pub.** 214 W. Fourth St. ☎ **512/457-0172.**

The name Fadó (say Fuh-*doh*) means "long ago" in Celtic, and homages to the auld sod abound in this usually packed watering hole. Polished wood blocks are carved with Celtic designs, Celtic warrior helmets and weapons dot the walls, and traditional Irish music plays every Sunday. But the free-flowing Guinness isn't warm, as it would be in the old country—nor is it nearly as inexpensive. When it gets too crowded inside, seek out the small outdoor patio with its own bar.

## LOCAL FAVORITES

**Cedar Door.** 910 W. Cesar Chavez. ☎ **512/473-3712.**

Think "Cheers" with a redwood deck looking out on Town Lake. The Cedar Door is Austin's favorite local, drawing a group of potluck regulars ranging from hippies to journalists and politicos. The beer's cold, the drinks are strong, and to lots of folks, it feels like home.

**Club de Ville.** 900 Red River. ☎ **512/457-0900.**

This is one of the few bars in the area where you can actually have a conversation without shouting. Settle in on one of the couches inside—the low red light is both atmospheric and flattering—or lounge under the stars, where a natural limestone cliff creates a private walled patio (which is taken over alternating Tues nights by karaoke). The cliff is also a great acoustical barrier for the bands that occasionally play here.

## A PIANO BAR

**Driskill Hotel.** 604 Brazos St. ☎ **512/474-5911.**

Sink into one of the plush chairs arrayed around a grand piano and enjoy everything from blues to show tunes in the upper-lobby bar of this newly opulent historic hotel. A pianist accompanies the happy-hour hors d'oeuvres (nightly 5 to 7pm), but the ivory thumping doesn't get going in earnest until 9pm on Tuesday through Saturday, when people start singing along.

## A SPORTS BAR

**Earl Campbell's Restaurant and Bar.** 212 E. Sixth St. ☎ **512/482-0520.**

With an owner who won the Heisman Trophy while playing for the UT Longhorns, before going on to become a Hall of Famer for the Houston Oilers, this friendly bar has impeccable Texas sports credentials—not to mention good barbecue. This is *the* place for viewing Longhorn's home games (unless, of course, you're rooting for the other side).

## A WINE AND TAPAS BAR

**Málaga.** 208 W. Fourth St. ☎ **512/236-8020.**

Come to this sleek, sophisticated spot to sip some fine wines and nibble some Spanish appetizers (the swordfish bites are especially tasty). There are regular wine tastings, and a nice selection of wines by the glass and by 2-ounce flights is always available. Beware the Kristen, however, a bartender's secret-formula drink billed "as the pink lemonade your mother never made you": It goes down nice 'n' easy but packs a powerful punch. This place is not for the smoke sensitive.

## 4 Films

Not surprisingly, you can see more foreign films in Austin than anywhere else in the state. Nearly every cinema in town devotes at least one screen to something off Hollywood's beaten track. In the university area, the largest concentration of art films can be found at the **Dobie Theatre,** 2021 Guadalupe St., on the Drag (☎ **512/472-FILM**), and at the two venues of the **Texas Union Film Series,** UT campus, Texas Union Building and Hogg Auditorium (☎ **512/475-6656**). The **Village Cinema Four,** 2700 W. Anderson Lane (☎ **512/451-1725**), across from Northpark Mall, also exclusively showcases independent and imported fare. If you'd like something a little more substantial than popcorn with your flicks, check out the **Alamo Drafthouse,** 409 Colorado St. (☎ **512/476-1320;** www.drafthouse.com), offering all-you-can-eat pizza nights, two-for-one pasta date nights, and theme events like "Hong Kong Sundays" with kung-fu films, Chinese food, and Chinese beer—all at terrifically low prices.

Of the many cinematic events held in town, October's **Austin Film Festival** is among the most interesting. Held in conjunction with the Heart of Films Screenwriters' Conference, it focuses on movies with great scripts. One year, for example, the Coen brothers, who were conference participants, showed a reedited, remastered version of their debut film *Blood Simple.* For current information, contact the Austin Film Festival, 1604 Nueces, Austin, TX 78701 (☎ **800/310-FEST** or 512/478-4795; fax 512/478-6205; www.austinfilmfest.org; e-mail: austinfilm@aol.com).

# 16 Touring the Texas Hill Country

A rising and falling dreamscape of lakes and rivers, springs and caverns, the Hill Country is one of Texas's prettiest regions, especially in early spring when wildflowers daub it with every pigment in nature's palette. Dotted with old dance halls, country stores, and quaint Teutonic towns—more than 30,000 Germans emigrated to Texas during the great land-grant years of the Republic—and birthplace to one of the U.S.'s more colorful recent presidents, the region also lays out an appealing tableau of the state's history.

San Antonio lies at the southern edge of the Hill Country, while Austin is the northeastern gateway to the region. The following tour traces a roughly circular route from San Antonio, but it's only 80 miles between the two cities; distances in this area are sufficiently short that you can design excursions based on your point of origin and your particular interests. The highlights are covered here, but those with extra time will find far more to explore. For additional information, log on to **www.hillcountryoftexas.cc**, which covers the region and provides links to three of its major towns: Bandera, Fredericksburg, and Kerrville. To find out what's blooming in the area, and exactly where, phone the **Texas Travel Information Center** (☎ **800/452-9292**) in March, April, or May.

*Note:* Driving in the Hill Country can be a delight, but the speed limit on a number of roads without many passing lanes is 70 m.p.h. If you want to meander and enjoy the scenery, be prepared to pull over and let other cars pass, or you'll have a retinue of annoyed locals on your tail.

## 1 Boerne

From downtown San Antonio, it's a straight shot, 30 miles north on I-10, to Boerne (rhymes with "journey")—a good base for travelers, as it's near both a big city and some very rural areas. A popular health resort in the 1880s, the little (2.2 miles long) town was first settled 30 years earlier by freedom-seeking German intellectuals. It was named after German firebrand journalist Ludwig Börne. A gazebo with a Victorian cupola in the center of the main plaza often hosts concerts by the Boerne Village Band, the oldest continuously operating German band in the world outside Germany (it first tuned up in 1860). A number of the town's 19th-century limestone buildings house small historical museums, boutiques, and restaurants, and a

Main Street Project has added old-fashioned lamp posts and German street signs, but Boerne's biggest draw is its antiques shops—more than 20 line the "Hauptstrasse," or main street. For a self-guided tour, stop in at the **Greater Boerne Chamber of Commerce,** 1 Main Plaza, Boerne, TX 78006 (☎ **888/842-8080** or 830/249-8000; www.boerne.org).

## SEEING THE SIGHTS

Those who want to spend their time outdoors can explore four distinct ecosystems— grassland, marshland, woodland, and river bottom—via short treks on the **Cibolo Wilderness Trail,** City Park Road, off Hwy. 46 East next to the Kendall County Fair grounds (☎ **830/249-4616;** www.cibolo.org). A dinosaur trackway traces the route of *Acrocanthosaurus atokensis* and friends, whose fossilized footprints were uncovered when the area was flooded in 1997. If you like your strolls to include sand traps, the top-rated **Tapatio Springs golf course,** Johns Road exit off I-10 West (☎ **800/ 999-3299** or 830/537-4611; www.tapatio.com), is the place for you.

One of the most popular nearby attractions is **Cascade Caverns** (☎ **830/ 755-8080**); drive about 3 miles south of Boerne on I-10, take exit 543, and drive 2.7 miles east. This active cave boasts huge chambers, a 90-foot underground waterfall, and comfortable walking trails; guides provide 1-hour interpretive tours every 30 minutes. It's open Memorial Day to Labor Day daily 9am to 6pm; off-season Monday to Friday 10am to 4pm, Saturday and Sunday 9am to 5pm. It's also easy to tour the stalactite- and stalagmite-filled **Cave Without a Name,** 325 Kreutzberg Rd., 12 miles northeast of Boerne (☎ **830/537-4212;** www.cavewithoutaname. com). A naming contest held when the cavern was discovered in 1939 was won by a little boy who wrote that it was too pretty to name (the $500 he earned put him through college). Open Memorial Day through Labor Day daily 9am to 6pm; off season, daily 10am to 5pm.

Rafters and canoers like **Guadalupe River State Park,** some 13 miles east of Boerne, off Hwy. 46 on P.R. 31 (☎ **830/438-2656;** www.tpwd.state.tx.us), comprising more than 1,900 acres surrounding a lovely, cypress-edged river. Keep an eye out: You might spot white-tailed deer, coyotes, armadillos, or even a rare golden-cheeked warbler here.

Those whose tastes run to the above-ground, indoors, and Epicurean will want to drive 12 miles north of Boerne on FM 1376 to the **Sister Creek Vineyards** (☎ **830/ 324-6704**), located in a converted century-old cotton gin on the main—actually the only—street in Sisterdale (pop. 50). Among the bottles recently available for sampling, the 1998 pinot noir and 1999 cabernet sauvignon and merlot were especially good. Open daily noon to 5pm. Weave down the road afterward to the **Sisterdale General Store** (☎ **830/324-6767**), opened in 1954 and not changed very much since then. You can still buy a pickled egg to accompany a cold one (Coke or Bud) at the beautiful old handcrafted bar, made of East Texas pine.

## WHERE TO STAY

Now a lovely Victorian-style B&B, **Ye Kendall Inn,** 128 W. Blanco, Boerne, TX 78006 (☎ **800/364-2138** or 830/249-2138; www.yekendallinn.com), opened as a stagecoach lodge in 1859. The rooms ($99) and suites ($160) are beautifully appointed, but the former have their bathtubs in the middle of the room, near the bed, and commodes behind a screen. If you're traveling with a companion with whom you're not willing to be that intimate, book a suite.

The **Guadalupe River Ranch Resort and Spa,** P.O. Box 877, Boerne, TX 78006 (☎ **800/460-2005;** www.guadaluperiverranch.com), was owned by actress Olivia de Havilland in the 1930s, and served as an art colony for a while. This gorgeous spread

# The Texas Hill Country

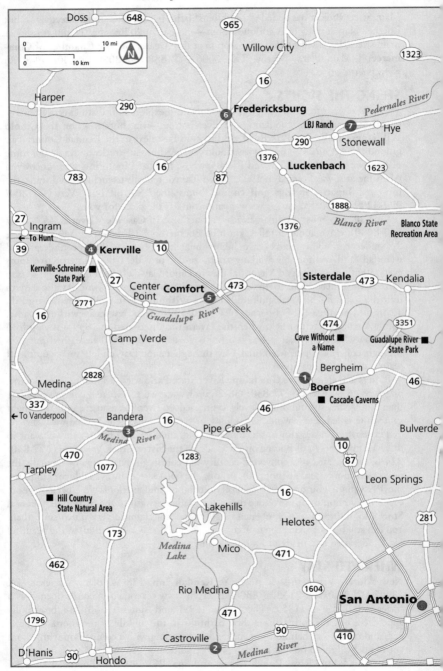

Doss
648
965
Willow City
1323
16
Harper
290
Fredericksburg 6
Pedernales River
LBJ Ranch 7 Hye
290
Stonewall
16
1376
Luckenbach
1623
783
87
1888
Blanco River
Blanco State Recreation Area
1376
27
Ingram
← To Hunt
39
Kerrville 4
10
Kerrville-Schreiner State Park
27
Center Point
Comfort
473
Sisterdale
473
Kendalia
2771
5
Guadalupe River
474
3351
16
Cave Without a Name
Guadalupe River State Park
Camp Verde
2828
Bergheim
1
Medina
337
Boerne
46
← To Vanderpool
Bandera
16
Cascade Caverns
3
Pipe Creek
46
Bulverde
470
Medina River
1283
10
1077
87
Tarpley
16
Leon Springs
Hill Country State Natural Area
Lakehills
281
173
Helotes
Medina Lake
Mico
471
462
Rio Medina
1604
1796
471
San Antonio
Castroville
90
D'Hanis
90
Hondo
2
Medina River
410

0  10 mi
0  10 km
N

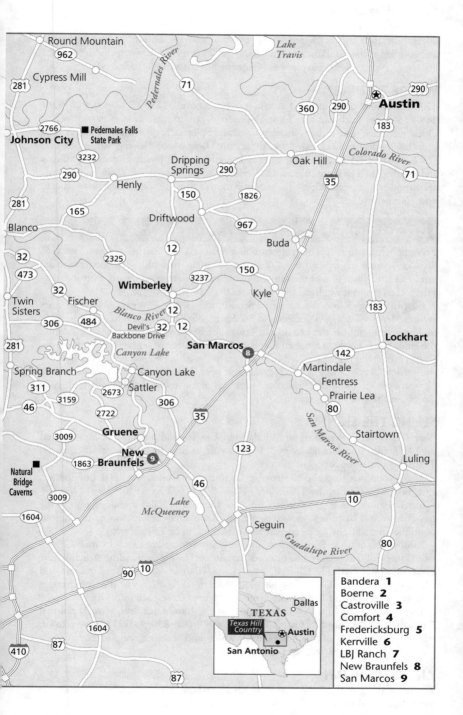

Round Mountain
962
Cypress Mill
281
Johnson City
2766
■ Pedernales Falls State Park
3232
290
Henly
281
165
Blanco
32
473
32
Twin Sisters
306
484
Fischer
281
Spring Branch
311
3159
46
3009
Natural Bridge Caverns
3009
1604

*Pedernales River*
71
*Lake Travis*
360
290
183
★ **Austin**
290
*Colorado River*
Oak Hill
35
71
Dripping Springs
290
150
1826
Driftwood
967
12
Buda
2325
3237
150
**Wimberley**
Kyle
183
*Blanco River* 12
Devil's Backbone Drive 32 12
*Canyon Lake*
**San Marcos** ⑧
142
**Lockhart**
Canyon Lake
2673
Sattler
306
Martindale
Fentress
Prairie Lea
80
*San Marcos River*
Stairtown
2722
35
**Gruene**
123
Luling
**New Braunfels** ⑨
1863
46
*Lake McQueeney*
10
80
1604
Seguin
*Guadalupe River*
90 10

1604
87
410
87

Bandera **1**
Boerne **2**
Castroville **3**
Comfort **4**
Fredericksburg **5**
Kerrville **6**
LBJ Ranch **7**
New Braunfels **8**
San Marcos **9**

**TEXAS**
Dallas
*Texas Hill Country*
★ **Austin**
**San Antonio**

offers abundant activities ranging from river rafting and porch sitting to getting wrapped and polished at the spa. Basic rates run about $299 per night for two, including a room, three meals, and snacks, but there are frequent specials and spa packages.

## WHERE TO DINE

**The Limestone Grill,** in Ye Kendall Inn (see above), 128 W. Blanco (☎ **830/ 249-9954**), sets an elegant tone for steaks, seafood, poultry, pasta, and even sandwiches. Open for lunch and dinner Tuesday to Saturday, brunch only Sunday, lunch only Monday; moderate to expensive. The more casual **Bear Moon Bakery,** 401 S. Main St. (☎ **830/816-BEAR**), is ideal for a hearty breakfast or light lunch. Organic ingredients and locally grown produce enhance the flavor of the inventive soups, salads, sandwiches, and wonderful desserts. Open Tuesday to Saturday 6am to 5pm and Sunday 8am to 4pm; inexpensive.

## 2 Castroville

Even though Castroville is even closer to San Antonio than Boerne—20 miles via U.S. 90 West—it has maintained more of a pristine, rural atmosphere. Residents who are not descended from one of the founding families have reported feeling a bit like outsiders, even after they've lived here for more than 20 years.

Castroville was founded on a scenic bend of the Medina River in 1844. Two years earlier, Henri Castro, a Portuguese-born Jewish Frenchman, had received a 1.25-million-acre grant from the Republic of Texas in exchange for a commitment to colonize the land. Second only to Stephen F. Austin in the number of settlers he brought over, Castro recruited most of his 2,134 émigrés from the Rhine Valley, and especially from the French province of Alsace. You can still hear Alsatian, an unwritten dialect of German, spoken by some of the older members of town, but the language is likely to die out in the area when they do.

## SEEING THE SIGHTS

*Note:* Castroville closes down on Monday and Tuesday, and some places are shuttered on Wednesday and Sunday as well. If you want to find everything open, come on Thursday, Friday, or Saturday.

Make your first stop the **Castroville Chamber of Commerce,** 802 London St., P.O. Box 572, Castroville, TX 78009 (☎ **800/778-6775** or 830/538-3142; www. castroville.com), where you can pick up a booklet that contains a walking tour of the town's historical buildings, as well as a map that details the location of the various boutiques and antique shops (they're not concentrated in a single area).

Almost 100 of the original settlers' unevenly slope-roofed houses remain in Castroville, some still occupied by the builders' ancestors. The oldest standing structure, the **First St. Louis Catholic Church,** went up in 1846 on the corner of Angelo and Madrid. Many of the European-style headstones in the **cemetery** at the western edge of town, where Henri Castro's wife, Amelia, is buried, date back to the 1840s.

Get some insight into the town's history at the **Landmark Inn State Historical Park,** 402 E. Florence St., Castroville, TX 78009 (☎ **830/931-2133;** www.tpwd. state.tx.us/park/landmark/landmark.htm), which also counts among its attractions a nature trail, an old gristmill, and a stone dam.

## AN HISTORIC INN

The centerpiece of the State Historical Park, the **Landmark Inn** offers eight simple rooms decorated with early Texas pieces dating up until the 1940s. Prices for a double with a private bathroom are $55; with a shared bathroom, $50. None of the rooms have phones or TVs, but they do have air-conditioning. A continental breakfast is included in the rate. Don't come here for luxurious appointments, but for a uniquely peaceful setting in the woods near the Medina River. *Note:* The inn is closed Tuesday and Wednesday, so no overnight reservations are accepted for Monday or Tuesday.

## WHERE TO DINE

Get a delicious taste of the past at **Haby's Alsatian Bakery,** 207 U.S. 90 East (☎ 830/931-2118), owned by the Tschirhart family since 1974, and featuring apple fritters, strudels, stollens, breads, and coffeecakes. Open Monday to Saturday 5am to 7pm.

A gourmet surprise in this rural area, **La Normandie Restaurant,** 1302 Fiorella St. (☎ 830/538-3070 or 800/261-1731), features a classic French menu, including escargot and coq au vin and the delicious house special veal *à la normande*. Strains of songs from Normandy, homeland of one of the proprietor/chefs, float through the pretty, lace-curtained cottage. There's a Tuesday buffet lunch, dinner Thursday to Saturday, and on Sundays a champagne brunch and dinner, if reserved by 3pm.

## 3  Bandera

North of Castroville and west of Boerne, Bandera is a slice of life out of the Old West. Practically everything and everybody here seems to have come straight off a John Ford film set. Established as a lumber camp in 1853, this popular guest-ranch center still has the feel of the frontier: Not only are many of its historic buildings intact—including **St. Stanislaus** (1855), the second-oldest Polish church in the country—but people are as genuinely friendly as any you might imagine from America's small-town past.

## WHAT TO SEE & DO

You can explore Bandera's distant past by picking up a self-guided tour brochure of historic sites at the **Bandera County Convention and Visitors Bureau,** 1808 Hwy. 16 South, Bandera, TX 78003 (☎ 800/364-3833 or 830/796-3045; www. banderacowboycapital.com), open weekdays 9am to 5:30pm, Saturday 10am to 4pm. But most people take advantage of the town's living traditions by strolling along Main Street, where a variety of crafters work in the careful, hand-hewn style of yesteryear. Be sure to stop in at the **Bandera Forge** (☎ 830/796-7184), a working blacksmith shop (you can design your own branding iron); the **Stampede** (☎ 830/796-7650), a good spot for Western collectibles; and the huge **Love's Antique Mall** (☎ 830/ 796-3838), a one-stop shopping center for current local crafts as well as things retro. **Country Accent Antiques,** Hwy. 16, 6 miles south of Bandera (☎ 830/535-4979), includes among its array of furnishings beds, benches, and gates crafted from wrought iron by Warren Lee. It's worth visiting for its herb garden and antique roses alone. Naturally, plenty of places in town can outfit you in cowboy duds, such as the **Trading Post,** 307 Main St. (☎ 830/460-3655), with a large selection of kiddie sizes.

If you want to break those clothes in, horseback riding options abound. The Convention and Visitors Bureau can direct you to the outfitter who can match you with the perfect mount. The CVB is also the place to check whether any rodeos or roping exhibitions are in the area. (They occur often in summer and less regularly in fall.)

## THE GREAT OUTDOORS

You don't have to go farther than **Bandera Park** (☎ 830/796-3765), a 77-acre green space within city limits, to enjoy nature, whether you want to stroll along the River Bend Native Plant Trail or picnic by the Medina River. Or you can canter through the

**Hill Country State Natural Area,** 10 miles southwest of Bandera (☎ 830/796-4413), the largest state park in Texas allowing horseback riding. The nearest outfitter is the helpful and reliable **Running R Ranch,** Route 1 (☎ 830/796-3984). Cost is $21 an hour for adults, $18 for those 12 and under. A visit to the nonprofit **Brighter Days Horse Refuge,** 682 Krause Rd., Pipe Creek, about 9 miles northeast of Bandera (☎ 830/510-6607), will warm any animal lover's heart. The price of admission to this rehab center for abandoned and neglected horses is only a bag of carrots or apples, but donations are most welcome.

About 20 miles southeast of town (take Hwy. 16 to R.R. 1283), **Medina Lake** is the place to hook crappie, white or black bass, and especially huge yellow catfish; the public boat ramp is on the north side of the lake, at the end of P.R. 37. The Bandera Convention and Visitors Bureau can provide the names of various outfitters for those who want to kayak, canoe, or tube down the Medina River.

Most people visit the **Lost Maples State Natural Area,** about 40 miles west of Bandera in Vanderpool (☎ 830/966-3413), in autumn, when the leaves put on a brilliant show. But birders come in winter to look at bald eagles, hikers like the wildflower array in spring, and anglers try to reduce the Guadalupe bass population of the Sabinal River in summer. Those seeking accommodations more upscale than the campground should try **Fox Fire Log Cabins,** 1 mile south of Lost Maples State Natural Area, HC 01, Box 142, Vanderpool, TX 78885 (☎ 830/966-2200; www.foxfirecabins.com), where two-bedroom cabins offer full kitchens, wood-burning fireplaces, and comfy antique-country furnishings (but new beds). Barbecue pits, volleyball and basketball courts, myriad outdoor activities, and low rates ($85 for two adults, $98 for four; children under 12 free) make this place ideal for families. Even higher on the lodgings food chain, the **Texas Stagecoach Inn,** HC 02, Box 166, Vanderpool, TX 78885 (☎ 888/965-6272 or 830/966-6272; www.bbhost.com/txstagecoachinn), is a beautiful 6,000-square-foot house that dates back to 1885. It's done in attractive ranch style, with some fun pieces from the 1950s. The location, on the banks of the Sabinal River, couldn't be more idyllic, and the hot breakfast buffets are elaborate. Rates range from $85 to $115 for a double.

## STAYING AT A GUEST RANCH

For the full flavor of this region, plan to stay at one of Bandera's many guest ranches; you'll find a full listing on the Bandera Web site. Note that most of them have a 2-night (or more) minimum stay. You wouldn't want to spend less time anyway; it'll take at least half a day to start to unwind and get attuned to the slower ranch rhythms. Expect to encounter lots of European visitors (you'd be amazed at how popular country-and-western dancing is in England). These places are great for cultural exchange, especially if you want to know things like what the best beers are in Texas and Germany.

At the **Dixie Dude Ranch,** P.O. Box 548, Bandera, TX 78003 (☎ 800/375-Y'ALL or 830/796-4481; www.dixieduderanch.com), a long-time favorite retreat, you're likely to see white-tailed deer or wild turkeys as you trot on horseback through a 725-acre spread; overnight trail rides can be booked in fall and winter. The down-home, friendly atmosphere keeps folks coming back year after year. Rates are $85 to $95 per adult per night.

Tubing on the Medina River and swimming in an Olympic-size pool are among the many activities at the **Mayan Ranch,** P.O. Box 577, Bandera, TX 78003 (☎ 830/796-3312 or 830/460-3036; www.mayanranch.com), another well-established family-run place, where corporate groups often come for a bit of loosening up ($120 per adult). Both ranches provide lots of additional Western fun for their guests during high season—things like two-step lessons, cookouts, hayrides, singing cowboys, or trick-roping exhibitions. Rates are based on double occupancy and include three home-cooked meals, two trail rides, and most other activities.

## WHERE TO DINE

When you're ready to put on the feed bag, try Main Street's **O.S.T.** (☎ 830/796-3836), named for the Old Spanish Trail that used to run through Bandera. Serving up down-home Texas and Tex-Mex victuals since 1921, this cafe has a room dedicated to The Duke and other cowboy film stars. Open daily for breakfast, lunch, and dinner; inexpensive to moderate.

**Billy Gene's,** 1105 Main St. (☎ 830/460-3200), serves up huge platters of down-home country standards like calves' liver and onions or meatloaf for seriously retro prices. Less health-defying food is available here, too. An open deck and huge windows afford excellent Medina River vistas. Open daily for all meals; inexpensive to moderate.

If you're just up for an old-fashioned milkshake or some fresh-squeezed lemonade, grab a stool at the soda fountain of the **Bandera General Store,** 306 Main St. (☎ 830/796-4925). Open 10am to 6pm Monday to Saturday, 10am to 4pm on Sunday.

One of the best country-western clubs in South Texas, the **Cabaret Dance Hall** (see below) has a cafe known for its good prime rib and Gulf Coast seafood.

## A COUPLE OF HONKY-TONKS

Don't miss **Arkey Blue & The Silver Dollar Bar** (☎ 830/796-8826), a genuine spit-and-sawdust cowboy honky-tonk on Main Street. When there's no live music (Gary Wright and the Roadkill Band are regulars), plug a quarter in the old jukebox and play a country ballad by owner Arkey. And look for the table where Hank Williams, Sr. carved his name.

Just down the road a piece, the old **Cabaret Dance Hall** (☎ 830/796-8166), established in 1936, was recently resuscitated. Larger than Arkey's, it can accommodate bigger-draw names like Don Walser (the "Pavarotti of the Plains"), Robert Earl Keen, and Chris Ledoux.

## EN ROUTE TO KERRVILLE

Each of the roads from Bandera to Kerrville has its distinct allure. The longer Hwy. 16 route—37 miles compared to 26—is one of the most gorgeous in the region, its scenic switchbacks introducing a new forest, river, or rolling ranchland vista at every turn (don't worry, the road is curvy, but not precipitous; you're at river level most of the time). Go this way, and you'll also pass through Medina. You won't doubt the little town's self-proclaimed status as Apple Capital of Texas when you come to **Love Creek Orchards Cider Mill and Country Store** (☎ 800/449-0882 or 830/589-2559) on the main street. Along with apple pies and other fresh-baked goods, you can buy apple cider, apple syrup, apple butter, apple jam, apple ice cream . . . you can even have an apple sapling shipped back home. Not feeling quite so fruity? The patio restaurant out back serves some of the best burgers in the region.

Military buffs and souvenir-seekers might want to take the more direct but also scenic Hwy. 173, which passes through **Camp Verde,** the former headquarters (1856–69) of the short-lived U.S. Army camel cavalry. Widespread ignorance of the animals' habits and the onset of the Civil War led to the abandonment of the attempt to introduce "ships of the desert" into dry Southwest terrain, but the commander of the post had great respect for his humpbacked recruits. There's little left of the fortress itself, but you can tour the **1877 General Store and Post Office** (☎ 830/796-4111), chock-full of camel memorabilia and artifacts from the past, as well as country-cute contemporary crafts. Buy some postcards and the fixings to have a picnic at the pleasant roadside park nearby.

## 4 Kerrville

With a population of about 20,000, Kerrville is larger than the other Hill Country towns so far explored. Now a popular retirement and tourist area, it was founded in the 1840s by Joshua Brown, a shingle-maker attracted by the area's many cypress trees. A rough-and-tumble camp surrounded by more civilized German towns, Kerrville soon became a ranching center for longhorn cattle and, more unusually, for Angora goats, eventually turning out the most mohair in the United States. After it was lauded in the 1920s for its healthful climate, Kerrville began to draw youth camps, sanatoriums, and artists.

### SEEING THE SIGHTS

It's a good idea to make your first stop the **Kerrville Convention and Visitors Bureau,** 2108 Sidney Baker, Kerrville, TX 78028 (☎ **800/221-7958** or 830/ 792-3535; www.ktc.net/kerrcvb), where you can get a map of the area as well as of the historic downtown district. Open weekdays 8:30am to 5pm, Saturday 9am to 3pm, Sunday 10am to 3pm. *Note:* If you're planning to come to Kerrville around Memorial Day weekend, when the huge, 18-day Kerrville Folk Festival kicks off, and also when the Official Texas State Arts and Crafts Fair is held, be sure to book far in advance.

The newly restored downtown area, flanked by the Guadalupe River and a pleasant park, is the most interesting part of town. For a glimpse of affluent Hill Country life in the early days, visit the **Hill Country Museum,** 226 Earl Garrett St. (☎ **830/ 896-8633**), a mansion built of native stone by Alfred Giles for pioneer rancher and banker Capt. Charles Schreiner. Open Monday to Saturday 10am to 4pm; admission $5 adults, $2 students. A collection of ball gowns is among the antique treasures. Old Republic Square (off Lemos, between Main and Water sts.) hosts a collection of quaint gift shops and boutiques, among them **Hill Country Western Wear** (☎ **830/ 257-7333**), selling chic cowpoke duds. The **Sunshine Antique Co.,** 820 Water St. (☎ **830/257-5044**), another restored turn-of-the-century building, lets you retreat to a charming tearoom after searching for treasures. More interested in the present than the past? **Artisans Group, Inc.,** 826 Water St. (☎ **830/896-4220**), sells beautiful contemporary crafts—but no food.

At the headquarters of **James Avery Craftsman,** about 3½ miles north of town on Harper Road (☎ **830/895-1122**), you can watch artisans work on silver and gold jewelry designs, many of which incorporate Christian symbols, then head for the retail shop.

Whether or not you think you like Western art, the **Cowboy Artists of America Museum,** 1550 Bandera Hwy. (☎ **830/896-2553;** www.caamuseum.com), is not to be missed. Lying just outside the main part of town, the high-quality collection is housed in a striking Southwestern structure. Open Monday to Saturday 9am to 5pm, Sunday 1 to 5pm; $5 adults, $3.50 seniors, $1 ages 6 to 18. Outdoor enthusiasts will enjoy the nearby **Kerrville-Schreiner State Park,** 2385 Bandera Hwy. (☎ **830/ 257-5392**), a 500-acre green space boasting 7 miles of hiking trails, as well as swimming and boating on the Guadalupe River.

### A NEARBY RANCH

You'll need a reservation to visit the **Y. O. Ranch,** 32 miles from Kerrville, off Hwy. 41, Mt. Home, TX 78058 (☎ **800/YO-RANCH** or 830/640-3222; www.yoranch.com).

# A Bit of Old England in the Old West

Several attractions, some endearingly offbeat, plus beautiful vistas along the Guadalupe River, warrant a detour west of Kerrville. Drive 5 miles from the center of town on Hwy. 27 West to reach tiny **Ingram.** Take Hwy. 39 West to the second traffic light downtown. After about ⅛ mile, you'll see a sign for the Historic Old Ingram Loop, essentially 2 blocks of antiques and crafts shops. Stop at **Miss Kitty's bar and drugstore,** which has every Avon product issued since the 1930s. Back on Hwy. 39, continue another few blocks to the **Hill Country Arts Foundation** (☎ 830/367-5120; www.hcaf.com), a complex comprising two theaters, an art gallery, and studios where arts and crafts classes are held. Every summer since 1948, a series of musicals has been offered on the outdoor stage. Continue 7 miles west on Hwy. 39 to the junction of FM 1340, where you'll find **Hunt,** which pretty much consists of a combination general store, bar, and restaurant that would look right at home in any Western. Now head west on FM 1340 for about ¼ mile. Surprise: There's a replica of **Stonehenge** sitting out in the middle of a field. It's not as large as the original, but this being Texas, it's not exactly diminutive, either. There are a couple of reproduction Easter Island heads here, too, but Al Shepherd, the wealthy eccentric who commissioned the pieces, died a few years ago, so there are unlikely to be any more local forays into ancient mysteries.

Originally comprising 550,000 acres purchased by Charles Schreiner in 1880, the Y. O. Ranch is now a 40,000-acre working ranch known for its exotic wildlife and Texas longhorn cattle. Daily activities include everything from organized hunts and cattle drives to horseback rides and hayrides.

## WHERE TO STAY

The **Y. O. Ranch Resort Hotel and Conference Center,** 2033 Sidney Baker, Kerrville, TX 78028 (☎ **877/YO-RESORT** or 830/257-4440; www.yoresort.com)—not near the Y. O. Ranch (see above), but in Kerrville itself—offers large and attractive Western-style quarters. Its Branding Iron dining room features big steaks as well as continental fare, but the saloon departs from Texas tradition with karaoke on Sundays. The gift shop has a terrific selection of creative Western-theme goods. Doubles range from $79 to $119, depending on the season.

**Inn of the Hills River Resort,** 1001 Junction Hwy., Kerrville, TX 78028 (☎ **800/ 292-5690** or 830/895-5000; www.innofthehills.com), looks like a motel from the outside, but it has the best facilities in town, including tennis courts, three swimming pools, a putting green, and free access to the excellent health club next door. Two restaurants and a popular pub complete the picture. Rates for doubles range seasonally from $79 to $99.

The **River Run Bed & Breakfast Inn,** 120 Francisco Lemos St., Kerrville, TX 78028 (☎ **800/460-7170** or 830/896-8533; www.riverrunbb.com), is of recent construction, but its native limestone and sloping tin roof hearken back to 19th-century German Hill Country architecture. A welcoming front porch, proximity to the Guadalupe River, rooms done in Texas country style, and big, down-home breakfasts make you feel way out in the country, but whirlpool tubs and TVs with (in the suites) VCRs remind you you're actually near the civilized center of town. Rooms range from $100 to $105; suites are $139.

## WHERE TO DINE

Because of its focus on salads and its somewhat froufrou look, more women than men tend to lunch at the **Old Republic Inn** in Old Republic Square, 225 Junction Hwy (☎ **830/896-7616**). But the guys are missing out on some incredible desserts. You can minimize the damage by getting a half order, but most people just end up trying two.

Although the menu at **Patrick's Lodge,** 2190 Junction Hwy. (☎ **830/895-4111**), is primarily French, and the tables are covered with white cloths, you can't accuse a restaurant with wood-paneled walls, mounted deer heads, and a view of Goat Creek of not being macho. Delicious Gallic classics such as escargot and filet mignon *au poivre* turn up alongside venison and chicken-fried steak. Prices are extremely reasonable, and the excellent wine list includes lots of local bottles.

## 5 Comfort

The most direct route from Kerrville to Fredericksburg is via Hwy. 16 North, but it's well worth detouring 18 miles southeast along Hwy. 27 to seek Comfort. True to its name, it's one of the most pleasant of the Hill Country towns. It has been said that the freethinking German immigrants who founded Comfort in 1852 were originally going to call it Gemütlichkeit—a more difficult-to-pronounce native version of its current name—when they arrived at this welcoming spot after an arduous journey from New Braunfels. The story is probably apocryphal, but it's an appealing explanation of the name, especially as no one is quite sure what the truth is.

The rough-hewn limestone buildings in the center of Comfort may compose the most complete 19th-century business district in Texas. Some of the offices were designed by architect Alfred Giles, who also left his distinctive mark on San Antonio's streets. The earliest church in town was built some 40 years after the first settlers arrived because during the initial period, the founders' antireligious beliefs, for which they had been persecuted in the old country, prevailed. Most of the settlers were also opposed to the Confederacy during the Civil War. The Treue der Union (True to the Union) Monument, on High Street between Third and Fourth streets, was erected in 1866 to commemorate 36 antislavery settlers killed by Confederate soldiers when they tried to defect to Mexico. Comfort seems to prefer its radicals safely in the past, however: A 1998 unveiling ceremony for a cenotaph erected to the Freethinker (Freidenker) founders in Comfort Park was postponed when it became clear that incoming celebrants would include atheists, socialists, and other contemporary adherents of the freethinking tradition. (After much in-fighting and dissension, the monument was eventually dedicated.)

## ANTIQUING

A majority of the town's high-quality and high-priced antiques shops are in the limestone buildings along High Street; more than 30 dealers gather at the **Comfort Antique Mall,** 734 High St. (☎ **830/995-4678**). But make your first stop the **Ingenhuett Store,** 830–834 High St. (☎ **830/995-2149**), set in an 1880 Alfred Giles building. The business has been owned and operated by the same German-American family since 1867. Along with groceries, outdoor gear, and sundries, the store carries maps and other sources of tourist information; you'll find everyone there extremely helpful. It's open far more frequently than the **Comfort Chamber of Commerce,** P.O. Box 777, Comfort, TX 78013 (☎ **830/995-3131**), on Seventh and High streets, which has very limited hours.

# Bats & Ostriches Along a Back Road to Fredericksburg

If you missed the bats in Austin, you've got a chance to see even more in an abandoned railroad tunnel supervised by the Texas Parks and Wildlife Department. From Comfort, take Hwy. 473 North 4 or 5 miles. When the road winds to the right toward Sisterdale, keep going straight on Old Highway 9. After another 8 or 9 miles, you'll spot a parking lot and a mound of large rocks on top of a hill. During migration season (May to Nov), you can watch as many as 2½ million Mexican free-tailed bats set off on a food foray around dusk. The viewing on the Upper Observation Area is free, and in past years, state-sponsored naturalist tours ($5 adults, $3 seniors, $2 ages 6 to 16) have been given on Thursday and Saturday evenings, June through October. There are 60 seats, filled on a first-come, first-served basis. Try the Old Tunnel Wildlife Management Area (☎ **830/995-4154;** www.tpwd.state.tx.us/wma/wmarea/tunnel) for current information.

Even if you don't stop for the bats, this is a wonderfully scenic route to Fredericksburg. You won't see any road signs, but have faith—this really will take you to town, eventually. You're likely to spot grazing goats and cows and even some strutting ostriches.

## WHERE TO STAY

One of the largest and most interesting antiques shops in town, **Comfort Common,** 818 High St., Comfort, TX 78013 (☎ **830/995-3030;** www.comfortcommon.com), doubles as a bed-and-breakfast. Reasonably priced accommodations in what was once the 19th-century Faust-Ingenhuett Hotel, built by Alfred Giles, are imaginatively decorated. All have private bathrooms and look out onto a peaceful garden. Rates run from $70 to $85 for the rooms, $95 for the suites. A separate cottage and log cabin rent for $110 and $125, respectively.

## WHERE TO DINE

The chef/owner of **Arlene's,** 426 Seventh St., just off High Street (☎ **830/ 995-3330**), used to be the food critic for the *San Antonio Express-News,* and her freshly made soups, quiches, sandwiches, and desserts prove she knew whereof she wrote. The converted old house is charming, and Arlene has the ability to pinpoint your place of origin as soon as you open your mouth. Hours are limited to Thursday through Sunday 11am to 4pm.

**Mimi's Cafe,** 814 High St. (☎ **830/995-3470**), also specializes in light repasts prepared daily on the premises. The chocolate French silk pie and apple cherry crisp are particularly popular. Mimi's is open Tuesday to Friday 11am to 2pm, Saturday 11am to 3pm, plus Fridays 6 to 8:30pm for steak dinners.

## 6  Fredericksburg

San Antonians and Austinites flock to Fredericksburg in droves on the weekends—and with good reason. It's got outstanding shopping, lots of historic sites (so you can pretend you're not just there to shop), and some of the most unusual accommodations around, all in a pretty rural setting.

Fredericksburg may be getting a bit trendy—"chick flick" producer Linda Obst lives here, and film-star sightings are becoming increasingly common—but the town also remains devoted to its European past. Baron Ottfried Hans von Meusebach was one of ten nobles who formed a society designed to help Germans resettle in Texas, where they would be safe from political persecution and economic hardship. In 1846, he took 120 émigrés in ox-drawn carts from New Braunfels to this site, which he named for Prince Frederick of Prussia. The town's mile-long main street is still wide enough for a team of oxen to turn around in (although that hasn't been tested lately). The permanent peace treaty Meusebach negotiated with the Comanches in 1847, claimed to be the only one in the United States that was ever honored, and the gold rush of 1849—Fredericksburg was the last place California-bound prospectors could get supplies—both helped the town thrive. Fredericksburg became and remains the seat of Gillespie County, the largest peach-producing county in the state—which explains the many roadside stands selling the fruit from late May through mid-August, and the variety of peachy products found around this area.

## SEEING THE SIGHTS
### IN TOWN

For a virtual preview, go to **www.fredericksburg-texas.com**. Once you're in town, the **Visitor Information Center,** 106 N. Adams, Fredericksburg, TX 78624 (☎ **888/ 997-3600** or 830/997-6523), can direct you to the many points of interest in the town's historic district. Open weekdays 8:30am to 5pm, Saturday 9am to noon and 1 to 5pm, Sunday noon to 4pm. Points of interest include a number of little **Sunday Houses,** built by German settlers in distant rural areas because they needed a place to stay overnight when they came to town to trade or attend church. You'll also notice many homes built in the Hill Country version of the German *fachwerk* design, made out of limestone with diagonal wood supports.

The unusual octagonal **Vareins Kirche** (**Society Church**) in Market Square once functioned as a town hall, school, and storehouse. A 1935 replica of the original 1847 building now holds the archives of the Gillespie County Historical Society. The Historical Society also maintains the **Pioneer Museum Complex,** 309 W. Main St., anchored by the 1849 Kammlah House, which was a family residence and general store until the 1920s. Open Monday to Saturday 10am to 5pm, Sunday 1 to 5pm; $3 for ages 12 and up. Among the other historical structures here are a one-room school-house and a blacksmith's forge. For information on both places and on the other historical structures in town, phone ☎ **830/997-2835.**

The 1852 Steamboat Hotel, originally owned by the grandfather of World War II naval hero Chester A. Nimitz, is now part of the **National Museum of the Pacific War,** 340 E. Main St. (☎ **830/997-4379;** www.nimitz-museum.org), a 9-acre Texas State Historical Park and the world's only museum focusing solely on the Pacific theater. It just keeps expanding and getting better, too. In addition to the exhibits in the steamboat-shaped hotel devoted to Nimitz and his comrades, there are also the Japanese Garden of Peace, a lovely gift from the people of Japan; the Memorial Wall, the equivalent to the Vietnam wall for Pacific War veterans; the Pacific Combat Zone, which includes the casing of the "Fat Man" atomic bomb among its artifacts; and the George Bush Gallery, dedicated in 1999. Displays in the Bush Gallery include a captured Japanese midget submarine and the flight helmet of Japan's leading ace; there's also a multimedia simulation of a bombing raid on Guadalcanal. Be sure to get one of the volunteers to give you a tour; the stories they tell of the veterans—Japanese as well as Americans—who have visited the facility are extremely moving. The Center for Pacific War Studies, a major research facility, is slated to open by 2003. Indoor exhibits open daily 10am to 5pm, outdoor exhibits daily 8am to 5pm; closed Christmas. Adults $5, students $3; children under 6 free.

If you're interested in saddles, chaps, spurs, sheriff's badges, and other cowboy-o-bilia, visit **Gish's Old West Museum,** 502 N. Milam St. (☎ **830/997-2794**). A successful illustrator for Sears & Roebuck, Joe Gish started buying Western props to help him with his art. After more than 40 years of trading and buying with the best, his collection is very impressive. Joe opens the museum when he's around; drop by and take your chances, or phone ahead to make an appointment.

## NEARBY

One of the many attractions in the Fredericksburg vicinity is **Lady Bird Johnson Municipal Park,** 2 miles southwest of town off Hwy. 16 (☎ **830/997-4202**), with an 18-hole golf course (which has a spiffy new clubhouse), six tennis courts, a volleyball court, a swimming pool (open summer only), and a 17-acre lake for fishing.

There's a winery in the heart of town, the family-run **Fredericksburg Winery,** 237 W. Main St. (☎ **830/990-8747**), which sells its own hand-bottled, hand-corked, and hand-labeled vintages, and specializes in dessert wines. But more respected are the three wineries nearby, all of which offer tastings and tours: **Oberhellmann Vineyards,** 14 miles north on Hwy. 16 (☎ **830/685-3297**); **Grape Creek Vineyard,** 9 miles east on Hwy. 290 (☎ **830/644-2710**); and **Becker Vineyards,** 1 mile farther east on 290 (☎ **830/644-2681**). Established in 1992, Becker is the newest, but many contend it's the best. Check **www.texaswinetrail.com** for details on these and other wineries in the Hill Country

A visit to the **Wildseed Farms,** 7 miles east on Hwy. 290 (☎ **830/990-1393; www.wildseedfarms.com**), will disabuse you of any naive notions you may have had that wildflowers grew wild. At this working wildflower farm, beautiful fields of blossoms are harvested for seeds that are sold throughout the world (26 states buy wildflowers from this company). For $3 you can grab a bucket and pick bluebonnets, poppies, or whatever's blooming when you visit. There's a gift shop and the Brew-Bonnet beer garden, which sells light snacks.

For a scenic loop drive, head northwest to **Willow City.** The 13-mile route, which leads back to Hwy. 16, is especially spectacular in wildflower season.

Take FM 965 some 18 miles north to reach **Enchanted Rock State Natural Area** (☎ **915/247-3903;** www.tpwd.state.tx.us/park/enchantd), a 640-acre, pink-granite dome that draws hordes of hikers. The creaking noises that emanate from it at night—likely caused by the cooling of the rock's outer surface—led the area's Native American tribes to believe that evil spirits inhabited the rock. *Note:* Because of the rock's popularity, a limit is placed on visitors. If the park is considered full, you will be asked to return around 4pm. It's best to call in advance to check.

## SHOPPING

Ladies and gentleman, start your acquisition engines. If you're pressed for time, concentrate on Main Street between Elk and Milam, although other sections are worth exploring, too. *Warning:* You may well OD on cuteness. More than 100 specialty shops, many of them in mid 19th-century houses, feature work by Hill Country artisans. You'll find candles, lace coverlets, cuckoo clocks, handwoven rugs, even dulcimers. Yuppies come from all over Texas to grab up the ultra-fashionable home furnishings sold at the six branches of the **Homestead stores** where European rural retro (chain-distressed wrought-iron beds from France, for example) meets contemporary natural fabrics. One of these outlets (Room #5) is devoted entirely to the color white. Log on to **www.homesteadstores.com** to get the picture—and the locations (five of the six are on Main Street)—or stop in the original store on 223 E. Main (☎ **830/997-5551**) for a map. You can also get an idea of just how chic the town has become by visiting **Parts Unknown,** 145 E. Main St. (☎ **830/997-2055**), a travel clothing store so exclusive that its other branches are in Santa Fe, Scottsdale, and Carmel. For something less effete, check out **Texas Jack,** 117 N. Adams St. (☎ 830/997-3213), which has outfitted actors for Western films and TV shows, including "Lonesome Dove," *Tombstone,* and "Gunsmoke." This is the place to stock up on red long johns.

Becoming increasingly well known via its mail-order business is the **Fredericksburg Herb Farm,** 405 Whitney St. (☎ 800/259-HERB or 830/997-8615; www.fredericksburgherbfarm.com). There's an outlet on Main Street, but the flower beds that produce salad dressings, teas, fragrances, and air fresheners (the chocolate mint smells good enough to eat) are only a short trip south of town; there's also a tea room, B&B, and day spa.

One of several such places to crop up in town recently, the **European Day Spa,** 623 S. Washington St. (☎ 877/997-5267 or 830/997-5267; www.europeandayspa.citysearch.com), has a list of treatments—everything from ear candling to heel massages—covering every stress imaginable.

## WHERE TO STAY

Perhaps even more than for its shopping, Fredericksburg is known for its appealing accommodations. In addition to the usual rural motels, the town boasts more than 250 bed-and-breakfasts and *gastehauses* (guest cottages). If you choose one of the latter, you can spend the night in anything from an 1865 homestead with its own wishing well to a bedroom above an old bakery or a limestone Sunday House. Most *gastehauses* are romantic havens complete with robes, fireplaces, and even spas. And unlike the typical B&B, these places ensure privacy, because breakfast is provided the night before (the perishables are left in a refrigerator). *Gastehauses* are comparatively reasonable; for about $100 to $150, you can get loads of history and charm. The four main reservation services are: **Bed & Breakfast of Fredericksburg,** 619 W. Main St. (☎ 877/396-9240 or 830/997-4712; www.bandbfbg.com); **Be My Guest,** 110 N. Milam (☎ 800/364-8555 or 830/997-7227); **Gastehaus Schmidt,** 231 W. Main St. (☎ 830/997-5612; www.fbglodging.com); and **Hill Country Lodging & Reservation Service,** 104 N. Adams St. (☎ 800/745-3591 or 830/990-8455; www.bnbglobal.com).

## WHERE TO DINE

Fredericksburg's dining scene is very diverse, catering to the traditional and the trendy alike. The former tend to frequent the **Altorf Biergarten,** 301 W. Main St. (☎ 830/997-7865), open Wednesday to Monday for lunch and dinner, and **Friedhelm's Bavarian Inn,** 905 W. Main St. (☎ 830/997-6300), open Tuesday to Sunday for lunch and dinner, both featuring moderately priced, hearty German schnitzels, dumplings, and sauerbraten and large selections of beer. The **Fredericksburg Brewing Co.,** 245 E. Main St. (☎ 830/997-1646), offers its home brews and friendly atmosphere, but the menu includes lots of lighter selections. Book one of the rooms upstairs, and you can relax in your own bed after a pizza and a pint of Pedernales Pilsner. Open daily for lunch and dinner; moderate. For blue-plate specials and huge breakfasts of eggs, biscuits, and gravy, the locals converge on **Andy's Diner,** 413 S. Washington St. (☎ 830/997-3744), open since 1957. Be sure to look up at the miniature train circling the restaurant. Open daily for breakfast, lunch, and dinner; inexpensive.

The more health-conscious turn up at the **Peach Tree Tea Room,** 210 S. Adams St. (☎ 830/997-9527), although they often order a slice of heavenly ice cream pie after their salads. Open Monday to Saturday for lunch only; moderate. A trio of recently established restaurants has local foodies in rapture. **The Nest,** 607 S. Washington St. (☎ 830/990-8383), open for dinner only Thursday to Monday, and the **Oak House,**

# Going Back (in Time) to Luckenbach

About 11 miles southeast of Fredericksburg on R.R. 1376, but light years away in spirit—it's as old hippie as its neighbor is nouveau yuppie—the town of **Luckenbach** was immortalized in song by Waylon Jennings and Willie Nelson. Well, okay, maybe it's misleading to call it a town. Luckenbach (pop. 25) pretty much consists of a dance hall and a post office/general store/bar. But it's a great place to hang out on weekend afternoons, when someone's almost always strumming a guitar, or Friday or Saturday evening, when Jerry Jeff Walker and Robert Earl Keen might be among the names who turn up at the dance hall. Tying the knot? You can rent the dance hall—or the entire town. Call ☎ **830/997-3224** for details. And to get a feel for Luckenbach, log on to **www.luckenbachtexas.com**, a hoot of a Web site.

Whenever you visit, lots of beer is likely to be involved, so consider staying at the **Luckenbach Inn,** 3234 Luckenbach Rd., Fredericksburg, TX 78624 (☎ **800/997-1124** or 830/997-2205; www.luchenbachtx.com), just ½ mile from the action, such as it is, and on a rise overlooking the wildflower-dotted countryside. The best of the accommodations, which range in price from $125 to $200, is the 1800s log cabin, large enough to sleep four. Rooter, the resident pot-bellied pig, is usually around to greet guests.

755 S. Washington St. (☎ **830/997-6223**), dinner only Tuesday to Sunday, just down the road from one another, are both set in lovely old houses, and both rely on fresh local ingredients for their updated American cuisine. The Nest is a tad more adventurous—and pricier. The contemporary-chic **Navajo Grill,** 209 E. Main St. (☎ **830/990-8289**), is the most cutting edge of the three, with dishes inspired by New Orleans (chef/owner Steve Howard has cooked at Emeril's, K-Paul's, and Nola), the Southwest, and occasionally the Caribbean. Open Tuesday to Saturday for lunch and dinner; expensive.

About 11 miles north of Fredericksburg on I-87, the **Hill Top Cafe** (☎ 830/997-8922) serves excellent Cajun and Greek food. You might find the owner, a former member of the band Asleep at the Wheel, very much awake at the piano. Open for lunch and dinner Wednesday to Sunday; moderate to expensive.

## 7 Lyndon B. Johnson Country

Welcome to Johnson territory, where the forebears of the 36th president settled almost 150 years ago. Even before he attained the country's highest office, Lyndon Baines Johnson was a local hero whose successful fight for funding of a series of dams provided the region with inexpensive water and power. Try to make a day out of a visit to LBJ's boyhood home and the sprawling ranch that became known as the Texas White House. Even those who don't usually feel drawn to the past are likely to find themselves fascinated by Johnson's frontier lineage. There are also quite a few restaurants in Johnson City, but consider bringing along a picnic to enjoy at the state park.

### LBJ HISTORICAL PARKS

From Fredericksburg, take U.S. 290 East for 16 miles to the entrance of the **Lyndon B. Johnson State and National Historical Parks at LBJ Ranch,** near Stonewall (☎ 830/868-7128 or 830/644-2252), co-run by the Texas Parks and Wildlife Department (www.tpwd.state.tx.us/park/lbj) and the National Park Service (www.nps.gov/lyjo). Tour buses depart regularly from the state park visitors center, which displays interesting memorabilia from Johnson's boyhood, to the still-operating Johnson Ranch. You probably won't spot Lady Bird Johnson, who spends about a third of her time here, but don't be surprised to see grazing longhorn cattle.

Crossing over the swift-flowing Pedernales River and through fields of phlox, Indian blanket, and other wildflowers, you can easily see why Johnson used the ranch as a second, more comfortable White House, and why, discouraged from running for a second presidential term, he came back here to find solace and, eventually, to die. A reconstruction of the former president's modest birthplace lies close to his (also modest) final resting place, shared with five generations of Johnsons.

On the side of the river from which you started out, period-costumed "occupants" of the Sauer-Beckmann Living History Farm give visitors a look at typical Texas-German farm life at the turn of the century. Chickens, pigs, turkeys, and other farm animals roam freely or in large pens, while the farmers go about their chores, which might include churning butter, baking, or feeding the animals. The midwife who attended LBJ's birth grew up here. As interesting as Colonial Williamsburg, but much less known (and thus not as well funded), this is a terrific place to come with kids. Nearby are nature trails, a swimming pool (open only in summer), and lots of picnic spots. Bring your pole (or rent one in Austin) if you want to fish in the Pedernales River.

Admission is $3 per person for bus tours; all other areas are free. All state park buildings, including the visitors center, are open daily 8am to 5pm. The Sauer-Beckmann Living History Farm is open daily 8am to 4:30pm. The Nature Trail, grounds, and picnic areas are open until dark every day. National Park Service tours of the LBJ Ranch, lasting from 1 to 1½ hours, depart from the state park visitors center daily 10am to 4pm (tours may be shortened or canceled due to excessive heat and humidity). All facilities in both sections of the park are closed Thanksgiving, Christmas, and New Year's Day.

It's 14 miles farther east along U.S. 290 to **Johnson City,** a pleasant agricultural town named for founder James Polk Johnson, LBJ's first cousin once removed. The **Boyhood Home**—the house on Elm Street where Lyndon was raised after age 5— is the centerpiece of this unit of the **Lyndon B. Johnson National Historical Park.** The modest white clapboard structure the family occupied from 1913 on was a hub of intellectual and political activity: LBJ's father, Sam Ealy Johnson, Jr., was a state legislator, and his mother, Rebekah, was one of the few college-educated women in the country at the beginning of the 20th century. From here, be sure to walk over to the **Johnson Settlement,** where LBJ's grandfather, Sam Ealy Johnson, Sr., and his great-uncle, Jessie, engaged in successful cattle speculation in the 1860s. The rustic dogtrot cabin out of which they ran their business is still intact. Before exploring the two sites, stop at the **visitors center** (☎ 830/868-7128)—from U.S. 290, which turns into Main Street, take F Street to Lady Bird Lane, and you'll see the signs—where a number of excellent displays and a touching film about Johnson's presidency provide background for the buildings you'll see.

The Boyhood Home, visitors center, and Johnson Settlement are all open 8:45am to 5pm daily except Christmas, Thanksgiving, and New Year's Day. Admission is free.

## WHERE TO STAY & DINE

The **Johnson City Visitor and Tourism Bureau,** P.O. Box 485, Johnson City, TX 78636 (☎ 830/868-7684; www.johnsoncity_texas.com), can provide information about dining, lodging, and shopping in town. Those interested in staying at a local B&B should call ☎ 830/868-4548.

For a unique retreat, drive north from Johnson City on 281 to Marble Falls, then head 15 miles east on FM 1431 to the town of Kingsland and **The Antlers,** 1001 King St., Kingsland, TX 78639 (☎ **800/383-0007** or 916/388-4411; www.theantlers. com), a restored turn-of-the-century resort occupying 15 acres on Lake LBJ. You've got a choice of bedding down in one of six antiques-filled suites in the 1901 railroad hotel, as President William McKinley did ($120 to $140); in one of three colorful converted train cabooses, parked on a piece of original track ($120); or in one of five appealing cabins scattered around the grounds ($100 to $150). Activities include strolling several nature trails, boating or fishing on the lake, or browsing the antiques shop in the main hotel building.

For fortification, cross the road to the **Kingsland Old Town Grill** (☎ **915/ 388-2681;** closed Mon to Tues), a good place for steak, regular or chicken fried. Look eerily familiar? This 1890s Victorian house served as the film set for the cult classic *The Texas Chainsaw Massacre.*

## EN ROUTE TO AUSTIN

If you're heading on to Austin, take a short detour from U.S. 290 to **Pedernales Falls State Park,** 8 miles east of Johnson City on F.R. 2766 (☎ **830/868-7304;** www.tpwd.state.tx.us/park/pedernal). When the flow of the Pedernales River is normal to high, the stepped waterfalls that give the 4,860-acre park its name are quite dramatic.

## 8 San Marcos

Some 26 miles south of Austin via I-35, San Marcos was first settled by a tribe of nomadic Native Americans around 12,000 years ago. Some scholars claim it is the oldest continuously inhabited site in the Western Hemisphere. Temporary home to two Spanish missions in the late 1700s, as well as to Comanches and Apaches (which explains the "temporary" part), this site at the headwaters of the San Marcos River was permanently settled by Anglos in the middle of the 19th century. Now host to Southwest Texas State University, the alma mater of LBJ—and the only university in the state to graduate a future president—San Marcos has the laid-back feel of a college town. It's also fast becoming a bedroom community of Austin, only half an hour away.

## WHAT TO SEE & DO

In the center of town—and, clearly, the reason for its existence—more than 1,000 springs well up from the Balcones Fault to form Spring Lake. On the lake's shore sits the **Aquarena Center,** 1 Aquarena Springs Dr. (☎ **512/245-7575**), renowned for its glass-bottomed boats from which you can view some of the rare flora and fauna (including five endangered species) supported by the astonishingly clear waters, which keep a constant temperature of 72°F. It's quite a sight to see the springs bubbling up at full force. Boat tours cost $6 adults, $5 seniors 55 and up, $4 ages 4 to 15; under 4 free. Above-water historical exhibits include the home of General Edward Burleson, who built the dam that created Spring Lake to power his gristmill, also preserved here. The first theme park in Texas and once home to Ralph the Swimming Pig, Aquarena Springs was bought by Southwest Texas State University in 1994; $16 million has been devoted to turn it into the "Texas Rivers Center at San Marcos Springs," an education and research facility. Phase I, demolition of the theme park structures to return the land to its pristine state, is scheduled to be completed by 2003.

There's no such goal for the **San Marcos River,** which begins at Spring Lake; it's often thronged with canoers and rafters. Between May and September, the local Lions Club (☎ **512/396-LION**) rents inner tubes and operates a river shuttle at City Park.

In addition to listing schedules and prices, the Web site **www.centurytel.net/smlc/** keeps tab of the water flow, which determines whether or not tubes will be rented on a given day.

When the Balcones Fault was active some 30 million years ago, an earthquake created the cave at the center of **Wonder World,** 1000 Prospect St., off Bishop (☎ **800/ 782-7653, ext. 2283,** or 512/392-3760; www.wonderworldpark.com). The stone steps by which you descend underground are sometimes steep, and the floor is often wet and slippery, so wear sturdy shoes. The end of the cave tour takes you to the so-called Anti-Gravity House, where you can see water flowing upward. Skip the petting farm, which is essentially a tram ride through an enclosure of depressed-looking deer. The cave tour is $11 adults, $9 ages 4 to 11; Anti-Gravity House, $3 all ages. Winter daily 9am to 5pm, (varying) longer hours in summer, spring, and fall; closed Christmas Eve and Christmas Day.

The more culturally (and caffeine) oriented should wander **Courthouse Square,** where several turn-of-the-century buildings are being restored. In fact, the entire downtown area is listed in the National Register of Historic Places. The San Marcos Fine Arts Center lies within gunshot range of the Old State Bank Building, robbed by the Newton Gang in 1924 and (most likely) by Machine Gun Kelly in 1933. The **Coffee Pot,** 129 E. Hopkins, Suite 100 (☎ **512/396-1689**), provides the most jolting experience here these days, although several gift shops and boutiques might give some an adrenaline rush.

To get an inside look at one of the town's two tree-lined residential districts, make an appointment to view the **Millie Seaton Collection of Dolls and Toys,** housed in the opulent 1908 Augusta Hofheinz mansion, 1104 W. Hopkins (☎ **512/ 396-1944**). Thousands of little eyes peer at you from the three stories crammed with figurines that Mrs. Seaton has been collecting since 1965, including some rare historical specimens; you're likely to recognize a few of them from your childhood.

Southwest Texas State University's Albert B. Alkek Library isn't old, but it's home to some of the state's most important literary artifacts as well as to a gem of a gallery, not to be missed if you're in town. The **Southwestern Writers Collection,** on the seventh floor of the library, 601 University Dr. (☎ **512/245-3861;** www.library.swt. edu/swwc/index.html), showcases materials donated by the region's leading filmmakers, musicians, and wordsmiths. You might see anything from a 1555 printing of the journey of Spanish adventurer Cabeza de Vaca to a songbook created by an 11-year-old Willie Nelson to the costumes worn by Tommy Lee Jones and Robert Duvall in "Lonesome Dove" (the collection was founded by Bill Wittliff, the screenwriter and producer of that famed TV miniseries). Lots of gleaming wood, Mexican tile, and bronze sculptures enhance the aesthetic experience. Open Monday to Friday 8am to 5pm (Tues until 9pm), Saturday 1 to 5pm, Sunday 2 to 6pm; weekdays only when the university is not in session. The **Wittliff Gallery of Southwestern & Mexican Photography** (☎ **512/245-2313**) exhibits not only works from its excellent permanent collection, but also temporary shows by other renowned photographers. Call ahead for directions to the building and parking garage. Same hours as the Southern Writers Collection (above).

## OUTLET SHOPPING

If truth be told, lots of people bypass San Marcos altogether and head straight for the two factory outlet malls a few miles south of downtown—the biggest discount shopfest in Texas. Take exit 200 from I-35 for both the **Tanger Factory Outlet Center** (☎ **800/408-8424** [San Marcos office] or 800-4TANGER [national office]; www. tangeroutlet.com) and the larger and tonier **Prime Outlets** (☎ **800/628-9465** or

## A Spectacular Drive

San Marcos is a convenient jumping-off point for one of Texas's most breathtaking drives. Take R.R. 12 West to R.R. 32 to reach the Devil's Backbone, a 15-mile, switchback-filled route affording spectacular Hill Country views.

The prettiest place to have a meal in town is the fountained courtyard at **Palmers,** 216 W. Moore (☎ **512/353-3500**), where you can sit among lovely native plants and trees and enjoy dishes ranging from fusilli pasta with herbed pesto or charbroiled ahi tuna to a hefty New York strip steak. Smaller "conservative" portions of many dishes are available; it's a smart option if you want to save room for the delicious Key lime or chocolate satin pie.

---

512/396-7183; www.primeoutlets.com), right next door. Among the almost 150 stores, you'll find everything from Donna Karan, Anne Klein, Calvin Klein, and Brooks Brothers to Samsonite and Waterford/Wedgwood. There's also a Saks Fifth Avenue outlet.

The **San Marcos Convention and Visitors Bureau,** 202 N. C. M. Allen Pkwy., San Marcos, TX 78666 (☎ **888/200-5620** or 512/393-5900), can provide you with information on mall bus transportation, as well as a complete list of places to eat and stay in town.

## WHERE TO STAY & DINE

A variety of accommodations at the **Crystal River Inn,** 326 W. Hopkins, San Marcos, TX 78666 (☎ **888/396-3739** or 512/396-3739; www.crystalriverinn.com), offers something for everyone. Nine rooms and three suites, beautifully decorated with antiques, occupy a large 1883 Victorian main house and two smaller historic structures behind it. There's also a fully furnished executive apartment across the street. Rates, which range from a low of $85 for a room during the week to a high of $150 for a two-bedroom suite on the weekend, include a full breakfast. The elaborately scripted (and enthusiastically acted) murder-mystery weekends are extremely popular.

## NEARBY WIMBERLEY

On the first Saturday of each month from April through December is **Market Day,** a huge crafts gathering that draws Austinites to Lion's Field in Wimberley, some 15 miles northwest of San Marcos.

To my mind, most of the shops and boutiques in the town itself are nothing special, but **Sable V Fine Art Gallery** (☎ 512/847-8975) and **Teeks Gallery and Gifts** (☎ 512/847-8868), both on the town square, are among the high-quality exceptions. **Heather Carter,** 15401 R.R. 12, No. 300 (☎ **512/847-0192;** www.hcarter. com), is a wizard with paper, handcrafting lovely notebooks that incorporate native plants. **Wimberley Glass Works,** Spoke Hill Road, 1.6 miles south of the town square (☎ 512/847-9348; www.wgw.com), stands out for its rainbowlike array of blown glassware; you can watch artist Tim de Jong at work much of the time.

Right next door is perhaps the best reason to come to Wimberley. The **Blair House,** 100 Spoke Hill Rd., Wimberley, TX 78676 (☎ **877/549-5450** or 512/847-8828; www.blairhouseinn.com), is a luxurious inn on 85 Hill Country acres, offering beautifully decorated rooms in a Texas limestone ranch complex. Talk about relaxing: Six of the eight rooms have Jacuzzis, and there's a massage room and sauna on the property. Innkeeper Jonnie Stansbury is a gourmet chef, and rates ($145 to $225 for a double) include her elaborate breakfasts and evening dessert and wine served in your room.

Most Saturday nights, she also offers outstanding, multi-course dinners ($50 per person) that draw people all the way from Austin. Book ahead.

If you're interested in other places to stay, eat, or shop in Wimberley, contact the **Chamber of Commerce,** 14100 R.R. 12, just north of the town square (☎ **512/847-2201;** www.wimberley.org).

## KOLACHE AND BARBECUE: A DETOUR TO LOCKHART

There are many reasons to make a scenic loop from San Marcos to Lockhart and back (or up to Austin), especially if you love food. If you take Hwy. 80 some 20 miles east to the town of Prairie Lea, you'll see the **Blue Ribbon Bakery** (☎ **512/488-2222**) on the south side of the road. Open only on Friday, Saturday, and Sunday, it's reputed to have the state's best *kolaches*—Czech pastries stuffed with cheese, fruit, poppy seeds, sausage, or ham, among other delicious fillings.

Continue about 7 miles to Luling and the junction of Hwy. 183; it's 15 miles north to Lockhart, Texas's smoked-meat Mecca. Many people swear by the barbecue at **Kreuz Market,** 619 N. Colorado (☎ **512/398-2361**), where the brisket, prime rib, and sausage come with little besides white bread; your food is slapped down on butcher paper, and the seating is family style. Open for lunch and dinner Monday to Saturday. Those who enjoy side dishes such as homemade coleslaw and pinto beans, have a preference for eating off plates, and don't like sharing tables, will be happier at **Black's Barbecue,** 215 N. Main St. (☎ **512/398-2712**), open daily for lunch and dinner. Although these two are the main contenders, **Chisholm Trail Barbecue,** 1323 S. Colorado (☎ **512/398-6027**), has its die-hard defenders; its niceties extend to a salad bar. Open Monday to Saturday for lunch and dinner. Kreuz's was established in 1900, Black's in 1932, and Chisholm Trail in 1978—enough time for all of them to have perfected their recipes.

But there's more to Lockhart than barbecue. At the center of town, the 1893 **Caldwell County Courthouse** is said to be the most photographed town hall in Texas. Although it's impossible to verify or refute the claim, there's no question that the ornate French Second Empire–style structure is photogenic: Its film credits include *The Great Waldo Pepper, What's Eating Gilbert Grape,* and *Waiting for Guffman.* You can pick up a guide to downtown Lockhart's historic structures, many of which house antiques shops, at the **Lockhart Chamber of Commerce,** 205 S. Main Street at Prairie Lea (☎ **512/398-2818;** www.lockhart-tx.org). Open Monday to Friday 9am to 5pm.

If you want to spend the night in this pretty rural town, the gorgeously restored **Albion Bed & Breakfast,** 604 W. San Antonio St., Lockhart, TX 78644 (☎ **512/376-6775;** www.austin360.com/ads/albion), will transport you back to its 1898 heyday. Gleaming parquet floors, intricate stained-glass windows, wrapped porches, and a veritable forest of long-leaf-pine woodwork are among the huge residence's many period details. Coffee and juice are brought up to the lovely antiques-filled rooms each morning, followed by a full breakfast in the dining room.

## PICKING OUT A HAT IN BUDA

There's not a whole lot happening in the town of Buda (pronounced *Byou*-duh), but if you get off I-35 at the Buda exit (exit 220, about halfway between Austin and San Marcos), you'll see **Texas Hatters** (☎ **800/421-HATS** or 512/312-0036; www. texashatters.com) on the access road on the east side of the highway. In business for more than 50 years, this Western hatter has had an unlikely mix of famous customers, from Tip O'Neill, George Bush, and the king of Sweden to Al Hirt, Willie Nelson, and Arnold Schwarzenegger—to name just a few.

## 9 New Braunfels

Some 16 miles south of San Marcos on I-35, New Braunfels sits at the junction of the Comal and Guadalupe rivers. German settlers were brought here in 1845 by Prince Carl of Solms-Braunfels, the commissioner general of the Society for the Protection of German Immigrants in Texas, the same group that later founded Fredericksburg. Although Prince Carl returned to Germany within a year to marry his fiancée, who refused to join him in the wilderness, his colony prospered. By the 1850s, New Braunfels was the fourth-largest city in Texas after Houston, San Antonio, and Galveston. New Braunfels doesn't rank nearly as high in population today, but it's not one of the Hill Country's quieter or quainter towns, either.

### WHAT TO SEE & DO

At the **New Braunfels Chamber of Commerce,** 390 S. Seguin, New Braunfels, TX 78130 (☎ **800/572-2626** or 830/625-2385; www.nbchamber.org), open weekdays 8am to 5pm, you can pick up the *Prosit Visitor's Guide,* which can help you take an antiques-lovers' crawl. Those who prefer the modern retail world should head for the **New Braunfels Marketplace,** 651 Business Loop I-35 North (☎ **830/620-6806** or 888/SHOP-333 in Texas; www.shopnewbraunfels.com), where factory outlet stores such as American Tourister, Bass, and Easy Spirit vie with several specialty shops for visitors' dollars. It's also home to the town's modern 12-screen cinema. Some of the stores in midtown straddle two eras: **Henne Hardware,** 246 W. San Antonio (☎ **830/606-6707**), established in 1857, sells modern bits and bobs, but maintains its original tin roof ceiling, rings for hanging buggy whips, and an old pulley system for transporting cash and paperwork through the back business office. It's said to be the oldest hardware store in Texas. **Naeglin's,** 129 S. Seguin Ave. (☎ **830/625-5722**), opened in 1868, stakes its claim as the state's longest-running bakery. If you missed Blue Bonnet's *kolaches* (see "*Kolache* and Barbecue: A Detour to Lockhart," above), you can try some here.

Henne's Hardware and Naeglin's are on a 40-point **historic walking tour** of midtown, also available at the Chamber of Commerce. Other buildings of note include the Romanesque-Gothic Comal County Courthouse (1898) on Main Plaza; the nearby Jacob Schmidt Building (193 W. San Antonio), built on the site where William Gebhardt, of canned chili fame, perfected his formula for chili powder in 1896; and the 1928 Faust Hotel (240 S. Seguin), believed by some to be haunted by its owner. These days, draughts pulled from the microbrewery on the Faust's premises help allay even the most haunting anxieties.

Several small museums are worth a visit. The **New Braunfels Museum of Art,** 199 Main Plaza (☎ **800/456-4866** or 830/625-5636), recently moved away from its sole concentration on porcelain Hummel figurines—although it still has the largest collection of them on public display—to include more contemporary art in other genres. Open Monday to Saturday 10am to 5pm, Sunday noon to 5pm; $5 adults, seniors $4.50, $3 students 6 to 18; under 6 free. Prince Carl never did build a planned castle for his sweetheart, Sophia, on the elevated spot where the **Sophienburg Museum,** 401 W. Coll St. (☎ **830/629-1572**), now stands, but it's nevertheless an excellent place to learn about the history of New Braunfels and other Hill Country settlements. Open Monday to Saturday 10am to 5pm, Sunday 1 to 5pm; $5 adults, students 18 and under free. The **Museum of Texas Handmade Furniture,** 1370 Church Hill Dr. (☎ **830/629-6504;** www.nbheritagevillage.com), also sheds light on local domestic life of the 19th century with its beautiful examples of Texas Biedermeier by master craftsman Johan Michael Jahn. They're displayed at the gracious 1858 Breustedt-Dillon Haus. The 11-acre Heritage Village complex also includes an 1848 log cabin and a barn that houses a reproduction cabinetmaker's workshop. Open June 1 to August, Tuesday to Saturday 10am to 4pm, Sunday 1 to 4pm, closed Monday except holiday Mondays; March to May and September to October, Wednesday to Sunday 1 to 4pm; winter, Saturday and Sunday 1 to 4pm, last tour begins at 3:30pm. Admission $3 adults, $1 children 6 to 12.

You can tour other historic structures, including the original 1870 schoolhouse and such transported shops as a tiny music studio, at the nearby **Conservation Plaza,** 1300 Church Hill Dr. (☎ 830/629-2943), centered by a gazebo and garden with more than 50 varieties of antique roses, which haven't been hybrid. Guided tours (included in admission) are offered every day except Monday. Open Tuesday to Friday 10am to 3pm, Saturday and Sunday 2 to 5pm; adults $2, 50¢ children 6 to 17; 6 and younger free. Also owned by the New Braunfels Conservation Society, the 1852 **Lindheimer Home,** 491 Comal Ave. (☎ 830/608-1512), is probably the best example of an early *fachwerk* house still standing in New Braunfels. Ferdinand J. Lindheimer, one of the town's first settlers—he scouted out the site for Prince Solms—was an internationally recognized botanist and the editor of the town's German-language newspaper. Museum hours are limited (summers, Thurs to Tues 2 to 5pm, closed Wed; rest of the year, weekends 2 to 5pm), but you can wander the lovely grounds planted with Texas natives (38 species were named for Lindheimer) if you can't get in to see the house.

## HISTORIC GRUENE

You can get a more concentrated glimpse of the past at Gruene (pronounced "Green"), 4 miles northwest of downtown New Braunfels. First settled by German farmers in the 1840s, Gruene was virtually abandoned during the Depression in the 1930s. It remained a ghost town until the mid-1970s, when two investors realized the value of its intact historic buildings and sold them to businesses rather than raze them. These days, tiny Gruene is crowded with day-trippers browsing the specialty shops in the wonderfully restored structures, which include a smoked meat shop, lots of cutesy gift boutiques, and several antiques shops. A brochure detailing the town's retailers, restaurants, and accommodations is available from the New Braunfels Chamber of Commerce (see above) or at most of Gruene's shops. The town's Web site, **www. gruene.net**, is stronger on graphics than on details.

## WATERSPORTS

Gruene also figures among the area's impressive array of places to get wet, most of them open only in summer. Outfitters who can help you ride the Guadalupe River rapids on raft, tube, canoe, or inflatable kayak include **Rockin "R" River Rides** (☎ 800/553-5628 or 830/629-9999) and **Gruene River Raft Company** (☎ 830/625-2800 or 625-2873), both on Gruene Road just south of the Gruene Bridge.

You can go tubing, too, at **Schlitterbahn,** Texas's largest water park and one of the best in the country, 305 W. Austin St. in New Braunfels (☎ 830/625-2351; www.schlitterbahn.com). If there's a way to get wet 'n' wild, this place has got it. Six separate areas feature gigantic slides, pools, and rides, including Master Blaster, the tallest, steepest uphill water coaster in the world. The combination of a natural river-and-woods setting and high-tech attractions make this splashy 65-acre playland a standout. Schedule varies, so call or check the Web site. All-day passes are $26.50 adults, $21.95 ages 3 to 11; 3 and under free.

Those who like their water play a bit more low-key might try downtown New Braunfels' **Landa Park** (☎ 830/608-2160), where you can either swim in the largest spring-fed pool in Texas or calmly float in an inner tube down the Comal River—at 2½ miles the "largest shortest" river in the world, according to *Ripley's Believe It or Not.*

There's an Olympic-size swimming pool, and you can rent paddleboats. Even if you're not prepared to immerse yourself, you might take the lovely 22-mile drive along the Guadalupe River from downtown's Cypress Bend Park to **Canyon Lake,** whose clarity makes it perfect for scuba diving.

## NEARBY CAVERNS AND ANIMALS

**Natural Bridge Caverns,** 26495 Natural Bridge Caverns Rd. (☎ **210/651-6101;** www.naturalbridgecaverns.com), 12 miles west of New Braunfels, is named for the 60-foot limestone arch spanning its entryway. More than a mile of huge rooms and passages are filled with stunning, multihued formations—still being formed, as the dripping water attests. The daring—and physically fit—can opt to join one of the recently established Adventure Tours, which involve crawling and, in some cases, rappelling, in an unlighted cave not open to the general public. Open 9am to 6pm June through Labor Day, 9am to 4pm rest of the year; closed Thanksgiving Day, Christmas Day, and New Year's Day; $12 adults, $10 seniors 65 and older, $7 ages 4 to 12.

Just down the road, the **Natural Bridge Wildlife Ranch,** 26515 Natural Bridge Caverns Rd. (☎ **830/438-7400;** www.nbwildliferanchtx.com), lets you get up close and personal—from the safety of your car—with some 50 threatened and endangered species from around the world. Packets of food sold at the entryway inspire even some generally shy types to amble over to your vehicle. Open daily 9am to 5pm, with extended summer hours 'til 6:30pm; admission $9.50 adults, $8 seniors 65 and older, $6 ages 3 to 11.

# WHERE TO STAY IN NEW BRAUNFELS & GRUENE

The **Prince Solmes Inn,** 295 E. San Antonio St., New Braunfels, TX 78130 (☎ **800/ 625-9169** or 830/625-9169; www.princesolmesinn.com), has been in continuous operation since it opened its doors to travelers in 1898. A prime downtown location, tree-shaded courtyard, downstairs wine bar, and gorgeously florid, high-Victorian–style sleeping quarters have put accommodations at this charming bed-and-breakfast in great demand. Three Western-themed rooms in a recently converted 1860 feed store next door are ideal for families, and there's an ultra-romantic separate cabin in the back of the main house. Rates range from $99 to $150.

For a river view, consider the **Gruene Mansion Inn,** 1275 Gruene Rd., New Braunfels, TX 78130 (☎ **830/629-2641;** www.gruenemansioninn.com). The barns that once belonged to the opulent 1875 plantation house were converted to rustic elegant cottages with decks; some also offer cozy lofts (if you don't like stairs, request a single-level room). Accommodations for two go from $85 to $135 per night. Breakfast, served in the plantation house, is $7.50 extra.

About 5 miles north of Gruene, the **Hunter Road Stagecoach Stop B & B,** 5441 FM 1102, New Braunfels, TX 78132 (☎ **800/201-2912** or 830/620-9453; www. lone_star.net/mall/stagecoach), offers accommodations in an 1848 log cabin and an 1850 German *fachwerk* house. As its name suggests, this was the stop for stagecoaches traveling between San Antonio and New Braunfels on the Butterfield line. Cedar-beamed rooms are furnished in primitive antiques, in keeping with the era, but all offer modern amenities such as private bathrooms, TVs, and telephones. A lovely 1850s garden highlights antique roses and native Texas plants; the herbs that grow here turn up in the breakfast dishes. Prices range from $95 to $150 for a double, with discounts available for stays of 2 days or more.

The **Bed & Breakfast & Getaways Reservation Service,** 295 E. San Antonio St., New Braunfels, TX 78130 (☎ **800/239-8282** or 830/625-8194; www. bedbreakfastgetaways.com), lists many other similarly cozy places in the area. If you're planning to come to town during *wurstfest* (late October through early November), be sure to book well in advance, no matter where you stay.

## WHERE TO DINE IN NEW BRAUNFELS & GRUENE

The oldest restaurant in New Braunfels, **Krause's Cafe,** 148 S. Castell Ave. (☎ 830/ 625-7581), serves substantial German dishes like sauerbraten, schnitzel, and home-made sausage in a homey diner-type setting. The **New Braunfuls Smokehouse,** 140 Hwy. 46 South, at I-35 (☎ 830/625-2416), has been around only since 1951; it opened as a tasting room for the meats it started hickory smoking in 1945. Savor it in platters or on sandwiches, or have some shipped home as a savory souvenir (www.nbsmokehouse.com). Open for breakfast, lunch, and dinner; moderate. The far newer **Huisache Grille,** 303 W. San Antonio St. (☎ 830/620-9001), has an updated American menu that draws foodies from as far as San Antonio. The pecan-grilled catfish and Yucatán chicken are excellent. Lunch and dinner daily; moderate to expensive. The latest arrival on downtown's fine dining scene, pretty **Giovani's,** 367 Main Plaza (☎ 830/626-2235), serves sophisticated Italian specialties, such as chicken with artichokes and veal saltimbocca, at very reasonable prices. Save room for the tiramisu. Lunch and dinner daily; moderate to expensive.

In Gruene, the **Gristmill River Restaurant & Bar,** 1287 Gruene Rd. (☎ 830/ 625-0684), a converted 100-year-old cotton gin, includes burgers and chicken-fried steak as well as delicious healthful salads on its Texas-casual menu. Kick back on one of its multiple decks and gaze out at the Guadalupe River. Lunch and dinner daily; moderate. The somewhat more upscale **Restaurant at Gruene Mansion,** 1275 Gruene Rd. (☎ 830/620-0760), serving German and continental cuisine, is a recent addition, but it looks like an old European hall. It also has an outside deck with a river view. Open Tuesday to Friday dinner only, Saturday lunch and dinner, Sunday brunch, lunch, and dinner; moderate to expensive.

## GRUENE AFTER DARK

Lyle Lovett and Garth Brooks are among the big names who have played **Gruene Hall,** Gruene Road, corner of Hunter Road (☎ 830/606-1281), the oldest country-and-western dance hall in Texas and still one of the most mellow places to listen to music. Some of the scenes in *Michael,* starring John Travolta, were shot here.

# Appendix A:
# San Antonio & Austin
# in Depth

**V**isiting places like San Antonio and Austin can be so much more rewarding when you know a little about their history and culture. With that in mind, here's a short introduction to these vast subjects.

## 1 San Antonio Today

The eighth largest city in the United States (pop. approximately 1,100,000), and one of the oldest, is undergoing a metamorphosis. For a good part of this century, San Antonio was a military town that happened to have a nice river promenade running through its decaying downtown area. Now, with the downsizing and privatizing of Kelly Air Force Base and the continuing growth in tourism (revenue: $3.51 billion per year), the city is increasingly perceived by outsiders as a place with a terrific river walk—and, oh yes, it has a strong military presence, doesn't it?

Although the city's outlying theme parks and central area attractions are also benefiting from increased visitation, downtown is by far the most affected section. The city's Henry B. Gonzales Convention Center doubled in size at the end of the last century, and its $187 million expansion is slated for completion by spring 2001. Historic structures are being transformed to accommodate visitors, too: The glorious Majestic Theatre was restored and reopened in the late 1980s, the Empire Theater followed in the late 1990s, and the Alameda and Aztec theaters should be ready to welcome audiences again not long into the new millennium. And every time you turn around it seems as though another old building has been converted into a hotel. Between restorations and new construction, nearly 3,000 guest rooms were added to downtown in the 1990s.

As a result of all this rapid development, a group of neighborhood property and business owners formed the Downtown Alliance, whose goals are an improved north/south–east/west transit system, a new visitor and transportation center, more parking spaces, greater access to the river from the street, and additional green spaces and sidewalk canopies for shade. Some of these aims, such as the expansion of the transit system and river accessibility, have already been achieved: Now the Riverwalk Trolley Station boasts an elevator that can move as many as 50 passengers down to the water.

Middle-class residential growth still lags behind commercial development in this area. San Antonians who moved downtown in the past decade initially patted themselves on the back for their prescience, but many are now beginning to second-guess the changes they helped bring about. Not only are there few residential services (the area still has no major supermarket, for example), but the huge success of the riverside Southbank and Presidio complexes, opened in the mid-1990s, destroyed what little quiet there was at night. Ordinances to cut down on late-night noise and the opening up of a dialogue between residents and businesses have begun to resolve that friction.

This is not to suggest there is no growth in any business sectors besides tourism. Boeing and Lockheed-Martin are among the aviation companies that have been attracted to Kelly Air Force Base, while other businesses like SBC (formerly Southwestern Bell) and oil giant Diamond Shamrock both moved their headquarters to San Antonio in the mid 1990s.

The North American Free Trade Agreement, signed in 1994, was also a boon for the city, which hosts the North American Development Bank—the financial arm of NAFTA—in its downtown International Center. Representatives from the various states of Mexico are housed in the same building as part of the "Casas" program. With its large Hispanic population, regular flights to Mexico City, cultural attractions such as the new Latin American wing of the San Antonio Museum of Art and the Centro Alameda project, and a history of strong business relations with Mexico, San Antonio is ideally positioned to take advantage of the increasing economic reciprocity between the two nations.

Even with its rosy outlook, the city is facing some major problems, ones it shares with other rapidly growing Southwest urban centers. San Antonio and Austin are 80 miles and political light-years apart, but the two cities are growing ever closer. Although they haven't exactly melded to form the single, huge metropolis that futurists predict, the increasing suburban sprawl and the growth of New Braunfels and San Marcos, two small cities that lie between San Antonio and Austin, are causing a great deal of congestion on I-35, which connects all four cities. San Antonio's Metropolitan Planning Commission is studying this problem; one of the solutions being considered is a light rail commuter train.

An even more serious concern is the city's water supply. Currently, the Edwards Aquifer is the city's only source of water; no one knows exactly how many years' worth of water it contains. Although an attempt on the part of the Sierra Club to impose pumping limits on the aquifer eventually failed, the result was federal regulation of the city's water use and renewed attention to the need for alternative water sources.

And, speaking of water, the increased traffic on the San Antonio River in recent decades has resulted in erosion of the canal walls below the River Walk serious enough to warrant major repairs—which means draining part of the river for an extended period. The busiest tourist areas won't be affected, but the north channel will be waterless from Lexington to Convent streets from December 2000 to November 2001, and from Convent to Houston streets from December 2001 to November 2002. Needless to say, the hotels (the Havana Riverwalk Inn, the Sheraton Four Points, the Hawthorne Suites, and the Adams Mark) and sights (the Southwest Center of Art and Craft) that bank on having filled banks nearby aren't overly happy about this project.

## 2 A Look at San Antonio's Past

**Dateline**
- **1691** On June 13, feast day of St. Anthony of Padua, San Antonio River discovered

*continues*

San Antonio's past is the stuff of legend, the Alamo being but the most famous episode. If it were a movie, the story of the city would be an epic with an improbably packed plot, encompassing the end of a great empire, the rise of a republic, and the rescue of the river with which the story began.

## ON A MISSION

Having already established an empire by the late 17th century—the huge Viceroyalty of New Spain, which included, at its high point, Mexico, Guatemala, and large parts of the southwestern United States—Spain was engaged in the far less glamorous task of maintaining it. The remote regions of east Texas had been coming under attack by the native Apache and Comanche; now with rumors flying of French forays into the Spanish territory, search parties were dispatched to investigate.

On one of these search parties in 1691, regional governor Domingo Teran de los Ríos and Father Damian Massenet came upon a wooded plain fed by a fast-flowing river. They named the river—called Yanaguana by the native Coahuiltecan Indians—San Antonio de Padua, after the saint's day on which they arrived. When, some decades later, the Spanish Franciscans proposed building a new mission halfway between the ones on the Rio Grande and those more recently established in east Texas, the abundant water and friendliness of the local population made the plain near the San Antonio River seem like a good choice.

And so it was that in 1718, Mission San Antonio de Valero—later known as the Alamo—was founded. To protect the religious complex from Apache attack, the presidio (fortress) of San Antonio de Béxar went up a few days later. In 1719, a second mission was built nearby, and in 1731, three ill-fated east Texas missions, nearly destroyed by French and Indian attacks, were moved hundreds of miles to the safer banks of the San Antonio River. Also, in March 1731, 15 weary families arrived from the Spanish Canary Islands with a royal dispensation from Philip V to help settle his far-flung New World kingdom. Near the protection of the presidio, they established the village of San Fernando de Béxar.

Thus, within little more than a decade, what is now downtown San Antonio became home to three distinct, though related, settlements: a mission complex, the military garrison designed to protect it, and the civilian town known as Béxar (pronounced bear), which was officially renamed San Antonio in 1837. To irrigate their crops, the early settlers were given narrow strips

and named by the Spanish; governor of Spanish colonial province of Texas makes contact with Coahuiltecan Indians.

- **1718** Mission San Antonio de Valero (later nicknamed the Alamo) founded; presidio San Antonio de Béxar established to protect it and other missions to be built nearby.
- **1720** Mission San José founded.
- **1731** Missions Concepción, San Juan Capistrano, and Espada relocated from East Texas to San Antonio area; 15 Canary Island families sent by Spain to help populate Texas establish the first civil settlement in San Antonio.
- **1793–94** The missions are secularized by order of the Spanish crown.
- **1820** Moses Austin petitions Spanish governor in San Antonio for permission to settle Americans in Texas.
- **1821** Mexico wins independence from Spain.
- **1835** Siege of Béxar: first battle in San Antonio for Texas independence from Mexico.
- **1836** The Alamo falls after 13-day siege by Mexican general Santa Anna; using "Remember the Alamo" as a rallying cry, Sam Houston defeats Santa Anna at San Jacinto.
- **1836** Republic of Texas is established.
- **1845** Texas annexed to the United States.
- **1861** Texas secedes from the Union.
- **1876** Fort Sam Houston established as new quarter-master depot.
- **1877** The railroad arrives in San Antonio, precipitating new waves of immigration.

*continues*

- **1880s** King William, first residential suburb, begins to be developed by German immigrants.
- **1939–40** Works Project Administration builds River Walk, based on plans drawn up in 1929 by architect Robert H. H. Hugman.
- **1968** HemisFair exposition—River Walk extension, Convention Center, Mansión del Rio, and Hilton Palacio del Rio completed for the occasion, along with Tower of the Americas and other fair structures.
- **1988** Rivercenter Mall opens.
- **1989** Premier of the newly refurbished Majestic Theatre.
- **1993** Alamodome, huge new sports complex, completed.
- **1995** Southbank and Presidio complexes open on the river.
- **1998** Opening of the Nelson A. Rockefeller Center for Latin American Art, a three-story, $11 million addition to the San Antonio Museum of Art; reopening of the Empire Theatre.
- **1999** San Antonio Spurs outgrow the Alamodome; funding approved for the new SBC Center.
- **2001** Completion of Convention Center expansion; reopening of the Alameda Theater.

of land stretching back from the river and from the nearby San Pedro Creek; centuries later, the paths connecting these strips, which followed the winding waterways, were paved as the city's streets.

## REMEMBER THE ALAMO

As the 18th century wore on, the missions came continuously under siege by hostile Indians, and the mission Indians fell victim to a host of European diseases against which they had no natural resistance; by the end of the 1700s, the Spanish mission system itself was nearly dead. In 1794, Mission San Antonio de Valero was secularized, its rich farmlands redistributed. In 1810, recognizing the military potential of the thick walls of the complex, the Spanish authorities turned the former mission into a garrison. The men recruited to serve here all hailed from the Mexican town of San José y Santiago del Alamo de Parras; the name of their station was soon shortened to the Alamo (Spanish for "cottonwood tree").

By 1824, all five missions had been secularized and Spain was, once again, worried about Texas. Apache and Comanche roamed the territory freely, and with the incentive of converting the native populations eliminated, it was next to impossible to persuade any Spaniards to live there. So, although the Spanish were rightly suspicious of Anglo-American designs on their land, when land agent Moses Austin arrived in San Antonio in 1820, the government reluctantly gave him permission to settle some 300 Anglo-American families in the region. Austin died before he could see his plan carried out, however. And Spain lost its hold on Mexico in 1821, when the country gained its independence after a decade of struggle. But Moses's son Stephen convinced the new government to honor the terms of the original agreement.

By 1830, however, the Mexicans were growing nervous about the large numbers of Anglos descending on their country from the north. They had already repealed many of the tax breaks they had initially granted the settlers; now they prohibited all further U.S. immigration to the territory. When, in 1835, General Antonio López de Santa Anna abolished Mexico's democratic 1824 constitution, Tejanos (Hispanic Texans) and Anglos alike balked at his dictatorship, and a cry rose up for a separate republic.

The first battle for Texas independence fought on San Antonio soil fell to the rebels; Mexican general Martín Perfecto de Cós surrendered after a short, successful siege of the town in December 1835. But it was the return engagement, that glorious, doomed fight against all odds, that forever captured the American imagination. From February 23 through March 6, 1836, some 180 volunteers—among them Davy Crockett and Jim Bowie—serving under the

> *From all manner of people, business men, consumptive men, curious men, and*
> *wealthy men, there came an exhibition of profound affection for San Antonio.*
> *It seemed to symbolize for them the poetry of life in Texas.*
> —Stephen Crane, *Patriot Shrine of Texas* (1895)

command of William Travis, died trying to defend the Alamo fortress against a vastly greater number of Santa Anna's men. One month later, Sam Houston spurred his troops on to victory at the Battle of San Jacinto with the cry "Remember the Alamo," thus securing Texas's freedom.

## AFTER THE FALL

Ironically, few Americans came to live in San Antonio during Texas's stint as a republic (1836–45), but settlers came from overseas in droves: By 1850, 5 years after Texas joined the United States, Tejanos (Mexican Texans) and Americans were outnumbered by European, mostly German, immigrants. The Civil War put a temporary halt to the city's growth—in part because Texas joined the Confederacy and most of the new settlers were Union sympathizers—but expansion picked up again soon afterward; the coming of the railroad in 1877 set off a new wave of immigration. Riding hard on its crest, the King William district of the city, a residential suburb named for Kaiser Wilhelm, was developed by prosperous German merchants.

Some of the immigrants set up Southern-style plantations, others opened factories and shops, and more and more who arrived after the Civil War earned their keep by driving cattle. The Spanish had brought Longhorn cattle and *vaqueros* (cowboys) from Mexico into the area; now Texas cowboys drove herds north on the Chisholm Trail from San Antonio to Kansas City, where they were shipped east. Others moved cattle west, for use as seed stock in the fledgling ranching industry.

Over the years, San Antonio had never abandoned its role as a military stronghold. In 1849, the Alamo was designated a quartermaster depot for the U.S. Army; in 1876, the much larger Fort Sam Houston was built to take over those duties. Apache chief Geronimo was held at the clock tower in the fort's Quadrangle for 40 days in 1886, en route to exile in Florida, and Teddy Roosevelt outfitted his Rough Riders—some of whom he recruited in San Antonio bars—at Fort Sam 12 years later.

As the city marched into the 20th century, Fort Sam Houston continued to expand. In 1910, it witnessed the first military flight by an American; early aviation stars like Charles Lindbergh honed their flying skills here. From 1917 to 1941, four Army air bases—Kelly Field, Brooks Field, Randolph Field, and Lackland Army Air Base—shot up, making San Antonio the largest military complex in the United States outside the Washington, D.C., area. Although Kelly was downsized and privatized, the military remains the city's major employer today.

## A RIVER RUNS THROUGH IT

As the city moved farther and farther from its agrarian roots, the San Antonio River became much less central to the economy; by the turn of the century, its constant flooding made it a downright nuisance. When a particularly severe storm caused it to overflow its banks in 1921, killing 50 people and destroying many downtown businesses, there was serious talk of cementing the river over. In 1925, the newly formed San Antonio Conservation Society warned the

# The Lay of the Land

Three geographical zones meet in San Antonio: The Balcones Fault divides the farms and forests of east Texas from the scrubby brushland and ranches of west Texas, and the Edwards Plateau drops off to the southern coastal plains. Frederick Law Olmsted's description in his 1853 *A Journey Through Texas* is more poetic. San Antonio, he writes, "lies basking on the edge of a vast plain, through which the river winds slowly off beyond where the eye can reach. To the east are gentle slopes toward it; to the north a long gradual sweep upward to the mountain country, which comes down within five or six miles; to the south and west, the open prairies, extending almost level to the coast, a hundred and fifty miles away."

city council against killing the goose that was laying the golden eggs of downtown economic growth. And in 1927, Robert H. H. Hugman, an architect who had lived in New Orleans and studied that city's Vieux Carré district, came up with a detailed plan for saving the waterway. His proposed River Walk, with shops, restaurants, and entertainment areas buttressed by a series of floodgates, would render the river profitable as well as safe, and also preserve its natural beauty. The Depression intervened, but in 1941, with the help of a federal Works Project Administration (WPA) grant, Hugman's vision became a reality.

Still, for some decades more, the River Walk remained just another pretty space; not until the 1968 HemisFair exposition drew record crowds to the rescued waterway did the city begin banking on its banks. Over the next 20 years, commercial development of the Big Bend section took off, culminating in the huge Rivercenter shopping and hotel complex in 1988. The South Bank complex and Presidio Plaza, opened in the mid-1990s, are being joined in the first years of the new millennium by riverside entertainment Meccas in the Crockett and Houston streets areas. Instead of falling victim to the city's suburban spread, the place where San Antonio began was revitalized by its river—just as the Conservation Society had predicted.

## 3 Multicultural San Antonio

It isn't just a buzzword on academic campuses: Multiculturalism is very real in San Antonio. As the only major Texan city founded before Texas won its independence from Mexico, its history encompasses diverse groups with distinct goals: Spanish missionaries and militia men, German merchants, Southern plantation owners, Western cattle ranchers, and Eastern architects. All have left their mark both tangibly, on San Antonio's winding downtown streets, and more subtly, on the city's culture and cuisine.

With its German, Southern, Western, and, above all, Hispanic influences—the city is nearly 60% Mexican-American—San Antonio's cultural life is immensely rich and complex. At the New Orleans–like Fiesta, for example, San Antonians might break confetti eggs called *cascarones,* listen to oompah bands, and cheer rodeo bull riders. Countless country-and-western ballads twang on about "San Antone"—no doubt because the name rhymes with "alone"—which is also America's capital for Tejano music, a unique blend of Mexican and German sounds. And no self-respecting San Antonio festival would be complete without Mexican tamales and tacos, Texan chili and barbecue, Southern hush puppies and glazed ham, and German beer and bratwurst.

The city's architecture also reflects its multiethnic history. After the Texas revolution, Spanish viga beams began to be replaced by southern Greek revival columns, German *fachwerk* (half-wooden) pitched roofs, and East Coast Victorian gingerbread facades. San Antonio, like the rest of the Southwest, has now returned to its Hispanic architectural roots—even chain hotels in the area have red-clay roofs, Saltillo tile floors, and central patios—but updated versions of other indigenous building styles are also popular. The rustic yet elegant Hill Country look, for example, might use native limestone in structures that combine sprawling Texas ranch features with more intricate German details.

## 4 San Antonio in Books & Film

### BOOKS

Before Frederick Law Olmsted became a landscape architect—New York's Central Park is among his creations—he was a successful journalist; his 1853 *A Journey Through Texas* includes a delightful section on his impressions of early San Antonio. William Sidney Porter, better known as O. Henry, had a newspaper office in San Antonio for a while; two collections of his short stories, *Texas Stories* and *Time to Write,* include a number of pieces set in the city, among them "A Fog in Santone," "The Higher Abdication," "Hygeia at the Solito," "Seats of the Haughty," and "The Missing Chord."

O. Henry wasn't very successful at selling his newspaper, *Rolling Stone,* in San Antonio in the 1890s, but there's a lively literary scene in town today. Resident writers include Sandra Cisneros, many of whose powerful, critically acclaimed short stories in *Women Hollering Creek* are set in the city (the color of her house, in the King William district, has caused a huge local uproar—see chapter 6 for details); novelist Sarah Bird, whose humorous *The Mommy Club* pokes fun at the yuppies of the King William area; and mystery writer Jay Brandon, whose excellent *Loose Among the Lambs* kept San Antonians busy trying to guess the identities of the local figures they (erroneously) thought were fictionalized therein. Stephen Harrigan's *The Gates of the Alamo* is a gripping, fictionalized version of Texas's most famous battle. For a hard-boiled detective take on the city, check out *Tequila Red* and other novels by Rick Riordan set in an appropriately seamy San Antonio.

### FILMS

For a bit of the myth surrounding the city, you might want to rent *The Alamo* (1959), starring John Wayne as Davy Crockett. (Apparently, Wayne had considered shooting the film in Mexico, but was told it wouldn't be distributed in Texas if he did.) Neither *The Alamo,* nor the earlier *San Antonio,* starring

### ❷ Did You Know?

- More jars of salsa than ketchup are consumed in the United States today.
- The first military flight by an American took place at Fort Sam Houston in 1910; in 1915, the entire U.S. Air Force—six reconnaissance planes—resided at the fort.
- The Fairmount Hotel in San Antonio is the heaviest building ever moved.
- Barbed wire was first demonstrated in San Antonio's Military Plaza.

Errol Flynn, were shot in San Antonio, but the 1935 *Fall of the Alamo*—not available on video—was. A number of early aviation movies used Fort Sam Houston as a location, among them the 1927 silent film, *Wings,* the first film to receive an Academy Award for best picture.

Some of the better-known films set in San Antonio in the past 3 decades are *The Getaway* (1972), *Sugarland Express* (1973), *Race with the Devil* (1975), and *Cloak and Dagger* (1983). *Ace Ventura: When Nature Calls* (1995) was filmed in and around the city; the African safari park scenes were shot just outside San Antonio. The 1996 remake of *Lolita* (released in this country in 1998), starring Jeremy Irons and Melanie Griffith, was shot largely in the area, as was *Selena* (1997), based on the life of the Tejano star. Scenes from Richard Linklater's *The Newton Boys* (1998), with Matthew McConnaughey and Ethan Hawke, use the Alamo City as a location, but the city has a far more prominent role in *Still Breathing* (1998) with Brendan Fraser (look for the shots of the Alamo and the Rose Window at the San José Mission). *All the Pretty Horses* (2000), featuring Matt Damon and Henry Thomas and directed by Billy Bob Thornton, and *Miss Congeniality* (2000), with Sandra Bullock, Benjamin Bratt, and Candice Bergman, are among the latest shoots to get the locals gawking.

## 5  Austin Today

Born on the frontier out of the grandiose dreams of a man whose middle name was Buonaparte, Austin spent its formative years fighting to maintain its status as capital. Texan hubris and feistiness remain key to Austin's character today—from state legislators who descend, squabbling, on the town every other year, to the locals fighting to save the golden-cheeked warbler from the developer's bulldozer.

Arguably the state's intellectual center—and undeniably its high-tech Mecca—Austin indulges in the good life with pure Texas excess. It has the largest travel store in the state, gigantic health food emporiums, and supermarket-size privately owned bookstores—not to mention the most movie screens and restaurants per capita in the country.

Much of Austin's success is attributable to the country's huge digital boom. The city's many high-paying computer-related jobs have been a draw to out-of-staters, quite a few of them Californians with lots of disposable cash. And although the majority of Austin's new residents are moving to the suburbs, the current economic expansion, which shows little sign of abating, has also fueled a resurgence in the central city. Downtown, the restoration of the capitol and its grounds, plus the choice of a world-renowned architect for a new Austin Museum of Art, are part of this process, as are the refurbishing of the old State Theatre and the reopening of the Stephen F. Austin Hotel, a 1924 property that's giving the (also newly refurbished) Driskill Hotel, once the only grand historic lodging in town, a run for its money. The convention center is doubling in size too, and with the opening of the Bob Bullock Texas History Center and (a few years down the road) the Jack Blanton museum across the street, downtown and the University of Texas are forming a vital central city nexus. The transformation of the historic Brown building into an apartment complex and the ongoing conversion of former warehouses and commercial lofts into residential housing are even more crucial signs that downtown is returning to the land of the living.

In addition, the debut of the Austin-Bergstrom International Airport south of downtown in March 1999 is enhancing the development of an area that had already started to make a comeback. South Congress Street (dubbed SoCo, of course) is drawing an increasing number of hip galleries and boutiques, and the airport is attracting more restaurants and hotels to this older area. And, in an ultimate Austin act of recycling, the abandoned hangers of the old Robert Mueller airport are being rented out for film production, which means more jobs and more activity in a once-decaying north-central neighborhood.

But there are many signs that Austin is becoming a victim of its own success. Locals complain that the people moving in from California drive like they're still in L.A.; formerly bicycle-friendly streets are no longer as hospitable to two-wheelers. The low-key, libertarian atmosphere of the city may be changing; there's now a gated residential complex right down the street from the famed Continental Club. In the mid-1990s, with thefts in microchips and circuit boards rising, the Austin Police Department introduced a high-tech crime unit.

With rising rents, many of the struggling musicians who gave Austin's music scene its vitality can no longer afford to live here. Gentrification is similarly resulting in the displacement of the poor and older people on fixed incomes. While newer arts venues move into downtown, older ones like the Capitol Theater in the warehouse district are being pushed out by high rents. Many of the restaurants in that newly burgeoning area are owned by groups of California investors rather than locals, and some funky midtown restaurants like Kerbey Lane are spinning off characterless counterparts in the city's northwest industrial section. And although the new airport prides itself on its use of local concessionaires, the restaurants and hotels that are springing up alongside the facility are chains.

What's more, downtown is by no means ready for large-scale residential growth. There are no supermarkets in central downtown; parking is very limited (especially for a city that, despite decent public transportation, remains totally auto dependent); and many downtown restaurants still close their doors on the weekends, when there's no business traffic.

One of the most pressing problems is out-of-control traffic. Although the freeways are perpetually being expanded, they can't keep pace with the ever-burgeoning population; in downtown, construction is forcing detours on already choked narrow streets. There's currently no solution in sight. A proposed light-rail system was voted down in 2000—in part, its opponents said, because it was too little too late; in part because they worried that Capitol Metro, the city transport system, wasn't up to the task of building it; and in part because . . . well, this is Austin, and getting everyone to agree on a project is like trying to pin down a certain presidential election that put the city on the national map.

## 6 Austin History 101

A vast territory that threw off foreign rule to become an independent nation—remember the Alamo?—Texas has always played a starring role in the romance of the American West. So it's only fitting that Texas's capital should spring, full-blown, from the imagination of a man on a buffalo hunt.

### A CAPITAL DILEMMA

The man was Mirabeau Buonaparte Lamar, who had earned a reputation for bravery in Texas's struggle for independence from Mexico.

**Dateline**

- 1730 Franciscans build a mission at Barton Springs, but abandon it within a year.
- 1836 Texas wins independence from Mexico; Republic of Texas established.
- 1838 Jacob Harrell sets up camp on the Colorado River, calling the settlement

*continues*

Waterloo; Mirabeau B. Lamar succeeds Sam Houston as president of Texas.

- **1839** Congressional commission recommends Waterloo as site for new capital of the republic. Waterloo's name changes to Austin.

- **1842** Sam Houston succeeds Lamar as president, reestablishes Houston as Texas's capital, and orders nation's archives moved there. Austinites resist.

- **1844** Anson Jones succeeds Houston as president and returns capital to Austin.

- **1845** Constitutional convention in Austin approves annexation of Texas by the United States.

- **1850s** Austin undergoes a building boom; construction of the capitol (1853), Governor's Mansion (1856), and General Land Office (1857).

- **1861** Texas votes to secede from the Union (Travis County, which includes Austin, votes against secession).

- **1865** General Custer is among those who come to restore order in Austin during Reconstruction.

- **1871** First rail line to Austin completed.

- **1883** University of Texas opens.

- **1923** Santa Rita No. 1, an oil well on University of Texas land, strikes a gusher.

- **1937** Lyndon Johnson elected U.S. representative from Tenth Congressional District, which includes Austin.

- **Late 1930s to early 1950s** Six dams built on the Colorado River by the Lower Colorado River Authority, resulting in formation of the Highland Lakes chain.

*continues*

In 1838, when our story begins, Lamar was vice president of the 2-year-old Republic of Texas; Sam Houston, the even more renowned hero of the Battle of San Jacinto, was president. Although they shared a strong will, the two men had very different ideas about the future of the republic: Houston tended to look eastward, toward union with the United States, while Lamar saw independence as the first step to establishing an empire that would stretch to the Pacific.

That year, an adventurer named Jacob Harrell set up a camp called Waterloo at the western edge of the frontier. Lying on the northern banks of Texas's Colorado River (not to be confused with the larger waterway up north), it was nestled against a series of gentle hills. Some 100 years earlier, the Franciscans had established a temporary mission here; in the 1820s, Stephen F. Austin, Texas's earliest and greatest land developer, had the area surveyed for the smaller of the two colonies he was to establish on Mexican territory.

But the place had otherwise seen few Anglos before Harrell arrived; for thousands of years, it had been visited mainly by nomadic Indian tribes, including the Comanches, Lipan Apaches, and Tonkawas. Thus, it was to a rather pristine spot that, in the autumn of 1838, Harrell invited his friend Mirabeau Lamar to take part in a shooting expedition. The buffalo hunt proved extremely successful, and when Lamar gazed at the rolling, wooded land surrounding Waterloo, he saw that it was good.

In December of the same year, Lamar became president of the Republic. He ordered the congressional commission that had been charged with the task of selecting a site for a permanent capital, to be named after Stephen F. Austin, to check out Waterloo. Much to the dismay of residents of Houston—home to the temporary capital—who considered Waterloo a dangerous wilderness outpost, the commission recommended Lamar's pet site.

In early 1839, Lamar's friend Edwin Waller was dispatched to plan a city—the only one in the United States besides Washington, D.C. designed to be an independent nation's capital. The first public lots went on sale on August 1, 1839; by November of that year, Austin was ready to host its first session of Congress.

Austin's position as capital was far from entrenched, however. Attacks on the republic by

Mexico in 1842 gave Sam Houston, now president again, sufficient excuse to order the national archives to be relocated out of remote Austin. Resistant Austinites greeted the 26 armed men who came to repossess the historic papers with a cannon. After a struggle, the men returned empty-handed, and Houston abandoned his plan, thus ceding to Austin the victory in what came to be called the Archive War.

Although Austin won this skirmish, it was losing a larger battle for existence. Houston refused to convene Congress in Austin. By 1843 Austin's population had dropped down to 200 and its buildings lay in disrepair. Help came in the person of Anson Jones, who succeeded to the presidency in 1844. The constitutional convention he called in 1845 not only approved Texas's annexation to the United States, but also named Austin capital until 1850, when voters of what was now the state of Texas would choose their governmental seat for the next 20 years. In 1850, Austin campaigned hard for the position and won by a landslide.

## A CAPITAL SOLUTION

Austin thrived under the protection of the U.S. Army. The first permanent buildings to go up during the 1850s construction boom following statehood included an impressive limestone capitol; two of the buildings in its complex, the General Land Office and the Governor's Mansion, are still in use today.

The boom was short-lived, however: Although Austin's Travis County voted against secession, Texas decided to join the Confederacy in 1861. By 1865, Union army units—including one led by General George Armstrong Custer—were sent to restore order in a defeated and looted Austin.

But once again Austin rebounded. With the arrival of the railroad in 1871, the city's recovery was sealed. The following year, when Austin won election as state capital, it was delivered.

Still, there were more battles for status to be fought. Back in 1839, the Republic of Texas had declared its intention to build a "university of the first class"; in 1876, a new state constitution mandated its establishment. Through yet another bout of heavy electioneering, Austin won the right to establish the flagship of Texas's higher educational system on its soil. In 1883, the classrooms not yet completed, the first 221 members of what is now a student body of more than 50,000 met the eight instructors of the University of Texas.

- 1960s High-tech firms, including IBM, move to Austin.
- 1972 Willie Nelson moves back to Texas from Nashville; helps spur live-music scene on Sixth Street.
- 1980s Booming real-estate market goes bust.
- 1995 Capitol, including new annex, reopens after massive refurbishing.
- 1997 Completion of the refurbishing of the capitol's grounds and of the Texas State Cemetery.
- 1999 Opening of Austin-Bergstrom International Airport.
- 2000 Driskill Hotel revamp completed, the Stephen F. Austin Hotel reopens, and plans to turn Robert Mueller Airport into film production studio approved.
- 2001 Debut of the Bob Bullock Texas State History Museum.

**Impressions**

*Like the ancient city of Rome, Austin is built upon seven hills, and it is impossible to conceive of a more beautiful and lovely situation.*
—George W. Bonnell, Commissioner of Indian Affairs of the Republic of Texas (1840).

The university wasn't the only Austin institution without permanent quarters that year: The old limestone capitol had burned in 1881, and a new, much larger home for the legislature was being built. In 1888, after a series of mishaps—the need to construct a railroad branch to transport the donated building materials, among them—the current capitol was completed. The grand red-granite edifice looking down upon the city symbolized Austin's arrival.

## DAMS, OIL & MICROCHIPS

The new capitol notwithstanding, the city was once again in a slump. Although some believed that quality of life would be sacrificed to growth—a view still strongly argued today—most townspeople embraced the idea of harnessing the fast-flowing waters of the Colorado River as the solution to Austin's economic woes. A dam, they thought, would not only provide a cheap source of electricity for residents, but also supply power for irrigation and new factories. Dedicated in 1893, the Austin Dam did indeed fulfill these goals—but only temporarily. The energy source proved to be limited, and when torrential rains pelted the city in April 1900, Austin's dreams came crashing down with its dam.

Another dam, attempted in 1915, was never finished. It wasn't until the late 1930s that a permanent solution to the water-power problem was found. The successful plea to President Roosevelt for federal funds on the part of young Lyndon Johnson, the newly elected representative from Austin's Tenth Congressional District, was crucial to the construction of six dams along the lower Colorado River. These dams not only afforded Austin and central Texas all the hydroelectric power and drinking water they needed, but also created the seven Highland Lakes—aesthetically appealing and a great source of recreational revenue.

Still, Austin might have remained a backwater capital seat abutting a beautiful lake had it not been for the discovery of oil on University of Texas (UT) land in 1923. The huge amounts of money that subsequently flowed into the Permanent University Fund—worth some $4 billion today—enabled Austin's campus to become truly first-class. While most of the country was cutting back during the Depression, UT went on a building binge and began hiring a faculty as impressive as the new halls in which they were to hold forth.

The indirect effects of the oil bonus reached far beyond College Hill. Tracor, the first of Austin's more than 250 high-tech companies, was founded by UT scientists and engineers in 1955. Lured by the city's natural attractions and its access to a growing bank of young brainpower, many outside companies soon arrived: IBM (1967), Texas Instruments (1968), and Motorola's Semiconductor Products Section (1974). In the 1980s, two huge computer consortiums, MCC and SEMATECH, opted to make Austin their home. And wunderkind Michael Dell, who started out selling computers from his dorm room at UT in 1984 and is now the CEO of the hugely successful Austin-based Dell Computer Corporation, spawned a new breed of local "Dellionaires" by rewarding his employees with company stock.

Willie Nelson's return from Nashville to Austin in 1972 didn't have quite as profound an effect on the economy, but it certainly had one on the city's live-music scene. Hippies and country-and-western fans could now find common ground at the many clubs that began to sprout up along downtown's Sixth Street, which had largely been abandoned. These music venues, combined with the construction that followed in the wake of the city's high-tech success, helped spur a general downtown resurgence. True, the oil and savings-and-loan crashes of the mid-1980s left many of the new office towers partially empty, but—wouldn't you know it?—within a decade, the comeback kid of cities had already made a complete recovery.

## 7  The Austin Sound

When they're not exercising—and often even when they are—Austinites are listening to music. The city has gigantic record stores, a shop devoted solely to music art, and more than 100 live music venues. One of the most appealing aspects of the local scene is the wide range of good sounds to be found at unexpected, totally original places—barbecue joints, Mexican restaurants, and converted gas stations. The atmosphere almost everywhere is assiduously laid-back—legends like Bob Dylan and Joan Baez still perform at intimate spots like the Backyard—and covers in the smaller clubs are still relatively low.

Some music aficionados may have heard about Austin in the mid-1960s, when hootenannies at Threadgill's frequently drew a young Janis Joplin, but the city's reputation for alternative country began when Willie Nelson came back to town in the early 1970s. He, Waylon Jennings, Jerry Jeff Walker, and Asleep at the Wheel's Ray Benson were followed by a new generation of progressive country rockers, including Jimmie Dale Gilmore, Butch Hancock, Joe Ely, Ian Moore, Rick Treviño, Junior Brown, and Nanci Griffith.

Not that country is all that Austin has to offer—this ain't just Texas; this is Austin, the self-proclaimed Live Music Capital of the World. Blues greats like Stevie Ray Vaughan, alternative bands like the Butthole Surfers, and early punk rockers such as the Big Boys have all stitched their patch into the quilt of Austin music. What's the next big sound to spring from this musical Mecca? That's just what the many music promoters who attend the city's annual S×SW (South by Southwest) conference, the music industry's most influential confab (see box in chapter 15 for details), want to find out.

The strength of its live music scene, combined with Austin's livability, attracted many musicians away from the established music cities of Los Angeles, New York, and Nashville in the 1980s and early 1990s, but the starving artist influx has slowed (and the exodus has started) as the city gets increasingly expensive. Still, there's no cause for alarm yet. On any given night, pretty much any type of music you could ever want to hear—from reggae to jazz, funk to folk, metal to hip-hop—is bound to be on stage somewhere in town.

## 8  Celluloid Austin

It's not as obvious a presence as the music scene, but cinema, especially of the offbeat sort, has given Austin a certain celluloid clout. The city first earned its credentials as an independent director–friendly place in 1982, when the Coen brothers shot *Blood Simple* here. But it was not until University of Texas graduate Richard Linklater captured some of the loopier members of his alma mater in *Slackers,* thus adding a word to the national vocabulary, that Austin really arrived on the *cineaste* scene. Although his later work, like *The Newton Boys,* is solidly mainstream, Linklater is still associated with the independent and experimental work of the Austin Film Society, which he founded in 1985. He's often spotted with Robert Rodriguez, who shot all or part of several of his films (*Alienated, The Faculty,* and *Spy Kidz*), in Austin, along with Quentin Tarantino, who owns property in town. Mike Judge, of "Beavis and Butthead" fame, also lives in Austin.

The city is home, too, to the annual Austin Film Festival, which premiered in 1993. The only such gathering that focuses on the paper behind the celluloid, it's held in tandem with the Heart of Films Screenwriters Conference (see chapter 15). And the come-lately film component of S×SW (see chapter 15), originally just a music conference, gets larger every year. Past panelists have included Linklater and John Sayles, whose film *Lone Star* had its world premiere here.

But the most recent development may be the most exciting yet: In 2000, the City Council approved the lease that will turn the old Robert Mueller airport into Austin Studios, a film/video/multimedia production facility. Six hangars (from 14,000 to 21,000 sq. ft.) will be used for set construction, wardrobe, and soundstages—and there are acres of open tarmac for parking. Projects that have already signed on include *The Rookie,* starring Dennis Quaid.

Of course, the city has long had an undercover Hollywood presence. If you don't recognize Austin in many of the big-budget films that were shot here—more than 75 in the past 2 decades—it's because the area offers such a wide range of landscapes, filling in for locations as far afield as Vietnam and Canada. But Texas features prominently in a number of the following Austin area productions: *Texas Chainsaw Massacre* (1972); *Honeysuckle Rose* (1980, Willie Nelson and Dyan Cannon); *The Best Little Whorehouse in Texas* (1982, Burt Reynolds and Dolly Parton); *Songwriter* (1984, Willie Nelson and Kris Kristofferson); *Nadine* (1987, Jeff Bridges and Kim Basinger); *D.O.A.* (1988, Meg Ryan and Dennis Quaid); *The Ballad of the Sad Cafe* (1991, Vanessa Redgrave and Keith Carradine); *What's Eating Gilbert Grape* (1993, Johnny Depp, Juliette Lewis, and Leonardo DiCaprio); *A Perfect World* (1993, Kevin Costner and Clint Eastwood); *Courage Under Fire* (1996, Meg Ryan and Denzel Washington); *Michael* (1996, John Travolta, William Hurt, and Andie McDowell); *Waiting for Guffman* (1997, Parker Posey, Christopher Guest, and Eugene Levy); *Hope Floats* (1998, Sandra Bullock and Harry Connick, Jr.); *The Whole Wide World* (1998, Vincent D'Onofrio and Renee Zellweger); *Home Fries* (1998, Drew Barrymore); *Where the Heart Is* (1999, Natalie Portman, Sally Field, and Ashley Judd); and *Miss Congeniality* (2000, Sandra Bullock and Michael Caine).

Austin has also been showcased on the tube. "Lonesome Dove," featuring Robert Duvall, Tommy Lee Jones, and Anjelica Houston, is the most famous of many miniseries shot in the area, but the more recent "True Women," which traces three generations in the Austin area, is the more historically accurate. Austinite Bill Wittliff, who directed "Lonesome Dove," was also responsible for "Ned Blessing," another miniseries that looked back to 19th-century Austin. The contemporary town was the setting for MTV's "Austin Stories," a short-lived series that reaped lots of critical acclaim before it was canned in 1998. And the Public Broadcasting Service has kept the city on the small screen since 1975, when the network first began taping concerts by renowned country-and-western performers for "Austin City Limits."

## 9 Recommended Books & Recordings

### BOOKS

The foibles of the Texas "lege"—along with those of Congress and the rest of Washington—are hilariously pilloried by Molly Ivins, Austin's resident scourge, in two collections of her syndicated newspaper columns: *Molly Ivins Can't Say That, Can She?* and *Nothing But Good Times Ahead.* George W. Bush was her more recent target in *Shrub.* For background into the city's unique music scene, try Jan Reid's *The Improbable Rise of Red Neck Rock.* It's been followed more recently by Barry Shank's scholarly tome, *Dissonant Identities: The Rock 'n' Roll Scene in Austin, Texas.* Serious history buffs might want to dip into Robert Caro's excellent multivolume biography of Lyndon B. Johnson, the consummate Texas politician, who had a profound effect on the Austin area.

William Sydney Porter, better known as O. Henry, published a satirical newspaper in Austin in the late 19th century. Among the many short tales he wrote about the area—collected in *O. Henry's Texas Stories*—are four inspired by his stint as a draftsman in the General Land Office. Set largely in Austin, Billy Lee Brammer's *The Gay Place* is a fictional portrait of a political figure loosely based on LBJ. The more recent *Strange Sunlight* by Peter LaSalle details corruption during the real estate boom years in Austin.

The city's most famous resident scribe, the late James Michener, placed his historical epic *Texas* in the frame of a governor's task force operating out of Austin. The city is also the locus of several of Austin resident Mary Willis Walker's mysteries, including *Zero at the Bone* and *All the Dead Lie Down,* and of *The Boyfriend School,* a humorous novel by San Antonian Sarah Bird.

It's only logical that the king of cyberpunk writers, Bruce Sterling, should live in Austin; he gets megabytes of fan mail each week for such books as *Islands in the Net, The Difference Engine* (with William Gibson), and *Holy Fire.* His nonfiction work, *The Hacker Crackdown,* details a failed antihacker raid in Austin.

Don't care to spend so much time in the present and future tense? Check out the charming mysteries penned by Susan Wittig Albert. Her amateur sleuth, China Bayles, runs an herb shop in Pecan Springs, a quaint central Texas town much like her own home town of Wimberley, not far from Austin. Her latest book is *Lavender Lies.*

## RECORDINGS

Janis Joplin, who attended UT for a time, and the late Stevie Ray Vaughan (enshrined in a statue overlooking Town Lake) both got their starts in Austin clubs. Since 1980, the list of artists who signed on to major record labels while living in Austin includes Asleep at the Wheel, the Butthole Surfers, Timbuk 3, Lucinda Williams, Lee Roy Parnell, Joe Ely, Jerry Jeff Walker, Hal Ketchum, and Jimmie Dale Gilmore. Local hero Willie Nelson has his own recording studio on the outskirts of town, and it's not surprising that the offbeat Lyle Lovett is an Austin resident.

# Appendix B:
# For Foreign Visitors

The pervasiveness of American culture around the world might make you feel that you know the USA pretty well, but leaving your own country still requires an additional degree of planning. This chapter will help prepare you for the more common problems that visitors may encounter.

## 1 Preparing for Your Trip

### ENTRY REQUIREMENTS

Immigration laws are a hot political issue in the United States these days, and the following requirements might have changed somewhat by the time you plan your trip. Check at any U.S. embassy or consulate for current information and requirements. You can also plug into the **U.S. State Department**'s Internet site at **http://state.gov**.

**DOCUMENTS**   The U.S. State Department has a **Visa Waiver Pilot Program** allowing citizens of certain countries to enter the United States without a visa for stays of up to 90 days. At press time they included Andorra, Argentina, Australia, Austria, Belgium, Brunei, Denmark, Finland, France, Germany, Iceland, Ireland, Italy, Japan, Liechtenstein, Luxembourg, Monaco, the Netherlands, New Zealand, Norway, San Marino, Slovenia, Spain, Sweden, Switzerland, and the United Kingdom. Citizens of these countries need only a valid passport and a round-trip air or cruise ticket in their possession upon arrival. If they first enter the United States, they may also visit Mexico, Canada, Bermuda, and/or the Caribbean islands and return to the United States without a visa. Further information is available from any U.S. embassy or consulate. Canadian citizens may enter the United States without visas; they need only proof of residence.

Citizens of all other countries must have (1) a valid passport that expires at least 6 months later than the scheduled end of their visit to the United States, and (2) a tourist visa, which may be obtained without charge from any U.S. consulate.

**Obtaining a Visa**   To obtain a visa, the traveler must submit a completed application form (either in person or by mail) with a 1½-inch-square photo and must demonstrate binding ties to a residence abroad. Usually you can get a visa at once or within 24 hours, but it might take longer during the summer rush from June through August. If you cannot go in person, contact the nearest U.S. embassy or consulate for directions on applying by mail. Your travel agent or airline office may also be able to provide you with visa applications and instructions. The U.S. consulate or embassy that issues your visa will determine whether you will be issued a multiple- or single-entry visa and any restrictions regarding the length of your stay.

British subjects can get up-to-date passport and visa information by calling the **U.S. Embassy Visa Information Line** (☎ **0891/200-290**) or the **London Passport Office** (☎ **0990/210-410** for recorded information).

**Immigration Questions**   Telephone operators will answer your inquiries on U.S. immigration policies or laws at the Immigration and Naturalization Service's Customer Information Center (☎ **800/375-5283**). Representatives are available 9am to 3pm, Monday to Friday. The INS also runs a 24-hour automated information service, for commonly asked questions, at ☎ **800/755-0777.**

**Driver's Licenses**   Foreign driver's licenses are mostly recognized in the United States, although you may want to get an international driver's license if your home license is not written in English.

**MEDICAL CONCERNS**   Unless you're arriving from an area known to be suffering from an epidemic (particularly cholera or yellow fever), inoculations or vaccinations are not required for entry into the United States. If you have a disease that requires treatment with narcotics or syringe-administered medications, carry a valid signed prescription from your physician to allay any suspicions that you may be smuggling narcotics (a serious offense that carries severe penalties in the United States).

For HIV-positive visitors, requirements for entering the United States are somewhat vague and change frequently. According to the latest publication of *HIV and Immigrants: A Manual for AIDS Service Providers,* although INS doesn't require a medical exam for everyone trying to come into the United States, INS officials may keep out people who they suspect are HIV-positive. INS may stop people because they look sick or because they are carrying AIDS/HIV medicine.

If an HIV-positive noncitizen applying for a non-immigrant visa knows that HIV is a communicable disease of public health significance but checks "no" on the question about communicable diseases, INS may deny the visa because it thinks the applicant committed fraud. If a non-immigrant visa applicant checks "yes," or if INS suspects the person is HIV-positive, it will deny the visa unless the applicant asks for a special waiver for visitors. This waiver is for people visiting the United States for a short time, to attend a conference, for instance, to visit close relatives, or to receive medical treatment. It can be a confusing situation, so for up-to-the-minute information concerning HIV-positive travelers, contact the Centers for Disease Control's **National Center for HIV** (☎ **404/332-4559;** www.hivatis.org) or the **Gay Men's Health Crisis** (☎ **212/367-1000;** www.gmhc.org).

**CUSTOMS REQUIREMENTS**   Every visitor over 21 years of age may bring in, free of duty, the following: (1) 1 liter of wine or hard liquor; (2) 200 cigarettes, 100 cigars (but not from Cuba), or 3 pounds of smoking tobacco; and (3) $100 worth of gifts. These exemptions are offered to travelers who spend at least 72 hours in the United States and who have not claimed them within the preceding 6 months. It is altogether forbidden to bring into the country foodstuffs (particularly fruit, cooked meats, and canned goods) and plants (vegetables, seeds, tropical plants, and the like). Foreign tourists may bring in or take out up to $10,000 in U.S. or foreign currency with no formalities; larger sums must be declared to U.S. Customs on entering or leaving, which includes filing form CM 4790. For more specific information on U.S. Customs, call your nearest U.S. embassy or consulate, or the **U.S. Customs** office at ☎ 202/927-1770 or www.customs.ustreas.gov.

## INSURANCE

Although it's not required of travelers, health insurance is highly recommended. Unlike many European countries, the United States does not usually offer free or low-cost medical care to its citizens or visitors. Doctors and hospitals are expensive, and in most cases require advance payment or proof of coverage before they render their services. Policies can cover everything from the loss or theft of your baggage and trip cancellation to the guarantee of bail in case you're arrested. Good policies also cover the costs of an accident, repatriation, or death. See "Insurance," in chapter 2, for more information. Packages such as **Europ Assistance** in Europe are sold by automobile clubs and travel agencies at attractive rates. **Worldwide Assistance Services, Inc.** (☎ 800/821-2828) is the agent for Europ Assistance in the United States.

Although lack of health insurance may prevent you from being admitted to a hospital in nonemergencies, don't worry about being left on a street corner to die: The American way is to fix you now and bill the living daylights out of you later.

**INSURANCE FOR BRITISH TRAVELERS**  Most big travel agents offer their own insurance and will probably try to sell you their package when you book a holiday. Think before you sign. **Britain's Consumers' Association** recommends that you insist on seeing the policy and reading the fine print before buying travel insurance. **The Association of British Insurers** (☎ 020/7600-3333; www.abi.org.uk/) gives advice by phone and publishes the free *Holiday Insurance,* a guide to policy provisions and prices. You might also shop around for better deals: Try **Columbus Travel Insurance Services Ltd.** (☎ 020/7375-0011; www.columbusdirect.net) or, for students, **Campus Travel** (☎ 0870/240-1010; www.usitcampus.co.uk/).

**INSURANCE FOR CANADIAN TRAVELERS**  Canadians should check with their provincial health plan offices or call HealthCanada (☎ 613/957-2991) to find out the extent of their coverage and what documentation and receipts they must take home in case they are treated in the United States.

## MONEY

**CURRENCY**  The U.S. monetary system is painfully simple: The most common bills (all ugly, all green) are the $1 (colloquially, a "buck"), $5, $10, and $20 denominations. There are also $2 bills (seldom encountered), $50 bills, and $100 bills (the last two are usually not welcome as payment for small purchases). Note that a newly redesigned $100 and $50 bill were introduced in 1996, a redesigned $20 bill in 1998, and redesigned $10 and $5 notes in 2000. Despite rumors to the contrary, the old-style bills are still legal tender.

There are six denominations of coins: 1¢ (1 cent, or a penny); 5¢ (5 cents, or a nickel); 10¢ (10 cents, or a dime); 25¢ (25 cents, or a quarter); 50¢ (50 cents, or a half dollar); and, prized by collectors, the rare $1 piece (the older, large silver dollar and the newer, small Susan B. Anthony coin). A new gold-colored $1 piece was introduced in 2000.

**CURRENCY EXCHANGE**  The foreign-exchange bureaus so common in Europe are rare even at airports in the United States and nonexistent outside major cities. It's best not to change foreign money (or traveler's checks denominated in a currency other than U.S. dollars) at a small-town bank, or even a branch in a big city; in fact, leave any currency other than U.S. dollars at home—it might prove a greater nuisance to you than it's worth.

**CREDIT CARDS & ATMS**   Credit cards are the most widely used form of payment in the United States: **Visa** (BarclayCard in Britain), **MasterCard** (Eurocard in Europe, Access in Britain, Chargex in Canada), **American Express, Diners Club, Discover,** and **Carte Blanche.** You must have a credit or charge card to rent a car. There are, however, a handful of stores and restaurants that do not take credit cards, so be sure to ask in advance. Most businesses display a sticker near their entrance to let you know which cards they accept. *Note:* Often businesses require a minimum purchase price, usually around $10, to use a credit card.

It is strongly recommended that you bring at least one major credit card. Hotels, car-rental companies, and airlines usually require a credit-card imprint as a deposit against expenses, and in an emergency, a credit card can be priceless.

You'll find automated teller machines (ATMs) on just about every block—at least in almost every town—across the country. Some ATMs will allow you to draw U.S. currency against your bank and credit cards. Check with your bank before leaving home, and remember that you will need your personal identification number (PIN) to do so. Most accept Visa, MasterCard, and American Express, as well as ATM cards from other U.S. banks. Expect to be charged up to $3 per transaction, however, if you're not using your own bank's ATM.

**TRAVELER'S CHECKS**   Although traveler's checks are widely accepted, make sure that they're denominated in U.S. dollars, as foreign-currency checks are often difficult to exchange. The three traveler's checks that are most widely recognized—and least likely to be denied—are **Visa, American Express,** and **Thomas Cook.** Be sure to record the numbers of the checks, and keep that information separately in case they get lost or stolen. Most businesses are pretty good about taking traveler's checks, but you're better off cashing them at a bank (in small amounts, of course) and paying in cash. You'll need identification, such as a driver's license or passport, to change a traveler's check.

## SAFETY

**GENERAL SUGGESTIONS**   While tourist areas are generally safe, U.S. urban areas tend to be less safe than those in Europe or Japan. You should always stay alert. It is wise to ask your hotel front desk staff or the city or area's tourist office if you're in doubt about which neighborhoods are safe. Avoid deserted areas, especially at night. Don't go into any city parks at night unless there's an event that attracts crowds, such as a concert or similar occasion.

Avoid carrying valuables with you on the street, and don't display expensive cameras or electronic equipment. If you are using a map, consult it inconspicuously—or better yet, try to study it before you leave your room. Hold onto your pocketbook, and place your billfold in an inside pocket. In theaters, restaurants, and other public places, keep your possessions in sight.

Remember also that hotels are open to the public, and in a large hotel, security may not be able to screen everyone entering. Always lock your room

**For Foreign Visitors**

---

**Travel Tip**

Be sure to keep a copy of all your travel papers separate from your wallet or purse, and leave a copy with someone at home should you need it faxed in an emergency.

door—don't assume that, once inside your hotel, you are automatically safe and no longer need to be aware of your surroundings.

**DRIVING**   Driving safety is important, too, especially given the highly publicized carjackings of foreign tourists in Florida. Question your rental agency about personal safety, and ask for a traveler-safety brochure when you pick up your car. Get written directions—or a map with the route clearly marked—from the agency showing how to get to your destination. (Many agencies now offer the option of renting a cellular phone for the duration of your car rental; check with the rental agent when you pick up the car.) And, if possible, arrive and depart during daylight hours.

Recently, more and more crime has involved cars and drivers. If you drive off a highway into a doubtful neighborhood, leave the area as quickly as possible. If you have an accident, even on the highway, stay in your car with the doors locked until you assess the situation or until the police arrive. If you're bumped from behind on the street or are involved in a minor accident with no injuries and the situation appears to be suspicious, motion to the other driver to follow you. Never get out of your car in such situations. Go directly to the nearest police precinct, well-lit service station, or 24-hour store.

Always try to park in well-lit and well-traveled areas if possible. If you leave your rental car unlocked and empty of your valuables, you're probably safer than locking your car with valuables in plain view. Never leave any packages or valuables in sight. If someone attempts to rob you or steal your car, don't try to resist the thief/carjacker—report the incident to the police department immediately by calling ☎ **911.**

You may want to contact the **San Antonio Convention and Visitors Bureau,** P.O. Box 2277, San Antonio, TX 78298 (☎ **800/447-3372;** e-mail: sacvb@ci.sat.tx.us), or the **Austin Convention and Visitors Bureau,** 201 E. Second St., Austin, TX 78701 (☎ **800/926-2282**), ahead of time for advice on safety precautions.

## 2  Getting to the United States

Houston is the hub for international Flights into Texas. **Air Canada** (☎ **800/776-3000**) offers daily nonstop flights from Toronto and Calgary to Houston. **Continental** (☎ **800/231-0856**) and **British Airways** (☎ **800/ 247-9297**) both have nonstop service from London.

For further information about travel to San Antonio and Austin, see the "Getting There" sections of chapters 2 and 9, respectively.

**AIRLINE DISCOUNTS**   The idea of traveling abroad on a budget is something of an oxymoron, but travelers can reduce the price of a plane ticket by several hundred dollars if they take the time to shop around. For example, overseas visitors can take advantage of the APEX (Advance Purchase Excursion) reductions offered by all major U.S. and European carriers.

**IMMIGRATION AND CUSTOMS CLEARANCE**   Visitors arriving by air, no matter what the port of entry, should cultivate patience and resignation before setting foot on U.S. soil. Getting through immigration control may take as long as 2 hours on some days, especially on summer weekends, so be sure to have this guidebook or something else to read. Add the time it takes to clear Customs, and you'll see that you should make a 2- to 3-hour allowance for delays when you plan your connections between international and domestic flights.

In contrast, for the traveler arriving by car or rail from Canada, the border-crossing formalities have been streamlined to the vanishing point. People traveling by air from Canada, Bermuda, and some places in the Caribbean can sometimes clear Customs and Immigration at the point of departure, which is much quicker.

## 3 Getting Around the United States

**BY PLANE**   Some large airlines (for example, Northwest and Delta) offer travelers on their transatlantic or transpacific flights special discount tickets under the name **Visit USA,** allowing mostly one-way travel from one U.S. destination to another at very low prices. These discount tickets are not on sale in the United States and must be purchased abroad along with your international ticket. This system is the best, easiest, and fastest way to see the United States at low cost. You should get information well in advance from your travel agent or the office of the airline concerned since the conditions attached to these discount tickets can be changed without advance notice.

**BY TRAIN**   International visitors can also buy a **USA Railpass,** good for 15 or 30 days of unlimited travel on Amtrak (☎ 800/USA-RAIL). The pass is available through many foreign travel agents. Prices in 2000 for a 15-day pass were $295 off-peak, $440 peak; a 30-day pass cost $385 off-peak, $550 peak. (With a foreign passport, you can also buy passes at some Amtrak offices in the United States, including locations in San Francisco, Los Angeles, Chicago, New York, Miami, Boston, and Washington, D.C.) Reservations are generally required and should be made for each part of your trip as early as possible.

**BY BUS**   Although bus travel is often the most economical form of public transit for short hops between U.S. cities, it can also be slow and uncomfortable—certainly not an option for everyone (particularly when Amtrak, which is far more luxurious, offers similar rates). **Greyhound/Trailways** (☎ 800/231-2222), the sole nationwide bus line, offers an **International Ameripass** that must be purchased before coming to the United States or at the Greyhound International Office at the Port Authority Bus Terminal in New York City. The pass can be obtained from foreign travel agents and costs less than the domestic version. Passes for adults in 2001 are as follows: 7 days ($185), 15 days ($285), 30 days ($385), or 60 days ($509). Foreigners can get more info on the pass at www.greyhound.com or by calling ☎ 212/971-0492 (14:00 to 21:00 GMT) and ☎ 402/330-8552 (all other times). In addition, special rates are available for seniors and students.

**BY CAR**   The most cost-effective, convenient, and comfortable way to travel around the United States is by car. The interstate highway system connects cities and towns all over the country; in addition to these high-speed, limited-access roadways, there's an extensive network of federal, state, and local highways and roads. Some of the national car-rental companies include **Alamo** (☎ 800/327-9633), **Avis** (☎ 800/331-1212), **Budget** (☎ 800/527-0700), **Dollar** (☎ 800/800-4000), **Hertz** (☎ 800/654-3131), **National** (☎ 800/227-7368), and **Thrifty** (☎ 800/367-2277).

If you plan on renting a car in the United States, you probably won't need the services of an additional automobile organization. If you're planning to buy or borrow a car, automobile-association membership is recommended. **AAA, the American Automobile Association** (☎ 800/222-4357), is the country's largest auto club and supplies its members with maps, insurance, and, most important, emergency road service. The cost of joining runs from $63 for singles to $87 for two members, but if you're a member of a foreign auto club with reciprocal arrangements, you can enjoy free AAA service in America.

For details about San Antonio and Austin, see the "Getting Around" sections of chapters 3 and 10, respectively.

## Fast Facts: For the Foreign Traveler

**Automobile Organizations**  Auto clubs will supply maps, suggested routes, guidebooks, accident and bail-bond insurance, and emergency road service. The **American Automobile Association** (**AAA**) is the major auto club in the United States. If you belong to an auto club in your home country, inquire about AAA reciprocity before you leave. You may be able to join AAA even if you're not a member of a reciprocal club; to inquire, call AAA (☎ **800/222-4357**). AAA is actually an organization of regional auto clubs, so look under "AAA Automobile Club" in the white pages of the telephone directory. AAA has a nationwide emergency road service telephone number (☎ **800/AAA-HELP**).

**Business Hours**  Offices are usually open weekdays 9am to 5pm. Banks are open weekdays 9am to 3pm or later and sometimes Saturday mornings. Stores, especially those in shopping complexes, tend to stay open late: until about 9pm on weekdays and 6pm on weekends.

**Climate**  See "When to Go," in chapters 2 and 9.

**Currency & Currency Exchange**  See "Entry Requirements" and "Money" under "Preparing for Your Trip," above.

**Drinking Laws**  See liquor laws in "Fast Facts: San Antonio," in chapter 3, and "Fast Facts: Austin," in chapter 10.

**Electricity**  Like Canada, the United States uses 110 to 120 volts AC (60 cycles), compared to 220 to 240 volts AC (50 cycles) in most of Europe, Australia, and New Zealand. If your small appliances use 220 to 240 volts, you'll need a 110-volt transformer and a plug adapter with two flat parallel pins to operate them here. Downward converters that change 220–240 volts to 110–120 volts are difficult to find in the United States, so bring one with you.

**Embassies & Consulates**  All embassies are located in the nation's capital, Washington, D.C. Some consulates are located in major U.S. cities, and most nations have a mission to the United Nations in New York City. Foreign visitors can find telephone numbers for their embassies and consulates by calling directory information in Washington, D.C. (☎ **202/555-1212**).

There's a Canadian Consulate in Dallas at 750 N. St. Paul St., Suite 1700, Dallas, TX 75201 (☎ **214/922-9806**). Houston is home to a consulate for the United Kingdom at 1000 Louisiana St., Suite 1900, Houston, TX 77002 (☎ **713/659-6270**).

**Emergencies**  Call ☎ **911** to report a fire, call the police, or get an ambulance anywhere in the United States. This is a toll-free call (no coins are required at public telephones).

If you encounter traveler's problems, check the local telephone directory to find an office of the **Traveler's Aid Society,** a nationwide, non-profit, social-service organization geared to helping travelers in difficult straits. Their services might include reuniting families separated while traveling, providing food and/or shelter to people stranded without cash, or even emotional counseling. If you're in trouble, seek them out.

**Gasoline (Petrol)**  One U.S. gallon equals 3.75 liters, and 1.2 U.S. gallons equals 1 imperial gallon. You'll notice there are several grades (and price levels) of gasoline available at most gas stations, and you'll also notice their names change from company to company. The unleaded ones with the highest octane are the most expensive (most rental cars take the least expensive "regular" unleaded) and leaded gas is the least expensive, but only older cars can take this, so check if you're not sure.

**Holidays**  Banks, government offices, post offices, and many stores, restaurants, and museums are closed on the following legal national holidays: January 1 (New Year's Day), the third Monday in January (Martin Luther King, Jr. Day), the third Monday in February (Presidents' Day, Washington's Birthday), the last Monday in May (Memorial Day), July 4 (Independence Day), the first Monday in September (Labor Day), the second Monday in October (Columbus Day), November 11 (Veterans' Day/Armistice Day), the fourth Thursday in November (Thanksgiving Day), and December 25 (Christmas). Also, the Tuesday following the first Monday in November is Election Day and is a federal government holiday in presidential-election years (held every 4 years, and next in 2004).

**Languages**  Major hotels may have multilingual employees. Unless your language is very obscure, they can usually supply a translator on request. Many people in San Antonio are fluent in Spanish.

**Legal Aid**  The foreign tourist will probably never become involved with the American legal system. If you are "pulled over" for a minor infraction (for example, of the highway code, such as speeding), never attempt to pay the fine directly to a police officer; this could be construed as attempted bribery, a much more serious crime. Pay fines by mail or directly into the hands of the clerk of the court. If accused of a more serious offense, say and do nothing before consulting a lawyer. Here, the burden is on the state to prove a person's guilt beyond a reasonable doubt, and everyone has the right to remain silent, whether he or she is suspected of a crime or actually arrested. Once arrested, a person can make one telephone call to a party of his or her choice. Call your embassy or consulate.

**Mail**  If you aren't sure what your address will be in the United States, mail can be sent to you, in your name, c/o General Delivery at the main post office of the city or region where you expect to be (call ☎ **800/275-8777** for information on the nearest post office). The addressee must pick mail up in person and must produce proof of identity (driver's license, passport, etc.). Most post offices will hold your mail for up to 1 month, and are open Monday to Friday 8am to 6pm, and Saturday 9am to 3pm.

Generally found at intersections, mailboxes are blue with a red-and-white stripe and carry the inscription U.S. MAIL. If your mail is addressed to a U.S. destination, don't forget to add the five-digit postal code (or ZIP code) after the two-letter abbreviation of the state to which the mail is addressed.

At press time, domestic postage rates were 20¢ for a postcard and 34¢ for a letter. For international mail, a first-class letter of up to one-half ounce costs 80¢ (60¢ to Canada and 60¢ to Mexico); a first-class postcard costs 70¢ (50¢ to Canada and 50¢ Mexico); and a preprinted postal aerogramme costs 70¢.

**Newspapers/Magazines** National newspapers include the *New York Times, USA Today,* and the *Wall Street Journal.* National newsweeklies include *Newsweek, Time,* and *U.S. News & World Report.* San Antonio and Austin each have one major newspaper: the *San Antonio Express-News* and the *Austin-American Statesman.*

**Radio/Television** Nationally, there are six commercial over-the-air television networks—ABC, CBS, NBC, Fox, UPN, and WB—along with the Public Broadcast System (PBS) and the cable news network CNN. In big cities, viewers have a choice of dozens of channels (including basic cable), most of which transmit 24 hours a day. Most hotels have at least basic cable, and many offer access to "premium" movie channels that show uncut theatrical releases. You'll find a wide choice of local radio stations, each broadcasting particular kinds of talk shows and/or music punctuated with news broadcasts and frequent commercials.

**Safety** See "Safety" in "Preparing for Your Trip," above.

**Taxes** In the United States, there is no value-added tax (VAT) or other indirect tax at the national level. Every state, county, and city has the right to levy its own local tax on all purchases, including hotel and restaurant checks, airline tickets, and so on.

**Telephone, Telegraph, Telex & Fax** The telephone system in the United States is run by private corporations, so rates, especially for long-distance service and operator-assisted calls, can vary widely. Generally, hotel surcharges on long-distance and local calls are astronomical, so you're usually better off using a **public pay telephone,** which you'll find clearly marked in most public buildings and private establishments, as well as on the street. Convenience grocery stores and gas stations always have them. Many convenience groceries and packaging services sell **prepaid calling cards** in denominations up to $50; they can be the least expensive way to call home. Many public phones at airports now accept American Express, MasterCard, and Visa credit cards. **Local calls** made from public pay phones in most locales cost either 25¢ or 35¢. Pay phones do not accept pennies, and few will take anything larger than a quarter.

Most long-distance and international calls can be dialed directly from any phone. **For calls within the United States and to Canada,** dial 1 followed by the area code and the seven-digit number. **For other international calls,** dial 011 followed by the country code, city code, and the telephone number of the person you are calling.

Calls to area codes **800, 888,** and **877** are toll-free. However, calls to numbers in area codes **700** and **900** (chat lines, bulletin boards, "dating" services, and so on) can be very expensive—usually a charge of 95¢ to $3 or more per minute, and they sometimes have minimum charges that can run as high as $15 or more.

For **reversed-charge or collect calls,** and for person-to-person calls, dial 0 (zero, not the letter O) followed by the area code and number you want; an operator will then come on the line, and you should specify that you are calling collect, or person-to-person, or both. If your operator-assisted call is international, ask for the overseas operator.

For **local directory assistance** ("information"), dial 411; for long-distance information, dial 1, then the area code and 555-1212.

**Telegraph and telex services** are provided primarily by Western Union. You can bring your telegram into the nearest Western Union office (there are hundreds across the country) or dictate it over the phone (☎ **800/325-6000**). You can also telegraph money or have it telegraphed to you very quickly over the Western Union system, but this service can cost as much as 15% to 20% of the amount sent.

Most hotels have **fax machines** available for guest use (be sure to ask about the charge to use it), and many hotel rooms are even wired for guests' fax machines. A less expensive way to send and receive faxes may be at stores such as Mail Boxes Etc., a national chain of packing service shops (look in the Yellow Pages directory under "Packing Services").

**Telephone Directories**   There are two kinds of telephone directories in the United States. The so-called **White Pages** list private households and business subscribers in alphabetical order. The inside front cover lists emergency numbers for police, fire, ambulance, the Coast Guard, poison-control center, crime-victims hotline, and so on. The first few pages will tell you how to make long-distance and international calls, complete with country codes and area codes. Government numbers are usually printed on blue paper within the White Pages. Printed on yellow paper, the so-called **Yellow Pages** list all local services, businesses, industries, and houses of worship according to activity with an index at the front or back. (Drugstores/pharmacies and restaurants are also listed by geographic location.) The Yellow Pages also include city plans or detailed area maps, postal ZIP codes, and public transportation routes.

**Time**   The continental United States is divided into **four time zones:** eastern standard time (EST), central standard time (CST), mountain standard time (MST), and Pacific standard time (PST). Alaska and Hawaii have their own zones. For example, noon in New York City (EST) is 11am in Chicago (CST), 10am in Denver (MST), 9am in Los Angeles (PST), 8am in Anchorage (AST), and 7am in Honolulu (HST).

Most of Texas, including San Antonio and Austin, is on central standard time. The far western part of the state, around El Paso, observes mountain time (clocks are set 1 hour earlier). Daylight saving time, which moves the clock 1 hour ahead of standard time, is in effect from the first Sunday in April through the last Sunday in October (starting at 2 am), except in Arizona, Hawaii, part of Indiana, and Puerto Rico.

**Tipping**   Tips are a very important part of certain workers' salaries, but they are rarely included in the price of anything. The amount you tip should depend on the service you have received. Good service warrants the following tips: bartenders, 15% of the check; bellhops, $2 to $4; cab drivers, 15% of the fare; cafeterias and fast-food restaurants, no tip; chambermaids, $1 per person per day; checkroom attendants 50¢ to $1 (unless there is a charge, then no tip); gas station attendants, no tip; hair dressers, 15% to 20% of the cost; parking valets, $1; redcaps (in airports and railroad stations), $2 to $4; restaurants and nightclubs, 15% to 20% of the check.

**Toilets**   You won't find public toilets or "rest rooms" on the streets in most U.S. cities, but they can be found in hotel lobbies, bars, restaurants, museums, department stores, railway and bus stations, or service stations. Note, however, that restaurants and bars in resorts or heavily visited areas may reserve their rest rooms for the use of their patrons. Some establishments display a notice that toilets are for the use of patrons only. You can ignore this sign or, better yet, avoid arguments by paying for a cup of coffee or a soft drink, which will qualify you as a patron. Large hotels and fast-food restaurants are probably the best bet for good, clean facilities. If possible, avoid the toilets at parks and beaches, which tend to be dirty.

# Index

## FROMMER'S® COMPLETE TRAVEL GUIDES

## FROMMER'S® DOLLAR-A-DAY GUIDES

## FROMMER'S® PORTABLE GUIDES

## FROMMER'S® NATIONAL PARK GUIDES

## Frommer's® Memorable Walks

Chicago
London

New York
Paris

San Francisco
Washington, D.C.

## Frommer's® Great Outdoor Guides

Arizona & New Mexico
New England

Northern California
Southern California & Baja

Southern New England
Vermont & New Hampshire

## Frommer's® Born to Shop Guides

Born to Shop: France
Born to Shop: Hong Kong,
  Shanghai & Beijing

Born to Shop: Italy
Born to Shop: London

Born to Shop: New York
Born to Shop: Paris

## Frommer's® Irreverent Guides

Amsterdam
Boston
Chicago
Las Vegas
London

Los Angeles
Manhattan
New Orleans
Paris
San Francisco

Seattle & Portland
Vancouver
Walt Disney World
Washington, D.C.

## Frommer's® Best-Loved Driving Tours

America
Britain
California
Florida

France
Germany
Ireland
Italy

New England
Scotland
Spain
Western Europe

## The Unofficial Guides®

Bed & Breakfasts in California
Bed & Breakfasts in
  New England
Bed & Breakfasts in the
  Northwest
Bed & Breakfasts in Southeast
Beyond Disney
Branson, Missouri
California with Kids
Chicago
Cruises
Disneyland
Florida with Kids

Golf Vacations in the
  Eastern U.S.
The Great Smoky &
  Blue Ridge Mountains
Inside Disney
Hawaii
Las Vegas
London
Mid-Atlantic with Kids
Mini Las Vegas
Mini-Mickey
New England with Kids

New Orleans
New York City
Paris
San Francisco
Skiing in the West
Southeast with Kids
Walt Disney World
Walt Disney World for
  Grown-ups
Walt Disney World for Kids
Washington, D.C.
World's Best Diving Vacations

## Special-Interest Titles

Frommer's Britain's Best Bed & Breakfasts and
  Country Inns
Frommer's France's Best Bed & Breakfasts and
  Country Inns
Frommer's Italy's Best Bed & Breakfasts and
  Country Inns
Frommer's Caribbean Hideaways
Frommer's Adventure Guide to Australia &
  New Zealand
Frommer's Adventure Guide to Central America
Frommer's Adventure Guide to India & Pakistan
Frommer's Adventure Guide to South America
Frommer's Adventure Guide to Southeast Asia
Frommer's Adventure Guide to Southern Africa
Frommer's Gay & Lesbian Europe
Frommer's Exploring America by RV
Hanging Out in England

Hanging Out in Europe
Hanging Out in France
Hanging Out in Ireland
Hanging Out in Italy
Hanging Out in Spain
Israel Past & Present
Frommer's The Moon
Frommer's New York City with Kids
The New York Times' Guide to Unforgettable
  Weekends
Places Rated Almanac
Retirement Places Rated
Frommer's Road Atlas Britain
Frommer's Road Atlas Europe
Frommer's Washington, D.C., with Kids
Frommer's What the Airlines Never Tell You